FAB FIVE

Other books by Mitch Albom

Bo
The Live Albom
Live Albom II
Live Albom III

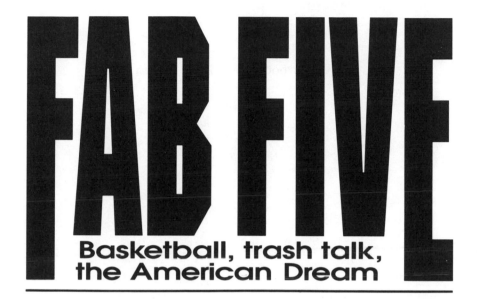

FAB FIVE

Basketball, trash talk, the American Dream

Mitch Albom

WARNER BOOKS

A Time Warner Company

Copyright © 1993 by Mitch Albom, Inc.
All rights reserved.

Warner Books, Inc., 1271 Avenue of the Americas, New York, NY 10020

W A Time Warner Company

Printed in the United States of America
First Printing: November 1993
10 9 8 7 6 5 4

Library of Congress Cataloging-in-Publication Data

Albom, Mitch.
    Fab five : basketball, trash talk, the American dream / Mitch
Albom.
        p.   cm.
    ISBN 0-446-51734-8
    1. University of Michigan—Basketball.   2. Michigan Wolverines
(Basketball team)   3. Basketball players—United States.   4. College
freshmen—United States.   I. Title.
GV885.43.U536A43   1993
796.323.63'0977435—dc20   92-51030
                                                                 CIP

*To David, for getting me into this,
and Janine, for getting me through it.*

CONTENTS

"Age looks with anger on the temerity of youth, and youth with contempt on the scrupulosity of age."

Samuel Johnson

"Let your nuts hang!"

Fab Five pregame chant

PROLOGUE

Traffic is at a standstill. Horns honk. Music blares. People line around the block, and beefy security guards in white T-shirts that read "Panther Protection Service," are holding back the mob. Something huge is happening inside the State Theatre on Woodward Avenue in downtown Detroit, June 30, 1993. It must be huge, because you don't get this many people out on a Wednesday night, not even in the summer.

"LET US IN!"

"CHRIS INVITED ME!"

"I'M ON THE LIST. YO, MAN. CHECK THE LIST."

Such commotion! And such women! It's as if every black female in the city aged 18 to 25 has shown up in a tight dress, plunging neckline, gold jewelry, poufed hair. The men respond in olive and maroon suits, with neat gold tiepins, and shoes that shine. Together they form a hurricane that swarms the theater, engulfing it, like one of those early rock-and-roll concerts in the 1950s.

The marquee reads, "CHRIS WEBBER DRAFT CELEBRATION."

The front panel says, "The Best Party in the Free World."

And here comes the man of the hour.

"IT'S CHRIS!"

"YOU THE MAN, CHRIS!"

"CONGRATULATIONS, CHRIS!"

Chris Webber, 20 years old, who grew up a few miles from here and as late as a week ago didn't have enough money in his pocket to buy a full tank of gas, now steps out from a new vehicle in a fine Italian camel-colored suit, with a rust handkerchief peeking out the front pocket. His shirt is tailored. His tie is silk. On his shaved head is a cap reading, "Golden State Warriors," the team that will make him rich. He waves at the crowd and hears it roar back at him.

"WHOOO, CHRIS!"

"ON YOUR WAY, CHRIS!"

Four hours earlier, before a nationwide TV audience, Webber was selected No. 1 in the NBA draft, meaning, at the very least, a $35-million contract, endorsement deals, an appearance on *The Arsenio Hall Show*. His father cried. His mother cupped his face when he kissed her. Chris, who still looks a lot like his fourth-grade picture—soft features, big eyes, and a winner's smile—had rented this theater in advance, because he felt sure something good was going to happen to him. Something good always happens.

Now, surrounded by an entourage, he eases through the lobby, parting the crowd like a shark fin.

"GOIN' TO THE LEAGUE, CHRIS!"

"DON'T FORGET TO HOOK ME UP, CHRIS!"

"WHASSUP, CHRIS?"

Flashbulbs explode. Everyone wants a hug. He stops to talk to a TV camera, the hot light blinding him momentarily.

"How's it feel?" a reporter asks.

"It's my dream," he says.

He moves to the staircase marked, "VIP Section, Passes Required," where two Panther Protection people grant him immediate passage. Up the stairs now, gawkers pointing, his entourage behind him like a bridal train. *He's here! He's here!* Music is thumping from the main room, rap, R&B, party music. A girl in a low-cut, red sequined dress sidles up to him, whispers "Hi." He says "Whassup?" and smiles.

"CHRIS! CHRIS!"

The mob, many of whom have never met Webber, is cheering now, urging him forward—"GO ON IN, CHRIS!"—and as he steps into the balcony that overlooks the already packed main floor, a king above his subjects, every eye in the place turns to spy him, the dancers, the drinkers, the videoids who've been watching a wall of TV sets replaying his brief but brilliant college career: Chris slamming a dunk, Chris blocking a shot, Chris going the length of the floor in his bright yellow Michigan uniform, baggy shorts, black shoes.

The DJ on the microphone can barely contain himself.

"The MAN is IN the HOUSE! The MAN is IN the—"

From the corner of his eye, Chris spots them. They stand out, taller than the rest. There's Jimmy, in a pale blue sports coat, and Juwan in a silk shirt, and Jalen in some kind of turquoise suit, the kind of suit only Jalen could wear, with his bald head and his earring. Only Ray is missing—he couldn't get a plane up from Texas—but Chris thinks of Ray when he thinks of them all, and when the others see him, their eyes lock in that group telepathy, and for a moment, all the noise in the theater swirls into the background, a seashell pressed against their ears. It's the same noise they heard when they were center of the storm in the national championship games, those huge domed stadiums, the whole world watching, and there they were, the young guns, the Shock the World boys, their throats dry, their nerves jangling, but somehow still tossing alley-oop passes and slam-dunking and hanging on the rims, the crowd going "AAAAAHHHHHHH!"

"Chris?" somebody asks, but he ignores it. He is moving toward them now as if no one else exists, and they are moving toward him, the smiles bursting—"You made it, boy!" one of them yells, and the others join in, "You made it! You made it!"—and they hug like soldiers on the plane ride home. Chris hugs Jalen. Chris hugs Jimmy. Chris hugs Juwan.

The DJ's voice echoes in their ears.

"The MAN is IN the HOUSE! How about it for CHRIS and the boys from the FAB FIVE!"

At the same time, not far away, in a small, single-level house on Bramell Avenue in Northwest Detroit, Michael Talley flops on his mother's couch. His droopy eyes are only half-open. The pop bottles are empty. The potato chip bags are down to crumbs. His friends from the neighborhood have gone, and his wife is off at her mother's place. She'll take care of the baby tonight, which is good; Mike doesn't feel like dealing with that crying right now. He is staring at the TV set, which flashes quietly.

"Damn," he says to himself. He had been hoping to hear his name from that box during the NBA draft tonight, hoping to hear some team say, "We want Michael Talley, we want the senior guard from the University of Michigan." Deep down, he knew it was a pipe dream. He had no agent. He'd gotten no calls. Unlike other seniors in college basketball, his playing time went down in his final year, because, well, the Fab Five needed their minutes, right? Now the league was looking right through him, an invisible commodity, him, Mike T, of all people, the kid they'd recruited out of high school so desperately you'd have thought he was the Messiah.

Tonight, with each passing pick, his friends told him, "Aw, you're better than that guy, Mike." "They're screwing you, Mike." He watched Chris Webber get drafted first, watched him take those long strides down that red-carpeted walkway, raising his fist like an Olympic hero. *Sure*, Talley thought, *Chris gets his.* And Talley had helped recruit Webber in the first place! Took him around on his campus visit. Said, "Come to school here, we'll both get a championship ring."

But Mike was two years older, and he was there first. He keeps saying that to himself. *I was there first. I was there first.* He grows angrier with each recital. He was once a hot recruit, he was once voted best high school player in the state, same as Webber. Why didn't things go in order, same as they always had? *I was there first!*

He remembers how his life changed when those kids showed up in the autumn of '91, Chris, Jalen, Juwan, Jimmy, Ray, how everything changed when they showed up, the coaches, the media, his career, everything. The Fab Five. Give us the Fab Five! Fab Five Fab Five Fab Five Fab Fi—

The hell with the Fab Five, he figures.

He reaches for the remote control, flicks off the set, walks up to his childhood room, and goes to sleep.

This is a story about extremes, city meeting suburbs, veterans meeting rookies, white meeting black, noise meeting quiet. It's a story about the Greatest Class Ever Recruited in college basketball, the Fab Five, and how a group like them will never come along again.

It's about youth, fame, basketball, media, ego, trash talk, and shocking the world.

But mostly it's about what happens when everyone's dream shows up at the same time.

And there's only one ball.

I

THE GREATEST CLASS EVER RECRUITED

1

Rinnnng! Rinnnng!

Steve Fisher, the head coach of the Michigan Wolverines, held the phone to his ear. His eyes darted nervously. Let's hope the kid is home, he thought. *Rinnnng!* Come on. Be home. At least the phone was ringing. Sometimes you got a busy signal all night. That was when mother or father got fed up and took the phone off the hook, or when the jealous younger brother pulled the cord out of the wall, or when the star recruit had his girlfriend over and didn't need to hear any sweet talk from coaches, not when he could get it from her.

Or maybe it was another school stealing the kid away?

Rinnnng.

Come on!

Around the corner from Fisher, in the other Michigan basketball offices, Brian Dutcher, the assistant coach, was also on the phone talking to a recruit, and Mike Boyd, another assistant coach, was also on the phone talking to a recruit, and Jay Smith, the youngest assistant coach, was also on the phone talking to a recruit. Their desks were stacked with brochures and tip sheets. As they spoke they made notes and checked 3 by 5 cards for references. Their voices all had the too-interested tone of someone trying to sell you something. If you eavesdropped from room to room, it sounded like a time-share pitch for condominiums . . .

"We sure would love to have you."

"This could be a great place for you."

"You'll love it here, the others do."

. . . or insurance salesmen . . .

"If you have a problem, we'll be there for you."

"A lot of the others promise you this and that, but can you trust them?"

. . . or political canvassing . . .

"Ask yourself, do you want to go four years under that guy?"

"The only reason they're bad-mouthing us is because they're jealous of our program."

It was, of course, none of this. It was simply another black-coffee night in the Great Recruiting Chase, the method by which college sports teams replenish their stock. Each fall and spring, they go to the well. And there was a sense of desperation in the empty buckets of the Michigan basketball team in the early fall of 1990. Last year's team did not win a conference title or go very far in the NCAA tournament. The current team did not look good. And while every program has a dip now and then, if you dip too low or too long, suddenly they're taking your name off the office door.

Back in Fisher's office, a breakthrough.

"Hello?" the voice said, answering the phone.

"Hello, Chris?" Fisher said, leaning forward.

Success!

"Coach Fisher here, Chris. Just calling to see how you're doing? . . . Uh-huh . . . Getting ready for the season? . . . That's good . . . How's school going? . . . Uh-huh . . . Talked to your dad last week, told him how much we wanted to have you here, I guess you know that . . . So are you still thinking about signing early? . . . Yeah . . . Well, I know this is the place for you, Chris, I know it, I just have to convince you of it . . . Uh-huh . . . Well, you're a special kid, Chris, and we all think that here, me, Coach Boyd, Coach Dutcher, Coach Smith, we were talking about you just this afternoon . . ."

Fisher rubbed his jowls and did his best to sound upbeat. Never let them hear your frustration. Never sound too desperate. As he listened to his latest recruiting fantasy speak, he happened to glance at the wall, a picture of the greatest basketball night of his life, the 1989 national championship. There he was, holding his blond-haired sons, Mark and Jonathan, and standing next to his wife, Angie. His own hair was sweaty, his smile was a mile wide. The picture was so real that when he looked at it, he almost heard noise coming from the background . . .

"THIS IS IT! THIS IS FOR THE NATIONAL CHAMPION-SHIP!"

Here was Steve Fisher, eighteen months earlier, inside the Seattle Kingdome, in front of 64,000 people, sipping water to calm his nerves. It was overtime in the national title game, the place roaring with noise, Fisher's own heart thumping so hard it was ready to burst through his rib cage. He stood on the sidelines, with that cup of water, as his point guard, Rumeal Robinson, launched a free throw that would tie the game.

Up . . . and . . . GOOD!

Fisher clapped. Robinson raised a fist, then went back to the line and shot another—up . . . and . . . GOOD!

Michigan had a one-point lead.

And three seconds left on the clock.

Seton Hall threw the ball in bounds. They tried a desperation shot. It was a high arching jumper and as it fell toward the basket, Fisher thought it was going to kill him, he thought it was going in. Had it gone in, his whole life would have been different. He might never have become famous. Might never have become rich. Might never have the job he has.

A whole life, riding on the arch of a basketball . . .

It missed.

"MICHIGAN WINS THE NATIONAL CHAMPIONSHIP! MICHIGAN WINS THE NATIONAL CHAMPIONSHIP!"

Fisher turned to the stands, still holding the water cup, and looked for his wife. He shook a fist in the air as if banging on a bomb shelter door. They'd won! They'd won! He spun back to the court, the dancing players, the camera lights, and suddenly Steve Fisher, in only his sixth game as a head coach, was hit with this rush, this euphoria, a tingling he had never felt before.

There is no feeling like it. It is a drug. The purest high in sports. Ultimate victory. Champions of the world. For one moment, you face the best on the planet and you leave them behind.

Coaches would die for this feeling. And to taste it once is to want it forever. Fisher bathed in it all night long, when his players hugged him, when Angie kissed him, when his children leapt into his arms, when Brent Musburger from CBS patted him on the back and asked, in front of a worldwide audience, how the rookie coach felt.

"Brent, I am the happiest man alive," the rookie coach replied.

The happiest man alive. Oh, if Steve Fisher could live forever in the snapshot from that drizzly Monday night, April 3, 1989, devoted husband, loving father, and, let's not forget, the winner, the champion, the best in the business.

What could be better than this? Today he was perfect.

Then came tomorrow.

Fisher hung up the phone and rubbed his neck.

"How we doin'?" he asked back in the office.

Dutcher, the assistant and recruiting specialist, gave the thumbs-up sign. "Good conversation. Juwan's still looking strong, Fish."

"Good," Fisher said. "Hey, Mike, how we doin'?"

"Spoke to Ray Jackson. Still trying to get the King kid on the phone," Mike said.

"I can't believe we have a chance with Jimmy King."

"Trust me, we do. How'd it go with Chris Webber?"

Fisher shrugged and looked at him, with a long silent gaze, the way he often looked at people with a long silent gaze. In this case, he didn't need to say what he was thinking. They needed these kids. They needed players desperately. The coffeepot was empty and the junk-food bags were tossed in the corner. Entries had been made in the recruiting logs—

Called Ray Jackson . . . Spoke with him, spoke with father . . . Father had a cold . . . Mother's birthday coming up . . .

Jay Smith came over with an artistic creation, a photo of Chris Webber, the No. 1 player in the country, overlaid on the Michigan emblem. He was thinking of sending it to Chris, maybe get his attention a little bit.

"What do you think?" Smith asked.

"If it works," Fisher said, "I love it."

He went back to his office and dialed another number.

Understand that Fisher never would have gotten his magic night in Seattle if his boss, Bill Frieder, hadn't been fired just before the tournament.

Frieder had been an eccentric and somewhat suspicious basketball coach at Michigan, who liked to write recruits as early as eighth grade. A jumpy guy by nature, Frieder was getting even jumpier with the new athletic director, Bo Schembechler—the football coaching legend—who would pound his fist and holler, "GOD DAMN IT! I WANT A SQUEAKY-CLEAN BASKETBALL PROGRAM. IS THAT UNDERSTOOD?"

Frieder understood. Bo didn't trust him. Although Frieder had never been found to have committed any violation, he liked to run a loose ship, let the kids be kids, let the boosters be boosters. He felt Bo's stare on the back of his neck like a laser.

A job opened at Arizona State, sunshine, easier academic standards, great money, big fat contract.

And no Bo.

Frieder grabbed it.

Unfortunately he grabbed it two days before the start of the 1989 NCAA tournament, which, for many teams, is the only part of the season that really matters. Frieder flew to Phoenix, accepted the job, then telephoned back to Ann Arbor to inform Schembechler.

"Now, don't worry," Frieder told him, "I'm on my way back. I'll coach the team through the end of the tournament."

"The hell you will!" Schembechler snarled, the blood rising in his temples. "No Arizona State man is going to coach this team. A *Michigan* man will coach this team."

Exit Bill Frieder.

And enter Fisher, the 44-year-old assistant, an apple-cheeked fellow with thinning brown hair, gentle eyes, and a Barney Fife voice, who took his son to school in the morning and went to church on Sundays and who had never been a college head coach in his life. Fisher had grown up in a small town in southern Illinois, learned basketball the old-fashioned way, from his dad. And as a coach, he taught with the passion of a father working with his son in the driveway.

Had Frieder stayed, Fisher probably would have left for a small Division I school somewhere, tried to build a program.

But now Schembechler was handing Steve Fisher the Michigan Wolverines, one of the premier college basketball teams in America.

Temporarily, of course.

"Here," Bo said, "coach the tournament. Do the best you can."

Well. In the first weekend, the Wolverines beat Xavier and eased past South Alabama. They came back the following weekend to outlast North Carolina and blow out Virginia. They came back a week later at the Final Four and stunned Illinois with a last-second basket, then beat Seton Hall in overtime on those Rumeal Robinson free throws.

And they cut down the nets.

National champions.

"MICHIGAN—KING OF THE COURT," read the cover of *Sports Illustrated*. The Wolverines were everybody's favorite underdog. They went to the White House, shook hands with the President. Fisher appeared on *Good Morning America*, ESPN, CBS. He was hailed as a breath of fresh air, an anathema to the joyless businessmen many college coaches had become.

After a brief waiting period, Schembechler did what most people expected: he gave Fisher the job full-time.

"You did a hell of a thing in that tournament, Steve," Bo told him. "You've earned the position. I'm raising your salary from $42,000 to $95,000. You'll have a shoe deal, a summer camp deal, and a TV and radio deal, which I will negotiate, if you like. The whole package should be worth between $300,000 and $400,000. That OK?"

OK? Was he kidding? The new head coach at Michigan? With six games on his résumé? Fisher was dizzy. Nothing like this had ever happened to him before, and he tried to approach it with his typical steady, even-gazed approach. But that was like capping an oil well. Head coach? National champions? Six games?

President Bush invited Steve Fisher and Angie back to the White House. Fisher even phoned his alma mater, Illinois State—who had been interested in him as a coach—from the back of a Secret Service limo. *"Sorry, I really appreciate the offer, but I'm going to take this little job here at Michigan . . ."* The back of a Secret Service limo?

Fisher got a six-figure shoe contract from Nike, and was invited to their annual party weekend in Newport Beach, California. Here he was strolling in the cool sunshine, chatting with Michael Jordan and Charles Barkley, getting the star treatment from hotshot Nike execs.

Back in Ann Arbor, Fisher got a nice car to drive, and he bought a beautiful house with his suddenly large income. People slapped his back, said, "Hi, coach."

What a life.

All he had to do was live up to his legend.

Which, of course, was impossible. He learned that the next year. The Wolverines lost the first game of the season, and they lost the last game of the season, and six more in between. They were eliminated in the second round of the 1990 tournament by a little-known, hotshot team named Loyola-Marymount.

And Fisher, like a pageant queen who surrenders her crown, was suddenly in search of an identity. He was no longer the Best in the Business. He was just another coach trying to get there.

The exodus of players began. Three seniors, Robinson—the hero from the championship game—plus big men Terry Mills and Loy Vaught went off to the NBA. And junior Sean Higgins, whom Fisher sorely needed to return, jumped to the NBA as well.

Suddenly Michigan had craters in its lineup. What made matters worse, the Wolverines most-desired high school recruit, a 7-foot scoring machine named Eric Montross, whose father went to Michigan and whose grandfather went to Michigan and who was supposed to be in the bag for Fisher, chose North Carolina instead. Some said it was unavoidable, that the kid was under too much pressure. Others said Fisher blew it.

Whatever. It worried Fisher. A veteran head coach knows the ups and downs of his damnable life. He has a swig of whiskey, chews a Maalox, bites the bullet. But Fisher had just had the rainbow in his lap, and now it was gone. He saw how quickly glory could evaporate. He went to the Nike affair, but the attitude was different: he was just one of the masses. And around Ann Arbor, he could hear whispers: *"We made a mistake. He can't recruit like Frieder. See what happened with Montross? Without talent, he's nothing, just a dressed-up assistant coach."*

Fisher may be, in his own words, "pure white bread," but he isn't dumb. He was scared. With a year-to-year contract—Michigan has never given any coach a long-term deal—and with a weak team coming back, he knew that patience was not something he could count on. There is only one way to improve your lot in college basketball: improve your personnel. And so there was one thing and one thing only that could save Fisher, get him back to the nirvana of the 1989 snapshot.

The best recruiting year anyone could imagine.

The Greatest Class Ever Recruited.

"We're focusing on one thing next year," Fisher had told his staff earlier in the summer. "Recruiting. Everyone is gonna work. Everyone is gonna push. We're gonna stay up late, we're gonna make all the calls, make all the visits. This is our emphasis, our No. 1 priority. This is what we need.

"We need players."
Players.
Players.
Players.
And the most important would be the first.

STAR SKETCHES
of Top Fifty High School Senior Basketball Players

JUWAN HOWARD   C/F   6-10   230
Hometown: Chicago, Ill.

"Jammin' Juwan" is rated the #1 prospect in the Windy City, and he was the most impressive senior player at last summer's prestigious Nike/ABCD Basketball Camp in Princeton, N.J. Yet another of the many outstanding power forwards in this class, Howard has the size and heft to successfully play on the block at the collegiate level. He is an excellent inside–outside scorer, and has a soft, accurate shooting touch with true three-point range. He is very mobile and runs the court extremely well. According to Coach Richard Cook, "Juwan takes great pride in his game and always plays very hard." He is a solid student and plans to study business management or radio-TV communications in college. He serves as president of the Senior Boys' Council at Vocational High. Howard narrowed his long list of colleges to Michigan, Arizona State, Pittsburgh, DePaul, Illinois, and Dayton.

— from Bob Gibbons' *All Star Sports* newsletter, 1990–91,
a tip sheet for college recruiters

2

"These look good, Ms. Howard," Brian Dutcher said, staring at his plate. He had a smile plastered on his face, the Official Recruiting Smile, and even though the plate was full of watery greens with a rather pungent smell, you couldn't wipe that smile off with sandpaper.

"Collard greens," Jannie Mae Howard said, chomping her cigarette. "You mean you ain't never had no greens before?"

"No, ma'am."

"Well, you gonna have some tonight."

She laughed, and so he laughed, and they all laughed—Dutcher, Steve Fisher, Mike Boyd, Lois Howard (Juwan Howard's aunt), Richard Cook (Juwan's high school coach), Donnie Kirksey (his high school assistant coach), Juwan himself, and most important, Jannie Mae Howard, his grandmother, the woman in charge, the woman who could Sway the Decision. In recruiting, there was always one person who could Sway the Decision, and without that person, you were dead.

"Yeah, coach, you gonna have some greens tonight."

"Coach Dutch gonna have him some *soul* food."

Dutcher, a devoted member of Fisher's staff, with Kurt Russell looks and boundless energy when it came to recruiting, laughed again and took his seat at the table. His plate was packed with pork roast, spaghetti, corn bread, and, of course, the greens. He pawed a forkful, chewed, and made a happy face, like out of a soup commercial.

"Hey, these are great."

"He likes them greens, Grandma."

"Course he like 'em."

"Really, these are great."

Dutcher was thrilled. Things were going well. Juwan Howard, the tall, neatly dressed kid with the thick eyebrows and the goatee, well, he could be The One! The big name Michigan signed to get the ball rolling! He was 6 foot 10, with a deep voice and a sweet jump shot, and was ranked the No. 1 high school center in the country. Lots of schools were after him. But Michigan had been following him longer than most. Dutcher had spotted Howard as a sophomore in a Chicago summer league, had watched the way he moved without the ball, none of the awkwardness you usually see in young kids his size.

"Steve, this kid can *play*," Dutcher reported.

Those are the magic words.

The pursuit began. Letters. Phone calls. Dutcher called almost every day during Juwan's junior year, just to say hello, talk about life, school, girls, whatever.

"Michigan would love to have you, Juwan."

"You could do great things here."

"We can't wait for you to visit."

Dutcher also mailed Juwan at least two handwritten notes per week. He sent articles that spoke of Michigan's excellent academic reputation—*"Thought your grandmother would like to see this"*—and he cut up make-believe headlines on mock *USA Today* sports sections.

HOWARD SIGNS WITH MICHIGAN

Go Blue!
Coach Dutcher

Still, the biggest thing, the most important element of the Great Recruiting Chase—at least according to Dutcher—was to let them see you. So, during the 30-day visitation period in the summer of 1990, Dutcher had watched Juwan play 28 days in a row—*and he wasn't even allowed to speak to him.* Those are the NCAA rules. Lookee, but no talkee. The NCAA has rules about everything.

So here was Dutcher, in his shorts and very noticeable Michigan T-shirt, standing like a sentinel on the side of the court, watching Juwan, smiling at Juwan, never saying a word, but making sure nobody else got to say a word either.

Twenty-eight days?

"Hey, that's the way the game is played," Dutcher would say in his snappy, salesmanlike voice. Every major college coaching staff has at least one guy like Dutcher, the "recruiting expert," the guy who specializes in throwing his net into the water and coming up with a catch. As the son of former Minnesota coach Jim Dutcher, Brian had spent hours as a boy in the Gophers' basketball office, listening to his father's assistants deal with recruits. He had learned the lessons well. In fact, he claimed to have a whole system now for body language when he went to see a recruit play. If the kid waved, it was a good sign. A smile was even better. Two smiles meant you had him.

The Nod and Wink Show!

"Don't waste time on kids who don't want you," Dutcher would declare, as if reciting the Scouts Oath, "and don't waste time on kids who don't have the grades to make your school. But if you find a kid who can play, and he wants you, and you want him . . ."

Go after him like a bloodhound.

And know his biggest influence.

For Juwan Howard, the report read, "Grandmother."

"You think I could have some more of these, um . . . greens, Ms. Howard?" Dutcher said now, holding out his plate.

"Coach," she said, laughing, "you like 'em so much, you go on and help yourself."

Jannie Mae Howard, the daughter of sharecroppers in Belzoni, Mississippi, had four babies by her nineteenth birthday, so she knew about motherhood, particularly young motherhood. When her teenage daughter Helena came home one night complaining about nausea, Jannie Mae sighed.

"It's that food down at the restaurant where I'm working, Mama," Helena said. "The smell of it makes me sick."

"It ain't the food, Helena. You're pregnant."

The doctors confirmed it. Helena quickly married the father, Leroy Watson, Jr., a phone company worker who had just come back from the army. And they lived for a while in the upstairs room at Jannie Mae's place on Chicago's South Side. But when Juwan was born, it was obvious the responsibility was too much for them. Helena was only 17, a junior in high school. When she brought the child home from the hospital, they didn't even have a crib for him. Jannie Mae told them to use the chest upstairs, open it up, get a pillow and a blanket, make sure it was sturdy.

For the first week of his life, Juwan Howard slept in a drawer.

Over the years, although his mother visited, Jannie Mae raised Juwan as her own. And he adored her. He sat by the kitchen table and watched her cook. He curled on the couch and fell asleep in her lap. She would tap her leg just enough to rock him to sleep, then light another cigarette and rub his head. She called him "Nookie," no one is sure why, but when she called, he listened.

"Nookie, go get me some cigarettes from Red's store."

"Aw, Grandma, I don't feel like—"

"What you say, boy?"

"Yes, Grandma."

They lived in several low-income projects, all on the South Side. At one point, they lived above a barbecue place, and they went to bed each night to the smell of the sauce. When Juwan came home one day with a homemade tattoo on his shoulder—"Dr. J," it read, after the basketball star—Jannie Mae let him have it, said he was too young to be scarring himself like that. And when the South Side gangs started calling, Jannie Mae locked the door, putting a sundown curfew on her grandson.

Jannie Mae Howard saved Juwan from an otherwise desperate street life, and she did it with love. For his grandma, Juwan went to school. For his grandma, he worked at his game. Jannie Mae was Juwan's guiding light.

And if she liked a college, Juwan liked a college.

Brian Dutcher knew this.

Not everyone was so smart. When Lute Olson and the Arizona staff came to Chicago to recruit Juwan, they mistakenly thought he and his coach were the only important people in the room. They directed the conversation toward the men. Jannie Mae, feeling ignored, went out on the porch and smoked cigarettes until they finished. On their way out, Olson asked if she had any questions.

"What the hell you asking me now for?" she said, blowing a cloud of smoke. "You ain't asked me a damn thing the whole night."

Their mouths fell.

They were dead.

Jannie Mae wasn't Juwan's only influence, however. There was also a fast-talking, round-headed marketing major named Donnie Kirksey, and getting him on your side took more than smacking your lips at his cooking. An opportunist from his loafers to his cellular phone, Kirksey had attached himself to Juwan early, joining the staff at Chicago Vocational High School, as an unpaid assistant coach, and befriending young Howard when he was a freshman. Kirksey had been a player at CVS, too, back in the early '80s. But he never had Juwan's kind of talent.

"You gotta be smart, Juwan," he would say. "You got a chance to get out of this neighborhood. You can't mess with no bad influences."

Donnie decided that he was a good influence, and so, in addition to coaching Juwan, he let Juwan stay at his house, which was close to the school. And when Juwan got a driver's license, he let him use his car. For a kid like Juwan, coming from the disciplined poverty of his grandmother's place, this was big stuff. Here, at Donnie's house, he could act all grown-up, have girls visit, stay up late. Donnie took him to a friend's summer cottage. Donnie took him to Bulls games.

The two of them grew close, and when recruiting heated up, word went out that Donnie Kirksey was the contact for Juwan Howard. He took many of the calls. He intercepted most of the letters. When recruiters came to CVS to see practice, Donnie let them know, "You talk to me about Juwan."

One school, Kirksey claims, offered him $25,000 to get Juwan to commit and $10,000 for every month he stayed enrolled.

"He's not for sale," Donnie told them. And that was true: it was more like the barter system. Donnie hoped that steering Juwan to the right school would help him achieve his *own* dream: getting on a major college coaching staff. Was he qualified? No. But stranger things had happened. Juwan, after all, was a prize recruit.

This goes on all over America, outsiders attaching themselves to high school basketball talent, hoping to ride their coattails to the big time. After all, most of the top prospects dream of playing in the NBA, and some of them make it, with rookie contracts worth anywhere from $1 million to $40 million. If a buddy, a confidant, or a favorite homeboy just happens to be around when the rainbow ends, well, there's no telling what might spill into his lap.

"Kirksey is really influential," Dutcher had warned Fisher. "We need to have him on our side."

So they recruited Kirksey as well. They phoned him. They encouraged his dreams of getting into the business. In the summer between Juwan's junior and senior years, Fisher actually hired Donnie Kirksey to work at his summer basketball camp in Ann Arbor, and paid him well. Would he have hired a volunteer assistant coach from Chicago under other circumstances? Of course not. But there was a plus with hiring Kirksey.

He brought Juwan with him.

The Michigan staff had wanted desperately to get Juwan to that camp, because, once he was there, they could spend time talking to him without violating the NCAA rule that allows only one official recruiting visit to campus.

Problem was, they weren't allowed to pay Juwan's camp fee, which was around $300, and Juwan didn't have the money, let alone a plane ticket.

Donnie had the idea.

"I could come work at the camp, be a speaker, or a teacher," he said. "You could pay me, and . . ."

And what he did with the money was his business, right? If, let's say, he wanted to pay for Juwan to attend, and maybe give him a ride in from Chicago?

The deal was made. Kirksey, whose entire coaching experience consisted of two years as an unpaid high school assistant, was brought in as an "expert" at Fisher's camp. And with him came a 6-foot-10 kid with a goatee and a beautiful turn-around bank shot.

This is not illegal—it has been done before—but it shows how far coaches will go in pursuit of the Next Great Recruit. Maybe years back, Fisher would have frowned on this practice. But that was before the Monday night in Seattle, 1989, when his whole life changed, when he drank from the Holy Grail, and when people began expecting him to do it again, real soon.

It isn't breaking the rules, schools do it all the time, he told himself.

And they needed this kid so badly!

The plan worked to perfection. Donnie was paid handsomely for three and a half days' work at the camp (his tasks included speaking to the kids about, ironically, "the dangers of the streets"). And Juwan had a great time in Ann Arbor, doing the camp, walking along the treelined campus, checking out the music stores and cafés, admiring the girls. This was a far cry from the noisy streets of South Chicago. And Fisher, Dutcher, and crew made Juwan feel like the most important kid in the world. Juwan was so likable, an only child who yearned for the closeness of a family.

One night Dutcher brought his wife and two baby daughters with him.

"This is your family, Juwan," Dutcher promised, putting his kids on Juwan's lap. "Think of my daughters as your baby sisters. You come here, you'll watch them grow."

Juwan ate it up.

When Juwan took his "official" recruiting visit to Michigan in the fall of his senior year—his second actual stay—he was already quite fond of the maize and blue. On that same weekend, Fisher brought in Jimmy King, the star guard from Texas. He had the two of them stay together, go to the football game together, party on campus together. This was a smart move by Fisher. Because, when all is said and done, getting teenage basketball players to pick a school is very much like getting teenagers to go to a party: *"Who else is going? If he's going, I'll go."*

And much to Fisher's pleasure, Juwan and Jimmy got along well, Juwan making jokes, Jimmy laughing and shrugging in his shy Texas way. They'd even talked about rooming together if both became Wolverines.

Dare he think about getting both of them?

No. First Juwan. Juwan! Juwan! Fisher and Dutcher wanted him most of all. They continued to indulge Kirksey, who was calling all the time now. When an opening occurred on Fisher's staff, Kirksey phoned and asked to be interviewed as a candidate. And even though Kirksey had a résumé that wouldn't get him in the door of any other major college coaching program, Fisher agreed to interview him, and paid for him to come to Ann Arbor—the same weekend Juwan and Jimmy made their visits.

This was a joke, a clear indulgence of a guy who had a star recruit wrapped around his finger. But this is the way the game is played—and it was awfully close to signing day, so Kirksey interviewed with Fisher, he interviewed with Jack Weidenbach, the U-M athletic director, he got the full treatment, even though, without his connection to Juwan, Donnie Kirksey was, in essence, useless to Michigan.

Fisher even tried to get Kirksey a job with Nike, through his friendship with Sonny Vaccaro, their top impresario.

And all this helped Michigan get closer to reeling in the big one. Juwan! He could make any program an instant contender. And on top of that, he was a great kid, polite, neatly dressed, with good study habits, a love of children, and a charming way with people (always good for the media relations!). Oh, if he would only commit!

"Juwan, you know how much we want you here at Michigan," Fisher had told him at the end of his weekend. "You could have an immediate impact."

"Thanks, coach," Juwan said. "I'm pretty sure I'm coming. I'm supposed to take some other visits, but you guys are my first choice."

"Well, we'd love to have you."

"OK."

"We'll be in touch."

"All right, then."

"Take care."

They said goodbye.

Fisher looked at Dutcher.

"*What* other visits?"

"Wake up, Nookie, you don't wanna be late."

This was the day. November 14, 1991. Time for Juwan to make his announcement. His grandma woke him, as she always did. He'd never used an alarm clock.

"And wear somethin' nice today," she added. "You gonna talk to those reporters, remember."

"OK, Grandma."

Juwan got dressed, choosing a rayon shirt and tan slacks. He ironed them, as he always did, and fussed with his hair until it was just right. He thought about all the colleges that wanted him, Illinois, Arizona, Arizona State, DePaul, Dayton, maybe a hundred others, and then he thought about Michigan, his choice. He felt confident. He felt good. He would tell the press today, and that would be the beginning of the end of this no-money life. He smelled his grandma's breakfast, mixed with her cigarette smoke.

"When I make the NBA one day," he told himself, looking in the mirror, "I'm gonna take care of Grandma. Buy a big house in the suburbs."

He came downstairs, gulped breakfast, kissed her goodbye.

"I love you, Grandma."

"Hmmm-mmm. Go on now."

He and Jannie Mae had signed the letter of intent this morning, so everything was legit. He felt good, he felt relieved. At school, he met with reporters and told them his decision.

"I think Michigan is a great school, and I'll be able to contribute to their program."

At practice, he ran through drills with an excited sense of purpose. And afterward, he clowned around with his buddies, feeling good, his life in order, time to kill now.

When he returned to 135th Street, the streetlamps were on. He parked his car and saw several people outside his apartment, which was strange. He recognized one woman. Friend of the family's. She seemed upset. He rolled down the window.

"Oh, Juwan, I'm so sorry for you."

"What do you mean?"

"You don't know?"

She looked shocked. "I, um, I shouldn't be the one to tell you."

"Tell me what?"

"You should find out in ther—"

"Tell me what?"

The woman began to cry. "I'm sorry, Juwan. Your grandmother . . . she . . ."

Juwan shivered. A hurt began to rise from a part of his belly he never knew he had. It lifted him from the car and up the steps.

"Naw," he said, looking in. "NAW!"

He burst through the door, and the weeping faces told him it was true. Jannie Mae Howard had collapsed in the kitchen that afternoon while talking to her daughter about Juwan's future. A heart attack, they said, massive. She was dead by the time she reached the hospital. Lois was crying. His mother was crying. They hugged Juwan. They said, "Mama's gone." Juwan felt like he was falling into a deep hole. He stumbled to his room and pounded the walls. She couldn't be gone! Not today! Not now! She was all he had! What about the future? He could still smell her cigarettes. He could still feel her leg shaking as he fell asleep in her lap. She couldn't be gone! How could she be gone?

"NAWWWWWWWWW!"

At the funeral, he wore a dark suit, and watched the stream of mourners walk past the coffin. He felt more alone than ever. From the corner of his eye, he spotted two white men, coming down the aisle. Coach Fisher. Coach Dutcher. They'd come to pay respects. Juwan felt an inexplicable tug in their direction.

"Look, Grandma," he whispered, the first of a million conversations with her spirit. "Look who came. They really do want me. I made the right choice, huh?"

Fisher and Dutcher nodded solemnly. Under the strangest of conditions, they had gotten their man.

Juwan Howard was a Michigan Wolverine.

And suddenly he needed them as much as they needed him.

STAR SKETCHES
of Top Fifty High School Senior Basketball Players

JIMMY KING 2G 6-4 185
Hometown: Plano, Tex.

King is our pick as the #1 player in the Lone Star State, and the nation's premier off-guard prospect. At John Farrell's huge 80-team bonanza, the Nike/Las Vegas Invitational Tournament, King was the most outstanding senior backcourt player. In Vegas he literally did it all, hitting clutch three-pointers, rebounding, passing, stealing the ball, and thrilling the crowd with a spectacular "Michael Jordan imitation" unlimited hang time "grandslam dunk." When asked about his future, King said, "I just let things fall into place. I try not to play to impress college scouts . . . that's not my style." Style is exactly what this youngster has, along with great talent, and a brilliant future. He is a good student and a first-class young man. His final colleges are Notre Dame, Kansas, Michigan, and Georgetown.

—from Bob Gibbons' *All Star Sports* newsletter, 1990–91,
a tip sheet for college recruiters

3

The same week Juwan saw his life change in Chicago, Jimmy King was wrestling with his own dilemma down in Plano, Texas. He flopped on his bed. He turned over and sighed. This college stuff was making him crazy. He wasn't talking to his father, they were fighting again, they passed in the hallways like feuding children. Same with his mother. They barely spoke—and all because of this recruiting business. Dad wanted Notre Dame. Mom wanted Michigan. Jimmy wanted Kansas. Everybody wanted something. The phone never stopped ringing. The answering machine was completely jammed. Recruiting letters came by the bundle—not that Jimmy even read them anymore.

This shit is crazy, he thought. He burrowed into a pillow, the way he used to do when he was a kid. Jimmy's face hadn't changed that much since those days. He still had the gap between his teeth, the high ears, and the mischievous eyes that narrowed when he smiled. But his basketball sure had changed, and that made all the difference.

A shooting guard, Jimmy King, like Juwan Howard, was the No. 1 rated high school recruit at his position. He was, in Steve Fisher's mind, nearly a fantasy. A guy this good would go all the way from Texas to Michigan to play? It was almost too much to imagine! At the Nike tournament over the summer, with 80 teams from around the country taking part, Jimmy King was easily the dominant backcourt player, stealing the ball, passing, rebounding, three-point shooting, and, of course, dunking. He was great at dunking, a leaping gnome, soaring, twisting, windmilling, making the drop. As a kid, he practiced on an eight-foot rim, watching tapes of Michael Jordan and imitating his exact moves, having his friends take Polaroid snapshots of him to make sure he was getting it right. Jimmy was a stickler for details.

So when he sprouted to 6 foot 4 and could dunk for real, it already felt natural. His friends used to challenge him. "Betcha can't dunk from here." They'd put a foot down somewhere on the court, and Jimmy would run, take off from wherever the foot was, and slam it.

Ca-bannng!

If only this college decision were that simple. There were just a few days before early signing period began. He'd have 10 days to put his name on a letter of intent; otherwise, he'd have to wait until spring, and right now, waiting until spring seemed like asking for an extra year in prison. His head was spinning! The Kings had agreed to 14 home visits from 14 different schools. Neighbors took to hanging around the front of their house, just waiting to see who'd emerge from the limo or the rent-a-car, maybe Jerry Tarkanian from UNLV, or Rick Pitino from Kentucky, or Fisher from Michigan. So many famous coaches came, showed their videos, made their speeches about how great Jimmy was and how great Jimmy would fit in and blah, blah, blah, that, quite honestly, Jimmy had a hard time keeping track of who said what. While John Thompson from Georgetown was visiting, a woman whom the Kings had never met knocked on the door. She acted like a friend, walked in, asked Thompson for an autograph, got it, and left. No one even knew her name.

Jimmy thought about the phone call the other day from Juwan Howard, the Chicago prep star he'd befriended on his visit to Michigan.

"Hey, roommate," Juwan had called him, telling him he'd chosen U-M. "I did it, now you gotta do it."

"I'm thinking about it."

"C'mon, man. I need a roommate. Pick Michigan."

"I'm thinking."

"Don't let me down, boy."

Jimmy liked Juwan. That was a plus for Michigan. And he liked Fisher, who was always calling, saying how at home Jimmy would feel, even though Ann Arbor was far away. He knew Michigan was recruiting Chris Webber, the No. 1 player in the country. It might be fun to play with him.

But Jimmy liked Kansas, too. On his visit there, Roy Williams, the coach, walked him into the pitch-black locker room, and when he flicked on the lights, there was a Jayhawks uniform with Jimmy's name and number hanging in a locker, with the shorts, the sneakers, the locker name tag. There were spotlights on it, too, so it looked like something out of a trophy case. You half expected angels to sing!

Jimmy thought that was cool.

His mom thought it was show biz. She sat on the living room couch while her son tossed and turned inside his room. Such pressure! And Plano, Texas, was not a place where you took pressure lightly. Unlike Juwan Howard's South Side of Chicago, where not making it was the plague, here in Plano, a blossoming Dallas suburb with a median income of $57,000, not making it fast enough was the enemy. A few years back, there had been a rash of teen suicides blamed on the town's undue emphasis on achievement. Eight teenagers killed themselves in a year. One Texas newspaper ran the headline "Plano: Where Suicide Is Preppy."

And even though the King family was not on the corporate fast track—Jimmy Sr. worked as a technician for the phone company, Nyoka was an analyst for Blue Cross/Blue Shield—and even though the town was 95 percent white and they were black, just the same, pressure was pressure, be it basketball or books. Nyoka worried as she leafed through the college material she had already leafed through so many nights.

"What do you think?" she asked her husband, who was watching the big-screen TV.

"I think he wants Kansas," he said. "You know, he got all caught up in that uniform thing. And then they sent him that box of rubber bands, remember, when they found out he liked to wear 'em on his wrists? That whole big box full, with his name on every one?"

"That's so unimportant. Why should that impress him?"

"Why?" He laughed. "Because he's 17 years old, that's why. He's just a kid."

She sighed. He was just a kid. A special kid, she thought. She remembered the time he came home and announced he was going on a diet. He was 7 years old.

And the night they found him, as a grade schooler, reading articles about basketball camps in his bedroom.

"What are you doing?" Jimmy Sr. had asked.

"This is the Five Star camp," young Jimmy said, showing them a picture. "It's the best one. It's the one I'm going to one day."

His voice hadn't even changed yet!

So Jimmy usually knew what he wanted. But this decision! It was shaking up the family! Nyoka prayed for a speedy conclusion.

Inside his bedroom, Jimmy ran through the pros and cons one last time. He made a cut. Forget Notre Dame. When was the last time they were in a Final Four?

No, it was between Kansas and Michigan. He put his head in the pillow, squeezed his eyes shut, and went back and forth like a paddleball: Kansas, Michigan, Kansas, Michigan, Kansas, Michigan . . .

His parents looked up when they heard the door open.

"I made up my mind," Jimmy announced, much the way he had when he told them of his childhood diet. "It's Michigan. I'm going to Michigan."

His mother jumped in happiness. His father smiled and congratulated him.

"We're very proud of you," Nyoka said.

"It's a good school," Jimmy Sr. said.

"And we have a lot of family up in South Bend, and that's only a few hours away, so they can come see you."

They insisted he call all the other coaches immediately. Tell them. Make it official. It was the adult thing to do, they said. So, one by one Jimmy dialed the numbers, and one by one he broke the news. Even Coach Williams. That hurt Jimmy the most. So long, Kansas uniform.

Finally, all that was left was to call in his acceptance. He dialed Steve Fisher's house. Fisher's wife, Angie, said her husband was in the car, with the other coaches, but don't worry, please, stay put, he'll call right back on the car phone.

Riiinnng.

"Jimmy? Coach Fisher here."

"How you doin'?"

"Fine. Just great. My wife said you called."

"Well, I made up my mind. I'm coming."

". . . Really?"

"Yup."

"YEEEEE! Wwooooeeee! Yoooowhooo! . . . YES! YES!"

Jimmy looked at the phone. He couldn't believe it. His big, mature, adult decision, and the coaches were screaming like kids in the backseat of the car.

Shit's crazy, he thought.

4

Texas, Steve Fisher marveled. How'd we ever end up in Texas? He remembered the first time he'd even thought about recruiting in the Lone Star State, when he was still working for Frieder. Mike Boyd, the other assistant, had said in a meeting, "We should branch out to Texas. The top players there are willing to leave, because the local schools pay too much attention to football."

Fisher hadn't thought much about it at the time. But now? Well, now Texas could be part of his salvation. Jimmy King? The guard that made coaches drool? Fisher never thought Michigan could get Jimmy King. But Michigan got him. That made two top-rated players at their positions, Juwan and Jimmy, a center and a shooting guard. Bringing them to visit school together had been a small stroke of genius. And it was only November!

For most coaches in most recruiting years—Fisher included—a pair of blue-chippers would be cause enough for celebration. But Fisher still nourished hopes for The Prize, the No. 1 player in the country, Chris Webber, who had excited the whole Michigan staff by telling the press after the signing of Juwan Howard, "I guess that means Steve Fisher can recruit, huh?"

When Chris Webber spoke, people listened—even if he was 17 years old.

Meanwhile, Boyd wasn't done in Texas. He had another kid on the line, about to commit.

Ray Jackson.

And how lucky was that?

Although Ray Jackson would one day become an integral part of Michigan basketball, Fisher's staff didn't even know who he was when they found him. Boyd had been in Texas for the Great Houston Shoot Out—a tournament for high school players—scouting another Jackson, Lukie Jackson, son of Luke Jackson, the former Philadelphia 76er. And a guy came up to Boyd, out of the blue, started talking.

"You with Michigan?"

"Uh-huh," Boyd said.

"Here to see Jackson?"

"Yep."

"Well, you're gonna see one hell of a player."

"Yeah."

"That kid can really play."

"I know."

"Personally, I think Ray Jackson may be the best player we got around here."

"Ye . . . uh . . . *Ray* Jackson?"

Boyd flipped through his lineup list. Sure enough, on another team was another Jackson. Ray, not Lukie. Boyd closed his eyes. Hadn't he gotten a phone call about a Ray Jackson from a former Michigan player not too long ago? Must be fate, he figured.

He went early to watch the game.

And—lookie here—this kid was outstanding. A thickly built player whose shirt just seemed to naturally pull from his shorts. He had silky moves and a quickness that was deceptive. He rebounded, played defense, scored inside, scored outside. He was laughing, relaxed, naturally athletic: you could see it in his easy stride and his fluid motion. He had 12 points in the first five minutes.

Boyd shook his head.

The things you find out.

"What'd I tell you about Jackson?" that same guy said after the game was over.

"You were right," Boyd said.

Thank God you mentioned his first name, he was thinking.

The next day, Boyd came to the gym and got his second surprise. Turns out Ray Jackson had been a Michigan fan all his life. He was now wearing a Michigan hat. And when he saw Boyd, he waved.

He waved? On his own?

Brian Dutcher would have fainted.

Ray Jackson could be catch No. 3.

And Fisher might have to start wearing cowboy hats.

TEXAS HIGH SCHOOL
BASKETBALL SCOUTING REPORT
"It Makes Good Court Sense"

6–5 plus   **RAY JACKSON**   **Austin L.B.J.**

Can go out on the floor and hit the three. SAT 840. Parents are in education. Solid family. Ray went to summer school and did well. Should make it. Lots of heavy letters coming in. Claims he wants to leave, but U.T. is hard to beat IF and WHEN they decide to go after a local kid. Plays hard and is very unselfish with good passing skills. High Div. I 3-man. Bright future.

—from Texas High School Scouting Report, a tip sheet for
college recruiters

5

Ray Jackson was conceived in a prayer.

"Please, Lord, give me a son," his father had whispered back in the winter of 1973, when his own athletic dreams were about to die. Ray Sr. had been a star defensive lineman at Southwest Texas State, an honorable mention All-American, good enough, he felt, to be drafted by the NFL. When he wasn't, it crushed him. He let himself go. Drank beer. Fell out of shape. A few months later, he got a letter from the Green Bay Packers, asking if he'd like to try out. He looked at his flabby body and he almost cried.

He never went. And he never heard from another NFL team. He was depressed. He sulked. He felt his lone shot at the big time was gone. So he closed his eyes and asked God for a son, an heir to his dreams. As he was a religious man, accustomed to quoting the Bible and praying at every meal, he was not surprised when, a few weeks later, his wife, Gladys, who had already borne him two daughters, told him the strangest thing: despite their efforts at birth control, she was pregnant again. Could he believe that?

And they had a son.

So young Ray Jackson came to earth with a purpose, and the purpose was sports. And sure enough, despite a chubby childhood and an easygoing, almost sleepy demeanor, Ray was a star at every sport he tried. He could play football, and run fast enough to set track records in junior high school. When he started basketball, the leaping came so naturally that his first dunk took place in an informal morning pickup game at the high school where his father worked. Ray, who was maybe 12 years old, was wearing jeans and loafers. He jumped.

Slam!

Jeans and loafers?

By the time he reached Lyndon Baines Johnson High School in

Austin, he was a star just waiting for a uniform. He made varsity as
a freshman, and by the end of the season, Ray was a starter. He was
athletic enough to throw a ball off the wall, catch it on the bounce,
and slam it through the rim. The following year, when recruiters
came to check out an older player, Mike McShane, Ray's coach, said
to them, "You oughta watch this kid Ray Jackson. You're gonna
love him."

They watched him shoot. Watched him drive the lane and twist
in midair. They nodded.

"How old is he?" they asked.

McShane thought for a minute. He realized he didn't know.

"Hey, Ray. How old are you?"

"I'm 14," he said.

McShane blinked. "C'mon. Stop lying. You're a sophomore."

"Coach, for real, I'm 14."

The recruiters took out their notepads.

From that point on, McShane took a special interest in devel-
oping Ray at every position. He played him at small forward, power
forward, shooting guard, and point guard, just so Ray would be
ready for when the colleges came calling. And they did come calling.
Letters flooded the office. The gym phone became the Ray Jackson
Hot Line. Oklahoma. Georgetown. Colorado. Houston. Texas.
Texas A&M.

And Michigan.

Ray had always loved Michigan. First he loved their colorful
football helmets and then he loved their basketball team, when it
won the 1989 national championship. He wore Michigan shirts and
hats as part of his wardrobe. "Those are my boys," he would drawl,
pointing to the maize and blue "M."

So when Ray saw Mike Boyd at the Houston Shoot Out, he
made sure to acknowledge him. He had no reason to be coy. He
wasn't like that, anyhow. If Ray liked you, he let you know. He said
"Whassup?" and he smiled that easy smile that seemed to pour from
his lips like syrup. Ray knew Michigan was looking at Jimmy King,
the Plano kid everyone said was the best player in the state. Ray had
never met Jimmy, but he certainly knew about him. Who in Texas
didn't?

If Michigan wanted Jimmy King at guard, then Ray could play
forward. That's what Ray figured. Ray was blessed with the ability
to adjust, to take life at the languid pace that the Texas heat often

demanded. Like his father, he had an infectious laugh, first deep, then high-pitched, his eyes squeezing shut as his mouth opened wide, a huge laugh, you couldn't help but laugh with him. Sometimes he had to stand up he was laughing so hard. He'd get out of the chair, slap it a few times, and plop back in it.

So the anxiety that Jimmy King felt in Plano was not matched in the small bedroom in the ranch house on Starstreak Road in Austin, behind the 7-Eleven and across from the Precision Tune Up Shop.

He knew what he wanted.

He wanted to go to Michigan.

There were people at his school who doubted he could make it. People who said a kid like him, from a predominantly black, lower-middle-class Texas high school, couldn't hack it at a huge, northern, mostly white campus. They also whispered that he wasn't smart enough to handle the academics. Ray took that personally and vowed to show them all.

But Ray didn't change for anyone. He once listed his hobby as "sleeping," and sure enough, when Steve Fisher and Mike Boyd arrived a little early for their in-home recruiting visit, Ray's mother, Gladys, had to knock on her son's bedroom door.

"Ray, wake up quick, the people from Michigan are here."

"Mnnnn . . . nnn . . . huh?" Ray said.

He'd been napping.

A month later, Ray Jackson, Jr., fulfilled his father's vision by accepting an athletic scholarship to Michigan, during the early signing period.

Their coaches had never seen him play a regular high school game.

"You'll show 'em," his father said. "God will lead the way."

And Ray felt good, because, after all, his father had been right about everything else.

6

Silence can indeed be golden, at least when the silence means your critics are choking on their words. Steve Fisher read the newspaper accounts of his early-signing-period success and had to keep from gloating. All those people who said he couldn't recruit—*Look at what happened with Montross!*—where were they now? Silence! Why, even the major scouting services were rating his recruiting catch of Juwan Howard, Jimmy King, and Ray Jackson as fifth-best incoming class in the country. And he wasn't done yet! There was still the big prize, Chris Webber, 6 feet 9 inches of titanic basketball talent, right down the road, in downtown Detroit. Fisher knew his chief competition on Webber was his archrival, Michigan State, but he'd also heard rumors about Kentucky, Duke, Minnesota, even the University of Detroit Mercy. And since Webber hadn't signed with anyone in the early period, he was in the stew for four more months. The school that got Chris Webber would be the envy of all the others. Fisher made sure his Michigan staff stayed relentless. Writing letters. Making the phone calls:

"Michigan is where you belong, Chris . . . And I know you're a family-loving person, right? . . . Well, this way your family can come and see you every game . . . So how's your schoolwork coming?"

There were others besides Webber. And they were just as close and just as convenient. Jalen Rose and Voshon Lenard were star guards from Detroit, they went to the same high school, and both were ranked in the top 25 in the nation. Michigan was on their short-lists.

A good year to be in this state, Fisher thought.

"Steve, we gotta focus on our backyard now, just focus on our backyard," Dutcher suggested, sounding like a field sergeant looking through binoculars. "We did our job out of state. Now we focus on our backyard. We can get those kids. We can get Webber and Rose and Lenard."

"Do they want to come to games?" Fisher asked.

"Heck, yeah."

"Let's make sure they get tickets whenever they want."

"They will."

"Get 'em up here, where we can talk to them."

"Exactly."

Fisher sighed. "I just hope we win when they're watching."

It was a major concern. People forget that while coaches are out shopping for next year's class, they still have to be running this year's team. Or is it the other way around?

Whatever. Fisher's future roster was looking better than his current one every day. The Wolverines were heading toward a miserable season, at least by Michigan standards. Led by 6-foot-1 guard Demetrius Calip—and when you're led by a 6-foot-1 guard, it doesn't bode well—they lost three games during the preconference season, then dropped four straight to open the Big Ten. They were out of the running before it even got started. Michigan State, their archrival, beat them in the conference opener by 15 points in East Lansing. Ohio State, another archrival, beat them by 10 in Ann Arbor. So thin was the Michigan talent that Fisher ended up starting a bald-headed forward named Freddie Hunter, who the year before was playing in the intramural leagues, on a team called "Freddie and the Seven Dwarfs."

On top of that, Fisher was now working short-handed. Mike Boyd had left the staff at the end of September, to take the head coaching job at Cleveland State. Boyd had always felt a little jilted that Fisher got the big office when Frieder left. Fisher knew that. Mike would make a fine head coach, he thought, and he deserved the chance somewhere, and besides, he certainly had done enough, recruiting-wise, for Michigan, being the main guy on Jimmy and Ray. Even after Boyd quit, he called those two, just to tell them, "I still think you should go to Michigan. I meant it before, and I mean it now. It's the best place for you."

That was nice. But now, with Boyd gone, Fisher had a gap. More than just a missing assistant coach, Fisher didn't have anyone black on his staff, and in recruiting, that can be death. College basketball is a racially charged sport, with a tinderbox balance. You often have predominantly black teams at predominantly white universities, where predominantly white head coaches construct staffs that have at least one black assistant coach. This, as ridiculous as it sounds, is to keep at least some slight mirror image between those who play and those who coach them. Is it tokenism? Of course. It is also considered a recruiting imperative. Without at least one black coach on the staff, other schools may quickly suggest, to black recruits, that you are a racist school, or that the last guy left because the head coach "had a problem with blacks." It didn't have to be true. It never had to be true. All you needed was the appearance of something. And the fact was, Fisher now had a staff of three white assistants.

But he had a plan.

Indiana came to town and beat the Wolverines. And Illinois came to town and beat the Wolverines. It seemed like everybody beat the Wolverines. Fisher was enduring more defeat halfway through this season than he'd endured in his entire head coaching career.

One night, as the season wound down, several players were sitting around "study table," which is a private area in the West Engineering Building where U-M athletes go to study and get academic assistance (it has also been described as a place for jocks to hang out, with desks). Anyhow, these players—including sophomore forward Tony Tolbert, freshman center Rich McIver, freshman forward Sam Mitchell, and sophomore center Eric Riley—were talking about the much ballyhooed incoming class. The famous Juwan Howard, the famous Jimmy King, the less famous Ray Jackson, and who knows, in the next few weeks, maybe the nation's No. 1 prep player, Chris Webber, and his buddy Jalen Rose.

"What does that mean for us?" one of them said.

Tolbert, the team comedian, grabbed a piece of paper and motioned for the others to gather round. He wrote their names down.

"Let's see," he said, "what does it mean for us? Well, there's 200 minutes a game, right? So if Chris Webber comes here, he's getting 40 or 39, you know that. So Sam"—*scratch*—"that leaves you one minute a game."

Sam laughed. It was nervous laughter.

"And Rich, baby, you with the wrong team"—*scratch*—"you ain't gonna play at all. You barely playin' now."

More laughter.

"Eric, I hear they promised Juwan Howard the starting center job, so"—*scratch*—"maybe 10 minutes a game for you."

Hahaha.

"And let's see. Me. Tony . . . hmmm . . ."

He drew the letters big enough for all of them to see.

"T–R–A–N–S–F–E–R."

They exploded, laughing until it hurt.

And nobody thought it was funny.

STAR SKETCHES
of Top Fifty High School Senior Basketball Players

JALEN ROSE   G/F   6-7   190
Hometown: Detroit, Mich.

School: Southwestern High School/Coach: Perry Watson

Last year this "sweet-shooting Rose" led Southwestern High to a perfect 27-0 record and the No. 2 national ranking according to *USA Today*. This was the first state championship for Coach Perry Watson, who had taken his Prospectors teams to the finals in seven of the past eight years, without winning a title. We rate this "lithe lefty" among the nation's premier swing men and three-point shooters. Rose is very adept at squaring up quickly, and firing three-point shots off his dribble. He is very proficient in all the fundamentals, and is an outstanding ball handler and passer. Coach Perry Watson praises his all-around talent, and his dazzling one-on-one abilities.

—from Bob Gibbons' *All Star Sports* newsletter, 1990–91,
a tip sheet for college recruiters

7

In coaching circles, Steve Fisher is known as a nice fellow, the kind of guy who'll drop you a note of congratulations, or call with genuine concern if you have a problem. This is an accurate picture of the man.

But Steve Fisher wants to succeed as much as the next guy, and while he never blatantly broke the rules in the pursuit of the Greatest Class Ever Recruited, he took advantage of them several times.

The first time was with Donnie Kirkscy.

The second was with Perry Watson.

Watson, a frequently aloof man with a stocky build, narrow eyes, and a trademark Fu Manchu mustache, was the coach of the Detroit Southwestern Prospectors, one of the best high school basketball teams in America. In his 13 years at that school—where he himself had once been a star—his teams won over 300 games and barely lost 30. He was remarkably influential in getting the city's most talented players to play for him—Southwestern was one of Detroit's "open" schools—and he was equally influential in helping decide where those players went to college. Under the defense of "protecting my kids" (Perry was always big on that phrase) he would often intercept college recruiters, control their access, and be present in homes when they spoke with the parents.

If he was on your side, you loved Watson.

If he wasn't, you hated him.

There were reasons to be on Watson's side in the fall of 1990. He had two of the nation's top recruits on his Southwestern team, Jalen Rose and Voshon Lenard, both excellent guards, and Michigan and Michigan State were interested in both. Watson also had the ear of Chris Webber, The Prize, the nation's No. 1 recruit, who played for another high school, but knew Watson from the AAU and summer league games. Detroit may be a big city but it's a small town when it comes to youth basketball. Sooner or later you end up at the same tournament, or the same summer league, in the same gym or the same church, and everyone worth knowing gets to know everyone worth knowing.

Watson was worth knowing.

Because he knew everybody.

Which is how this story comes together. When Mike Boyd left the Wolverines' staff in September, Fisher had a vacancy to fill. He needed someone to recruit in the inner cities. He needed someone to relate to the black recruits. He needed, truth be told, a black coach, like Perry Watson, because, as mentioned, almost no college basketball program headed by a white coach does not have at least one black assistant. And most of the time, that assistant does the lion's share of recruiting in black homes. That may be backward, and in a way, even racist, but that is how it works. Black coaches, the thinking goes, will make a black family feel more at ease about sending their son away to school.

And while Perry Watson had not been particularly friendly to the Michigan program in recent years—his last recruit to go there was Antoine Joubert, seven years earlier—all that was about to change.

Fisher was going to hire Perry Watson as his assistant.

The nation's most influential high school coach was going to college.

Fisher could have done it in September, and there were strong rumors that he would. But Fisher did not hire Watson in September. He did not hire him in October, or November or December. He left the job open the entire year and never formally offered it to anyone.

This might seem strange, since Fisher needed help recruiting, and his depleted team needed all the coaching it could get. But if you look closely, you see that not hiring Watson in the fall was actually a brilliant move by Fisher.

And it may have been the final bait that hooked the Greatest Class Ever Recruited.

Had Fisher hired Watson in September, two things would have happened:

1. Watson would never have gotten to coach his 1990–91 Prospectors, something he desperately wanted to do. This was a once-in-a-lifetime team with a shot at No. 1 in the nation.

2. Watson would have been subject to the same NCAA recruiting restrictions as the rest of them. He'd have to join the Nod and

Wink Show, alongside Fisher and Dutcher, even with kids he knew as well as Rose, Lenard, and Webber. No talking to them, except at specific times. No giving them rides or visiting with their parents.

On the other hand, if Watson *wasn't* hired yet, if he was left alone in his high school job, he could coach his team *and* do whatever he wanted, talk to whomever he liked, exert the same influence he always had on kids who looked up to him.

And Jalen Rose, the cocky, bald-headed player with the long limbs, long shorts, and hands-in-the-cookie-jar grin?

Jalen looked up to Perry most of all.

Jalen was a special kid, who seemed to know, right from the start, that he was blessed by the basketball gods. As a child, he would get up early on Saturday mornings and dribble the ball up and down the street of his Detroit neighborhood, his socks pulled high to his knees, pretending he was Julius Erving. He would talk about how good a player he already was and how good he was going to be. Having learned how to stick up for himself verbally in a home where he was the youngest child, Jalen was a master mouth on the court. He told his childhood friends to "Check up, fool" when they were trying to stop him. And as soon as he released the shot, he'd bark, "Get off me, punk." There was no game too intimidating. No players too big to jaw. The first time he met Chris Webber, they were both 11, both trying to make a church league team. Chris was much taller. Jalen dribbled up to him, sneered, and said, "Welcome to the big time."

Eleven years old?

That was Jalen. He was yelling "Check up!" and "Don't bring that shit in here!" before his voice cracked. He liked to break-dance, wore Starter jackets, and wasn't above taking the money his mother gave him for a haircut, having his head shaved instead by a guy he knew down the street, then using the money for potato chips and video games. Jalen had a wicked grin, and eyes that could stare you down, but he was smart, and he seemed to have a premonition about his basketball talent: when he and his friend Willie Robinson challenged kids in the neighborhood to two-on-two games, Jalen called his duo "the Dream Team."

As it turned out, with his long angular limbs and great feel for the ball, Jalen would indeed develop into a dreamy talent, worthy of the Great Recruiting Chase. He sprouted in junior high, his legs shooting out like pasta coming through a machine, longer, longer, growing into his destiny.

Soon he could not only talk the game, he could play it.

In Detroit, if you are any good, you will wind up sooner or later in the storied gym at St. Cecilia's church. A poster for urban renewal on the outside, it is first-class hardwood and glass on the inside, and has been home to some of the finest basketball talent in the country, one of those places that the NBA stars remember years later and shake their heads and laugh. "Man," they say, "there was some serious hoopin' in the Saint."

Jalen was all for serious hoopin', even as a kid, and so he found his way to St. Cecilia's quickly, sitting at first, watching the older kids play, but eventually working himself into a few early games. It was at St. Cecilia's that he first got to know Perry Watson. Jalen liked Perry's goatee, which reminded him of Magic Johnson. And he liked the fact that Perry coached famous players. Jalen would always ask about Anderson Hunt, one of Perry's best kids at Southwestern, who later went on to UNLV.

"I can be as good as Anderson Hunt," Jalen would squeak.

"Maybe you can," Perry would answer. "If you keep working."

"I'm gonna play for you one day, and show you I can be better than Anderson Hunt."

Week after week, month after month, Jalen would come to St. Cecilia's, play early, then sit behind the bench when Perry's teams played, watching Perry work, listening to him coach. Chris Webber would come down sometimes as well, and the two kids whispered about how much they wanted to play for "Coach Perry" in high school. By this point, Rose and Webber were playing on the same AAU team, and getting to know each other well enough to tie their futures together. They promised they would both go to Southwestern. This suited Perry just fine—get the most talent, win the most games—but he was careful not to publicly recruit them. That was against the rules.

Besides, Perry didn't need to talk up Southwestern; he had plenty of friends who would do it for him. One friend, a slickly dressed former autoworker named Ed Martin—known by some as "that gambler who kept a wad of bills stuffed inside his sock"—would attach himself to kids like Chris and Jalen, call himself their "godfather," and provide little favors to help entice them to Southwestern High School. Martin was big on baked goods, and often delivered cakes and pastries to the homes of good young ballplayers. He had them in his car and he would pop the trunk and open a fresh cake right there, in the parking lot of some gym, sharing pieces with parents of star recruits, talking about why they should attend Southwestern. Or he would deliver bottles of liquor. Good stuff. Expensive stuff. If you think parents and kids aren't influenced by cakes, liquor, and money, you must live in the suburbs.

Ed Martin knew both Chris Webber and Jalen Rose, and when Chris was deciding where to go to high school, Martin would give him rides from place to place and try to convince him that Southwestern (and Watson) was the right choice. He flashed big wads of money in front of Mayce Webber, Chris' father, just to impress him. He gave them a big sell.

Jalen didn't need a big sell. He was a city kid. He wanted a city school. He wanted Perry Watson as his coach.

He went to Southwestern.

"Here," Jeanne Rose, Jalen's mother, had said to Perry before Jalen's freshman year. "I'm handing my son over to you now. He's in your hands. Anything goes wrong, I'm blaming you."

Nothing went wrong, at least not as far as basketball was concerned. Rose continued to talk nonstop, but he developed a game to go with it. He blossomed into a major talent, a terrific rebounder, long-range shooter, great ball handler. He had a feel for the game, he could play anywhere on the floor. During the state championship game his junior year, the Prospectors' big center, Elton Carter, was hurt and couldn't compete. Jalen, a skinny 6 foot 7 and more naturally a guard or small forward, slid into the post, played like a big man, did turn-around bank shots, and banged inside for rebounds. The Prospectors won the title. Jalen was the star.

For that alone, Watson would have loved Jalen forever. But they had far more than the Prospectors in common. They would talk about life, talk about problems, take trips together to see other players. Perry, by that point, had become a surrogate father to Jalen, whose real father, former NBA star Jimmy Walker, had skipped town before Jalen was born. Jalen was haunted by that absence more than he admitted. Maybe more than he knew. He looked to Perry for traditional father things, such as protection.

Once, during a game with archrival Cooley High, Jalen was clotheslined by a Cooley player while going for a layup, and the way he hit the floor, people thought he was dead. He was in convulsions.

Perry rode with him to the hospital, stayed through all the tests, and talked to the doctors, who said Jalen should stay overnight, just for precaution. Jalen's mother was there. So was his brother.

A nurse came out and said Jalen was asking for Perry.

"I wanna go home," Jalen told him.

"You can't," Perry said. "The doctors want you to—"

"I wanna go home. I don't wanna stay. Get me out."

Perry got him out. Took him home. And the next day, using pillows to prop up his head, Jalen rode with Watson in his BMW down to Toledo, to watch Chris Webber play in a basketball game.

Any notion that Perry Watson wasn't going to be influential with Jalen's college decision was simply naive. Perry was there, sitting on the old couch in the cramped front room of the Roses' small home on Appoline Street, in Northwest Detroit, answering questions when recruiters visited. Like Juwan and Jimmy, Jalen was rated by many scouting services in his senior year as No. 1 in the nation at his position, swing man. He was 6 foot 8, and when he played guard, he simply played above his opponent's head. Jalen had also been chased by nearly every school you can name. Phone calls. Letters. But he let Perry intercept almost everything. Jalen had his eye on two schools, UNLV and Syracuse, both of which ran up-tempo offenses and had reputations for being rather light on discipline.

Unfortunately, both schools were also headed for probation due to NCAA violations.

Scratch those two off the list.

Going into his senior year, Jalen Rose was up for grabs.

So the chase was on. And it became twice as frantic when Chris Webber, his buddy, was suddenly telling recruiters that he really would like to go to school with Jalen. This meant coaches that might not have otherwise rushed to the cocky, trash-talking guard were now all over him. Hey. To get Webber, they would have recruited Dumbo the elephant.

But Watson was still in control.

And Watson was going to Michigan. By February of 1991, everyone in the business seemed to know this, even though nothing official had been announced. Watson was still free to talk to Rose whenever he wanted—while recruiters had to wait nervously back on campus. And, to really get their goat, Watson could talk all he wanted to Chris Webber, too. And he did. Perry would often call Chris and give him pointers about his game, send him notes on conditioning, diet. A little odd for a kid from another high school, you might say.

But it had an effect on Chris. Two years later, Webber would admit, "I believed Coach Watson was going to Michigan, I'm not gonna lie. And that had a big effect on me, because I got along with him better than I did with Coach Fisher."

Chris' father, Mayce Webber, would say, "I knew Perry was going to Michigan the day after Mike Boyd left."

One night in February, Michigan was hosting Purdue, and Chris and Jalen came together. When the student section spotted them, they chanted, "Webber! Webber!" and "Rose! Rose!" The kids grinned.

Michigan played tough that night, but lost to the Boilermakers in double overtime, their eleventh defeat of the season. Afterward, Chris and Jalen stopped by the locker room, and Fisher called them into his office.

"You see what happened tonight," he said. "If you guys were here, we'd have won this game. We really need you."

They nodded. Rose nudged Webber.

"Tell him, man."

"Tell him what?"

"You know, tell him we're coming."

"Ah, man, no, you tell him."

"You tell him."

Webber laughed. Jalen laughed. Fisher laughed, hiding the thrill that had just shot through his body. Did they say they were coming? Were they kidding? Should he ask? Should he not ask? They said they were coming? Didn't they say they were coming?

They waved goodbye and went back to high school.

It was the first of a million times that Jalen would leave Fisher guessing.

On March 23, 1991, the guessing would end, at least as far as Rose's college recruitment was concerned. At the Palace of Auburn Hills, home of the Detroit Pistons, the Southwestern Prospectors had just beaten Northern to capture their second straight high school basketball state championship. Jalen had scored 25 points, grabbed 18 rebounds, and celebrated by throwing his fists in the air and whooping with his teammates. Southwestern would be named the nation's best high school team. Watson would be named the nation's best high school coach. It was everything they wanted.

In the postgame press conference, someone immediately asked Jalen what college he was planning to attend.

"I don't wanna talk about that now," he said, eyeing his teammates. "We're just here to talk about the win tonight."

But, later, as the questions wound down, he was asked again.

"Well, to be truthful, I'm going to Michigan," he said.

Michigan?

"Yep."

Reporters swarmed him. Michigan? That meant the Wolverines had Juwan Howard, Jimmy King, Ray Jackson, and Jalen Rose, four blue-chippers, three of them the best in the nation at what they did. Whoa! Jalen Rose was going to Michigan?

A few months later, Perry Watson surprised no one by saying he, too, was joining his star player in Ann Arbor, as Michigan's newest assistant coach.

How do you like that?

Another Dream Team.

TV Script, Chris Webber Piece

REPORTER: *By collegiate standards, Chris Webber's 6-foot-5 frame is just average. But Webber is nowhere near college. In fact, he's not even in high school! Chris is a 13-year-old eighth grader whose height makes him a terror on the basketball court.*

FATHER: *They say he might reach 7 foot 2.*

HIGH SCHOOL COACH: *Potential-wise? The sky is the limit.*

REPORTER: *Webber towers over the opposition—a sequoia amongst saplings.*

STARTLED KID: *He's a monster! It's like playing against a monster!*

REPORTER: *What's it like having size 16 sneakers and having free rein around the rim?*

CHRIS: *It's pretty fun most of the time, 'cause I can practice dunking.*

REPORTER: *Chris is still a growing boy.*

FATHER: *My great-great-grandfather was huge—7 foot 6, or somewhere in that area.*

REPORTER: *The hottest high school commodity is undecided about where he'll go to high school, but he has already made his mind up about college!*

CHRIS: *I'd like to go to Michigan State.*

REPORTER: *Is that positive?*

CHRIS: *Uh, yeah. It's positive.*

—from WDIV-TV feature piece on Chris Webber, then an eighth
grader, in the winter of 1987

8

"OK, everybody, smile."

Click!

While Jalen Rose was making his big announcement at the Palace, not far away, at the posh 1940 Chop House restaurant in Detroit, the flashbulbs were popping. It was a private party for the Country Day High School basketball team. Balloons. Streamers. Kids throwing arms around each other.

Downstairs, a crowd of reporters paced like wolves.

"Isn't he ready yet?"

"What's taking so long?"

"Yeah. Is this a press conference or a slumber party?"

Chris Webber, the object of their attention, 6 foot 9 in his stocking feet, huge hands, great leaping ability, enormous wingspan, unbridled enthusiasm, great smile, good grades, nice family, The Prize, the Golden Fleece, the nation's No. 1 high school basketball player, wanted a few more minutes to clown around with his pals. Earlier in the day, they had won the Class B state championship, in Chris' last game. He dominated, naturally, scoring 27 points and winning the MVP trophy—all this despite an injured ankle.

Now he was scheduled to announce his college decision. Four TV stations, every Detroit newspaper, and several radio outlets were downstairs. Wire services were on alert. Footage was being assembled by local affiliates. Talk shows from as far away as Lexington, Kentucky, were awaiting the information. *Where's he gonna go? Where's he gonna go?*

The question had dogged him like an odor since freshman year. *Where's he gonna go?* The summer before, he had been on a date in a movie theater, and in the middle of the film, a guy from behind tapped him on the shoulder and said, "Aren't you Chris Webber? . . . Did you pick a college yet?"

Today, finally, the answer. Michigan State had been an early favorite. So had Duke, the reigning national champion, and the University of Detroit–Mercy, a city school with a black head coach.

And Michigan.

"Can you imagine if it's Michigan?" a reporter said. "Juwan Howard, Jimmy King, Ray Jackson, Jalen Rose, *and* Chris Webber at one school? They'd be unstoppable."

The others nodded impatiently.

Upstairs, Chris' father, a tall auto factory worker with a pencil-thin mustache, watched his son in typical amazement. So calm. How did the boy stay so calm?

"MAYCE WEBBER?"

"That's me."

"Telephone call, downstairs."

He descended the staircase, waved at the mob of reporters, went through the doors, around the corner, saw a pay phone off the hook. He picked up the receiver.

"Hello?"

"Chris is going to Michigan, isn't he?"

"Who's this?"

"It's a mistake, Mayce. Don't let him do it. We'll give you $40,000. Send him to us."

"Forty thousand dollars?"

"That's right."

"What school you with?"

"I'm a friend of Mississippi State."

"Mississippi State?"

"Mississippi, Mayce. Remember? You were born here. You owe us, Mayce. Your boy should play back home."

"You're crazy."

Mayce hung up and returned to the party.

Two minutes passed.

"MAYCE WEBBER! PHONE CALL!"

Down the stairs, nod at the reporters, around the corner, pick up the receiver.

"Hello?"

"Make it $100,000."

"A hundred thousand dollars?"

"Mayce, take the money, man."

"I can't take no money."

"Why not? Tax-free. How long will it take you to make that money working in an auto plant?"

Mayce flinched.

"My boy ain't for sale."

He hung up, climbed the stairs, went back to the party. They were setting up a podium at the end of a narrow hallway. Any minute now, Chris could start his press conference. Then this madness would be over.

"MAYCE WEBBER! PHONE CALL!"

Damn.

Down the stairs, past the reporters, around the corner.

"Yes?"

"One hundred and fifty thousand."

"What?"

"One hundred and fifty thousand. Plus a house. Plus a job. You'd be sick to turn that down, Mayce."

"Listen, man, I was born in Mississippi. I know Mississippi. There ain't that much money in the whole state of Mississippi."

"We'll take care of you, Mayce."

"Uh-huh."

"I'm serious."

"Listen . . ."

"I'm serious."

Mayce rubbed his head, which was starting to hurt.

Serious? They were always serious when it came to that one blessed child, the Lord of the Rims, the No. 1 recruit in the nation who could do it all, and was going to do it for somebody's program next year. You didn't need to say his name. It was on the wind, blowing across America, in scouting sheets and camp reports and newspaper copy, from asphalt playgrounds to carpeted coaches' offices. It got people talking, it lit up phone lines on radio talk shows— *"What about this kid in Detroit? Do we have a chance at getting him?"*— the name, the reputation, the promise, the Lord of the Rims, like a small tornado he touched campus after campus, swirling papers around the basketball office, kicking up a dreamy dust that blew out over the highways and cascaded into the open windows of rented Chryslers or Chevys that the recruiters were driving, another day of checking the high schools and the summer leagues, searching for a kid like this one, the draw, the franchise, the anointed, the savior, the miracle, the carpet ride to March Madness!

"Oh, man, could you imagine . . ." they tease themselves as they punch up another radio station and swig another Diet Pepsi and keep driving. *Could you imagine?* And, with nobody around, they do imagine, just once, even if they haven't got a chance in hell of getting this kid, even if he wouldn't consider their program if it fell into his lap, they imagine it, because it feels good to imagine it, opening night, next fall, there he is, wearing their uniform, as the announcer calls the starting lineups . . .

Chris Webber!
Chris Webber!
Chris Webber!
Chris Webber!

Mayce Edward Christopher Webber III emerged from the womb like a big card folded into a small envelope, his left foot bent back to the knee, because he was simply too large for his mother to carry. At 10 months he was walking. At 13 months he was catching a ball in his oversized hands. He had a voracious appetite, going through bottles, then jars, then plates of food, and he outgrew clothes before they had a chance to fray. Doctors told his parents he would reach 7 feet tall. By nursery school, he was boy-sized; by kindergarten, he was towering over other children. Compared to the average kid, watching Chris grow was like watching a dinosaur.

But inside the giant, bony frame lived a soft soul, an obedient child with a sense of responsibility that astounded even his parents. You told him not to go down steps, he didn't go down steps. You told him not to touch the stove, he didn't touch the stove. Each time Doris Webber was pregnant (she would bear three more sons and a daughter) Chris somehow knew she needed sleep, and he would feed his baby brothers peanut butter off a spoon to keep them quiet while she napped. Chris changed diapers and fed bottles and held his siblings' hands when they went to the grocery store. They often slept in the same bed, all five of them, even though two other beds were available. During thunderstorms they would huddle together on a blanket in the small front room; Chris, the big brother, was looked up to for protection.

People in their lower-middle-class Detroit neighborhood would tease the Webbers about their almost corny relationships, calling them "the Waltons" and "the Brady Bunch." They would tease Chris about his clothes, which his mother often sewed herself. She paid no attention. Doris had firm ideas about home and childhood, and in addition to regular church visits, she created "quiet time," every day, one hour, in which her children were not permitted to talk, watch TV, or do anything besides read or think. Doris' intentions were to prepare them for places where there would be nothing to do—since both she and Mayce worked, and couldn't afford day care, she would often have to take all five kids with her—but in Chris' case, the hour gave him a chance to think about himself, his life, his size, what people said to him. It was this forced contemplation, one hour, every day, year after year, that would later blossom into a consciousness that set him apart from the rest of the Fab Five.

"Mommy," young Chris asked one day, "does the devil like his friends?"

"What do you mean?"

"Well, if the devil is a bad man, then how can he like his friends?"

See what happens when a kid has time to think?

He started his basketball in sixth grade, in a summer AAU program, mostly because he was tall, and tall kids are supposed to play basketball. He was so bad he quit after the second night. His father nudged him back. Curtis Hervey, a local coach, saw the boundless potential in Chris, who was already over 6 foot, but he also saw his soft personality. Chris would help people up if he knocked them down, he would apologize for fouls, and when someone blocked his shot or trash-talked him, he was ruined for the rest of the day.

Hervey decided to toughen him up.

"Get this kid," he whispered to Luwan Bell, a taller, brutish player who would later go on to play at the University of Detroit–Mercy. "Hit him. Talk about his mama. Whatever. Don't let up."

Bell agreed, and day after day, he would torture Webber, insulting him, blocking his shots, handing them back, blocking them again. Chris cried. Walked off. But over time, he learned to thicken his skin.

And slowly he learned the game.

Hervey would schedule private sessions with Webber, bring orange juice and sandwiches, stay in the gym for hours, teaching him post-up moves, how to jump off the proper foot, how to use his body for rebounds. He also formed an AAU team and took Chris and his teammates—which included a cocky kid named Jalen Rose—on trips and tournaments out of the city. They played in St. Louis, in Seattle, in Chicago. Their team was called "the Super Friends," and by the summer of Chris' seventh-grade year, they were practicing sometimes through the night, two hours on, two hours' rest, two hours on, two hours' rest. In the national play-offs, they faced a team from New York that featured 13-year-old Jamal Mashburn, who would go on to star at Kentucky. The following summer, they shared a tournament with a team from Utah, and a 14-year-old giant named Shawn Bradley, who would go on to star at Brigham Young.

Webber, Mashburn, and Bradley would one day become millionaires in the same room on the same night, as three of the top four picks in the 1993 NBA draft.

But they were all kids then.

They had no idea what was in store for them.

The first to make contact was Jud Heathcote, the bellicose, white-haired Michigan State coach who had once guided Magic Johnson to an NCAA championship. Heathcote saw a local TV news piece on this eighth-grader down in Detroit named Chris Webber, who was already dunking and blocking shots as if swatting flies. When asked in that piece where he wanted to go to college, Chris gurgled, "Michigan State." And even though his voice was squeaky when he said it, well, it's never too early for a savior, right? Heathcote invited the Webber family to East Lansing. They watched a game, marveled at the arena, cooed at the pictures of Johnson in the trophy cases. They were shy and impressed, and oh, if Heathcote were only able, man, he could have signed the kid right there, aged 13.

Instead, Chris went home, and the chase was on. Bill Frieder, Michigan's coach, began showing up at Chris' eighth-grade games at Temple Christian School, front row center. Eighth grade?

The phone began ringing in the Webber home on Biltmore Street in Northwest Detroit; it would not stop for the next four years. Letters arrived, sometimes 10 at a time—all this before Chris' *junior high graduation.*

Dear Chris,

You are an excellent basketball player and a fine young man. We would very much be interested in having you attend our university one day . . .

Dear Chris,

We have followed your success in junior high and are confident you'll make a great high school player. Have you considered our university for your college years? . . .

Dear Chris,

Congratulations on a great junior high career! . . .

This is how unique Chris Webber was: there are starters on Final Four teams today who didn't get as much attention picking a college as Webber got picking a high school.

Doris Webber, an intense, loving woman who grew up in Detroit and worked as a special-ed teacher, was unimpressed. She had plans for her son; she wanted him out of the inner city, in a private school, someplace where learning was the primary focus.

Mayce Webber, a blue-collar man his whole life, was torn between listening to her and listening to everyone else on the street.

"You can't send him to no private school, Mayce, the boy has a chance to go to the NBA!"

"You gotta send him to Southwestern, Mayce. Let Perry Watson guide him."

"You gotta send him to Cass, Mayce. Develop his basketball!"

"Private school? You're throwing the boy's life away."

One night, during a weekend game at St. Cecilia's gym, a man in a leather cap asked Mayce to come outside. He wanted to talk. In an alley, with no one around, he pulled out a wad of bills. Told Mayce it was $10,000.

"What the hell you doin', man?" Mayce said.

"Take it, Mayce. Nobody's gonna know. Send your boy to Renaissance High, and there'll be more of it."

"You're giving me $10,000?"

"I ain't giving you anything. Nobody knows we're here. Take it."

It was the first—but hardly the last—financial inducement Mayce Webber would turn down. Nearly two dozen money offers were made for Chris' high school acceptance alone, always on the sly, always untraceable, a phone call, a whisper, someone bumps into you. One night the phone rang, and a man who only said he was "from Indiana" offered Mayce $20,000, a job, and a new house in the Hoosier State—move the whole family down—in exchange for Chris' high school enrollment.

"You with Bobby Knight?" Mayce had asked.

"No," the guy snapped. "Bobby Knight ain't the only damn basketball coach in Indiana, you know."

While Mayce shook his head, and his other children wondered what the fuss was all about, Doris signed up Chris, against his will, for the admission test to Country Day High School, a private school on rolling green hills in the Detroit suburb of Beverly Hills. Doris had always wanted to go there as a child, but could never afford it; she was determined that Chris get the chance.

Kurt Keener, the basketball coach at Country Day, accustomed to the sloppiness of small-time competition, remembers glancing over the test list, seeing the name, and doing a double take, like a man who discovered four extra zeros in his paycheck.

"Uh, excuse me," he said to the secretary, "is this *the* Chris Webber?"

Thirteen years old, he was already *"the."*

When summer ended, basketball junkies were stunned to learn that young Chris Webber had indeed enrolled in Country Day High School. Almost everyone had figured him for Southwestern and Perry Watson. But Doris Webber was a stronger force than even Watson, and she got her wish: first week of September, Chris put on the required navy-blue blazer with the school's insignia, and the white shirt, and the school tie, and began a high school experience unlike anything he had ever known.

Here, on the Country Day campus, kids arrived in BMWs and Audis. They took Christmas vacations in Hawaii, the Caribbean, Europe. They were more competitive in the classroom than on the playing field.

They were mostly white.

"Are you the new basketball player?" they would ask when Chris, by now 6 foot 5, walked down the hall.

"No, I'm here on a golf scholarship," he would snicker.

Chris did not want to be at Country Day. For most of his time there, despite enormous success, and the kind of popularity a teenager dreams about, he hated it. He felt out of place. In the summer, Chris was playing night games with Jalen Rose and Voshon Lenard and former Detroit high school stars who were then in major colleges, like Steve Smith at MSU and Derrick Coleman at Syracuse, and sometimes even Isiah Thomas and Vinnie Johnson from the Pistons would show up. Chris and friends would drink fruit punch and eat barbecue potato chips and blast rap and funk music and talk about the league. There was almost no contact with white kids or white coaches.

And then autumn came and he was back in the Country Day uniform, playing with mostly white teammates who couldn't last a minute in a Saturday night run at St. Cecilia's, hearing classmates tell of vacations that he could never take.

One time a girl in Chris' junior class came in crying. Someone had stolen her car, right from the school parking lot. The class was aghast. But when she went out a few hours later, there was a new Mercedes, in the same spot, with a big red ribbon around it.

Happy Birthday. From your parents.

They had stolen her car on purpose.

Chris was sick.

But being cloistered in an academic abbey didn't keep recruiters from finding Webber. On the contrary, Chris was responsible for more famous coaches driving around Beverly Hills, MI, asking directions to "this Country Day place," than any 100 players before him. They all came, in pursuit of The Prize, the biggest names, Mike Krzyzewski from Duke, John Thompson from Georgetown, Lute Olson from Arizona, Rick Pitino from Kentucky. Of course Heathcote was there, and also Fisher, who, in Chris' junior year, took over the Michigan Wolverines. They stood in the gym, sometimes five of them at once, arms folded, doing the Nod and Wink Show. Not that it mattered.

Chris had long ago stopped making eye contact.

By junior year, everyone knew that Webber—who could block 15 shots a night—was overqualified for Class B high school basketball. He could score 40 points by halftime if he wanted. So he was just waiting to pick a college. That, and trying to duck the mobs of fans who were already asking for his knee pads, his wristbands, and his socks after games, figuring this kid's gonna be big one day, let's get it while we can.

Life on Biltmore Street became daily chaos. Noise. Yelling. Knocking. And ringing. The Webbers did not want to change their phone number, which was listed, because Doris' father was ill, and they were worried he might get confused. But everyone had it, and everyone dialed it. Recruiters knew no manners. They called during waking hours and sleeping hours and you couldn't hang up the phone without it ringing again within three seconds. After a while, the Webbers just walked around the house to the sound of bells.

As Chris narrowed his choices, the pressure increased, and requests turned to pleas. One coach called to tell Chris he was getting divorced, his life was in shambles, "but man, Chris, if you would only come to our school, everything would turn around for me." Another coach, upon learning Chris' family was religious, said, "You know, Chris, I was reading the Book of Palms the other day . . ."

The Book of Palms?

There was no safe haven. Recruiters, boosters, advisers, all formed this little army that seemed to smell Webber coming. They waited outside gymnasiums. They doubled attendance at his church. Chris began sleeping at friends' houses, just to avoid the contact. Mayce couldn't go anywhere without getting advice. The mall, the gas station—life had come down to one sentence, four words, and you could hear them coming the moment you made eye contact.

Where's Chris gonna go?

Where's Chris gonna go?

All during this time, Fisher, who had been heavily recruiting Juwan Howard and Jimmy King, never let his eyes stray far from The Prize. As it was pretty common knowledge that Webber wanted to stay near home, so his family could see him play, Fisher felt Michigan had the edge on all the other schools except one.

Fisher worried mostly about Michigan State.

And Jud Heathcote worried mostly about Michigan.

They kept tabs on each other like the Soviets and the Americans during the cold war.

At the start of his senior year, Chris seemed to be leaning toward East Lansing, not Ann Arbor. Mayce Webber had always had a fondness for Heathcote, whom he found funny, and when Chris took his official visit to East Lansing, where he already knew many people, he had a great time. Tom Izzo, Heathcote's handsome young assistant and main recruiter, with the energy and enthusiasm to rival Brian Dutcher at Michigan, drove Chris home after that visit and was delighted with the conversation.

"You know, coach, for the first time I really feel happy."

"That's great, Chris."

"I'm thinking about committing early to your school."

"Hey, you know we'd love to have you."

"Yeah. I'm thinking about it. I really am."

Izzo could hardly contain himself. He felt a special closeness with Chris. They talked about more than basketball. They talked about life, friendship, the future. Izzo thought he was the greatest recruit he had ever met—and he thought Chris liked him, too. In truth, Webber simply had the ability to make everyone he met feel special.

But real or imagined, Izzo was excited. He raced home and told Heathcote, who was also thrilled. Chris Webber signed up early? What could be better than that? The Spartans might even get Jalen Rose, maybe the top guard prospect in the country, since they had started recruiting him heavily at Chris' request. Heathcote wasn't sure Rose was the best type of kid for his program, but the way he saw it, if Webber wants Rose, they'll go for Rose. Chris Webber, as Jud would one day say, "is worth 10 players."

Meanwhile, things did not look rosy for Michigan. Chris had taken his official visit there and had seemed distant, at least to Fisher and his wife, Angie. The kid barely spoke! To make matters worse, they went to a football game Saturday afternoon, and while Chris visited the press box, the adults took their seats. A fan behind them started yakking.

"Hey, isn't that Steve Fisher?" he said, loudly enough for the Webbers to hear.

"Yeah," someone said.

"Man, he hasn't done anything lately."

"Yeah, he can't recruit like Frieder."

"I hear he doesn't even have a chance with Chris Webber."

Angie was dying inside. God! Of all the people to sit behind them! She glanced at Doris Webber, trying to gauge her reaction. Fortunately, Doris had long ago stopped listening to people at sporting events. Still, both Angie and Steve were embarrassed by the incident, and worried about the whole visit, and when the weekend was over, Fisher had only one hope: that Chris would not sign with anyone early. Because, if he did, it wouldn't be Michigan.

This is when the last big break took place for Fisher's Greatest Class Ever Recruited. It came as a result of the ludicrous fever that follows star recruits, and the desperate measures schools attempt in order to gain an edge.

Here's what happened: Chris took a visit to Minnesota, just 10 days before the early signing period. While there, he went to a football game, Minnesota vs. Michigan State at the Metrodome. He visited a private box and took a seat, which, technically, is not allowed by the NCAA, although Webber didn't know it at the time.

Meanwhile, sitting in the booth next door—how's this for coincidence?—was the Michigan State contingent, including Clarence Underwood, their recruiting coordinator.

"Clarence, look, that's Chris Webber!"

"He's not allowed in a private box!"

"And he's wearing a Minnesota sweatshirt. They're not allowed to give him one of those!"

"They're breaking the rules."

"We should get a picture."

"Yeah, somebody get a picture."

"Somebody find a photographer. Quick!"

A female photographer was found. She was sent down to the field and asked to shoot up into the box, with a long-distance lens, so as not to be obvious, like some spy scene out of a Robert Ludlum novel. She followed instructions. Took the pictures. Snap! Snap!

They had their evidence.

And in that single, passionate moment of self-righteousness, Michigan State kissed Chris Webber goodbye.

When Underwood returned to East Lansing, he immediately told Jud Heathcote of his discovery.

"What do you think?" Underwood said.

"What do I think?" Heathcote answered. "I think it's useless. Webber's not going to Minnesota. It's us or Michigan. Why make a fuss like that for? Get rid of the film. Don't tell anyone."

Too late. Someone from the NCAA called that day (how *do* they find these things out?) and someone called again a week later, and Underwood, given his job, could hardly lie about photographs.

Next thing Chris Webber knew, the NCAA was paying a visit, pictures in hand. They gathered Chris, his father, Keener, and representatives from Minnesota at Keener's house, after school, and for three hours grilled them with questions. The meeting got ugly, with

Chris rising several times and screaming, "You're treating us like criminals. What'd we do? What'd we do?"

He blamed Michigan State for turning them in.

And he swore, that evening, he would never go to that school.

All of which put Fisher and Michigan back in the driver's seat. To his credit, Fisher played it smart, never dogging Webber, showing him respect, selling the school to the parents and the need for players to the son.

When Mayce asked Fisher, "Is my boy gonna start immediately?" Fisher was diplomatic:

"I can't promise anybody to start, but if he can start for other schools, I can't see why he wouldn't start for us."

A good answer. Mayce appreciated that. And, of course, Chris liked the idea that Jalen and Perry would probably join him in Ann Arbor. He was talking more and more to Jalen these days, discussing options, making plans.

Poor Michigan State! Desperate to stay in the chase, Heathcote and Izzo apologized profusely to the Webbers, insisting it was not their idea to squeal on them. They continued to come to all the permissible games, and invited Chris and Jalen to come to East Lansing anytime. But they were slipping, and they knew it. Izzo was absolutely livid that MSU should pay a price for a Minnesota act, while Michigan, just down the road, was getting away with Perry Watson acting as, in Izzo's words, "an unofficial recruiter every single day for Chris and Jalen. Anyone who doesn't think so is buying the biggest sandbag in the world."

Sandbag or not, Chris moved closer and closer to picking Michigan. And the addition of Juwan Howard and Jimmy King only enhanced his feelings. Chris wanted to play with talent.

"You know, if we all went to Michigan," he said to Jalen one night, "we could win a championship our freshman year."

Which brings us back to the 1940 Chop House, in downtown Detroit, with Mayce Webber rubbing his head, this guy on the phone offering $150,000, a house, and a job. Mayce thought about Monday, when this would all be over, and he'd be back in the GM plant, moving stock around. Did he say $150,000?

He stopped. He thought of Chris, upstairs, so calm, so happy, ready to meet the press.

After all they'd been through? How could he crack now? One day, Chris would go to the NBA, make $30 million, and $150,000 would be pocket money, he figured.

"How about it, Mayce?" the phone voice said again. "I'm serious."

"Me, too."

He hung up. Climbed the stairs. And never said a word about the offer. He found his son, hugged him, and squeezed alongside him near the podium, where the mob of reporters had gathered, awaiting the word, sweating into their notepads.

"Um, I've made my decision," young Chris said, leaning into the microphone. He pulled a maize and blue hat from a plastic bag and tugged it on his head with a dazzling smile.

"I'm gonna be a Michigan man."

Friends applauded. Mayce exhaled. People ran to the phone to spread the news: the nation's No. 1 high school player had just joined the most impressive collection of high school talent anyone could remember. Michigan now had the best recruiting class in the country.

While most journalists were calling Michigan sources for a comment, one reporter, from East Lansing, placed a call to Tom Izzo, the MSU recruiter. Izzo had been sitting alone in his three-bedroom house, all day, hoping against hope, maybe something will happen, maybe he'll change his mind.

"He picked Michigan, Tom," the reporter said. "I'm sorry."

"Uh-huh. Thanks."

Izzo hung up, sat on the floor, and wept.

9

Steve Fisher was never much for big celebrations, so Angie, his wife, got the wine. It was a special vintage, which they'd discovered on a vacation following the 1989 national championship, the last big thing they'd had to celebrate. She popped the cork and reread the label. "Coach's Insignia" from a place called, believe it or not, "Fisher Vineyards."

"Let's toast," Angie said, lifting her glass.

Steve smiled. The sun was setting in Ann Arbor, and spring had begun to melt the snow along the streets. The campus was coming back to life, and so were the coffee shops and delis along South University and State streets. Michigan is one of the largest universities in the world, indistinguishable from the town it inhabits—you could almost say that Ann Arbor is its campus—with frat houses sitting up the block from suburban cul-de-sacs, and student booksellers sharing walls with clothing and department stores. Whenever you drive, you see cars with maize and blue bumper stickers. Wherever you walk, you see students mixed with townspeople. It is a liberal city, but a serious academic environment. Michigan is ranked in the top 10 nationally in everything from medicine to journalism.

It was not urban, it was not Texas, and so, in the case of the five upcoming basketball recruits, it would be different from anything they had ever experienced. But that didn't stop the student body from buzzing about their arrival. Michigan loved its Wolverines' sports. And the snagging of Chris Webber, Jalen Rose, Juwan Howard, Jimmy King, and Ray Jackson had people more excited about basketball than they had been, well, since Fisher won those six magical games in 1989.

Inside the large Tudor house on Scottwood Road, Fisher tried to keep his mind from racing. Had he really pulled this off? Was someone going to smack him and say, "Wake up, you're dreaming"? Was he really the same man who, just last year, suffered all that criticism as the guy who couldn't recruit?

In one remarkable five-month stretch, Fisher and his coaching staff had reeled in the biggest haul of talent anyone could remember. Haul? It was the mother lode! A recent high school ranking had Chris Webber the No. 1 player in the nation, Juwan Howard No. 3, Jalen Rose No. 6, Jimmy King No. 9, and Ray Jackson No. 84—with Chris, Jimmy, and Juwan the best at their positions. All five were going to Michigan? You get one of those a year, you congratulate yourself.

All five?

People had been calling Fisher nonstop to congratulate him. How'd he do it? Five blue-chippers? And the smallest one was 6 foot 5?

This was better, they crowed, than North Carolina's famed recruiting class last season—which included Eric Montross. This was better than Indiana's crop a few years ago, which produced a national champion.

This was like giving birth to quintuplets, only these quintuplets could shoot, slam, muscle for rebounds, and run the floor like greyhounds. What was more, each could play a different position. There were two potential guards in the mix, Rose and King, two potential forwards, Webber and Jackson, and a potential center, Howard. The symmetry was obvious: in one season, Steve Fisher had recruited a team.

"Cheers," Angie said.

Fisher raised his glass to join her. Again, the enormity of it all! It washed over him like a slow delicious wave. Five blue-chippers!

"Cheers," he answered.

They clinked their glasses.

For a moment, they just sat together, sipping wine, enjoying the quiet. In the serenity of his dark-wood living room, he tried to imagine that blessed moment when he, Steve Fisher, would take charge of the Greatest Class Ever Recruited.

Or would it be the other way around?

II

BIRTH OF THE FAB

1

"Freshmen against y'all."

"Nah, man, let's just play."

"Uh-uh. Freshmen against y'all."

It was fall of 1991, and the Michigan campus was swollen with students. The trees along State Street and "the Diag"—the popular student path that shortcuts past the library—were ablaze with colored leaves, dying a winter's death.

Inside Crisler Arena, where the basketball team plays, something else was dying: the tradition that new guys wait their turn. In most college sports programs, freshmen are grunts. They fetch balls. Hand out water. Carry the bags. And look up to the upperclassmen, who, they figure, can teach them a few things.

That is the norm.

But this was not normal.

This was a pickup scrimmage, the returning players and the five new kids that would make up the 1991–92 Michigan basketball team. Practice had not officially begun, but players were encouraged to get together and work out on their own.

Already, a shift in the power structure was under way.

A hard-fought rebound led to a scuffle between Chris Seter, a senior forward, and Jimmy King, one of the new kids. Seter had yelled, "I don't care who you think you are, you're a freshman around here!"

To which Jalen Rose, the new 6-foot-8 point guard, who sported a shaved head and a fake-diamond earring, and had a habit of yelling "Money!" whenever he fired a shot, immediately responded with a suggestion.

"OK, he's just a freshman. How 'bout we play freshmen against y'all?"

The upperclassmen shook their heads. This Rose kid had already gotten on their nerves with his I'm-in-charge-here attitude. Now he was drawing a line down the middle of the team. Freshmen against the rest? The veterans had been privately avoiding this since pickup games began. They had nothing to gain. In most schools, the older players would win this challenge easily; but in most schools, the veterans didn't post a 14–15 record last season, while the freshmen were winning every high school honor known to man.

"C'mon," Rose repeated, dribbling the ball for emphasis. "Whassup? Freshmen against y'all."

"All right," someone finally said. "Let's go."

And they drifted apart, crossing invisible lines, those who had worn the Michigan uniform before, those who hadn't. Michael Talley, the junior guard, slapped a few of his older teammates on the butt, as if to say, no problem, we can handle these punks, let's just do it. Seter blew a mouthful of aggravated air and dug in.

"Here we go," Rose whispered to Chris Webber.

"Let's run, baby," Juwan Howard said, flipping the ball to King, his roommate, who nodded over at his Texas partner, Ray Jackson.

Whoooooommmppph! A pilot light ignited. Four 18-year-olds and one 17-year-old were making like a doo-wop group dropping naturally into harmonies, creating a basketball far richer than anything they could do apart. Rose looked for Webber, found him with an alley-oop pass, and Webber slammed it with authority. Howard, the big kid from Chicago, took a nice feed in low, turned, and banked one in. Ray Jackson and Jimmy King, the Texas connection, came flying down on fast breaks, two blurs, seemingly out of control, collecting themselves at the last instant to jam it home and swing on the rim. Steals. Slams. They banged bodies on defense and grunted when they fought for rebounds. Sneakers squeaked up and down the hardwood floor, punctuated now and then by a "Whoooo!" holler from one of the freshmen.

The upperclassmen could not match their baskets. And they could not match their enjoyment. The freshmen were having a party out there! They nodded and pointed to each other, backpedaling after baskets as if their union were the most natural thing in the world.

"GAME!"

They won easily.

"GAME!"

They won again.

"Can't check me," they taunted.

"Money!"

Jesus, they do a lot of talking, the upperclassmen thought.

When the last round ended, the ball swishing through the net, there was no applause, there was no sound at all, only heavy breathing. Chris pulled on his shirt and wiped his mouth. Jalen spit and rubbed it into the floor with his sneaker. By the time Steve Fisher, their coach, poked his head inside—*"Just checking, how you fellas doing, all right?"*—it was all over. No box score. No record. No film.

And yet something very tangible had happened that afternoon. They knew it, you could ask them. Outside, the colored leaves were falling, and students in Michigan sweatshirts huddled against the autumn chill. Here, inside an otherwise empty Crisler Arena, quiet thunder had just struck.

The Fab Five had been born.

2

Let's talk about the shorts.

You don't fly the friendly skies from Bangor to Tijuana looking for that last great high school player without learning a thing or two about basketball fashion. Brian Dutcher learned this much: shorts. Big shorts. Long, loose, look-like-your-older-brother's shorts. They were in. Michael Jordan wore them, yanked on them, and as Jordan goes, so goes the basketball world. Dutcher saw a tournament in Illinois where the kids' shorts hung to their shins. He saw a game in Indiana where players deliberately untucked their tops as camouflage, then pulled their shorts halfway down their butts.

Big shorts. Down to the knees. Fly in the breeze. Kids loved them. And since Dutcher prided himself on his ability to relate to the players—and since the greatest class on the planet was coming to Ann Arbor . . .

He called the equipment manager, Bob Bland.

"Hey, Bob. When you order this year's uniforms, get an extra four inches on the shorts, OK?"

"An extra four inches?"

"Yeah."

"On the shorts?"

"Right."

"If you say so."

Just four inches. That's all. Yet in the two years that Webber, Rose, King, Howard, and Jackson would capture the college basketball headlines, all they would do, all they would accomplish, nothing would attract more attention—or symbolize their rebellion—more than those shorts. Big nylon shorts that covered their thighs. Big nylon shorts that sat halfway down their buttocks. Big nylon shorts that made them look as if they were playing, sometimes, inside a Hefty bag. Fisher had not been in favor of the shorts. He winced when Dutcher suggested them. Had this been the old days of Michigan sports, where players were supposed to be honored to simply wear the uniform, the idea of changing style for fashion's sake would be unthinkable. *It was good enough for Cazzie Russell, it's good enough for you!* But these were not the old days, and these were not just any kids, and Dutcher could be so persuasive, and Fisher could be talked into things, and, well . . .

"They'll love 'em, Steve," Dutcher had promised.

And sure enough, when the freshmen arrived on Media Day, and found these new maize uniforms with these extra-long shorts hanging in their lockers, the reaction was thumbs-up.

"Check these out," said Juwan.

"Fresh shorts!" said Ray.

Only Jalen, ever the dealer, held his shorts up to his long skinny frame, and frowned. He looked over to Chip Armer, the hefty, 6-foot-9-inch senior who barely played.

"Yo, man," Jalen whispered, sliding up to Armer. "Lemme trade you shorts."

"Huh?"

"Lemme trade you shorts. You can wear mine. I like 'em *extra* long."

"Uh . . . OK."

Armer wore a 46. Jalen was a 37.

So here was what you saw when the 1991–92 Michigan basketball team emerged from the locker room for its first official encounter with the media: four seniors, four juniors, three sophomores, and five freshmen, Juwan Howard, Jimmy King, Ray Jackson, and Chris Webber, in long maize shorts . . .

. . . and Jalen Rose in a tent.

"Over here! Over here!" the photographers hollered, cameras clicking wildly. "All five freshmen! Can we get all five freshmen! Stand this way . . . Now side by side! Chris in front! . . . Nice shorts! . . ."

The upperclassmen watched in amazement. So this was what it was going to be like. In most programs, the media needs information sheets to identify the rookies. Here they needed one to remember the veterans.

Some of the older players wandered to the far end of the gym and shot baskets by themselves. Nobody interviewed them. Rob Pelinka, the junior guard, came over to Dutcher and pointed to his uniform.

"What about me?" he said. His baggy shorts had not arrived yet—his, and a few other upperclassmen's—so they were issued the regular kind, which now, in comparison, looked like European bathing suits.

"They're coming," Dutcher said. "Sorry. They screwed up the order."

Pelinka walked away. It was not the first time the upperclassmen felt like the show was starting without them.

For this, they would not blame the new players.

They would blame Steve Fisher.

3

Boom, boom, on your black ass, bitch
And here's another hit from my shit . . .

Jalen bopped his head and sang along with the music. Explicit rap was his favorite, and he blasted it over the locker room stereo system during the first weeks of practice. Geto Boys. EPMD. Naughty by Nature. The other freshmen would come in, sliding their shoulders to the beat, and pretty soon it was a regular feature.

Inside his office, Steve Fisher heard the thumping bass lines, but, for the moment, chose to ignore the naughty lyrics—if he understood them. Rap music was not a big part of Fisher's CD collection.

Did he have a CD collection?

Steve Fisher was the other end of rap. He was, in his own words, "pure vanilla," a guy who liked to eat at Dairy Queen, went to church every Sunday, looked like Jimmy Carter, sounded like Don

Knotts, and was maybe the last man on earth you'd expect to round up five supersonic black basketball players from the inner cities and Texas playgrounds, and assemble them into the Greatest Class Ever Recruited.

In fact, compared to the backgrounds of his new star players, Steve Fisher grew up on the set of *Our Town*. He was raised in Herrin, Illinois, a tidy little coal mining town not far from the Kentucky border that, during Fisher's childhood, had a Roman Catholic church, the Polar Whip Drive In, and not a single traffic light. There was no crime to speak of. No drive-by shootings. Kids had to sneak off to smoke cigarettes. Fisher, the second of four children, was woven comfortably into small-town life, delivering newspapers as a boy, playing on all the sports teams, going fishing with his grandfather on Crab Orchard Lake.

His father was a stoic, German-Irish government worker, his mother, a short, fiery Italian woman. Steve—who took after his father—learned quickly that people can coexist without being the same.

This would help immensely with the Fab Five.

So would the fact that, despite his Richie Cunningham background, Fisher was a good player himself in high school, a wiry point guard who might have gone on to a major college program had he not hurt his knee in his senior year. Fisher accepted his knee injury with the same "Nothing I can do about it" attitude that would define his personality later in life. He had, as his older brother, John, would put it, "an unbelievable ability to play the hand that was dealt him."

He went to Illinois State, on a partial athletic scholarship, and decided to become a coach. His goal was to one day make it to Division I basketball. That's all. He wasn't thinking about national championships. He wasn't thinking about recruiting a kid like Chris Webber.

Back then, Fisher was a skinny jock with wire-rim glasses, fond of Levi's and junk food. He went through the tumultuous 1960s without the slightest bit of tumult. He didn't protest the war. He wasn't into free love. He wore no beads or headbands. He didn't even like the Beatles. His bum knee and a low lottery number kept him out of the draft, and when he graduated Illinois State, he took a job at Rich East High School in Park Forest, Illinois, as assistant varsity basketball coach and varsity tennis coach.

He was happy.

He stayed there 11 years.

It was at Rich East that Fisher—who took over varsity basketball in 1971—coached his first black player, a talented transfer named Roscoe Young, Jr. Fisher's hometown, Herrin, had been almost exclusively white, nearly all of his college teammates were white, and he was so naive to black culture at that point—and this was 1971—that when he asked Roscoe to tell him about another kid who was running around the track, Fisher said, "Who's that colored fellow over there?"

"He's not colored, coach," Roscoe said, "he's black."

This began Fisher's education.

He learned. One of Fisher's strengths—and weaknesses—is the pliable nature of his personality. He will bend. He will tolerate a lot. But he will also change.

His future critics would be surprised to learn that Fisher, back at Rich East, was quite a disciplinarian. Having himself been coached in high school by a man who whacked his players' butts with a paddle if they didn't listen, Fisher had no problem being strict. When a player was slacking off in the classroom, he would grab his uniform and curl it around his fist, drawing the kid closer and closer as he said, "I . . . want . . . you . . . going . . . to . . . class!"

When he first started coaching, Fisher interrupted the action every two minutes for instructions or criticisms. But when his star player summoned the courage to come to him and say, "Coach, you do so much interrupting we never get a chance to play during practice—and then we don't know how to play during the game," Fisher listened. He admitted he was wrong. And he loosened the reins.

And his teams won.

Another idea that would resurface with the Fab Five.

Fisher met his future wife, Angie Wilson, at that school. She liked him because he was focused, stable, and when he got embarrassed by something, his round cheeks would turn beet red. On a seminar questionnaire, he had listed his goals in life as (1) to be a Division I coach, (2) own a nice house, (3) drive a Cadillac. This was perfect for Angie, who herself was not a fast-lane person.

They dated for several years, and on New Year's Day, 1974,

Fisher was over at her apartment, watching the Rose Bowl. She drew up a piece of paper and slipped it in front of him.

> *If we don't get married this summer,*
> *I am leaving you.*
>
> *Check a box:*
> *X—Yes, I will marry you.*
> *X—No, I won't marry you.*

Fisher checked yes.
Angie kissed him, and called her mother.
He continued to watch the game.

So he has always been good with what's put in front of him. Taking the 1989 Wolverines to the national championship was proof of that.

And now fate—and a hell of a recruiting effort—had left him in charge of the most highly acclaimed freshman class in history. And he had to figure out all these major issues: Who would start? How could he keep the others happy?

What about the rap music?

Were he a control freak, like some coaches, he would have laid down the law about behavior, about discipline, about how you talk, how you dress, what music plays in the locker room. But had he been a control freak, he would not have gotten the likes of Chris, Jalen, Juwan, Jimmy, and Ray to commit to his program. They didn't want to play for John Thompson or Bobby Knight. They didn't want someone, as football coaches often put it, "breaking them down and building them up." These were five confident kids, with strong personalities. Fisher's strength—and the thing the freshmen liked about him—was that he ruled with an iron stomach, not an iron fist. He tolerated. He was flexible. While some coaches' power is in their movement, Fisher's was in his ability to stand still, to endure rough moments, confident they would pass.

He would suffer much criticism for this approach—especially with his loud and flamboyant group of freshmen. But, to turn Norman Maclean's description of midwestern life on its side, when it came to Steve Fisher, "a river ran around him."

He would let the Fab Five be themselves.

For better or for worse.

4

As the season approached, there was one question on all the players' minds: Who is going to start? Or, in the case of the upper-classmen, who *isn't* going to start? It was a touchy issue, and the two groups—new players, old players—would never talk about it in mixed company.

"I wonder if Fish is gonna go with me," Juwan said one night in the dorms.

"He's got to play us if we're the best, right?" Jalen said.

"Man, I know I ain't startin'," Ray said in his Texas drawl. "I'm thinking they forgot they recruited me."

"Maybe he won't start any of us," Chris said.

They stared at him.

And they laughed.

"What are you worried about, boy?" Jalen said, sneering. "You know *you're* gonna start. You're a lock."

"Yeah," said Jimmy. "You were starting before you even got here."

"Yeah."

"Chris be like, 'Oh, please, coach, can I start, I was the No. 1 player in the country last year,' " Juwan said, laughing.

"Naw, naw!" Chris said, smiling despite himself. "It's not like that."

But it was. They could all see it. Chris was different. Even in a roomful of stars, he stood out.

Michigan athletics had an impressive roster. Tom Harmon, who won the Heisman Trophy. Cazzie Russell, who starred in the NBA. Jim Harbaugh, who quarterbacks the Chicago Bears. Mike Barrowman, who captured an Olympic gold medal. They were all famous when they left.

But none of them ever *arrived* with the fanfare of Chris Webber.

Remember, Chris was a statewide legend at a university in which 70 percent of the undergrads are from the state. People used to drive a hundred miles to see Webber play in high school. Kurt Keener, his coach at Country Day, purposely arranged games all over Michigan—Battle Creek, Saginaw, Grand Rapids, even Traverse City, way up north, a five-hour drive—just so the population could be exposed to his prize player. The gyms were sold out weeks in advance. Citizens in those towns would rush the bus when it arrived, waiting for Webber to step off so they could get a glimpse of him. *Look at how big he is! Hey, he's nice-looking, too! And so polite! Did you see that dunk!*

He was a basketball rendition of Elvis Presley on the Louisiana Hayride, a local legend about to burst like a nova. Already, he had been featured on network TV and in *Sports Illustrated.*

So when he arrived in Ann Arbor, there was no sitting on the egg of his fame; he was hatched. People asked for autographs as he carried bags into his dorm. Faculty wanted to know if they had him in their classes. When he went to study table, the stars from the football and baseball teams all wanted to talk to him.

The women were always calling.

"It's funny," he said of the attention one day after practice, "I haven't even played yet."

But he would. There was no doubt about that. With his huge hands, his lightning reflexes, and this certain gleam of stardom that seemed to burst off his teeth whenever he smiled, this was one freshman even the upperclassmen couldn't deny.

What about the others? The newspapers had started calling them "the Fab Five"—even though it was not an original moniker, having been used before on a U-M team in the '80s—but none besides Chris were guaranteed a starting spot.

So practice was becoming brutal. The upperclassmen gave no quarter during drills. No one wanted to lose his starting position. These older Wolverines may not have posted a great record the year before, but they were not exactly water boys. Michael Talley had been a consensus All-American his senior year at Detroit's Cooley High, every bit as heralded as Rose was two years later. Rich McIver was a Player of the Year in Texas. Eric Riley and Kirk Taylor were All-State players in Ohio. James Voskuil, Sam Mitchell, and Jason Bossard were All-State in Michigan, Rob Pelinka was All-State in Illinois.

Such is the level of big-time college basketball. There are no slouches, even on losing teams. Each of the Michigan upperclassmen had come through the chute with the highest of accolades. Some went further than others. But none of them wanted to move over for a freshman.

Even if that freshman could dunk from the foul line.

"Get off me, bitch," Juwan would yell.

"Shut up, punk," Riley would answer.

"I'm schooling you today," Jalen would threaten.

"Not today, boy," Mitchell would answer.

Arguments started. Small fights broke out. Chris Seter, the rarely used 6-foot-9 forward, nearly came to blows with Jalen, who had been bragging about how good he was going to be. Seter told him he wasn't there yet. Another time, Jason Bossard, a bulky sophomore guard, got tangled with Jimmy King and knocked him to the ground.

"Hey, I don't give a shit who you are!" Bossard yelled as his teammates grabbed him. "I've been here two years, and you just got here."

That pretty much summed up the sentiments. Usually, the heat from these confrontations would blow off by the end of practice, and no harm, no complaints. In fact, coaches often encourage such competition, within reason. Builds courage, they figure.

Still, there were funny moments, too. Fisher, who wasn't exactly hip to the new airy fashion look, constantly yelled at Ray and Jimmy about their shorts.

"Ray, will you pull your pants up, for pete's sake!" he would holler.

"Jimmy, I told you yesterday, get your shorts off your ass!"

Everybody would laugh at this, and even Fisher would have to grin. And then there was the time Chip Armer, the large but rather stiff center, went to shoot left-handed and somehow—and this is really quite a mystery—blocked his own shot with his right hand. The gym burst into hysterics. The freshmen were laughing so hard they ran up into the stands to scream. Fisher was trying not to say anything, to save Armer the embarrassment, but his cheeks got so red from holding it in he finally exploded like a balloon.

"Ohhhhhhh SHIIIT!" they all hollered, tears coming from their eyes. "Oooooohhh . . . oooohhhhh . . . shiiiiit!"

At times like that, they were like any other college team, private laughs, private jokes, wonderful moments that pulled them together as a unit. You would never know they were some sort of historical embryo.

"How do they look, honey?" Angie would ask him as the season opener approached.

"I don't know," he said honestly. "I really can't tell you."

And he couldn't. Fisher went to sleep each night with an excited but unclear feeling. So much raw talent. So much unharnessed speed, strength, leaping ability.

At times they were wonderful, the best, they looked like God's own basketball children.

And at times he had to tell them to pull their pants up.

5

Cobo Arena, in downtown Detroit, just across the river from Canada, was once the home of the Detroit Pistons. This was before the 1968 race riots, which spurred massive exodus and left vacant buildings the unofficial symbol of the Motor City. Today the Pistons play out in the suburbs, and Cobo is used mostly for conventions, auto shows, and an occasional religious revival meeting. At times it sits empty altogether, bordered by a waterfront that is eerily quiet.

But on December 2, 1991, Cobo Arena made a small piece of history: it was host to the first official game of Michigan's Fab Five Freshmen.

Basketball-wise, it was hardly a night to remember.

In front of a small, loosely mixed crowd of 9,989 people, the Wolverines and the University of Detroit–Mercy Titans were introduced. Some fans pointed at Michigan's oversized shorts and laughed. *"Got enough material there, fellas?"* Others were anxious to see what these ballyhooed U-M kids could do. To polite applause, Chris Webber and Jalen Rose, the homegrown kids, trotted out for the starting lineup, alongside junior guard Michael Talley and senior forward Freddie Hunter, a walk-on. Juwan Howard started at center, a mild surprise. Fisher didn't decide until shortly before game time, benching Eric Riley, the junior who had been second in the conference in rebounding and blocked shots last season.

"Eric, I'm going to go with Juwan," Fisher told his junior center, trying to make it sound matter-of-fact. "You'll get a lot of time off the bench. I need you to be as ready as you always were."

Riley said "OK." But he was crushed. In his mind, he had lost his position, and there are few things more humiliating to an athlete.

Which doesn't mean that Fisher made the right move. Michigan won the opening tap, and here is how the Fabulous Era began: Juwan threw the ball right into the arms of two U of D players. Turnover.

Next time he touched it, he threw it out of bounds. Turnover.

Next time he touched it—*shreeee!*—he was called for traveling. Turnover.

Three chances, three mistakes. What a start. At this rate, they could lose by 100.

Less than one minute into the new season, Fisher yanked his first freshman.

He resisted the urge to check his birth certificate.

Howard took a seat, shaking his head, and slumped next to Perry Watson, who patted him on the back and whispered, "Don't worry about it." Fisher tried to tell himself the same thing. *Patience. You're gonna need patience.* Whatever magic these freshmen had produced in those private scrimmages, it was absent now, under the lights and cameras and the referee's whistle. Rose had a shot blocked. Webber tossed an air ball. Fisher shuffled players in and out, always mindful of having too many new kids out there at once.

The game was ugly. Fortunately, U of D wasn't much of a threat. With only one player taller than 6 foot 6, the Titans gave the Wolverines second and third chances on rebounds. So when the Wolverines weren't busy dropping the ball, or throwing it behind people, or taking too many steps with it—they committed 34 turnovers, which is sort of like hitting every other car on the highway—they were able to dunk and drive and drop a few jumpers. The crowd was occasionally impressed, especially when Webber took an alley-oop feed from Rose and thunder-slammed it in a single swooping motion. Still, the overall product was sloppy—that's being polite—and Fisher was relieved when the final buzzer sounded.

For the record, Webber finished his first college game with 19 points, 17 rebounds, and *seven* turnovers. He also fouled out.

Howard finished with 13 points, nine rebounds, and six turnovers. He also fouled out.

And U-M won, 100–74.

A TV announcer called it "high school basketball at the collegiate level." Reporters joked about breaking the all-time turnover record. Fisher left the arena with a sigh, and more questions than he'd had when the evening began.

"I didn't think anybody played particularly well," he said diplomatically.

Patience, he told himself. Patience.

Game two was also on the road, in Cleveland, against Cleveland State, coached by Mike Boyd, who, of course, in his own way, was largely responsible for the Fab Five's existence. Boyd smiled at Jimmy and Ray during warm-ups, and remembered not too long ago when he was recruiting them for U-M.

Now he had to try and stop them.

The game was pretty much a reward for Boyd's loyal years in Ann Arbor. When a major program like Michigan plays a smaller program like Cleveland State, the former usually gains an easy victory, the latter gains prestige, broadcast money, and a big ticket night. It's the least you can do for an ex-assistant, right?

And indeed, the arena was packed, a near sellout, with 13,055 curious fans. Once again, Chris, Jalen, and Juwan started for U-M. And once again, the game was a mess. The Wolverines' first four possessions were a backcourt violation, a pass thrown out of bounds, a missed jumper, and an offensive foul. Juwan again seemed to be a Not Ready for Prime Time Player, making just one of seven shots. Michigan turned the ball over 27 times, an improvement over the opening night fiasco, but hardly acceptable.

They still won, 80–61.

Boyd shook hands warmly with Fisher afterward. "Don't worry, they'll be something when they start clicking, Steve."

"Yeah. I hope so."

Fisher headed for the bus. After two shaky road wins, the Wolverines were only two games away from the biggest challenge of the nonconference season, the Duke Blue Devils, the defending national champions, who were coming to Ann Arbor the second weekend in December. People were already talking about that game. Fisher shuddered. "We're not ready for a team like that right now," he told his staff. "Hell, we're barely getting past U of D."

There were other problems, too. Backups like bulky forward Sam Mitchell were worried about their future. Sam had been the last man off the bench in this game. And he'd barely played in the season opener. He remembered that meeting at study table last spring, when Tony Tolbert wrote Sam's name on the pad, then scribbled a "1" for minutes. Maybe he was right. Already, Sam could see that playing behind Webber, Howard, Riley, and James Voskuil wasn't going to leave him much time. He glanced around the sparkling new Cleveland State Convocation Centre, with its forest-green-and-white paint job. He thought about the Vikings and Coach Boyd.

"Man," Sam said to himself, "I could be starting for these guys, easy."

By the following season, he would be.

6

Not long after the semester began, Juwan and a friend from Chicago named Lamont "Juice" Carter were walking near the Michigan track when they heard the pop of a gun. Instinctively they dove to the ground and covered their heads.

"Shit," Juice said, looking up.

"What?" said Juwan.

It was only a starter's pistol, shooting into the air. They got up, two city kids, embarrassed and dirty. Still, the fact that they both hit the ground, even here, on the picturesque Michigan campus, spoke volumes.

"This place is really different," the freshmen would say that first semester. They may have been the Greatest Class Ever Recruited, but it didn't take long for Chris, Jalen, Juwan, Ray, and Jimmy to feel like strangers in a strange land.

Michigan is a huge university set among the tall burr oaks that surround Ann Arbor. The Huron River runs just outside of town, and people picnic on its banks. It's a long way from the bad side of Detroit or Chicago.

Enrollment in the university is around 36,000. Maybe 2,600— or eight percent—are black.

Three out of every four students are white.

This alone was a jolt to kids like Juwan, Jalen, and Ray, who were used to almost exclusively black high schools and neighborhoods. Jalen freely admitted, "I never had a white teammate before I got here. And I never had any white friends."

All Michigan freshmen are required to live in the dorms. And here, too, the Fab Five were in the minority. Jalen roomed with Chris, Juwan roomed with Jimmy. Ray roomed with sophomore Sam Mitchell, all in South Quad, alongside all the other pimple-plagued, mostly white freshmen new to campus. Many of them would come gawking outside the players' doors, hoping to sneak a peek at Chris Webber, who enjoyed a cult hero status in Michigan. Jalen couldn't understand that, any more than he could understand why his neighbors complained about playing rap music late into the night. "What's their problem?" he asked.

There were other adjustments. Academics were demanding— even though the freshmen players had a significant safety net, a mandatory four-nights-a-week study table, and an academic adviser named Bob Clifford, who would visit them after practice and call at night to remind them of papers and exams. And then there were the three-hour practices, and the planes and hotels of a road trip. All this was sharply different from high school.

Mostly, there was this whole different value system of the campus around them. People forget that big-time college basketball, in many cases, takes its stars from one environment and asks them to perform in another.

So while many Michigan students filled the cappuccino shops with talk of research grants and entry-level management positions, the Fab Five hung out in the gym or at the Touchdown Cafe, talking about the studs they knew in the NBA.

And while many Michigan students picked up the political and business sections of the newspaper to discuss the latest developments, the Fab Five grabbed the sports section and read about themselves.

And when time came for social bragging, many of Michigan's more affluent students compared cars, or family incomes, and who had it the best.

The Fab Five bragged about the 'hood.

And who had it the worst.

Jalen boasted of Detroit parties he'd been to that were broken up by gunfire. Chris spoke of violence in a Detroit movie theater, where he got "wrecked" and had his jacket stolen off his back. Ray told of kids he'd grown up with who were in prison now, drugs, robberies. Juwan recalled one time, on 135th Street, when he hung his stuff on the clothesline in the morning, and an hour later it had all been stolen.

Only Jimmy, having grown up in Plano, had few horror stories to tell. And of course, he was teased unmercifully.

"Jimmy, you're like that TV show *Dallas*, with all the money!" the others would laugh.

"Naw, naw, Plano's not like that."

"Yeah, you rich. You got like oil wells and everything."

"Aw, you don't know nothing about it."

Jimmy sulked. It bothered him. In a virtual flip-flop from the university around them, the freshmen acted as if there was nothing worse than having had it good.

7

The freshmen may have been running the show, but the official captain of the Wolverines was a bald-headed, 22-year-old senior psychology major who was paying for his own education. Freddie Hunter was probably the least likely candidate to lead the Greatest Class Ever Recruited. He wasn't even on scholarship! The coaches had discovered him in the intramural leagues, heading a team called "Freddie and the Seven Dwarfs," scoring at will against flabby students who just wanted to get a little exercise. Hunter had played in high school, he was 6 foot 5, and so desperate were the Wolverines for talent—remember, this was after Rumeal Robinson, Terry Mills, Loy Vaught, and Sean Higgins all departed, and Eric Montross took a pass—that he was brought to Crisler and made the team immediately. He wound up starting 12 games in the 1990–91 season.

Now here he was, leading calisthenics and team prayers, and trying to influence the most famous group of freshmen that had ever walked into a Wolverines locker room.

"I like your bald head, man," Jalen had told him. "It brings out the dog in you."

Well. At least Freddie had that going for him.

He didn't have the monthly room-and-board check, or the tuition refund, or any of the other financial niceties that the star recruits enjoyed; when all five of them committed, and several fifth-year seniors returned, there were simply no scholarships left. Fisher apologized. What could he do?

So Hunter, who grew up in Detroit, worked and studied and

worked and played basketball, and at times he must have wondered where the fairness was in life, especially when the freshmen behaved like, well, freshmen. As captain, Hunter had wanted the team to huddle up before each game and give a traditional "Go Blue!" cheer.

The freshmen said uh-uh.

"Go Blue?"

"That's baby shit."

"We need somethin' real."

"Somethin' fresh."

They played around with expressions. Eventually they found one, in the lyrics of a rap song by Ray's favorite group, the Geto Boys.

"LET YOUR NUTS HANG!"

Let your nuts hang?

8

A cold wind blew outside Crisler Arena, where students had camped the night before, hoping for good seats to Saturday's game. It was final-exams week, the malls were stuffed with Christmas shoppers, and everything about the blustery day suggested football season. In fact, there was a football story brewing. Michigan's flashy wide receiver, Desmond Howard, was a favorite for college football's biggest prize, the Heisman Trophy. The results would be televised on CBS, after the basketball game. Inside Crisler, special screens had been set up for viewing. Many joked that the vote would be more dramatic than the game.

Fisher feared they were right. Duke was the reigning national champion, the model program. If they had written *In Search of Excellence* about college basketball, the cover would have been a Blue Devil, holding a ball in one hand and a calculus book in the other. Powerful. Smart. Confident. Even Fisher had sighed, "We're approaching this game as if we're playing the Chicago Bulls."

What he didn't know yet was his freshmen would rather play the Chicago Bulls than the pretenders they had faced so far. Eastern Michigan, Chicago State, Cleveland State, and the University of Detroit—Mercy? Come on. These were kids who were used to playing summers against NBA stars, big names like Isiah Thomas, Mark

Aguirre, Steve Smith. They got up for that kind of competition. They tolerated the rest. Much to Fisher's dismay, the Fab Five did not believe that all opponents were created equal. To them, the schedule was divided this way:

1. Games That Mattered.
2. Games to Be Endured.

Duke was definitely a No. 1.

In fact, they already hated the Blue Devils. Duke was so . . . composed! So disciplined, so well mannered, so well coiffed! Regular shorts, regular haircuts, always in suits coming to and from games. Duke's coach, Mike Krzyzewski, was the Zen master for intelligence over insolence; his star players, the handsome forward Christian Laettner and the buck-toothed point guard Bobby Hurley, were two polite white kids with all the fundamentals. Laettner was so good-looking he didn't even sweat like other people. He looked like a Calvin Klein model who'd just been spritzed.

Besides, wasn't Duke the team that stopped the University of Nevada–Las Vegas juggernaut last season? UNLV was what basketball was all about to Jalen, Chris, Ray, Juwan, and Jimmy, loose and jamming and free-spirited and in-your-face. Yet Duke, in its prissy superiority, had defeated the Runnin' Rebels in the Final Four, biggest upset of the year, these punky kids from Durham, North Carolina, with no names on the back of their uniforms, jumping and pointing the No. 1 fingers and cutting down the nets.

It made the Fab Five sick.

"I hate it when Fish talks about Duke like they're unbeatable," Webber mumbled to Rose during warm-ups. "How come he doesn't give us more credit? We're good, too."

"I know it," Rose agreed.

"I'm gonna show him today."

"I know it."

"No stopping us today."

"I know it."

The arena filled. The cameras rolled. And a nationwide audience got its first look at the Greatest Class Ever Recruited, as the CBS announcers read their names aloud. The student crowd, grateful to be out of the cold, was not going to sit there quietly. They roared during the introductions. They sang "The Victors" with the band. The noise reached a fever pitch as Fisher gave his last instructions to his hungry troops.

"Let's give everyone a touch on the first play, OK? Work it around! Everyone a touch! Let's go!"

The ball was tossed, Chris tapped it to Juwan, who took two dribbles and fired a shot with nobody underneath.

Clank!

Everybody a touch?

"I must be talking to myself," Fisher thought, flopping back in his seat. "I swear I must be talking to myself."

It got worse from there. Webber fouled Grant Hill on Duke's first basket. Rose picked up two fouls in five minutes, then got a third and sat almost the rest of the half. Howard continued his habit of bad starts, traveling, then traveling again. Jimmy King, who didn't start but came in quickly off the bench, was hitting his long-range baskets, but not often enough. Duke cruised to comfortable leads, nine points, 13 points, even 17 points. The crowd noise quickly died. It was embarrassing. Fisher's pregame fear—"I just pray we don't get blown out on national television"—seemed a sure bet, and the referees were not kind to the young Wolverines, blowing whistles at anything that even *looked* like an infraction. After one such tweet, fans threw trash on the floor, and Fisher had to grab the PA microphone and address the crowd: "THIS IS MICHIGAN. WE'VE GOT GREAT FANS. CHEER. DON'T THROW ON THE FLOOR."

On the other hand, he thought, if you refs made a decent call, maybe they wouldn't.

Duke went into halftime with a 43–33 lead, and it would have been a lot worse if not for a late spurt of Michigan baskets just before the buzzer. The only thing that kept fans from giving up altogether was the occasional flashes of brilliance—and insolence—that the freshmen had showed.

Especially Webber.

He had dunked over Laettner early in the game and had mouthed off to him: "You're weak. You ain't nothing. I just dunked on you on national television. How'd it feel?"

"Go away, little schoolboy," Laettner said.

Webber did not go away. He slammed again between Hill and Laettner. He blocked one shot by Antonio Lang, then blocked the follow-up and caught it in midair. Unlike many of his teammates, he was playing a terrific game. The star was stepping into the spotlight. So there was hope.

In the locker room, Fisher told them they had to stay focused, stop turning the ball over so much, calm down, play like they were capable of playing.

"It's only a 10-point lead, we can overcome it," he said.

And they surprised him.

They listened.

"All right, time to play, time to play," Jalen exhorted as they took the floor, cleansed of that first half. A minute later, Jalen scored his first basket of the day, a short jumper, and the Wolverines came together. Something about Rose. He was a catalyst, his confidence was contagious: when he had it, the team had it.

And suddenly they all had it. Webber spun and slammed. He took a pass from Jalen and slammed again. He took an alley-oop from Michael Talley and rammed it so hard through the rim it almost spun back out. Webber stared at Laettner as he ran downcourt after that one, a death stare, a gunslinger stare, and the fans were on their feet, cheering. A spark had been ignited.

Things began to tilt.

Duke's lead was cut to seven, then to five. The Blue Devils were making uncharacteristic mistakes. Laettner threw a pass away. Brian Davis double-dribbled, and Jalen taunted him. "Double, double, you in trouble."

Webber slammed down an offensive rebound. Rose tossed in a driving leaner. King sank a three-pointer. They had sync. They had rhythm. It was like watching a house being built in a single afternoon. You looked at the scoreboard and—whoa, what's this?—Michigan, barely old enough to vote, had a lead over the best team in the nation, and there were less than five minutes to go!

With the shot clock winding down, Webber found himself outside the three-point line, top of the key, no one open for a pass. "Oh, no," Fisher thought. But Webber squared like a guard and fired away, a shot that seemed to take three minutes to arrive at the rim. What was he doing? A three-pointer? The Big Man? What's he doi—

Swish!

"THAT'S THE STUFF LEGENDS ARE MADE OF!" screamed CBS analyst Billy Packer.

The crowd went berserk, leaping, slapping hands, giddy as a Christmas morning. They sensed that moment that is universal to all great upsets: the subtraction of fear by the underdog.

Michigan could actually win it.

The Wolverines were up, 74–71, less than a minute left, when a pass was poked away and Rose and Laettner went to the floor for the loose ball. They grabbed it together. Whistles blew. Laettner laughed and tried to yank away the ball. He said, "Give it up, little fella." You don't say that to Rose, who yanked the ball back, and they were tugging and yelling, then Jalen was on his feet, his fists clenched.

"You ain't all that!" Jalen yelled.

"Grow up," Laettner said.

The referees jumped between them.

"You ain't nuthin'! You want it? You gonna get it."

"Go away."

"You want it? You gonna get it."

Rose, in his mind, was only doing what he'd always done, in St. Cecilia's and Bishop Borgess and the Northwest Activity Center and all the other hardwood hotboxes of his youth: never, ever, let anyone embarrass you in your house. Laettner was laughing at him? Not acceptable.

Critics would not understand this. But Jalen didn't care. This was war. The game had grown so intense, so full of slapping hands and diving bodies, that there were only free throws scored for the rest of regulation. Hurley made a pair after Talley fouled him diving for a loose ball. Rose made a pair after Hurley fouled him to avoid a sure dunk. With 37 seconds left, Michigan still led by three, 76–73, and Laettner pulled up outside the three-point line. He had made shots like this his whole career, killer shots in critical moments, but this one clanked off the front of the rim, and all Michigan had to do was grab it, grab it, and they had the win in hand. Grab it! Grab it! But the rebound was high, and Hurley got it on one bounce. Without a dribble, he launched a desperation three-pointer. Webber came flying over to try and block it, swallowing Hurley whole . . .

The shot missed badly off the iron. But Webber, desperate to block it, landed on Hurley instead, knocked him to the floor, and the refs blew the whistle. Fisher dropped his head. Disaster.

A three-point attempt gets three shots when fouled.

Hurley could tie the game at the line.

And he did. One. *Swish.* Two. *Swish.* Three. *Swish.* Michigan had a last chance to win in regulation, a desperation heave by Webber from 60 feet away. The crowd held its breath, the ball flew in a strong low arch. It smacked off the front of the rim, and the buzzer sounded.

Overtime.

Although Jimmy King came off the court laughing—"That's all right, dog," he said, consoling Webber, "we got 'em, we got 'em,"—they did not have 'em, and they would not win this game. Duke went back to its basketball surgery, drawing reach-in fouls and going to the free throw line. When Webber tried to poke the ball away from Laettner, the whistle blew again, and Laettner smacked his fist in the air and hollered "YES!" That was five fouls. Webber was out. The crowd moaned. Webber had scored 27 points, grabbed 12 rebounds, and blocked three shots. He was arguably the best player on the floor—for either team—and he was 18 years old. He bit his lip and dropped sadly into his seat.

It was catch-up from that point on. Duke made all 10 of its free throws. And when Rob Pelinka's heaving three-point shot at the buzzer missed badly, the Fab Five had lost their virginity, suffered their first collegiate defeat—against a Duke team that would prove the old saying "The first cut is the deepest."

"You played well," Fisher told them in the locker room. "We made some mistakes that cost us, but you showed leadership, and pride . . ."

Fisher chose his words carefully. He could see the hurt in their faces. "Listen," he said, "you're not as bad as you think you are right now. But you're also not as good as people will say you are. I want you to remember that."

Across the hall, in the Duke locker room, he was being proven prophetic.

"We knew they were good," said Hurley, "we just didn't know they were *that* good already."

"We escaped today, pure and simple," Grant Hill said, shaking his head. "They're the best team we've faced in two years."

"They're better than Vegas."

Better than Vegas? This was exactly the kind of compliment Fisher feared. He foresaw the sudden headlines about his phenomenal freshman class. Predictions of greatness. Expectations that were unrealistic. He worried that the public would think the Wolverines had actually won this game, simply by making it close.

Still, he had learned something today, and he thought about it as he watched his players dress. These freshmen had an extra gear when it came to big games. They knew when it mattered, and they turned it up. Hell. This was the best team in the country they'd just played, and his kids were genuinely angry that they didn't win by 20.

Fisher thought back to his 1989 Michigan championship team. They, too, seemed to live for the big moment. That's what it takes, he told himself.

Now.

How could he bottle it?

9

Ann Arbor emptied for Christmas break, because, like most college towns, it breathed in and out with student schedules.

College athletes are not so lucky. There is always some other tournament to go to, more games, more competition. The Wolverines had only two free days to race home for Christmas, buy presents, do a little mistletoe kissing with girls they left behind, and get back to campus in time to leave for the Red Lobster Classic in Orlando, Florida.

Still, two days was enough time for Ray Jackson. Maybe too much. He flew home to Austin, with its warmer winter breezes, and his childhood friends, and his beloved father, who gave him a hug. And part of Ray didn't even want to go back to college. Of all the freshmen, he had played the fewest minutes and was the least sought after for interviews or autographs. His parents and friends had come to Ann Arbor for the Duke game, but Ray barely got in. He couldn't face them afterward. Although sitting the bench would be completely understandable for most freshman athletes, Ray was so upset he left the locker room without taking a shower and went straight home alone. When people asked him about the Fab Five, Ray would sigh and say, "It ain't no Fab Five, it's Fab Four plus whoever they stick in there."

That hurt, but it hurt even more when he went back to Texas, where he'd been a star. Austin was suddenly a bittersweet memory for Ray. Everywhere he went, people asked the same thing. "Why aren't you playing more? You should be the man!"

"Yeah," he said, shrugging, looking down. "I know."

Jud Heathcote, the Michigan State coach, says freshman year is the most unhappy for all basketball players, and not just because many of them are not starting, but because they're not *starring*.

He's right. Remember that almost every recruit who pulls on a college uniform was a major star in high school and is used to the spotlight.

Six months earlier, Ray Jackson had been burning up the nets in Austin. People came to see him, they whispered and pointed when he took the court. Now some other high school star was the new rage, and Ray was far away, playing 12 minutes a game. It hurt.

"What do you think I should do?" Ray asked his father, the football coach.

"Nothing you can do right now," he said. "Just do what they ask you. Make the most of your opportunities."

"But they ain't giving me a chance."

"Son, lemme ask you something. Who gave you your basketball ability?"

Ray thought for a minute. He remembered all the morning rides with his father in the car, going to school, with the gospel music on.

"God," he said.

"That's right. God gave it to you. Now, if God gave it to you, how can anybody take it away from you?"

"I guess they can't."

"They can't. Nobody can. Not Michigan. Not Fisher. Nobody."

Ray sighed. His folks told him to hang in there, stuffed him with Christmas goodies, kissed him goodbye.

"At least Orlando's warm," Ray told himself, going to the airport. "I don't have to deal with that snow shit for a few days."

Orlando would prove that everything is relative. For while Ray was moping about the start of his Michigan career, Sam Mitchell, his roommate, was reaching the end of his.

Already, Sam hadn't played in the last three games. He hoped that would change in Florida. But after the first game of the mini-tournament—in which Michigan beat Brigham Young—Sam was caught after curfew with a girl.

So was Juwan Howard.

Two separate incidents. Same violation. They weren't in bed

with the girls, just hanging around in the parking lot past the designated in-room hour.

"We can't have this, men," Fisher yelled at the team meeting. "The players caught will be punished. That's why we have rules."

Juwan was worried. For Sam, this was rock bottom. He was going nowhere on this team, and he knew it. Now this?

When most of the players gathered in a hotel room that night, Sam looked beaten. He told them he was transferring.

"I'm outa here. You guys know I can't get no minutes. I'm only a sophomore. If I transfer, I can still have a career."

His teammates nodded, including the freshmen. Surprisingly they were welcome in this meeting. Very little blame was directed at the new kids, not for playing time. Deep down, the older players knew if they were given those minutes, they'd take them, too.

It was the coaches they blamed.

"Do what you gotta do, Sam," Chris said.

"Yeah, ain't no fun if you ain't playing," Ray said, half talking to himself.

There was a knock at the door. It was Fisher, asking what's going on, break it up. Fisher didn't like players-only meetings, and this one quickly scattered. But the upperclassmen were saddened by Sam's announcement, and they went to sleep thinking about what it meant for the rest of them. It was the first crack in the foolish hope that this team could be big enough for everyone.

The following night, in the championship game, the crack grew larger. Juwan Howard was "punished" for his curfew violation by not starting. Eric Riley took his place. But six minutes into the game, Juwan was inserted. And he had sat next to Perry Watson the whole time before going in, getting tips, keeping his head in the game. Juwan wound up playing 24 minutes, two more than Riley, even though Juwan missed every shot he took in the second half.

Sam Mitchell, meanwhile, sat at the farthest end of the bench and never unzipped his sweats.

The game was ugly, turnovers, bad shots, poor ballhandling, but Michigan, taller and stronger, still won by a dozen, 63–51.

When the press asked why Fisher had started three freshmen, but not Howard, he said, laughing, "I was fearful you were going to keep bugging me for the fifth freshman, so I thought I'd go back to three."

His frivolity stung players like James Voskuil, Eric Riley, Rich

McIver, and Michael Talley. Why not tell them what really happened? Why not say one of the freshmen screwed up? They felt a bond had been broken, that things were going to be different this year, no matter how much they protested. The freshmen would be in one category, and everyone else in another.

Fisher himself had often stated, "Everyone on this team will be treated fairly, but not the same."

When Sam Mitchell left the arena that night, the other players knew what Fisher meant.

The Fab Five had claimed their first victim.

In the early 1960s, Steve Fisher had been a promising high school point guard in Herrin, Illinois. Numerous colleges were interested in him, including such faraway schools as Colorado and Arizona. One night, a young coach from Army came to watch him play in a Christmas tournament, maybe consider recruiting him. Serious type. Wore an Ohio State watch.

Bobby Knight.

Fisher was that good. Then, during a game in his senior year, he slipped on some water and felt a sharp pain in his knee. The trainers came out, slapped some red-hot analgesic on it, and the next day, Fisher couldn't even walk.

Although he didn't know it then, he had torn the anterior cruciate ligament—the most deadly of knee injuries, the type that ends careers—and while he pushed himself back to the team, he played on one leg the rest of the year. He couldn't cut sharply. He couldn't drive. His scholarship offers dried up, and he was left to pick a school on his own—he chose Illinois State—and get a partial scholarship. He played for the team, but he rarely started. By junior year he was pretty much a bench fixture, his dreams of a big-time career over.

"How can I get more time?" he would ask his coach.

"Just hang in there, keep working hard," the coach would say.

Fisher knew, deep down, that he was just being polite. The truth was, with his bum knee, Fisher simply wasn't as good as some of the other players out there. And he never would be. In his typical fashion, he seemed to absorb this, outwardly, without any fuss whatsoever. *Play the hand you're dealt.*

One time, his older brother, John, came to see Illinois State play Washington University in St. Louis. He sat in the stands, waiting for his kid brother to get in, but Steve never did. John remembered

how great a player Steve had been in high school, and the countless
hours he practiced those drills their father gave them on the backyard
hoop. He was convinced Steve should be playing, and afterward he
went to the locker room.

Most of the players were in the showers. John approached the
coach and introduced himself.

"How come my brother isn't playing?"

Before the coach could answer, they heard a yell from across the
room.

"HEY!"

It was Fisher, standing there in a towel. He had seen John and
had overheard the question. He glared at his brother. Although Steve
almost never showed anger, you could hear it in his voice now. The
words came between clenched teeth.

"That's . . . none . . . of . . . your . . . business. I'm doing my
job. He's doing his job. Stay out of it!"

John got the message. He left quickly. Steve may have harbored
resentment deep down, but he had been taught over the years that
you don't question authority, you trust your coach. If you're unhappy with the results, work harder.

He didn't like it, but he endured.

Now, as the man in charge of the Michigan Wolverines, he tried
to use that experience in dealing with disgruntled players. But for all
the nice things said about teamwork and character, the unwritten
rule of college sports—back in the '60s when Fisher played, and
through the '70s, '80s, and '90s—was clear: the best players play.

The others wait.

Fisher didn't feel guilty about this—after all, he wanted to win,
wasn't that what he was supposed to do?—but he wasn't beyond
feeling bad for the sophomores and juniors whom he had relied upon
so much last year, when the team was dismal. He would often call
that team "the happiest group of athletes I ever coached," despite
their losing record, because there was little jealousy, everybody was
trying as hard as he could.

Now with the Greatest Class Ever Recruited, minutes and shots
were sliding with every game, toward the newcomers. But hey.
They were winning. They were 8-1, about to begin the Big Ten
portion of the season. Whenever Fisher started to feel too sentimental
about the upperclassmen, he thought back to last year's record: 14
and 15.

A few more of those, and he wouldn't be anyone's coach.

So when Sam Mitchell told Fisher he wanted out, Fisher wasn't surprised.

"I wish you'd stay, Sam, we still could use you."

"Naw, coach. I want more playing time. I want to go someplace I can start."

Fisher called Mike Boyd at midnight and set plans in motion for Mitchell to transfer to Cleveland State—which he ultimately did.

The next day Fisher called in Freddie Hunter, the walk-on captain.

"I have good news," Fisher said. "A scholarship has become available."

Might as well turn a liability into an asset.

III

"WHEN ARE YOU GONNA START ALL FIVE? . . ."

1

And now, on your TV sets, Dick Vitale.

The creature from another planet.

"The topic of conversation in my classroom is BASKETBALL SEASON, BABY! Were gonna break down the season into the TRI-MESTER! The first part is the PRECONFERENCE, the second part is the BIG TEN, the third part is the BIG DANCE, THE POSTSEASON, BABY!"

Hmmm.

The creature is bald, with unblinking eyes, waving his arms like a caffeinated lawyer. He is standing in front of a blackboard in what they call, on ESPN, a "feature piece."

He is clearly insane.

"I'm gonna hand out grades to the FABULOUS FIVE, BABY, even though Steve Fisher says, 'DON'T CALL THEM THE FABU-LOUS FIVE!' But Steve, they are FANTASTIC!

"Chris Webber gets an A-PLUS for the preconference schedule, he's the best freshman IN THE COUNTRY!

"JALEN ROSE gets an A-PLUS!

"JIMMY KING gets an A!

"JUWAN HOWARD gets an A-MINUS!

"RAY JACKSON, superathlete, an A-MINUS!"

Hmm.

The creature has worked himself into a lather now, waving his glasses, pointing with a stick.

Caution: Keep your hands and feet away from his mouth.

"The big question now is WHAT GRADES WILL THEY GET as we go to the BIG TEN? How do they handle THE ROAD? How do they handle ADVERSITY? IT ALL BEGINS TONIGHT, BABY, Iowa and Michigan, it's READY TO ROCK AND ROLL!

"This is PROFESSOR VITALE saying BYE BYE FROM HIS CLASSROOM . . ."

Hmmm.

We now return you to the planet earth and your regularly scheduled programming.

Dick Vitale! Dick Vitale! Could you go anywhere without hearing about Dick Vitale? Or hearing someone imitate Dick Vitale! Or seeing his mug on the TV screen, yakking at you like some kind of wind-up doll on acid? Vitale was—and is—synonymous with college basketball fever, the unbridled passion, the go-nuts, stick-your-fingers-in-the-air, get-your-big-face-right-in-front-of-that-camera-lens hysteria. Fans are infatuated with the guy.

And in the winter of 1991, Vitale became infatuated with the Fab Five.

Don't forget that, before he became a broadcaster for both ABC and ESPN, Vitale was once a coach himself, at the University of Detroit Mercy, and later, briefly, with the Detroit Pistons. So he knew the Michigan area, had a special love/hate relationship with it. When the Fab Five came along, with their press clippings, their flamboyance, their predictions of greatness, and their heavy Detroit influence, well, Vitale chomped into them like a hungry trucker chomps into a sandwich.

Now he was set to broadcast their first conference game, inside the raucous Carver-Hawkeye Arena in Iowa City. Vitale had run into Steve Fisher before the game and laughed at his serious expression.

"Don't look so nervous, Steve! You got more talent than anybody."

Fisher had nodded and smiled at Vitale, his usual approach to powerful media people—make peace, not waves—but inside, he couldn't help but worry. The conference is a unique part of the season, like a separate act in a three-act play: the first act is the nonconference schedule, in which you occasionally play a tough team (like Duke) but mostly play pushovers to pad your record. The last act is the tournament, in which you pray you get lucky, win six games, and go to heaven.

The middle act is the conference schedule, your own league, your backyard, one home game, one away game. Fisher had yet to win a conference title. He wanted one badly. Winning the national championship is great, the Big Enchilada, but you can win one and easily never win another. Conference championships demonstrate staying power. The great coaches win them over and over. Knight. Smith. Thompson. Krzyzewski.

Fisher wanted to be a great coach. So he wanted to win his league. This is tough. The Big Ten is particularly fierce competition. Whether it's one half of the arena taunting the other in a Michigan–Michigan State showdown, or Knight's chair-throwing tantrums with his Indiana Hoosiers, or Purdue's Gene Keady screaming at his players down in West Lafayette, or the tidal waves of noise when Ohio State is torturing an opponent inside St. John Arena, whether it's Monday night, Thursday night, or Saturday afternoon, from border to border in the states of Michigan, Illinois, Iowa, Indiana, Minnesota, and Ohio, the Big Ten is the real deal, 18 games, two against everybody, let the strongest survive.

If Fisher could win the title in this conference, it would solidify his reputation as a good coach rather than a lucky one.

And with this crop of freshmen, he had a chance.

Or at least he thought so, until a few days before the Big Ten opener, when Jalen Rose, his leading scorer and cocky floor general, was late for a team meeting.

Twenty minutes late.

"I overslept," Jalen said.

Damn it, Fisher thought. Now what? He knew the upperclassmen were sensitive over what had happened with Sam Mitchell. He knew he had to take action.

"Jimmy King and Mike Talley will be our starting guards Thursday night," Fisher announced. "Jalen, you'll come off the bench."

Jalen stared blankly. It was the first game since ninth grade that he would not open.

He didn't say a word.

And now here they were, in Iowa City, where the landscape was flat and frozen, and the cars were parked snow tire to snow tire outside the arena. Inside, the crowd was already chanting with the marching band, shaking gold and black pom-poms, booing when Michigan was introduced, exploding when their beloved Hawkeyes ran onto the floor. This is college basketball in the Great Midwest, tractors and snow, family values, and the Big Ten, where every opponent becomes as hated as a man who would steal your lover. Fisher clapped his hands together and let the noise wash over him.

"LET'S GO! LET'S GO!" he yelled as the buzzer sounded to end warm-ups.

Chris, Jimmy, Eric Riley, Freddie Hunter, and Michael Talley tucked in their jerseys and came out for the opening tap. If Fisher had been in the habit of saying prayers before tip-off, now would have been a good time. The Wolverines hadn't won in this building in three years. And their leading scorer was on the bench.

Michigan won the tap, but on the opening possession, King had his shot blocked. Iowa came down and scored. Next possession, King threw a pass away.

"Come on, Jimmy!" Fisher yelled.

Webber picked up a quick foul. The crowd cheered. Michigan was having a hard time with Iowa's pressing defense. Webber, trying to lead a fast break, got whistled for a second foul on a charge. He glanced at the bench as if to say, "What's going on?" The Wolverines looked lost, out of rhythm, nervous, sloppy. They were scrambling just to score a basket.

Three minutes and 18 seconds into the game, Fisher had seen enough.

"Jalen!" he barked.

And Rose, his purgatory ended, came out with his arms dangling, half trotting, half walking, rolling his big head on his skinny neck as if nothing had ever happened. *Just tying my shoes, fellas. You ready to go?*

And he proceeded to melt the arena.

He took a pass from Talley and sank a leaning basket. Swish. He squared from the three-point line and bombed away. Swish. He took a fast-break feed from Ray Jackson and threw up a four-footer. Swish. He went to the corner and hurled another three-pointer. Swish. On his way downcourt, he passed the Iowa bench, his shoulders deliberately drooped, and he winked. "I'm on fire out here!" he taunted them.

It was his night. He hit from everywhere. He tossed in a lane leaner, he banked a driving layup, he got tripped at half-court by Iowa's Acie Earl, went flopping onto his head, came up, walked to the foul line, and drained two free throws. Jalen was a blur on the floor, taking a high dribble, accelerating toward the hoop. His skinny frame and flapping shorts and shaved head made him look, at times, like a long blue pencil with an eraser on top, but the pencil had 14 points at halftime. And got even better.

When Iowa tied the score, Jalen hit a jumper. When Iowa pulled ahead, Jalen made a beautiful bounce pass to Talley for a layup. When Iowa pulled ahead again, Jalen heaved a three-pointer that rattled the rim on its way through. With less than a minute left, he led a break, ran to the foul line, pulled up, and fired. Swish. Michigan had a lead. Jalen had 30 points.

"This kid is unreal," Jay Smith mumbled.

"I know it," Perry Watson said. He smiled. He'd seen enough games like this coaching Jalen in high school.

Iowa tied the game and it went into overtime. Fine by Rose. "More time for me," you could hear him say. By this point, all thoughts of punishment had long since vanished from Fisher's head. Rose was not leaving. He played every second. And at the most critical juncture, Michigan clinging to a two-point edge, he took a fast-break feed, flew body-to-body with Iowa's Troy Skinner— freshman against senior—pushed the ball off the backboard, through the net, and landed to the sound of a referee's whistle. Jalen flapped his left index finger. "And one, and one . . ." he said.

And one. He'd been fouled to boot. He sank the free throw, a three-point play, it was 78–73, and the Big Ten season was about to open happily for the Michigan Wolverines.

Jalen Rose was having the best night of his career.

As a sub.

"That was our plan all along," Fisher told the press afterward, when his team had won the game, 80–77. "We wanted to save Jalen from early fouls, hide him on the bench, bring him in so that they wouldn't know who he was, and have him score 34 points. Hahaha."

The upperclassmen winced again. More cutesy cover-up. Jalen, however, felt vindicated. While the other freshmen seemed over- whelmed by their first Big Ten road game, Jalen seemed to enjoy the bedlam. He scored nine points more *than all his freshman teammates combined*.

"You showed 'em who you were tonight," Watson said, giving Rose a squeeze.

Who he was.

An interesting question.

It was 1973, a cold January night, when Jeanne Rose, a single mother of three, who lived in Detroit and worked as a clerk at Chrysler, felt the stirrings of her fourth child, felt her water break, and called her brother Len—"Hurry up, I'm having the baby"—to drive her to the hospital. He raced over in his small green Fiat, helped her in, and slammed on the accelerator. The hospital was 10 miles away. By the time they pulled up to the curb, Jeanne was deep into contractions.

"Hang on!" Len urged.

"I'm trying!" she said.

Len ran and got the nurses. They came racing out with a stretcher. But as they slid Jeanne out from the car seat, all of a sudden the baby, a boy, popped into the world, right there in the parking lot. It happened so quickly the nurses fumbled him, bumping him against the curb, leaving a bruise above his nose for a year.

This was not a normal birth, but then, not much Jalen Rose did was normal, from the time he almost drowned trying to jump across a swimming pool, to the time he was arrested in a drug bust while playing video games. Of all the Fabulous Freshmen, he was at once the most puzzling, disturbing, fascinating, and charming, whether dressing like a rap star, mouthing off to opponents, or hugging a teammate and almost choking him with those long stringy arms. Like the magician Merlin in British mythology, Jalen could become almost anything he wanted, a dazzler, a screamer, a liar, a child, a friend, an enemy.

But much of who he was seemed to come directly from the genes of a man he does not know and has never met.

Jimmy Walker.

His father.

Jimmy Walker was a college All-American at Providence, and a flashy, lean, first-round draft pick for the Detroit Pistons in 1967. He was a great player, known for confidence in his ballhandling. His patented move was "the spin," in which he came at you full force, then swung the other direction, 180 degrees, leaving you in his fumes. He was also a dead-eye shooter. And, like the son he would father, he was a talker. One time, during a game, he was hitting baskets with such accuracy he ran up to the ref and said, "Hey, you better do something, there's something wrong with this ball."

"What?" the ref said.

"It keeps going in."

Among the Pistons, Walker was also known to party all night, sleep all day, take a bath, and be ready to go. He liked his women, had plenty of them, and fathered at least four children that people knew of, without ever marrying the mothers, or taking much, if any, financial responsibility.

He hooked up with Jeanne late in his Pistons career—although he was married at the time—and for a while, they made a popular couple. But, true to form, he was gone by the time the baby came.

And Jeanne never mentioned him again.

"Jalen" is a hybrid, partially for Jimmy—the "Ja" part—with the "len" for Len, to honor the car-driving uncle. So the kid's very name suggests a tug between what he had and what he missed. Jalen never met his father. To this day, he has never spoken to him.

Still, genes are genes, and the father lived inside the son. Those who knew them both could see the connection, in their gap-toothed smiles, their gangly arms, their love of on-court conversation, and, mostly, their movements with a basketball. One day, when Jalen was 11, he was playing at St. Cecilia's gym in Detroit, mouthing off to the other kids, heaving shots, mouthing off again. Sam Washington, the smiling, heavyset legend who ran the leagues there seemingly forever, had been watching Jalen. He remembered Walker. He remembered when Walker used to play in this same gym, how he yelled "Just in time!" when someone would try to block his shot, meaning, just in time to watch it go in.

Sam went into his office, set up a movie projector, found a film, then called for Jalen. He shut the door.

"See that?" Sam said, turning on the machine.

On the wall, Jalen watched a young man with a short Afro dribbling downcourt, then spinning 180 degrees and losing his defender with ease. The man shot long-range jumpers. He threw wonderful passes.

"That's your father," Washington said. "I knew him. He could really play."

He shut the projector.

"And so can you."

Jalen bit his lip. He had heard of Jimmy Walker, mostly from his brothers and sister, but until that moment, had never seen the man play basketball. Now, in that office, he felt a surge of something. Anger? Pride? Destiny? He left the gym, but he couldn't stop thinking about it. A few weeks later, he found a bubble gum card of his father's career, and he kept it in his pocket wherever he went. Sometimes, in outdoor pickup games, he would reach back to finger the card, and say to himself, "I'm gonna be you today." He would see that figure on the office wall, hear the projector clicking softly.

Although he never told his mother about the card—she never spoke about Walker, and he respected her silence—he took it with him everywhere, and would flash it sometimes like a badge, to gain entrance to the playground when the older kids had the court.

"Go on home, you too small."

"I ain't small. Check this out."

"Jimmy Walker?"

"That's my father."

"You Jimmy Walker's boy?"

"Un-huh."

"Well, come on then, let's see if you can play like him."

And in he went. Jalen never ran from competition, and playing better players made him better. In a small way, that card helped further his career. For two years, he kept it with him, memorized it, fingered it until it was crinkled and frayed. At night he would put it in a box, or leave it in the pants he was going to wear the next morning.

Then, one day, he went to check his pockets, and he couldn't find it. He looked everywhere. Nothing.

The most important influence Jalen Rose never had.

Gone again.

You had to understand this about Jalen in order to fully grasp the way he acted at Michigan. He simply saw himself inside the game. He saw his destiny, he saw his past and his future, he saw his father making moves on that wall in the St. Cecilia gym office. There was never any fear in Jalen Rose once he crossed the court line. He could make mistakes, he could miss shots, he could throw bad passes, he could embarrass his coaches—it didn't matter. He would laugh, point at his chest, whisper to the defender, "I just did that to keep you in the game," then come back and do something spectacular. He knew, he just knew, that he would eventually get it right, that basketball was his calling in life, and this not only let him rise to the occasion—to answer the Iowa benching with those 34 points—but it also earned him the private awe of every other player in that uniform, even the older ones, even those who didn't like him, because they couldn't do what he could do. Like soldiers on the eve of a battle, they knew this crazy bastard might be the difference between them coming home alive or dead.

And so—begrudgingly in some cases—they awarded him admiration, respect, and fear.

And he became their leader.

2

REPORTER: *When are you going to start all five freshmen, Steve?*

FISHER: *I don't know. Some nights I think I should be adding instead of subtracting.*

Over the next few weeks, the Michigan team would play every kind of basketball except consistent. It was impossible to predict their performance. They would lose at home. Win on the road. Blow a lead. Come back from behind. At times they looked like prison walls couldn't contain their talent: they made impossible driving shots, beautiful no-look passes, rim-rattling dunks.

But then they'd come back with stupid plays, forgetting to box out, missing defensive assignments, racing upcourt and taking the first shot that came to mind, and shots were always coming to mind. They lost to Minnesota, on the road, and to Purdue, at home. Then they went to Champaign, Illinois, and beat the Illini, with Jalen scoring 17. Jalen had been high scorer in each of the first four conference games. But his frequent lapses in judgment were largely responsible for the Wolverines' most dismaying statistic of all: an average of 19 turnovers per game.

"Men, we've got to concentrate for 40 MINUTES!" Fisher would exhort in practice, yelling as they ran drills. "We can't win playing 30 MINUTES OF BASKETBALL!

"Protect the basketball! Respect the basketball!"

Fisher knew coaching five freshman stars wasn't going to be easy. After all, in high school, all they had to do was show up and dominate. Bad passes were made up for with phenomenal catches. Guys like Chris simply had to touch the ball to dunk it.

This was a different level. But with the five of them banding together, he had trouble sometimes holding their concentration. Or getting them to accept that something they were doing was . . . (*gasp*) . . . wrong!

"You see how you didn't step up there, Chris?" Fisher would say, pointing to the screen during a film session.

"Yeah, but . . ." Chris would begin.

"You see how you didn't box the guy out that time, Chris?" Fisher would say.

"Yeah, but . . ."

Chris always had a reason for his mistakes. And he was used to having his reasons accepted. He was definitely the motivate-through-encouragement type. This was one reason Chris chose Michigan and Fisher over schools like Indiana, North Carolina, Georgetown, and even Michigan State—whose coaches are known to be excellent, but also volatile and loud.

Fisher could get loud, but he picked his spots—and his players. Jimmy, for example, also didn't like to be yelled at. If Fisher or Jay Smith got overly critical, Jimmy might spin and snarl, "OK, I got it! I got it!"

Interestingly, of the five, Jalen probably took straight criticism the best. Then again, he earned it the most. Depending on his mood, Jalen could be heavenly or hellish in practice. If he decided to play the team clown—tossing wild shots during shooting drills, yelling "Flurries!" when they fell, or "Money! Cash money!," laughing, coaxing the other guys into a frenzy—well, at those times the coaches wanted to strangle him.

But at other times Jalen asked the most intelligent questions. He even made a few suggestions for their game plan. Fisher saw how much Jalen understood the game instinctively—it was like talking to a fish about life underwater.

Fisher had his staff scan the out-of-town newspapers for motivational articles during the conference season. They would paste and underline clips that said Michigan was "too young" or "too immature" or "too brash" or "too many hot dogs."

There was no shortage of material.

"When are you going to start all five freshmen?" reporters would ask.

"Don't know," Fisher would say.

"Why don't you want to start all five freshmen?" they would ask.

"No reason," Fisher would say. "They're just not all ready."

To this point, Fisher had steadfastly held to no more than three freshman starters. It was easier that way. Less media fuss, less complaints from the upperclassmen. Still, he knew the time was coming when he couldn't hold back Jimmy King and Ray Jackson, who were showing flashes of what made them such high recruits in the first place. The upperclassmen ahead of them—Michael Talley, the 6-foot-1 guard, and James Voskuil, the 6-foot-8 forward—did not need to start to be effective, Fisher felt.

Of course, they would disagree.

3

The last big recruit Bill Frieder signed before bolting to the Arizona desert was a Detroit kid named Michael Talley. At the time, Talley was quite a prize.

Now, two years later, he was about to disappear.

"Mike T," as they called him, had droopy eyes, a shaved head, and a frequent pout. He grew up 40 miles and a galaxy away from Ann Arbor, on the Northwest Side of Detroit, where a stray bullet is as likely a cause of death as a car accident. His father left when he was young, his mother raised him, and Mike avoided trouble mostly by hanging around Haley Middle School, where a family friend, Greg Bronson, worked as a janitor. Bronson would open the gym for Mike or Talley every day, and the kid would play his favorite game, throw the ball ahead of him, chase it the length of the floor, pretend he was on a fast break with three seconds, two seconds, one second, SHOOT! . . .

Then throw the ball the other way and start over.

Talley would do this until he was gasping for air, stop, wait, then do it again, hours at a time. When he reached junior high, coaches noticed his coordination, speed, dribbling skill, and, no surprise, ability to finish a fast break. Soon they were after him. Talley chose Cooley High, one of the best basketball schools in the city, and even moved to his grandfather's house in order to live in the required district. A starter from his freshman year, Talley led Cooley to three state championships, and in his senior season, was voted "Mr. Basketball," meaning the best prep player in the state of Michigan. He got used to people making a fuss over him, because he was 6 foot 1, he was fast, and he could take just about anybody to the hole.

Recruitment was heavy, with colleges around the country pursuing him, calling him, writing him, wooing him. Talley used to sneak into the Cooley athletic office during lunch hour just to see how many new letters came that day. Michigan and Michigan State were in the thick of the chase (much the way they would be with Chris Webber). And when Frieder—who had been buzzing around Talley for years—finally snagged him, it was considered a major coup for the maize and blue. Stardom was predicted. Michael Talley would be the Next Great Wolverine.

Then Frieder left.

"Mike, I'm really sorry," he said when he called before leaving for Arizona. "It's still your decision if you want to go to Michigan."

What could Talley do? No one ever talks about the recruits coaches leave behind when those coaches look for the Next Great Job. They woo these kids, sweet-talk them, get them to say the magic word, "Yes," then abandon them at the altar. Talley had already committed to Michigan. To back out now would cost him a year of eligibility. He wanted to stay near home. Frieder assured him that the new coach, Steve Fisher, would treat him well.

Talley had little choice but to trust him,

The first two years, things were OK. He started every game his sophomore season.

Then came the Greatest Class Ever Recruited.

Now Talley, a junior, was on the bubble. He had started this season until injuring his hand in the Duke game. He missed the next game completely. And down in Orlando, he came off the bench for the first time since he was a freshman. He immediately asked for a meeting with Fisher.

"How come I'm not starting?" Talley said. "I was injured. You shouldn't lose your starting job because you're injured."

"You won't," Fisher told him. "You'll get a chance to start again."

Talley did, against Iowa, and he continued starting through the Indiana game, and for three games after that. But his time was gradually decreasing as Jimmy and Jalen played more and more. Where Talley once used to play 30 minutes a game, now he was down to around 14. He was nervous, out of sync, he would be ineffective in one stretch, get yanked, fret about getting yanked, go in, be ineffective, and get yanked again. Against Michigan State he missed all five of his shots, and against Ohio State, he missed all four.

"I'm thinking about going with King," Fisher told his staff in a meeting before the next game, against lightly regarded Northwestern.

"He's ready, as far as I can see," Dutcher said.

The other coaches nodded. What they were saying, in essence, was out with the old, in with the new.

And so, on a cold Wednesday night, February 5, before another sellout crowd at Crisler Arena, Steve Fisher benched Michael Talley for Jimmy King, giving him four freshmen in the starting lineup.

And Talley went berserk.

"Fuck this!" he told himself. "I can't even start now against fuckin' Northwestern? Hell with this place!"

He fumed on the bench. He bit his lip. He went straight home after the game, and skipped the next practice. Didn't call. Offered no explanation. This infuriated Fisher, who tolerated a lot, especially from his freshmen. But blatant breaking of the rules, without even making an excuse, was unforgivable. A meeting was scheduled for the next day, and Talley and his mother came to Fisher's office.

"Why weren't you at practice yesterday, Mike?" Fisher asked.

"I didn't feel right being there, after what happened with Northwestern," Talley answered.

"Not starting is no excuse for missing practice."

"You told me I wouldn't lose my starting position."

"I didn't say that, Mike."

"Yes, you did! Yes, you did!"

Talley began to shake. In his mind, that's exactly what Fisher had said. In Fisher's mind, he had said Talley wouldn't lose his position to injury. The tension was fierce. Talley would later say of that meeting, "There was no loyalty or trust between us anymore. I felt that was the end of it . . . it was like a sledgehammer across my head—boom! . . . We had meetings after meetings and still Coach could not just come out and say, 'I wanna start the Fab Five.' Just say it. 'I wanna start the Fab Five.' We all knew that's what he wanted to do . . ."

Talley thought about transferring, running away, he thought about how disloyal and disrespectful it was to bring five freshmen in and displace everyone else. Why couldn't they wait, as he had waited?

All this was racing inside Talley's head as he squirmed in the chair in Fisher's office.

Fisher didn't see it. He simply saw an older player who had been beaten out by a younger one. He saw the same thing that had happened to him in college. He remembered how he took it, quietly, respectfully, not questioning the authority.

Now here was a mouthy kid who missed practice deliberately.

"Mike, I'm not taking you to Notre Dame Sunday," Fisher said. "You're staying home."

Talley stared at him, without a word, and tried to imagine a way to fly out of the room.

When problems arise on college basketball teams, it is traditionally the place of the older players to straighten things out, lay down the law, enforce the great pecking order of seniors to juniors to sophomores to freshmen. This is how Glen Rice and Loy Vaught handled things with the 1989 Michigan championship team, this is how Steve Grote, John Robinson, and Rickey Green did it with the 1977 Big Ten title team, this is how Cazzie Russell and Bill Buntin did it with the celebrated 1965 squad, which went to the national championship game.

But none of those teams started freshmen.

Only one even started a sophomore!

The Wolverines of 1992 were being led by 18-year-olds like Jalen Rose, who spent much of the time cooing rap lyrics and dogging anyone in sight, and Juwan Howard, who, for philosophy, would quote you the movie *Scarface*, and Chris Webber, who was wide-eyed and childlike, learning something new about life every day. These were the players with minutes. So these were the leaders. Freddie Hunter, the captain of the team, the mature senior, hadn't taken his warm-ups off in half the games, and when he did, he almost never scored. How much influence can you have, soldier, if you barely participate in the war?

Thanks to the Greatest Class Ever Recruited, the older players were now like aging Broadway dancers sent to the back of the chorus line.

With Talley out, only James Voskuil remained in the lineup from last year's starters.

"Watch out, man," Eric Riley had teased him, after the four

freshmen helped key a blowout win over Northwestern. "They got me and Mike. They coming after you next."

Voskuil grinned, and wondered if he was serious.

4

Almost every night, Jimmy King called home to talk to his girlfriend, Tiffany Wilson. She had been a cheerleader at a rival high school back in Plano. They had met at a basketball game, and even though she was 4 foot 11 and he was 6 foot 5, and even though she loved to talk and he liked to keep quiet, they hit it off, and they kept their relationship going long-distance.

"What's it like being up there?" Tiffany, who attended a women's college in Texas, would ask him. "We see your games down here sometimes. They're talking about you guys with that 'Fab Five' stuff and everything."

"It's OK," Jimmy would answer. "It's different. I can't wait until they start all five of us."

"They will. You're too good. It's just a matter of time."

Jimmy was the most difficult player to get to know among the freshmen. He would slouch in the nearest available chair—head back, feet up, arms out—and would appear to be this very tall, very lazy slug. But underneath those sleepy lids, Jimmy was, next to Chris, the most acute observer on the team. He preferred to listen to someone first, check out his motivations, then see if he wanted to open up.

Often he did not.

But he opened up to Tiffany. They talked sometimes for two or three hours a night. He missed their dates back home at Cheddar's restaurant, where they had chicken-fried steak and potato skins and lemonade. He missed the summer nights at the middle school playground, when he would shoot baskets and she would rebound the ball and they would talk about dreams, about how one day he'd be in the NBA.

They all dreamed of the NBA, Jimmy, Jalen, Chris, Juwan, Ray. It was one more thing that united them—especially since they all had a legitimate chance to make it. They watched games together at night and figured where they might fit in come their draft year. Admitting you saw yourself on the Lakers or the Bulls was cool.

Admitting you had a girlfriend back home was not, at least not to outsiders. So if you asked the freshmen about their steadies— Jimmy, Jalen, and Ray each had one—they would smilingly deny their existence.

"Whatcha talking, girlfriend?"

"You must have me confused!"

"Shhhhh! Don't say that word!"

In truth, girls like Tiffany were the Fab Five's only link to reality when the fame began to swell. When you're 18 or 19 years old, it's important to have an anchor, someone from back home to talk to when things get crazy.

And once they all made the starting line—"It's just a matter of time"—things would get plenty crazy.

5

Sunday, February 9, 1992, was a historic day in the sports world. In Albertville, France, the XVI Winter Olympics were under way, the men's downhill race highlighting the schedule. In Orlando, Florida, at the NBA All-Star game, Magic Johnson, stricken with the AIDS virus, was returning to play one last time.

And in South Bend, Indiana, before a national TV audience, the Fabulous Freshmen of Michigan were causing people to poke each other, sit up in their chairs, and rub their eyes.

All five were coming out on the floor.

To start a basketball game.

Together.

No one knew how long it had been since a major college program tried this. But Fisher was doing it. Taking the plunge, starting all five—just days after he had finally consented to start four. He was inspired by, of all things, a phone call to his father earlier that morning.

Howard Fisher, the fundamental-loving volunteer coach who made Steve shoot free throws before dinner back in Herrin, Illinois, and who was so serious about Michigan basketball he stopped coming to games after a visit in 1989 when the Wolverines lost—Howard blamed himself, for distracting the coaches—and who now watched every game instead via a satellite dish back in Herrin, and then reran it on the VCR, making notes and sending them to his son, well, Howard had an idea about the lineup.

"How's the team look?" he had asked Steve before the Notre Dame game.

"I don't know, Dad. We're a little flat."

"Maybe you ought to start Ray Jackson."

"He's not ready yet."

"I think he is. I like the way that kid plays."

"I'm already starting four freshmen."

"So? Don't be afraid to start all five."

"I'm not afraid. Who says I'm afraid?"

"All right, I won't tell you your business."

"OK."

"Just don't be afraid to start all five."

On the bus ride to the arena, Fisher watched his players, their headphones in their ears, their eyes gazing out the windows. They had won five and lost four since the Big Ten opener. He wondered about the effect of Talley being left behind. Maybe his father was right. Maybe this was just the move for some new inspiration. Notre Dame didn't count in the conference standings, so it wasn't like risking a truly important game. And these freshmen loved to get up for national television, that he knew for sure. It was gonna happen sooner or later . . .

At the arena, Fisher pulled Voskuil aside.

"James," he said, "I'm starting Ray today. I just made the decision. Stay ready. Stay focused. You'll get your minutes off the bench."

Voskuil was stunned. He had heard his fellow upperclassmen predicting doom, saying their days were numbered; he had even seen what happened just a few days earlier with Talley. But as long as he was starting he hadn't believed it. He thought he was different. Now, suddenly, he was out, too. He felt burned and embarrassed, like he'd put his trust in the wrong advisers.

During the pregame speech, Fisher made no special announcement; he simply went through each starter's assignment. This was how he broke the news:

"Juwan, you're starting on No. 20, LaPhonso Ellis. He's good, we all know it . . .

"Jimmy, you're on Elmer Bennett, No. 12. He's fast, so watch for that . . .

"Ray, you start on Daimon Sweet . . ."

When Voskuil heard the words "Ray, you start on Daimon Sweet," he felt his belly churn. He couldn't look at anyone. He kept his eyes locked on the blackboard. Later he would say, "If I could have transferred right then, I would have. I felt humiliated."

The Fab Five, on the other hand, felt like a singing group that had just gotten its first record contract. Chris actually smiled when he heard Fisher say Jackson's name; the rest of them played it low-key until they broke for warm-ups. Then they gathered around Ray, locked arms in a tight huddle, like children planning a secret meeting in the tree house.

"This is what we've been waiting for," Chris said, his head half-buried in Jalen's armpit.

"Our time," answered Jalen, bobbing up and down.

"We all together now," said Jimmy.

"Show the world, baby," said Juwan.

"I'm with it," said Ray.

"Let's give 'em some shit."

"All right, dogs."

"Five freshmen."

"We ain't freshmen."

"Show 'em now."

"Let's do it!"

"LET YOUR NUTS HANG!"

And from the opening tap, they did, with an energy that hadn't been felt since that pickup game in October back at Crisler. Their feet were jumping, the sneakers squeaking sharply, their eyes darting from corner to corner, the ball moving in crisp, clean passes. Ray took a feed from Juwan on the first possession and made a blind dish to Chris coming baseline for a slam. Chris was fouled, and the freshmen slapped hands. A few minutes later, Ray stripped possession from Notre Dame's Sweet, and started the fast break, speeding down the left side, then lofting the ball toward the hoop, alley-oop. Webber soared, caught it one-handed, and—SHUMMMMP!—slammed it home, a perfect feed. The crowd went crazy—and this was in Notre Dame! Chris grabbed Ray's head on the way upcourt, unable to suppress his laughter.

"YEAH, BABY!" Chris yelled.

"UH-HUHHHHH!" Ray answered.

Like children running down a steep hill, the five of them were thrilled with their own sudden speed, and they used it not only for spectacular fast breaks but for rebounds and defense, sliding to help out, denying shots, poking passes. The unbridled enthusiasm that often looked mismatched with some of their more patient upper-classmen looked harmonious now, like complementary colors, all in the same mood, all of the same mind. They made sense together.

And they took over the game.

Juwan sank one jump shot after another. Chris slammed so hard the rim bent and would not snap back. On a fast break in the second half, Jalen came down the right wing, scooped the ball to Ray, who whipped it to Jimmy, who fed it back to Jalen, who pulled up and buried a four-footer. Good!

Even Fisher half grinned. They were in sync, in rhythm, a jazz quintet locked on a riff, drum, bass, piano, sax, trumpet, joining forces, making one united, swinging sound, and if you turned down the volume and just watched the picture, you still would hear it.

If you had your volume up, however, as most of America did, you heard something else: you heard Al McGuire, the former coach turned star NBC analyst, chiding the freshmen for their flamboyant behavior.

"You can tell they're freshmen, they go too much with the French pastry, too much with the hotdogging . . .

"Every play with them gets to be like Hiroshima, Nagasaki, every play has to be a large explosion . . .

"I never would have recruited five freshmen. I'd have thought it would cause too much of a problem . . .

"It's too early for jivin', men, too early for jivin'! . . .

"There goes another Harlem Globetrotter pass from Webber. No reason for that! It's French pastry! . . .

"Remember, Michigan fans, these are just kids. They'll give you thrills but they're also gonna give you Elvis Presley, Heartbreak Hotel . . ."

There was no Heartbreak Hotel on this day. Michigan won, 74–65. And the Fab Five scored every point. Every point? By freshmen? That's right. Chris had 17, Juwan had 14, Jimmy had 19, Jalen had 20. Ray had two baskets, three rebounds, and several steals in his starting debut.

Still, many Americans agreed with McGuire's opinions (especially when he kept repeating them). Why so much showboating? Why all that fist waving and mouthing off? And why did it always have to be an alley-oop or a reverse slam? *Bobby Knight's teams wouldn't do that!*

It didn't help that Notre Dame is America's college when it comes to sports, and the Fighting Irish's four starting seniors had just been whipped by five upstart freshmen.

French pastry. Hot dogs. The rap would shadow them forever. America loves youth, but hates impunity. And, thanks to their behavior—and broadcasts like McGuire's—the Fab Five were now synonymous with both.

6

Chris Webber was quickly becoming everybody's favorite interview. The media liked his thoughtful answers, his flashes of humor, and his candor after losses. Besides, he was the star. People wanted to hear what he had to say. In journalism, when the guy you *need* to talk to is also the guy you *like* to talk to, there's a word for him: godsend.

One time, after a game, Chris was talking with several white TV reporters about Michigan and Michigan State. He was being typically analytical. "I'm sure they're hearing a lot about the five freshmen at Michigan, and they're feeling ignored. Nobody likes to be ignored, so our games become a red-letter date on their schedule, and—"

He stopped when he saw a visitor, one of his old Detroit pals, a young black man, about to leave the locker room.

"Yo! Yo!" Chris yelled, his tone changing completely.

The TV lights turned off. The friend spun around.

"Whassup? Whassup?" Chris hollered. "Where them guys at?"

His friend made a joke.

"Oh, man, you ain't all that!" Chris said. "I buss your ass, I buss it, you know I will. I'ma get you later, you ain't all that, yo, yo, you hear me? Hahahaha."

The friend laughed, said he'd see Chris later. Chris sat back down, said, "Sorry," the lights flicked back on, and he returned to his perfect elocution.

It was a scene that repeats itself night after night, not only in the Michigan locker room but in most basketball programs across the nation. Some athletes call it "black voice/white voice." Two completely different tones, words, references, and attitudes—both seeming perfectly natural—depending on whom you are talking to. On the Michigan team, particularly with Chris, Juwan, and Jalen, you would hear one voice with TV media, another with print media, one with black reporters, another with white reporters. And a completely different voice when they were talking among themselves. The pronunciation changed. "Ain't" and "be" came and went. The word "nigger," which was as common as your average pronoun when the Fab Five shot the breeze together—"That nigger's crazy"; "C'mon, nigger, lemme have the ball"—was never spoken during media sessions.

Chris admitted he used different voices all the time.

"It's subconscious," he said after the TV people left. "You're trying to make the right impression. I think the media has a tendency to put the worst representation of the black community on TV. Like if there's a murder—and there could be a million black people standing around—they seem to always go to the lady with the rollers in her hair, who looks like she's on drugs, and they ask her what happened. She'll say, " 'Well, I be inside, and we be cookin' . . .' "

Chris sighed. "I just feel there's more to black people than ignorance. So when a white reporter comes up, we try to make—and maybe we overdo it sometimes—we try to make ourselves really clear, so that it's represented the right way."

Webber shook his head. He said it was weird, wasn't it, how fans wanted them to play basketball the way they'd been taught in the city but didn't want them to talk the way they'd been taught in the city. This, by the way, is one of the great hypocrisies of college athletics.

"White people are always telling me, 'Chris, you speak well.' But they're just saying that 'cause I'm black. If I was white, they'd expect it."

At least Webber, who went to a predominantly white, upper-class high school, had experience walking between two worlds, as did Jimmy King, thanks to his hometown of Plano, Texas. But Jalen, prior to arriving in Ann Arbor, had never played basketball with a white teammate. He had no white friends, and only a handful of white acquaintances, besides the three men on the coaching staff.

Juwan Howard came from similar circumstances, no white team-mates, no white coaches, urban upbringing; he made noticeable efforts during interviews with white reporters to check his speech, and use buzzwords like "most definitely" and "proper concentration" and "achieve our goal of victory."

On the other hand, you had players like Rob Pelinka, the junior guard, who grew up in the well-to-do suburb of Lake Bluff, Illinois; his high school was 95 percent white. Same thing for James Voskuil, the junior forward, who grew up in Grand Rapids, Michigan. Jason Bossard, the sophomore guard, was raised in a rural northern Michigan town, where the black population was almost nil. The first time he heard one of the Fab Freshmen say "nigger," he froze, expecting a fight to break out, until he realized the guy saying it was black.

"I didn't think that was, you know, allowed," he said later.

To top it off, you had a mixed-bag coaching staff as well. Fisher had grown up in white-bread America, Herrin, Illinois. Perry Watson, on the other hand, was inner-city Detroit, black high school, black friends, and for the previous 13 years at Southwestern, almost exclusively black athletes.

At times this made for a wonderful melting pot, with jokes and shared experiences that broke down many of the preexisting stereotypes. Between playing together, taking showers together, traveling together, well, if the whole world got along as well as most sports teams in general, racism wouldn't be half the problem it is today.

On the other hand, things were not perfect. And there was definitely racial tension on the Michigan Wolverines. With the freshmen collecting more and more of the playing time, there was already animosity. The fact that they were all black just provided another vent for frustration.

It didn't help when the freshmen ragged on white people.

"You guys are real smart, but you wouldn't last two minutes out on the streets," Jalen would tell Pelinka and Voskuil, who would laugh, but uncomfortably.

"White people don't need sex as much as black people, that's a fact."

"How come white people wear all them ugly golf clothes, like those purple pants you got, James?"

Much of this was done in fun. But the laughter died considerably when it came to basketball. Some of the white players felt they weren't getting the same looks on the floor that the black freshmen got. One of those white players, who asked specifically not to be identified on this point, said, "I went two months without Perry Watson saying a word to me. He definitely favored the black kids.

"That's not right. He's supposed to be coaching me, too."

7

Karen Beeman, the secretary in the basketball office, opened the letter, scanned it, and sighed. She put it in a pile with all the others. She had read a lot of critical mail in her time on the job—hey, she worked during the Frieder years—but this was definitely a new trend.

The shorts! What was with the shorts! More and more, the mail was going this way:

Dear Coach Fisher,
    I have been a loyal Michigan fan for 20 years. Never have I been so embarrassed as I am with your current basketball team. Why do they have to wear those baggy shorts? They look like clowns . . .

Dear Coach Fisher,
    I am a Michigan alum and have always supported the sports teams. But the way your freshmen are behaving is an embarrassment. First of all, why do they have to wear those baggy shorts?

Dear Coach Fisher,
    I hate the shorts, and I hate the hotdogging. Let the freshmen wait their turn, like everybody else. GO BLUE!

The interesting part was that many letters came from *supporters* of the program—people who wanted the Fab Five to win, but didn't feel comfortable in the way they were doing it. Too much showing off, they said. Not enough respect for tradition.

Michigan has the largest alumni association of any college in the nation, and there are few corners of the globe where you can't eventually find somebody wearing maize and blue. This pride in attachment is what makes Michigan strong, but also cements certain ideas of what the school should be. And, apparently, the team that was out there in the early winter of 1992, showing off, but playing only .500 ball in the conference, didn't fit the image.

Fisher generally ignored the critics' mail—even when he answered it. But there were other things not so easily ignored. In the much-anticipated first game against Michigan State, the Fab Five's behavior had indeed been on the brink of embarrassing. Michigan had won, 89–79—a dramatic come-from-behind performance that rivaled what they did against Duke—but Chris and Jalen, eager to beat the school that had so heavily recruited them, did their share of taunting and trash talking during the game. Webber bragged afterward about yelling at Heathcote, "DON'T YOU REMEMBER WHY YOU RECRUITED ME?" and "IS THIS YOUR BEST DEFENSE? YOU GOTTA HAVE BETTER THAN THIS!"

Meanwhile, the pro-Spartans crowd, which had once cheered "Web-ber! Web-ber!" to try to entice him to East Lansing, was, naturally, now rooting bitterly against Michigan and its big-deal freshmen, booing and hooting and thundering insults. When the game was over, and Michigan had won, Juwan answered the crowd, first by waving his arms, as if to say, "What you got to say now?" and then by grabbing his crotch in what he would later call "the Roseanne Arnold thing."

Should Fisher have controlled him? Yes. Should Juwan have been more mature? Of course.

Can we say that about many 18-year-olds and their coaches? Definitely.

But that kind of action did not escape the fans, and, more significantly, it did not escape the TV cameras and the reporters. In fact, thanks to the video highlight packages and wire services, Michigan's reputation was quickly spreading near and far as a team that not only tried to beat you but wanted to rub your face in it.

When the Fab Five & Co.—16-6 overall and 7-5 in the Big Ten—went to play Northwestern in Evanston, an article appeared in the *Chicago Tribune* with the following sentence:

"The Wolverines will continue to underachieve until some of their fabulous freshmen forget about trash talk and hotdogging and concentrate on acquiring the poise and discipline that characterize Ohio State and Indiana."

This just floored Fisher. It was one thing to tell him his kids talked junk. But to hold up other Big Ten programs in some sort of angelic comparison, well, that was too much. "Have they ever seen Indiana or Ohio State play?" he railed after that *Tribune* article. "They talk just as much as we do! This is really getting out of hand."

And the next day he saw just how far. The game against Northwestern had barely begun when Michigan got a fast break, and Jalen lobbed a pass to Jimmy King, who dunked. Jalen turned and ran back upcourt, smiling in his usual "gotcha" fashion, and Ed Hightower, one of the most respected referees in the game, came running right up to him and got in his face.

"None of that!" he scolded. "We won't have any of that showboating in this game."

"I'm just smiling," Jalen said.

"No smiling!" Hightower barked. "Smiling and laughing will not be tolerated on this court tonight."

Jalen was stunned. Fisher was stunned.

No smiling?

Hightower had plenty of company. It was bad enough that the Fab Five looked like a house party's worth of bad haircuts and extra fabric. OK. Maybe fans could live with that. But the talking! That was too much. And did these freshmen talk? They never shut up! They talked in the tunnel, they talked in the layup line, they talked during introductions, they talked before the jump ball, and yes, they talked—"*Can you believe this, Shirley, I mean, watch their mouths as they dribble out there, look, LOOK! They're jawing out there, for God's sake*—in the middle of the game!" Jalen Rose would drop a jump shot over his defender, watch it swish, and coo, "Damn, I'm good." Chris Webber would monster-slam over some helpless center, and on the way upcourt snicker, "You can't check me. You might as well go home now." Ray Jackson would lean over on the foul line, glance at the shooter, and say, "Everybody's watching, don't nut up." You couldn't hear this, of course, not from where you sat, but you could sometimes see it, especially when the cameras began to make a habit of lip-reading close-ups. And this was the final straw for the critics. Bald heads? OK. Long shorts? Maybe. But all this noise, this jaw-flapping, this yip, yap, shut-your-trap, verbal one-upmanship, from a bunch of kids who couldn't even drink a beer legally, well, that's gotta stop. It isn't good basketball! *Bobby Knight wouldn't allow that!*

They were wrong, of course. If there is one thing any real player learns before he ever sinks his first big jump shot, it is how to talk. Call it trash, call it jive, call it bragging, call it mouthing off, the spoken word is endemic to every asphalt, bent-rim, no-net playground in America.

"Check up!"

"That's off!"

"All net!"

"You're sorry!"

"Go home!"

"Get that weak-ass shit outa here!"

Basketball, played in places where today's stars come from—and even in places as innocent as YMCAs and college intramural leagues—is as much a game of attitude as it is execution. Get an edge. State your case. In his face.

And it is nothing new. Trash talk is not confined to big cities or urban jungles. Nor is it confined, contrary to some opinion, to the black race. Boston Celtics star Larry Bird, from French Lick, Indiana—Indiana? Isn't that where Bobby Knight coaches?—had long been known as one of the biggest trash talkers in the NBA. He would bury a three-pointer and yell at the opposing coach, "Hey, send someone out who can guard me, OK?" Larry Bird! Good old, hardworking, fundamentally sound Larry Bird?

U-M fans were very excited when Juwan Howard signed his letter of intent. They were ecstatic when Chris Webber and Jalen Rose both committed on the same day. They framed the papers trumpeting the arrival of the Greatest Class Ever Recruited.

Where did they think these kids were coming from, Palm Beach?

And how did they think they got to be so highly ranked? Not from playing against small-time talent, or shrinking away from brash competition.

Another thing to remember, in the case of the Fab Five, particularly Webber and Rose: many of the opposing players were familiar to them, in some cases even good friends. People forget how much contact there is through the summer leagues, the AAU, and the high school tournaments. By college, many of these "opponents" are buddies.

And one of the things you do with your buddies is talk junk.

Grant Hill, who traded chitchat with Chris during the Duke game, had hosted Chris during his recruiting visit to Durham, and Chris had even stayed at Hill's house back in high school. Bobby

Hurley was talking with Chris on the phone while Chris was still in high school. Jamal Mashburn, the Kentucky star, whom Jalen and Chris would one day dog in the Final Four, had played against them back in eighth grade. Jimmy Jackson, the archenemy from Ohio State, played in their summer leagues in Detroit. Voshon Lenard, the Minnesota star, was Jalen's high school teammate. Juwan Howard knew most of the nation's top freshman rivals—like Purdue's Glenn Robinson and Memphis State's David Vaughn—from playing against them in the Nike/ABCD tournament.

"People don't realize that these same guys we're dogging out on the court, we're laughing with in the tunnel and getting their phone numbers and making plans and stuff," Webber explained.

He was right. People didn't realize it.

All they knew is that they had never seen so many camera close-ups of moving lips during basketball games.

"Keep an eye on their mouths," the directors would say.

Yeah. You never know when they might be talking.

Or, heaven forbid, smiling.

8

Fisher might have thought the Hightower incident was the lowest point of the season. But, as they say about the weather in Michigan, you thought that was bad? Just wait a few minutes.

The next game, against Wisconsin, would truly signal rock bottom. As of 1992, Wisconsin had one winning season in the previous 10 years.

But on the night of February 26, the Badgers played above themselves, while the Fab Five played at the level of their shoestrings. They were awful. Outrebounded, outshot, outhustled, and outdone. The success-starved fans at Wisconsin loved every minute; they screamed as if it were a tournament game. Wisconsin was hot, made 25 of its 26 free throws, and got a sterling performance from freshman guard Michael Finley—a freshman was outperforming the Fab Five?—who scored 30 points, while his counterpart on Michigan, Jimmy King, had zero.

The Badgers blew out the Wolverines, 96–78.

Fisher was livid.

"Practice is gonna be hell tomorrow," Juwan mumbled on the way out.

Wrong. Hell began that evening. The team stayed in Wisconsin, and Fisher ordered a film session as soon as they got back to the hotel. Normally they wait until the audiovisual guys can cut down the tape; on this night they watched the whole game, from tap to buzzer, and when it was over, Fisher rewound it and made them watch it again.

"What's wrong with you guys?" he hollered. "Look at that. No way we should be outplayed like this!"

He tore into the team, and so did his assistants. Then he asked the players to speak. They began by making excuses. Then by saying they were tired. Pretty soon, it turned into one of those wee-hours, might-as-well-be-honest, who-the-hell-do-you-think-you-are bull sessions.

"I'm sick of the same food all the time!"

"How come we have to stay in a hotel at home?"

"All these guys complaining about playing time—why don't they shut up?"

"If you're not gonna try out there, why are you starting?"

Fisher let them talk. He responded when necessary. The meeting went past midnight, past 1 A.M., past 2 A.M., nobody leaving, the doors closed, the screaming muffled by the walls.

In every turnaround season, there is a moment like this, an emotional pivot. Either you swing the other way or you continue to sink.

The doors finally opened somewhere shy of 3 A.M., and the Michigan players, some of them hoarse from yelling, trudged back to their rooms and went to sleep.

It was the worst meeting of the year.

It was the best thing that could have happened.

From that point on—and really, for the rest of the season—the play was inspired. And even though Fisher shook up the starting lineup the next game, a road trip to Ohio State—he replaced the Texas kids, King and Jackson, with Talley and Voskuil—and even though they lost that game in teeth-gnawing fashion, turning the ball over three times in 31 seconds after controlling most of the game, there was no denying how much they now wanted to win.

Chris entered the locker room and kicked a door so hard it

almost came off its hinges. Then he punched it for good measure. Some of the freshmen were near tears. Fisher actually took this as a good sign. They hurt. They cared.

"Look at me, men!" Fisher demanded. "I'm proud of your effort, but I'm bitterly disappointed in that last five-minute stretch. You've got to learn to fight through that."

He moved toward Juwan, who had his head down. "LOOK AT ME!" he hollered. "YOU FOUGHT HARD. If you give me that kind of effort, good things will happen. Be determined that when you come back, and when you have easy shots, YOU'RE GOING TO MAKE THEM! When you have free throws, YOU'RE GOING TO MAKE THEM! When you have open 15-footers, YOU'RE GOING TO MAKE THEM!"

He lowered his voice. "Take a shower, and let's get out of here."

Jalen dressed slowly. He had committed two of the three turnovers in those disastrous 31 seconds. And he'd made just four of his 16 shots. He was bad. He knew it. There was none of his kidding around. The regular season was almost over, and for the first time in a long time, his team was not winning enough.

When reporters later asked him about the game, he was blunt.

"If I had played better we would have won."

Back in Ann Arbor, winter was reaching its final stretch, endless days of white-gray skies and the same old snow that had been there for weeks. Fisher resumed his morning routine, took his son to school, read his paper, drank his coffee, made his phone calls. But this was March, and that meant things were accelerating. There were only three games left in the regular season, three games before the NCAA tournament made its selections. And with an overall record of 17-8 (8-7 in the Big Ten) Fisher wasn't taking an invitation for granted. He remembered the feeling of being passed over the year before, with his losing team. It stung just to think about it.

He had other concerns as well. Recruiting was becoming a futile exercise. Almost everyone asked about the Fab Five, and despite Fisher's promise that the best players play—no matter what age— none of the top recruits wanted to go someplace where five great sophomores would be starting ahead of them.

"Do you think Chris will leave after this year or his sophomore year?" high school stars would ask him.

"I can't tell you," Fisher would say.

"How much playing time would I get if everybody comes back?" somebody would ask.

Fisher would force a smile.

The Greatest Class Ever Recruited was assuring itself no follow-up competition.

Meanwhile, Chris, Ray, Jimmy, Jalen, and Juwan were still causing a commotion. At Fisher's weekly luncheon with the M Club boosters (a common practice at most major schools, in which people who give significant money to help the program are rewarded with perks such as lunch with the coach, even though most coaches look forward to this the way they look forward to a rectal exam) he was asked about his team's antics on the court. Why so much talking? Was that really what "we" wanted from "our" program?

Fisher bit his lip. "I think it's been blown out of proportion," he said, using a coach's favorite explanation. "I consider the matter closed."

But the Fab Five were just getting started. Jalen, the ringleader, had revived his normal feistiness. He talked junk in practice. And the night before the game—against Indiana, another "disciplined" program that critics would compare to Michigan's—he even jabbed at Fisher.

"Hey, coach, I'm wearing a T-shirt under my jersey tomorrow, we straight?" he said.

"Oh, we're straight, all right," Fisher answered, "but you're not wearing a T-shirt."

"C'mon, coach. That was a recruiting requirement. If you had told me we couldn't wear T-shirts, I wouldn't be here."

"Jalen . . . stop harassing me."

Jalen grinned. "What if the T-shirt says 'We love Fisher'?"

"JALEN!" Fisher yelled, chasing him away.

If people only knew what I put up with, he thought.

That night, Fisher pulled out a surefire motivational tool. The tape of the 1989 championship game. He put it in the machine and said to his players, "I was going to wait until the tournament to show this. But I think it's time. Men, this is a team that found a way to win."

The screen lit up with images from Seattle. Glen Rice drilling three-pointers, Terry Mills banking a jumper. Rumeal Robinson at the free throw line in overtime, making the first shot, raising a fist, then sinking the game-winner, as a younger-looking Fisher clapped in encouragement.

The players were captivated. If one thing held their attention—even the Fabulous Freshmen—it was watching basketball success. When the tape ended and the lights came up, you could feel the rejuvenation. It was as if someone had smashed a gauntlet and said to this team, "You really want a title? Fine. Now's the time to get started."

They went to their rooms. Got up the next morning. And beat Bobby Knight's Indiana Hoosiers, No. 4 in the nation, in convincing fashion, 68–60.

They beat Purdue, 70–61.

And they beat Illinois, 68–59.

It was their longest winning streak in conference play.

And suddenly the regular season was over, and the tournament was just days away. Michigan—led by freshmen—had won 20 games, lost eight. They had inched back up to No. 14 in the national polls. Even some of the critics had cooled after the three straight victories. Maybe the kids were growing up. As the team gathered at Crisler Sunday night to watch the selection show on TV, and find out where Michigan would be seeded, and who it would play, Fisher allowed himself a small sigh of satisfaction. They might be young, loud, bald, and brash. But they were too good to ignore. An invitation would be coming to the Big Dance.

And once you're invited, anything can happen . . .

IV

THE PROMISED LAND

1

Before we worshiped at Michael Jordan's feet, before student athletes wore earrings, long shorts, and fat black sneakers, before Dick Vitale screamed his first "TIME OUT, BABEEEEE!," before college teams flew chartered planes across the country, before there was a San Juan Shootout and a Rainbow Classic in Hawaii, before college recruits came from Nigeria, Australia, Egypt, and Yugoslavia, before instant-replay scoreboards and three-point baskets and breakaway rims, before Magic at Michigan State and Bird at Indiana State, before Dean Smith biting his lip and John Wooden fixing his glasses, before UCLA played Houston in the Astrodome, the game that started the avalanche, got television hooked, before all this madness, this pressure, before the glory-dripping, money-soaked insanity that has become college basketball in the springtime, there were the Utah Utes.

The Utah Utes.

The Utes were a nice little team that, in 1944, took a train from Utah to New York City for the National Invitational Tournament and lost in the first round. Since they had come all that way, and since there was a war on—and who knew how much longer the world would last?—they decided to see the sights of the Big Apple.

Then they got a telegram. *"Would you like to play in the NCAA Tournament?"*

There was an opening, because one of the invited teams had dropped out. Vadal Peterson, the Utes coach, a thin-lipped, short-haired man, asked his players if they wanted to bother. "After all," he said, "it means an awful long train ride to Kansas City."

A vote was taken, and the majority said why not, let's go. So they left the Belvedere Hotel on West 48th Street, boarded a train from Grand Central Station, and eventually arrived in Kansas City.

Three victories later, they won the national championship.

* * *

No one votes on whether to accept an invitation to the tournament anymore. They pray for it, beg for it, lobby for it, dream about
it. The tournament! March Madness! Six wins and the crown is yours!
No matter who you are! No matter how low-seeded! Anything is
possible as long as you are invited, so when that invitation comes,
the bags are packed, the seats are booked, even though you've just
finished an entire regular season, maybe 30 games, and the kids are
tired and they all have classes. So what? Teams will fly anywhere to
be in the Big Dance, from Rhode Island to San Diego and back again
if necessary. They'll stay in sanctioned hotels, attend massive press
conferences, submit lists of accredited personnel to be admitted to
their practices, and if they win in the first and second rounds, they'll
do the same thing a week later, and if they win in the third and fourth
rounds, they'll do the same thing a week later—"We're going to the
Final Four!" That's all they need to say. Six plane trips, three hotels,
15 press conferences, 18 nights accommodations, 54 catered meals,
and they haven't even won yet!

You know what? They'll do it happily, willingly, no complaints
about the ride, because success breeds success, successful programs
attract successful athletes, and while the regular season is nice, and
conference titles are special, winning the tournament is what it's all
about. You do that, you have the big bowl of ice cream all the kids
want, the banner they want to play under.

National champions.

So it was that Steve Fisher's team gathered in the Crisler Arena
locker room in the second week of March to watch the selection
brackets on TV. There was pizza and soda and chips and pretzels. It
was a little like opening your birthday presents with a bunch of other
kids. Lots of smiles. And lots of comparing.

One by one, the teams were announced, how they were seeded,
where they would be going—there are eight subregional sites, four
regional ones, and of course, a single, stadium-sized arena for the
Final Four, in this case, the Minneapolis Metrodome.

Fisher, Dutcher, Smith, and Watson had all figured Michigan
for a No. 3 seed, maybe a No. 4—after all, they were ranked four-
teenth in the country—so when the Wolverines came up as the No.
6 in the Southeast, Fisher was not happy. Later, in private, he would

yell at his staff, "We got screwed! They're screwing us!" But here, in front of the kids, he simply nodded and told them to be ready. The first challenge, Friday night, in Atlanta, would be the Temple Owls, a 17-12 team that gave opponents fits with a tricky defense.

"You don't need me to tell you how much you want this," Fisher said with a special look at the freshmen. "Now, let's make sure we practice like it this week . . ."

As the players left, some of them with pizza slices hanging from their mouths, Fisher wondered what lay ahead for this most unpredictable of teams. So young. So vulnerable to mistakes. And yet so talented. God, at times they really did play like the best team in the country.

Fisher headed out to meet the media. No team had ever won a national championship with five freshmen, it was true. But one team had started *four* freshmen and won it all.

Nice little squad.

Surprised everybody.

The Utah Utes.

2

Steve Fisher wasn't any more superstitious than the next coach, but he'd take a lucky sign if you gave him one. And, despite his anger at the Wolverines' No. 6 seeding, he did feel a twinge of destiny with the location. The first two rounds of the Southeast regional would be in Atlanta and Lexington. These were the sites of Fisher's greatest achievement, the 1989 national championship run.

"I'm asking for the same hotel rooms," he said.

And he wasn't kidding.

Atlanta, in particular, held a lot of memories. Fisher's first win as a collegiate head coach. And one of the strangest team meetings in Wolverines history.

This, of course, was after Bo Schembechler had told Bill Frieder to take his new Arizona State job and get lost, stay the hell away from the Michigan players. But those same players had never said goodbye to the man who recruited them (and who, until two days earlier, had been their coach). So when Fisher received a call from

Frieder saying he was coming to Atlanta despite Schembechler's threats, could he please meet with the team in private, Fisher said all right. He gathered the players in a hotel room, told them, "There's someone who wants to speak to you."

He opened the door. Frieder entered, crying.

"I never wanted things to happen this way . . ." he began.

The kids were stunned.

That meeting—the day before the first game, when most teams are studying tape and memorizing defenses—served to change the mood of Fisher's Wolverines, to cast the tournament in another light. They proceeded to win, win, win, right to the championship. "We didn't feel the pressure other teams felt," Rob Pelinka recalled. "We felt different."

Now, three years later, they really *were* different, the first team to start five freshmen in the history of the NCAA tournament, and nobody was giving them much chance beyond the first round.

Fisher had privately told his staff, "If we win the first two rounds, I'll be excited. That's a good accomplishment for a team this young."

Then again, this was Atlanta, his lucky town. And he *was* at the same hotel. And, as it turned out, there *was* another inspirational visitor.

The Greatest.

Not Jalen.

The other Greatest.

"You'll never guess who we just saw," Chip Armer gushed to his teammates as he stepped from the elevator Thursday afternoon.

"Who?" asked Webber.

"Muhammad Ali."

"Don't mess with me!"

"I'm not messin'. He's here. Look. You can see him two floors down."

Webber and several others leaned over the open railing. Sure enough, Ali and his small entourage, in town for a promotional appearance, were walking to their rooms. The kids yelled, Ali looked up, and, recognizing them from their Michigan outfits, motioned for them to come.

Soon the whole team was inside Ali's suite. The former champion, crippled by Parkinson's syndrome, did little more than smile, pose for pictures, and do some of his trademark magic. But during one of his card tricks, he spoke.

"Need concentration . . . to do this," he whispered, "like . . . on a basketball court."

The players were captivated. Jalen immediately lobbed a verbal challenge.

"I hear Tyson said he coulda whupped you."

Ali lifted his head. He stared at Jalen.

"I wish . . . I was a dog . . ." he said slowly, "and you . . . was a tree."

Everyone froze.

Then they broke up laughing.

Jalen was actually speechless.

On their way out, each player shook hands with the legendary fighter. When Juwan approached, Ali pulled him close.

"Shock the world," he whispered, repeating the phrase that made him famous in the '60s.

Juwan beamed.

The meeting with Ali seemed to confirm to the Fab Five that they really were in the Big Time. Nerves began to kick in. Shoot-around was lively. Friday afternoon, during their pregame naps, Webber had a dream that he was a bald-headed child again, playing basketball with a fearless attitude. He woke up and nudged Jalen.

"I'm fixin' to cut my hair off."

"Huh?"

"Bald-headed. Help me out."

Jalen got the clippers. They sat in front of the mirror. And when the Wolverines arrived at the Omni, both Webber and Rose were smooth on top.

The arena was only half-full, as Michigan-Temple was not supposed to be much of a matchup. Those who bothered to show came mostly out of curiosity about these so-called Fabulous Freshmen. Fisher cautioned his players about Temple's difficult matchup zone—a tricky, dancing defense that looks like one thing until you go to pass or dribble, then looks like something else. He also spoke about the hype of the tournament, how young players often succumb to it.

"I know how good you can be," he said, "now go out there and show everybody else."

In the tunnel, the players huddled, and when they broke, Juwan uttered his new motto.

"Shock the world!"

They were on their way.

Temple was coached by John Chaney, a thickly jowled, raspy-voiced, 61-year-old man who looks like a basketball version of Yoda from *Star Wars*. His droopy eyes and philosophical press conferences have convinced people he's some sort of genius, but during the game, he's a plain old butt-kicker. He exhorted his players to take advantage of Michigan's inexperience. He screamed at them during time-outs, and in the half-empty arena, you could hear him several rows back.

"They're young! They're young! Get a lead and I can win this game for you!"

Temple got a lead, in the second half—after Michigan blew a 14-point first-half advantage—but then Rose went to work. He sank two of his trademark leaning bank shots. He buried a three-pointer. He made free throws.

"How come your coach crying so much?" Jalen snickered to Eric Brunson. "He's a crybaby. Tell him to shut up."

"At least my coach moves," Brunson answered.

"Yeah, he moves, but he gonna lose."

And Rose was right. Despite Chaney's promise, the Fab Five held their form, and they won their first tournament game by seven points, 73–66.

Rose led the way with 19. The freshmen scored all but two of Michigan's baskets.

In the press conference afterward, Chaney appeared unimpressed by the Michigan kids. "They overcame mistakes tonight," he sour-graped, "but I don't know if they can overcome the same mistakes against an equally talented team."

What he had in mind, no doubt, was mighty Arizona, the team playing the second game in the Omni that night, and a team that had, at one time, been ranked No. 1 in the nation. If the Wildcats won, they would face Michigan Sunday as a heavy favorite. Fisher expected it, and had his staff do some scouting in advance.

It turned out not to be necessary. Arizona has a history of being a raging ocean in the regular season and mop water in the postseason—and, true to form, it was upset Friday night by little-known East Tennessee State, 87–80.

So Sunday afternoon, instead of the marquee Michigan-Arizona showdown, it was the suddenly favored Wolverines against the virtually unknown Buccaneers. In body size alone, this was like skyscraper against mobile home. One East Tennessee guard was the 5-foot-11, appropriately named Jason Niblett. The other guard was 5-foot-6-inch Eric Palmer.

And these were the starters!

This would be no contest. Although Fisher warned against overconfidence, and showed film after film of the Buccaneers sinking three-point baskets against Arizona, he needn't have worried. Before you could say "East Tennessee who?" Jimmy King was soaring for open dunks, Juwan Howard was popping in turn-around baskets, and Jalen flew past one defender, went under the basket, came out the other side, and banked it in.

He was laughing.

The lead was 20 by halftime.

Before this game was over, even little-used subs like Jason Bossard, Chris Seter, and Chip Armer saw action. The final score was 102–90. The Wolverines dominated every important category, including 32 assists on their 38 baskets. When the buzzer sounded, Jimmy King raced down the tunnel and ran smack into a Michigan staff person who was holding an orange soda. It spilled all over King.

"Dang!" he yelled.

That was as close as anyone got to the Wolverines all day.

There is nothing like the feeling of having survived a round of the NCAA tournament and coming home for three days before the next round. Everyone is congratulating you. Everyone is calling. You can feel the buildup each day; it is tangible, like feeling your heart pumping blood when you first begin to exercise. And, of course, the media is suddenly everywhere.

Especially if you're a good story. And the Wolverines were. Shaquille O'Neal and his LSU Tigers had been eliminated in the first weekend; so had big names like Syracuse, Georgetown, Missouri, USC, Arkansas, and even Kansas, the top seed in the Midwest.

Many journalistic noses thus sniffed in the direction of Ann Arbor, where those five crazy freshmen had breezed through their first two games, and were heading to Lexington with shaved skulls and long shorts and lots of—what were they calling it?—trash talk.

"Sounds different," you could hear sports editors across

America saying in their Monday morning meetings. "Let's send somebody out there."

Little surprise that U-M's regular media session in Crisler was more than three times its usual size, with notable out-of-town reporters and TV cameras present.

"How are you able to play so well as freshmen?" someone from New York would ask.

"We're not freshmen on the court," Chris would answer.

"Aren't you nervous about this, being freshmen?" someone from Oklahoma would ask.

"We're not freshmen on the court," Juwan would answer.

"What's the biggest thing you worry about out there, being freshmen?" someone from Cincinnati would ask.

"We're not freshmen on the court," Jimmy would answer.

Despite the drone of it all, Chris, Jalen, Jimmy, Ray, and Juwan were basking in the attention. This was fun. This was what they'd expected when they signed on the line. ESPN sent reporters. So did CBS, which also announced that it wanted Michigan in the 10:30 P.M. slot Friday night, so it could televise the game to the nation.

"You know why *that* is," Jalen said, winking. "It's us."

It *was* them. The Fab Five were beginning to stir the nation the way they had stirred the city, the state, and the general region. It wasn't quite the cover of *Sports Illustrated*, or the spread in *Life* magazine for the Mercury astronauts. But they were officially the Colorful Angle, and the Colorful Angle is never overlooked in March Madness, not with ESPN and CBS and Dick Vitale and *USA Today* all atwitter for angles on "The Road to Minneapolis."

Meanwhile, the Michigan campus was buzzing.

Do you think they can do it? They're so young! Support began to swell. The criticism of their showboating and trash talking was slowly melting away now, because, hey, if that's what it took to win a title, well, the fans would be flexible. Students saw the Fab Five guys from across the street and honked their horns and waved.

"Yeah, we're cool with everybody now," Webber sneered.

His cynicism was well founded. When they were losing, playing erratically, the Fab Five were simply a young, brash, obnoxious collection of talent. But win a few tournament games, and suddenly you become *our* young, brash, obnoxious collection of talent. And that makes all the difference. Banners hung from dorm windows— "U-M All the Way in NCAA's"—and handwritten notices covered bulletin boards, seeking rides down to Lexington. Fisher was on the news every night. Webber or Rose or Howard or King was feature-profiled every day by one of the area newspapers. The fever had caught on. It was spreading.

After all, if the school learned anything from 1989, it was this: be prepared for miracles.

The Final Four was only two wins away.

Cynicism wasn't limited to the Fab Five. The upperclassmen on the team—who now, in order to reach their lockers, had to squeeze around reporters come to interview Chris or Jalen—accepted their reduced roles with a certain smirk. They nicknamed themselves "the Forgotten Five."

"We make our own history," James Voskuil said. "We go backwards."

Statistically, players like Voskuil, Freddie Hunter, Eric Riley, Chris Seter, Chip Armer, and Michael Talley had indeed gone backwards. In points per game, rebounds, blocks, and steals, some were at less than half the output they'd contributed in the 1990–91 season. The freshmen had usurped the minutes and the ball. The upperclassmen were a support group only.

Then again, last year at this time, they were home for the year.

Which is better? To be the star on a losing team or the reserve on a champion? The Forgotten Five wrestled with that one every day.

In a players-only meeting in Atlanta, the Wolverines had promised to stop drinking for the tournament. And no sex.

"We all about basketball now," someone had said.

"Yeah. Let's get serious."

"No cold ones."

"No beer."

"No women."

"After we win the Final Four, we get all the women we want."

They'd laughed, and Eric Riley had laughed along with them. Riley went along with just about everything the team did. But deep down, the 7-foot center, with large almond-shaped eyes that made him look at times like a giant Bambi, knew it was a little late for him to be swearing abstinence.

Riley had a child, a year-old son named Andrew. The boy had

been born just before the school year, and if losing his starting position to the Greatest Class Ever Recruited wasn't enough, Riley also had to play Daddy now, driving out to the mother's home in Ypsilanti and taking the baby for a night. It was something the Fab Five kids could never understand, and he kept it mostly to himself.

One day after practice, when the others had left, he sat in the stands and related the story.

"She was just a girl I was messin' with. Her name is Julie. I met her between freshman and sophomore years, summertime, she was over Loy Vaught's place. Said she'd just graduated high school.

"We were messin' around for about four months. She told me she was on the pill, so I'm like, OK, cool. Then one day, she calls me up and says, 'I'm pregnant.' I'm like, 'Get an abortion.' She says, 'I can't. I told my mother.' Her mother's religious and against it, and I was like, 'Damn.'

"I thought about it hard for two or three months before I told anybody. I was scared and everything. I finally told my mother, and she said, 'You wanna marry this girl?' I said, 'Hell, no.' That was like out of the question. So I just said I'm gonna take care of the baby when it comes."

It came in August of 1991. He got a phone call at his home in Cleveland.

"It's a boy," Julie said.

Eric hung up. He didn't call anyone. He drove north the following week—it took him that long to borrow a car—and when he got to the house, he felt an uneasy turning in his stomach. He rang the bell. Moments later, he was holding a baby in his arms.

His baby.

His son.

How strange, he thought. He'd always dreamed of that moment, passing out cigars to his friends—who, in his mind, would be NBA players—but here he was, alone, in Ypsilanti, no friends, no cigars, with a girl and her parents whom he didn't even like all that much. Each time he came to visit, they would chart his arrival and departure on a notepad, as if preparing for some lawsuit.

"Sheee," he said now, shaking his head. Riley was a guy to whom bad news just seemed to come, always at the worst time. On the day he was going to commit to Syracuse, he learned they'd signed four big men. On opening night this season, Fisher told him he was being replaced as a starter by Juwan Howard.

Now, in the middle of a nationally watched tournament run, Riley got a phone call from Andrew's mother, saying she needed more money to pay for a baby-sitter. He didn't deserve sympathy; he didn't ask for any. But the burdened look on his face said this was not about silly things like trash talk or long shorts. This was real.

Last season, when he was starting, Riley had dreamed of jumping straight to the NBA after his junior year, and earning enough money to stop worrying about bottles and baby-sitters.

Now he was another member of the chorus line behind the Greatest Class Ever Recruited.

"This ain't the way I thought things were gonna go at all," he admitted, looking out at the empty arena. "All the scouts will be watching. I need a big game, man. I need a big game bad."

Oklahoma State had started the year with 20 straight wins. The Cowboys reached No. 2 in the polls, led by All-American forward Byron Houston, a beefy 6-foot-7 force who had scored 56 points in the first two tournament games. OSU was considered a "hot" team, and also a good story. The coach was Eddie Sutton, the fluffy-haired former Kentucky coach who had been drummed out of Lexington over a recruiting scandal. Fifty-dollar bills. Nice little stack of them. Sent in a package to a recruit in Los Angeles.

The NCAA put Kentucky on probation and kept them out of the tournament for two years.

Sutton quit, under pressure. He was devastated—although most felt he was also guilty. He had been so enamored at the idea of coaching the Kentucky program that he once said, "I'd crawl on my hands and knees to Lexington."

That was about the way he left town.

His return was big news.

So was the arrival of the Wolverines. Lexington is a basketball-crazy city—Kentucky is a basketball-crazy state—and since Chris Webber had considered coming to school here, everyone knew about him, because everyone in Kentucky knows everything about potential basketball recruits. At the shoot-arounds on Thursday, more than 3,000 people showed up, in the middle of the workday, just to watch teams go through layup lines.

This was not lost on the Fab Five.

"Let's give 'em something," Ray whispered, eyeing the crowd.

"Do it," Jimmy urged.

And hoo-hah! Let the show begin. While other teams had pretty much gone through their drills like good soldiers, the Fab Five started a can-you-top-this dunkathon that had the Kentucky fans screaming like teenage girls at a rock concert.

Juwan slammed.

"Oooh!"

Jalen pump-slammed.

"Oooooooh!"

Jimmy took off from somewhere in Ohio and monster-jammed.

"OOOOOH!"

Chris did a windmill crusher. Ray did a 360 stuff. Michael Talley, Freddie Hunter, Kirk Taylor, and James Voskuil rammed home their own renditions.

"AAAAAH! OOOOOOH! YAAAYY!"

The players were laughing. The crowd ate it up. Fisher watched with his arms folded, saying nothing. This might be where the conservative Michigan fan comes flying out of the stands yelling, "You're the coach! Make them stop!" And it's true, a more disciplined coach might have never let them get started. "We're here to work," he might have barked. "No horsing around!"

But this was not the Wolverines' real practice—they, like the other teams, would do that in a closed gym someplace later on—and besides, Fisher was not like that, not this year, and not with this group. He saw a value in letting talent behave as talent will behave. Right or wrong, he took a passive approach when things weren't critical. And he let his stallions run.

Whommpfff!

Jimmy hammered another one.

"OOOOOOOOOH!"

3

Scott Knoll had the keys to the Fab Five's rooms.

He also had, at various times, plane tickets, films, someone's forgotten clothes, Steve Fisher's car keys, batteries for the Walkmans, someone's forgotten sunglasses, video players, tapes, Steve Fisher's youngest son, food, aspirin, someone's forgotten schoolbooks . . .

Scott Knoll—whom everyone called "Doogie" because his soft

blond hair, slight build, and perpetually innocent-looking face suggest the TV character Doogie Howser—was the student manager of the team. As such, his responsibilities were, well, anything. And during tournament time, anything had even broader boundaries.

The first thing he did, for example, upon arriving at the Lexington hotel, was go to Jalen and Chris' room and hook up the video games. Sega Genesis. Nintendo. He did this, actually, everywhere they went. City after city. Hotel after hotel. Jalen and Chris just figured, "He knows how to do it, he's willing to do it . . ."

He was there to help. The same way he was there to go door-to-door waking the players up in the morning, in case they overslept. The same way he was there to go door-to-door making sure they were in bed at night, in case they "overlooked" curfew. The same way, if one of the players forgot something, he was there to fetch it, or if they lost something he was there to find it. And Doogie was only one of a number of student managers, all ready, willing, and able to do the same to help the team. He was not paid for this. He got nothing for the sweat, aggravation, or countless hours—and often he worked until sunrise cutting videotape for the coaching staff—nothing save an occasional favor from the staff, some free meals, a nice trip, some pocket money whenever Fisher could slip him some for watching his kids or delivering something. But Doogie would end up needing a fifth year of college to graduate because of all the time he put in as student manager, and nobody took care of his tuition. He did this as a labor of love.

He was a small part of the safety net that protects and often coddles big-time college athletes, from academic advisers who are kept abreast of their progress constantly—catch a problem before their eligibility is affected—to trainers who massage their aching limbs, to student managers who can hook up a Sega Genesis.

"I don't mind," said Knoll, in his typically friendly fashion. "I know how to do it. I like it. It's just part of what I do."

And because he did it, right from the start, none of the freshmen figured there was anything special about it. He was there to help. There were always people there to help. It was part of the life of big-time athletics, and so, in Lexington, when Ray or Jimmy or Jalen said, "Doog, man, I'm outa batteries for my jams. I gotta have some, man. Can you get me some?" more often than not, he would.

The night before the Oklahoma State game, Doogie did his normal curfew check. Certain players, he admitted, hardly needed it. Rob Pelinka. James Voskuil. These guys were in bed before you asked, and up before you knocked.

Chris and Jalen, on the other hand, liked to play around. Pretend they weren't there. Or simply sleep through wake-up calls. So when he got to their room the night before the third game of the tournament they had dreamed about all their lives, he knocked, and at first there was no answer. He flashed on that worried feeling. Uh-oh. He knocked again.

Then he heard laughter, and the *dooodleweep, doodlewooop* of the video games. He knew everyone was in for the night.

4

SHREEEEEEK!
Fisher unfolded his arms and screamed.
"CHRIS! WHAT ARE YOU DOING?"

It was Friday night, second half of Michigan–Oklahoma State, the Rupp Arena crowd was a sea of noise, with a mob of Oklahoma State fans in their orange and black outfits pointing at Webber and hooting, "You! You! You! You!" Webber looked toward the roof and wiped the sweat off his upper lip. Already playing a terrible game, he had just committed his fourth foul.

"What's he doing?" Fisher moaned to his bench. Jay Smith and Brian Dutcher shook their heads. The players looked helpless. The Wolverines had let the Cowboys back into this game, after breezing to a large lead in the first half. Now they trailed, 37–36, and Webber was coming out. Four fouls? And still 19 minutes to go?

"Eric!" Fisher barked. "Get in there!"

Riley jumped to his feet. He had been sitting next to Perry Watson most of the night, and for some reason, Perry had been telling him, "If you want to impress the NBA, you're gonna have to do it from the minutes you get coming off the bench. Make the most of them."

Now he was running onto the floor with a chance to do just that. He had wanted a big game. Jalen grabbed him by the head and whispered, "Your time, E."

Next thing he knew, Riley was rebounding a Juwan Howard miss, tossing it up, and watching it fall through the net.

Score! Michigan had the lead back.

Next time down, Riley fought hard for the ball and was fouled while shooting.

"Good play! Good play, Eric!" Fisher yelled.

Two plays later, he rebounded a Jimmy King miss and banked it home. Riley hadn't scored more than four points in over three weeks, but he breezed past that mark and just kept going. Without worry as to time limits—Chris and Juwan were both in foul trouble—Riley was able to play aggressively, even make a few mistakes and not immediately tighten up and glance at the bench and see a sub running toward him. He used his size. He spun and shot. He slapped at rebounds until he captured them. During the 10 minutes that Webber was on the bench, the Wolverines actually outscored Oklahoma State, 17–13.

Eric Riley—a charter member of the Forgotten Five—was leading the way.

At one point, Byron Houston, trying to stop Riley, elbowed him in the face. Riley shrugged it off, but Jalen came racing over, stuck his bald, jack-o'-lantern head right in Houston's eyes, and said, "I was gonna be nice to you, but now that you elbowed my boy, I'm gonna dog your butt!"

So now Riley was really in the club.

The game went back and forth. Finally, with Michigan clinging to a 65–61 lead, under two minutes to go, a bad pass came Riley's way, it hung in the air, there were two men on him, and as he went for it, he was fouled. He turned and headed nervously toward the free throw line.

This had been his weak spot all night. He'd missed five out of six free attempts. Fisher knew it. He called Riley over and put an arm around him. "You're playing great basketball, Eric! Great basketball! Stay tough. Stay tough. You're playing great. You'll make these free throws. Just go do it."

Riley nodded. It was the nicest conversation he'd had with Fisher in a year.

And a smart piece of coaching. Riley stepped to the line, buoyed with confidence, and swished them both. It was 67–61. Riley now had his season high in points, 15, and his season high in rebounds, 10. He was sweating and panting like the old days. He had protected his team from disaster and had just given it a cushion.

Now it was up to Rose to bring it home.

No problem. Jalen was dropping layups, hitting free throws, and grabbing more rebounds than anybody on either team. In fact, the only thing more impressive than his basketball was his mouth.

He was in rare trash-talk form. He chided Houston, the All-American, who had dared to elbow Riley and, as if being punished, was having an awful night, shooting just two for 14.

"You can't be no real All-American," Jalen said. "You must be an impostor . . .

"Whole country watching, and this is gonna be the way they remember you? . . .

"Go ahead and shoot, you ain't making anything tonight anyhow . . .

"Say goodbye to college. You through."

Houston was ruined. And with that Cowboy roped and tied, Jalen went to work on Sean Sutton, the wiry, pointy-eared, senior guard who was also the coach's son. Sean Sutton had said he wanted to win this game to help avenge the "nightmare" he and his dad had endured in Lexington.

He had a new nightmare now.

The guy in the floppy shorts with the gap-toothed smile.

"This gonna be the way you go out?" Jalen taunted. "Disappointing your father in front of all these people?"

"You gonna be crying afterwards, saying how bad you feel 'cause you let your dad down."

"I can see it. I feel sorry for you."

Sutton tried to silence Jalen by canning a miracle shot in the closing seconds. But his last pass was stolen, Michigan held on, and Rose was laughing at the end. U–M 75, OSU 72.

The buzzer sounded.

The crowd roared.

Michigan was down to the final eight. They would play Ohio State next. For the right to go to Minneapolis.

"WHASSUP! WHASSUP!" Webber yelled, racing onto the floor.

"YEAH, BABY! YEAH, BABY!" Juwan hollered, raising his arms.

Fisher was overjoyed. His team had survived a major scare without Webber, something he'd never imagined.

God, he loved this town!

"You guys did a great job of hanging in there and staying ready on the bench," he told them in the locker room. "This was a team win. Congratulations. Let's get showered and get back. We've got another game on Sunday."

"Whoooo! Whooo!"

The press came storming in, and, for once, as many gathered around Riley as around Webber. The junior center answered the questions. He squinted in the bright camera lights. For that half hour, he didn't feel like a daddy, or a substitute, or a questionable NBA draft pick. He felt like a basketball player—and a kid.

Like the rest of them.

5

Over the years, when the Beatles were asked about the best time of their lives, they inevitably answered the year *before* they made it big, when their music was full of youthful energy, they knew they had something special, and they woke up every morning with goose bumps that this could be the Day the World Discovers Them.

The Fab Five hit that moment the day after the Oklahoma State win, during a press conference in the Patterson Ballroom of the Hyatt Regency in Lexington. The NCAA policy was you bring your coach and your five starters, so Fisher arrived with Chris, Jalen, Ray, Jimmy, and Juwan. Believe it or not, this was the first time all five freshmen had ever done a press conference together.

And this wasn't some chintzy, little bridge-table gathering. This was a ballroom! Chandeliers! A stage!

"Check it out," they mumbled to each other as they were marched to a long table, each spot reserved with a personal name tag and a microphone. They sat before several hundred reporters and photographers, who filled the chairs and lined the back wall. Lights flicked as the kids sat down. Cameramen shuffled noisily on a wooden platform. Every move the freshmen made seemed to engender a corresponding sound, clicks, flashes, whispers. A ballroom? A stage? Someone tapped the microphone, checking for power, and the thumping sound boomed over the loudspeakers. Conversation dropped to silence. Notepads appeared. Tapes began to hum. It was like the opening of a congressional hearing.

"I'd like to introduce the players at the table," the moderator began. "To my left, Jalen Rose, Jimmy King, Juwan Howard, Ray Jackson, and Chris Webber. And of course, Coach Fisher. We'll take any questions."

You could feel the mischief brewing. They glanced at the mob, then glanced at one another, nodding when their names were called. Jalen laughed, then looked down to hide it; the others caught on and laughed along with him.

The questions began. One by one, reporters rose to the microphone, first to ask about basketball, Ohio State, the previous meetings, but then about other things, personalities, team jokes, the hair, the shorts. With each answer, the players leaned closer into the microphones, taking greater interest, trying a line, trying another, swelling with the realization that all these people, all these adults from all these really major news organizations, were interested, truly interested, in them.

What do you do for privacy?

Juwan: "Oh, when we want privacy, we can get it. You'll see one of us sneak off by ourselves, maybe with a little girl, hahahaha, I'm just teasin'."

The reporters laughed.

Hmmm, Juwan thought.

Why do you do all that trash talking?

Jalen: "We're not trash talkin', we're . . . conversatin'."

More laughter.

Hmmm.

Who came up with the name Fab Five?

"You guys," Chris said.

More laughter.

Do any of you really expect to win four national championships in a row?

This was too perfect, a mush ball down the middle of the plate. With no hesitation, they leaned into the microphones, loud and clear for the folks back home.

Jalen: "Yes."

Jimmy: "Yes."

Juwan: "Yes."

Ray: "Yes."

Chris: (*pause, wait for laughter*) "Yes. Yes! What do you think I was gonna say?"

The Greatest Class Ever Recruited arrives on campus as freshmen: Ray Jackson, Juwan Howard, Jalen Rose, Jimmy King and Chris Webber. (© *Duane Black*)

As interim coach, Steve Fisher won the 1989 national championship. Bo Schembechler congratulated him and gave him the job full time. Fisher has been trying to recapture the moment ever since. (*Steve Nickerson*/Detroit Free Press)

Chris Webber's college selection was a media event, which he shared with his family. (© *Duane Black*)

Not coincidentally, Jalen Rose and his high school coach, Perry Watson, came together to Michigan.
(© *Julian Gonzalez*/Detroit Free Press)

Juwan Howard. (*Pauline Lubens*/Detroit Free Press) (INSET: *Courtesy of Lois Howard*)

Jimmy King. (© *Julian Gonzalez*/Detroit Free Press) (INSET: *Courtesy of the King family*)

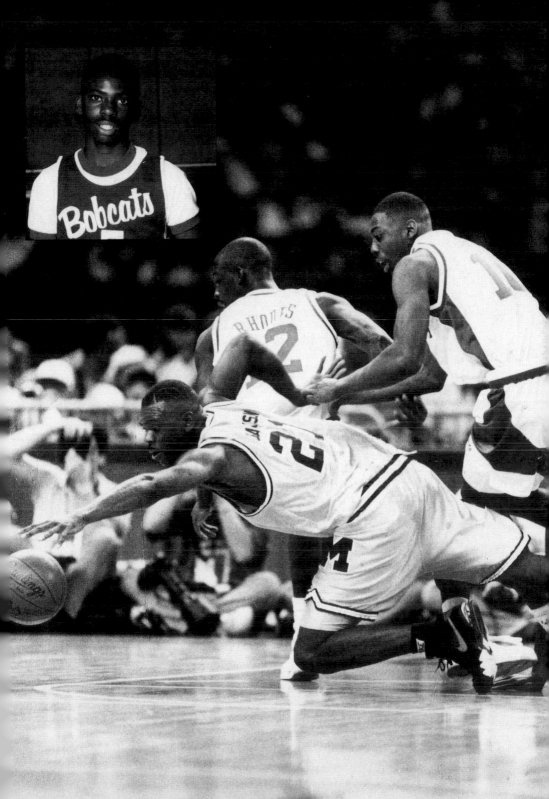

Ray Jackson. (© *Julian Gonzalez*/Detroit Free Press) (INSET: *Courtesy of the Jackson family*)

Rose and Webber were best friends, but high school rivals. (*Mark A. Hicks*)

At Michigan, they fulfilled their dream of playing on the same team. (*Kristoffer Gillette*)

Michael Talley and Eric Riley were two upperclassmen who took a seat to make room for the Fab Five. (*Kristoffer Gillette*)

Fisher had to challenge the Fab Five on court, and deal with their image off court. (© *Julian Gonzalez*/Detroit Free Press)

The media fell in love with the Fab Five during the 1992 NCAA championship. Ray, Jalen, Juwan, Jimmy and Chris were always entertaining. (*Kristoffer Gillette*)

Jalen's father, Jimmy Walker, an All Star for the Detroit Pistons in the 1970s, has never seen his son. (*Courtesy of Detroit Pistons*)

Jalen was used to life on his own, in the spotlight and out.
(© *Julian Gonzalez*/Detroit Free Press)

(© Jodi Buren)

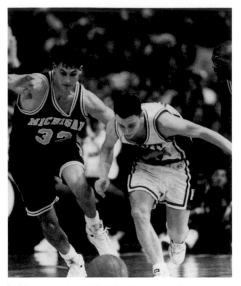

Duke was the Fab Five's nemesis, the one team they never beat. Bobby Hurley challenges James Voskuil. (© *Julian Gonzalez*/ Detroit Free Press)

Chris Webber wanted to beat Christian Laettner and Duke more than any other opponent. But the Blue Devils captured the 1992 championship. (© *Scott Takushi*/St. Paul Pioneer Press)

Fisher promised "to coach everyone fairly, but not the same." This sat better with some than with others. (*Kristoffer Gillette*)

Jalen Rose. (© *Julian Gonzalez*/Detroit Free Press) (INSET: *Courtesy of Jeanne Rose*)

Trash talking became symbolic of the Fab Five, but they often talked to each other as much as the opponents. (© *Julian Gonzalez*/ Detroit Free Press)

Jalen could always get a rise out of Chris or Jimmy. (© *Julian Gonzalez*/Detroit Free Press)

Celebrations like this one after the 1993 win over Michigan State brought a storm of criticism on the Fab Five. (*Kristoffer Gillette*)

OPPOSITE PAGE: Chris Webber (© *Julian Gonzalez*/Detroit Free Press) (INSET: *Courtesy of the Webber family*)

Jimmy King saved the season—and
the greatest comeback in Michigan
history— with this last-second shot
against UCLA in the 1993 tournament
(*AP/Wide World Photos, Inc.*)

Even unknown teams like Coastal Carolina
dreamed of knocking off Juwan Howard
and the Fab Five in the 1993 tournament.
(© *Julian Gonzalez*/Detroit Free Press)

The semifinal win over Kentucky in the 1993 Final Four was the Fab Five's last victory
together—and their most impressive. Jalen accepts congratulations afterwards.
(© *Julian Gonzalez*/Detroit Free Press)

OPPOSITE PAGE: The play that lives in infamy. With 11 seconds left in the
1993 championship, Chris calls a time-out he doesn't have. (*Joe DeVera*/Detroit News)
INSET: North Carolina's Eric Montross celebrates the violation, and the championship
that came with it. (*Joe DeVera*/Detroit News)

After the championship loss, Juwan was consoled by Randy Walkowe, one of many ill children he befriended during hospital visits. (*Steve Nickerson*/Detroit Free Press)

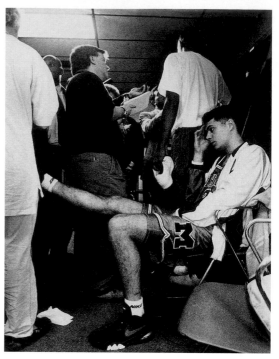

Rob Pelinka contemplates life after Michigan, after the crushing loss to North Carolina. He had law school ahead, but it was little consolation. (*Steve Nickerson*/Detroit Free Press)

Chris's dream of making the NBA came true when the Orlando Magic picked him No. 1 in the draft, then traded him to Golden State, in exchange for Anfernee Hardaway—who had encouraged Chris to leave school for the draft. They switched hats, and Chris was on his way. (*Daniel Lippitt*/Detroit Free Press)

Bingo. Freeze it. That was the moment. Replayed a thousand times on TV, splashed across newspapers, broadcast on every sports-talk radio station from Miami to Spokane. *Yes, yes, yes, yes . . . yes.* The room cracked up. Did you hear that! Such precocious kids! *Yes, yes, yes, yes . . . yes.* Like when Joe Namath guaranteed his Super Bowl win. Like when Moses Malone said "Fo . . . fo . . . fo," predicting his 76ers' play-off path to an NBA crown. Everybody loves a confident young underdog, especially one with a sense of humor, and from that moment on, the Fab Five could do no wrong in this tournament. Forget the midseason criticism. They were giving reporters exactly what they needed in this cluster-bomb affair: color, personality, fresh angles. *Hey! Listen to these guys!* Not like those other college drones that marched in under their coach's whip, say nothing funny, do nothing funny. Not a Bobby Knight team or a Dean Smith team. Here were these five freshmen, 18 and 19 years old, for goodness' sakes, and when they said something crazy, their coach just looked at them and rolled his eyes. Did they really expect to win it all?

Yes, yes, yes, yes . . . yes! Great stuff!

What about adversity?

Chris: "This team rises to adversity."

Are you worried about all these interviews?

Ray: "We've been interviewed. There's just more of y'all now."

How does your basketball rivalry with Ohio State compare to the football rivalry?

Juwan: "Hey, I'm from Chicago. I didn't even know there *was* a football rivalry."

Oh, they were loving it now, slapping each other, acting like smart-aleck kids with a substitute teacher, making funny answers seem even funnier. Snap. Flash. Click. Click. Flash. For the life of them they couldn't understand what the fuss was about, they were just talking the same junk they always did. But now the whole country instead of just the state of Michigan was listening; there was CBS and ABC instead of WXYZ and WDIV. It was fun, so the Fab Five played—they played with the media, and the media didn't care. Chris, Jalen, Ray, Jimmy, and Juwan were in that blessed cusp of new fame when your freshness covers all your sins, they were ripe, they were A New Story.

It would pass, of course, turn ugly, come back to bite them a year later. But no one knew that now. A half-hour press conference passed like a fingersnap. Five freshmen. An MTV moment. Don't trust anyone over 20.

Yes, yes, yes, yes . . . yes!

The media—and therefore, much of America—fell in love with the Fab Five that afternoon, right here, in the Patterson Ballroom of the Hyatt Regency in Lexington. The Beatles of Basketball! All hail!

All they had to do now was deliver.

Against a team they hadn't beaten all year.

During football season, Ohio State is the most hated Big Ten team on the Michigan campus. "I Hate Buckeyes" bumper stickers are always visible in Ann Arbor, as are "I Hate Wolverines" versions in Columbus. The famous "10 Year War" between Bo Schembechler and Woody Hayes' gridiron teams stoked the flames of this rivalry, with some of the fiercest football ever played, every yard seeming to come in blood. It has never abated. Michigan–Ohio State is traditionally the last game of the Big Ten football season, and it often determines who goes to the Rose Bowl, so it is critical.

Now, for the first time in history, the basketball rivalry had reached a similar showdown: the Wolverines would play the Buckeyes for the right to go to the Final Four.

The smart money was on Ohio State.

"We have to avoid what happened last time," Fisher warned.

"And the time before that," Dutcher added.

And the time before that.

And the time before that.

And the time before that.

Fisher hadn't beaten Randy Ayers' team since the first meeting in the 1989–90 season. Five straight losses. It was embarrassing. No school had dominated Fisher's squads this way.

Ayers, the young, handsome, mustached former college player, had replaced Fisher as the new darling of Big Ten coaches. He'd won National Coach of the Year last season, and Big Ten Coach of the Year this season and last season. His team was the conference champion, the No. 1 seed in the region, ranked No. 3 in the nation, with an All-American and Big Ten Player of the Year, Jim Jackson.

And whatever Ayers was telling his kids, it was working against Michigan. The first time they met this season, the Wolverines could only score 13 points in the first half—their lowest total in 40 years—

and that was in Ann Arbor! The second game, in Columbus, hurt even more; Michigan was playing well until late in the second half, when Ohio State stole the ball three times in 31 seconds and went from trailing to winning. It was brutal. The Michigan players had been so down after that one.

Then again, they hadn't lost since. Fisher took solace in that. He believed his kids when they said the last loss to the Buckeyes was the turning point in the season. He could only hope their new enthusiasm would somehow engender a different performance.

"Am I worried?" he said the night before. "I'm always worried."

The Fab Five weren't.

"We're gonna beat them this time," Webber promised, looking at the brackets in the local newspaper. "We had them scared last time. We're gonna beat every team we lost to this year before this is over."

He looked up for emphasis, as if this were the most natural statement in the world, then returned to the paper. Already, the Wolverines had balanced losses with victories against Indiana, Minnesota, Michigan State, and Wisconsin. Webber studied the remaining teams in the bracket, and traced the winners-meeting-winners scenarios with his finger, like a prospector tracing a treasure map.

He smiled.

"Yep. We're gonna beat Ohio State, and then we'll play Cincinnati, and then we're gonna beat the last team we haven't beaten yet."

Who's that?

"Duke. For the national championship."

How do you gauge manhood? How do you know the precise moment when a child leaps the great canyon, and begins to see life as the whole world, instead of just his corner of it? In most societies there is some sort of ritual, a ceremony, a performance. In basketball it is simply this:

You beat the guy who used to beat you.

And you beat him at his own game.

By their faces during introductions, you could tell the Fab Five were out to accomplish this against Ohio State. Remember, this was a team that never met an entrance it couldn't ham up. A little dance. A little laughter. But on Sunday afternoon, inside the steaming noise of Rupp Arena, they were dead serious. Even Jalen, who ran through the Wolverines' line punching elbows like a boxer, scowled at having to wait at half-court to shake hands with the opponent. No jokes. No smiles. They all wanted the same thing. Get it started, so they could get it over.

"Everyone's saying we can't do this," Chris mumbled when they locked heads in their huddle. "Everyone says they're better than us."

"Let's show 'em, baby."

"Now's the time."

"We didn't come all this way to lose."

Webber had his huge arms circled around all of them, and toward the end, he locked his hands, so that they were imprisoned in his massive wingspan, Ray, Jimmy, Juwan, and Jalen. He bounced them, like a father bouncing his children to comfort them on a stormy night. At times like this, Webber simply seemed bigger than them all, a Superman.

The ball was tossed.

And Superman was flying.

He dunked. He banged. He sucked in rebounds. He sent bodies crashing to the floor. Webber's mood was established early in the game, when he and Lawrence Funderburke, the Buckeyes' sophomore center, got tangled going for a rebound. Webber yanked himself away and made two fists, then quickly lowered them, but dogged Funderburke downcourt. "I'm on you, boy," he said.

They were pushing each other in the lane as the Buckeyes tried to set a play, but Webber kept one eye on the ball, and suddenly, in midshove, he slipped from Funderburke and raced over to senior forward Chris Jent, who was rising for a shot. Webber bent his knees and lifted off like a rocket, his arm almost coming out of his socket, high enough to dust the top of the backboard and—whack! Blocked!

Webber landed and went right into Jent's face. An executioner's stare.

"Remember that," Webber said. "I'll be here all day."

Which is how long it felt like this game lasted. The pace was so exhausting, the banging so intense, that it seemed like a demolition derby played at high speed. The lead changed hands 12 times in the first 10 minutes. Ohio State's point guard, Mark Baker, drove for a basket. Ray Jackson answered with a three-pointer. Baker hit a 12-footer. Jimmy King threw one in off the glass. Funderburke hit a turn-around jumper in the lane. Webber slammed. A baseline jumper by Juwan Howard with five seconds left gave the Wolverines a halftime lead of 37–31. But this was anyone's game.

Jalen had put a little personal flair on the contest when he scowled at Jimmy Jackson and said, "Nice move. I wanna be just like you when I grow up."

But it looked like Ohio State would laugh last.

Midway through the second half, with a respectable lead—57–50—the Wolverines began to lose it, to come apart, same as they had in Columbus the last time they played.

Jimmy King slipped and was called for traveling. Jalen threw the ball into a defender's hands. Webber missed the front end of a one-and-one. Miss. Turnover. Miss. Turnover.

Six and a half minutes went by and Michigan did not score a point. The Buckeyes ran off 11 straight. They led by four, 61–57, with just a few minutes left. The road to Minneapolis was reaching its exit ramp.

Time out, Michigan.

Fisher gathered them all together. The assistants scurried for their clipboards. Fisher waved them off.

"Listen," he told the team calmly. "I want you all to close your eyes."

Huh?

"Close your eyes. I want you all to think positive thoughts. Just positive things. You're good. You're good enough to win here. You're going to win. I want you to see yourself winning. Close your eyes. Take a deep breath."

The assistants glanced at one another. What was he doing? Now? At this moment? They were going Zen?

The players followed instructions. They shut their eyes, like Peter Pan, they thought good thoughts, happy thoughts, without a word of instruction about zones or rebounds or inbounds plays.

"OK," Fisher said calmly. "Now, let's go out and win it."

It was the kind of coaching move that Fisher, in his quiet way, never gets credit for. The Fab Five went out there and proceeded to do exactly what he'd given them confidence to do. They came back.

Jalen drove into the lane, hung in the air, and . . . swish! The drought was broken. Chris took a lob feed from Jimmy, between two players, knocked one down, and slammed it. Tie! Ohio State scored, but Rose came down the lane again in the final minute, tossed up a soft shot that rolled on the rim, came off, but Webber, almost smelling where it would go, used his body to clear the area, grabbed the ball, and banked it in.

The score was 63–63, and Ohio State had one last chance to win it.

The crowd was on its feet, the entire arena screaming itself hoarse, yelling for a miracle. The Wolverines hunkered down. Nine seconds left . . . eight . . . seven. Jimmy Jackson dribbled in on Ray, went to whip a pass to the corner, King came racing over, got a hand on the pass and the ball was loose, a pinball now, ricocheting off feet, knees, elbows, legs—grab it! grab it!—it rolled to Jent, who threw up a shot in a nervous arc—"MISS!" the Michigan bench yelled. It did miss, just short, clanked the near side of the rim, flew over the cylinder, and Webber rose and slapped it backward.

Once again, the Wolverines were going into overtime.

"Now we attack!" Fisher yelled. "They can't believe you're still here! They thought you were done! They don't want to face you now! Stay tough, and this game is yours!"

On their way out for the overtime jump ball, Chris slid up to Jalen and kissed him on the cheek, the way Isiah Thomas and Magic Johnson used to do in the NBA championships.

Mmmwah!

They both cracked up.

And they kissed Ohio State goodbye for 1992. Jalen hit the opening jumper. Jimmy bagged a three-pointer. Jalen sank two free throws after Jimmy Jackson fouled him.

"See you in the NBA," Jalen sneered at the Ohio State All-American.

"This is messed up," Chris added to Jackson. "You gonna end your career in the conference final, losing to us? That's the way you want to go out?"

Jackson sneered back, told them to shut up, but it didn't matter. Ray found Chris open on an Ohio State mistake, a backdoor cut. Chris was alone, took the feed, tossed it in easily, and was fouled late by Jent. It was 72–67, Michigan, and that was all the Wolverines needed. Webber ran straight into the arms of the bench players, and Jason Bossard, Eric Riley, and Rob Pelinka slapped his head and called out, "WE DID IT! WE'RE GOING TO THE FOUR!" Juwan was running upcourt in an exaggerated high-step, pumping his arms like a track hurdler with this huge smile on his face. Jalen was pointing. Ray was laughing.

A few minutes later, it was official: final score Michigan 75, Ohio State 71, and U-M fans stormed the floor and surrounded their heroes. Chris and Jalen were on the ground, hugging, and Chris came up with tears in his eyes. Hats were pulled out, "Michigan Wolverines, Final Four 1992," and Ray pulled one on, and then pulled another on top of it. The network TV people went scrambling for Fisher, who seemed almost dazed by it all. Behind him, Juwan was windmilling his arms, yelling at the crowd, "WE TOLD YOU! WE'RE GONNA SHOCK THE WORLD! DO YOU BELIEVE US NOW! DO YOU BELIEVE US NOW!"

Fisher beamed into the cameras, "I do. I believe them now."

There was no time for reflection, not in that pandemonium. But had there been, Fisher might have realized how the calendar almost assured that he would win this game. The date, after all, was March 28. Exactly one year ago, Jalen Rose was blurting out his college plans in the state championship locker room, and Chris Webber was holding his press conference in that crowded downtown restaurant.

One year ago, Fisher was clinking wineglasses with his wife, Angie.

One year ago, the five seeds had been planted. The Greatest Class Ever Recruited was coming to Michigan.

And now they were going to the Final Four.

6

Bill Wickett rubbed his eyes and blinked hard. Uh-oh. The numbers on his computer screen were starting to blend together. This happens when you're working through the night updating statistics on shots, rebounds, assists, steals, turnovers, blocks, shooting percentage, and personal fouls.

Wickett, only 24 years old—but aging fast—was the sports information director for the Michigan basketball team, who, along with head Sports Information Director Bruce Madej, spent the afterglow hours of U-M's tournament victories scurrying like an accountant to get numbers crunched, typeset, off to the printer, bound, and shipped to the next competition site, first Atlanta, then Lexington, now Minneapolis, where some kind soul retrieves them from the airport—*Hooray! The updated media guides are here!*—tosses them in a van, delivers them to the arena, stacks them atop tables in the media headquarters, just in time for a mob of reporters to storm in and grab them, like plates at a salad bar, because where would they be without the media guide! How else would we know that Jalen Rose had "a personal best of three blocked shots against Illinois," or that Juwan Howard "had the most electrifying game of his career at Indiana"?

No information is too small at the Final Four, nothing too mundane, too useless, too trivial, too inefficacious, not when the whole world is coming to the party, the Big Dance, the End of the Road.

And the interview requests! "The *New York Times* wants to come out, can they get 20 minutes with Chris?" . . . "*L.A. Times* wants to come out, can they get 20 minutes with Jalen?" . . . "*Sports Illustrated* is coming out, they want" . . . "the *Chicago Tribune* is coming, they want" . . . "CBS is coming" . . . "ESPN is coming . . ."

And the campus? It's Merchants Heaven! School spirit is jangling those cash registers, and sweatshirts, hats, caps, shorts, jerseys, anything with a logo is flying out the doors. There's an epidemic of school fever. Final Four carpools are posted on the ride boards, vans roll down the streets with "MINNEAPOLIS OR BUST" spraypainted on the sides, it's spring fever rolled into spring break, everyone going loopy, and they were especially loopy in Ann Arbor, April 1992, because of the Fab Five. What if they really pulled this off? What if they went out to Minneapolis and won the whole damn thing? Would history ever be able to record it? They were the Beatles of basketball, playing Shea Stadium, and you just had to be there!

In the ridiculous echo of all this, Chris, Jalen, Juwan, Ray, and Jimmy may have been the calmest kids on campus.

Understand that in their minds, this was not luck; this was where they were supposed to be. They were the best in high school. They planned on being the best in college. And they were not too young, not to their way of thinking. The Fab Five's heroes included Magic Johnson, who won a national championship at age 20 and an NBA championship at age 21, and John Singleton, the 22-year-old director of the acclaimed film *Boyz in the Hood*, and Naughty by Nature, the rap group whose members were 18, 19, and 20. Youth was not a deterrent. Youth was not what mattered. What mattered was getting to the big time, and doing what you were supposed to do once you got there—then acting as if you were meant to be there all along.

Chris loved to tell a story he heard about Michael Jordan, which summed up the attitude rather neatly:

It seems that some of the Chicago Bulls were teasing Jordan on a trip to L.A. about not being as world-famous as everyone said he was.

"Tell you what," Jordan said. "Pick anyone in the world, and I bet I can get in touch with them."

The first name yelled was Janet Jackson, the singing star. Jordan nodded, pulled out a small electronic Rolodex, punched a number, and dialed it.

"Hello, is Janet there? . . . No? . . . Well, would you do me a favor, please? Would you tell her MJ called, and he's in town, and she can call me at . . ."

He hung up. His teammates dogged him.

"Aw, that wasn't her number! . . . You just made it up . . . That don't prove noth—"

The cellular phone rang.

"Hello?" Jordan said. "Janet! Thanks for calling me back . . ."

The Fab Five loved that story. Chris loved it especially. To him, to all of them, that was what this whole thing was all about, getting to the top, knowing everyone else at the top, acting almost casual, the ultimate cool. Let other people do the staring. You belong.

"Living large," athletes often call it.

And Minneapolis, in the 1992 college basketball world, was as large as it got.

7

I never had any friends later on like the ones I had when I was twelve. Jesus, did you?

—Stephen King, from "The Body"

In the summer of their eighth-grade year, Chris Webber and Jalen Rose were teammates on a Detroit AAU team—"Super

Friends,'' it was called—and it took them to St. Louis for a tournament. One afternoon, they got a cap gun. Chris put a roll of caps in his pocket. Just for laughs, Jalen pulled the trigger against Chris' jeans.

The roll caught fire.

"Stop it!" Chris yelled.

"Hahaha. I got you!" Jalen said.

"Stop it, you're burning me!"

"Gotcha! Gotcha!"

The caps were exploding, one after another—*pop-pop-pop-pop-pop*—and suddenly smoke was coming from Chris' leg. He screamed. "Get 'em off me! Get my pants off me!" He was fumbling with his buckle, panicking, and Jalen dropped the gun and yanked open the clasp, pulled the jeans down away from Chris' body. They stepped on the pants to put out the fire. Chris was near tears. He rubbed his left thigh, where the flesh was burned.

He still has the scar today.

So you could say Jalen left his mark on Chris early, and when they arrived at their Minneapolis hotel, the Registry, in Bloomington, to a sea of fans, reporters, autograph collectors, and stargazers, Chris remained close on Jalen's heels, right up to the hotel room. People are surprised to learn that, of the two, Jalen is actually the leader, Chris the follower. This goes back to their first meeting, when Jalen introduced himself to Chris by saying, "Welcome to the big time."

Like most tall children, Chris was self-conscious at an early age, and he admired Jalen's feistiness and guts. He smiled innocently when Jalen told his stories, even if they were mostly lies. Hell, Jalen was bragging about girls when he was 11.

Jalen was, to Chris, the part of himself he often suppressed. Chris lived in the city, but Jalen really *was* the city, Jalen got in more trouble, took more chances, and generally was willing to do the stuff that Chris knew, deep down, his parents wouldn't approve of. Jalen talked junk. Jalen challenged the older kids. He would roll up his pant legs and leave his shoelaces untied and call you "punk" if you missed a shot. When you're 12 years old, and a boy, you fall in line behind a guy like Jalen.

And besides, Chris thought Jalen was funny.

Jalen, meanwhile, who didn't really trust that many people, liked Chris because, for one thing, he was equally competitive. You don't play hard, you can't be Jalen's pal. Also, Chris was from the 'hood in Detroit, a prerequisite for being a true Jalen friend. And they could talk. Jalen didn't have a father, not one that was around, anyhow, and his brothers were 10 and 13 years older than him. With Chris, he could open up, share secrets, talk about life one day in the NBA, his ultimate dream.

He knew it bothered Chris when he teased him about going to a private, predominantly white school in the suburbs, Country Day—"You're soft! You didn't play anybody tough in high school!"—but deep down, Jalen admired the intelligence and perseverance he knew that took. He himself had taken the test for admittance to Country Day, and had passed—he could have gone, too. But Jalen always seemed to know basketball was where he should put his chips. He convinced his mother he was better off at Southwestern because Perry was there, and Perry knew basketball. Still, Jalen put his arm around Chris back in eighth grade, when Chris began to cry, wondering why he had to go away to that white school, with all those rich people.

"Don't sweat it," Jalen had said, "we'll go to the same college and win a championship together."

Now here they were, lying on their beds in a Final Four hotel room.

"Tell me again how we're gonna get our parents those Cadillacs when we go pro?" Chris said.

"I told you," Jalen answered. "We get my mom over your house. Then we get your brothers to steal the cars."

"My dad'll be going crazy, calling the police and everything."

"Right. Then we run outside and say, 'Hey, come out here.' "

"Then we have somebody driving those two Cadillacs down the street, right?"

"With a big-ass bow on top."

"Yeah! Yeah! One of them big red bows that goes all the way around."

"Two big old Cadillacs."

"Same kind."

"And you and me just be standing there, laughing."

"Yeah. You look at your mom and dad and I'll look at my mom and we'll be like, 'Dang, I guess this is what you're driving now. Cadillacs.' "

"Yup."

"I can't wait."

"Me, neither."

Doogie and Dave Ralston, the trainer, came to double-check curfew. "Get some sleep," Ralston said. Chris and Jalen nodded, but when Ralston left they rolled their eyes. They would be up until 4 A.M., and it would have no effect on their play. They were on the twelfth floor of the Registry Hotel in Bloomington, Minnesota, here for their destiny, the championship of the world, and when the lights finally went out in their room, the small glow of dreams could still be seen flickering through the window.

8

The Cincinnati Bearcats, ranked twelfth in the nation, were almost as unique a story as Michigan. They were the Fab Five pushed through the Looking Glass.

The entire Cincinnati roster came from other schools, either transfers or junior college players. This meant that—unlike Webber, Rose, Howard, King, and Jackson, who had all been prize recruits back in high school—most of these Bearcats were the leftovers, the forgotten kids who couldn't make the top level for some reason.

Nick Van Exel, their speedy starting point guard, was listed as a junior, but this was his first year at Cincinnati, after two years at someplace called Trinity (Texas) Junior College. Herb Jones, their leading scorer, spent two years at Butler Junior College (Atlanta). Corie Blount, their starting 6-foot-10 center, was a JUCO transfer as well. Anthony Buford, one of their best players, grew up in Michigan but was ignored by the Wolverines and the Spartans and wound up playing for the University of Akron, before following his coach, Bob Huggins, to the Bearcats.

Like basketball orphans, they had something to prove and nothing to lose. They flexed. They boasted. And they talked trash. Terry Nelson, a forward who wore a shaved head and actually worked part-time as a stand-up comedian, said his roots in the tough end of Los Angeles had more than prepared him for this game.

"Michigan won't say nothing on Saturday I haven't already heard."

Then, in front of all the microphones, Nelson, 6 foot 5, made a prediction.

"Chris Webber will not dunk on me. He'll be looking up from the floor before he dunks on me."

Whoo, boy.

Here we go.

Webber—who reads everything—was fuming before he ever got to the arena. During warm-ups, he was shooting free throws, keeping an eye out for Nelson, when a reserve Cincinnati player named B. J. Ward walked past and mumbled, "Yeah, you better practice those free throws."

Chris went ballistic.

"Who the hell are you? Jalen, who the hell is this guy?"

Jalen looked at the guy's back.

"No. 32. Ward."

"No. 32?" Chris said. "Are you on the scouting report? Juwan, was this guy on our scouting report?"

Juwan shook his head. "No, he wasn't."

"You ain't even on our scouting report? We just spent an hour on your team, and your name didn't even come up. You must be the thirteenth man or something. You must be a scrub."

"I'm no scru—"

"You must be a scrub, you gotta be, 'cause we didn't even hear your name."

Ward sneered. He mumbled something about having dunked on Chris in a high school All-Star game. But he could barely get a word in. Chris was going off on him now, right here, in the Minneapolis Metrodome, with the crowd filing in. Several Wolverines stopped their dribbling and watched.

"You're weak, man!" Webber yelled. "You're just weak! Don't you criticize my game. Don't you even—you know what, you know what? I don't even wanna see you again until you write me a 10-page paper on why you can't play!"

"I ain't writing you no—"

"And send me a highlight tape! You send me a highlight tape of you playing, just a tape of you playing in the park! You tape yourself playing in the park, and send me the tape, and after me and my friends review it, we'll let you know if you can play! You ain't nothing but a scrub.

"Now, get outa here. I got nothing to say to no scrub."

Ward forced a laugh and walked away. Webber's eyes were daggers, his mouth pursed in anger.

"Man, I don't know if this is good," Rob Pelinka whispered to a teammate. "He's getting too charged too early."

As it turns out it was a perfect icebreaker. And quite appropriate. Michigan and Cincinnati would be in each other's face all day.

As the players circled for the opening jump, the jawing started again. Webber finally found Nelson and slid within earshot.

"I'm gonna dunk on your ass all night long," Webber said.

"You try it, I'll break your legs."

"That ain't funny. I got a future, and you don't."

You almost hated to see the game start.

But it did, and Cincinnati went right to its trademark: the press.

A pressing defense means the defenders stick to you the moment you bring the ball in bounds. And, sometimes, in the corners and the side lanes, two and three defenders will swarm the ball handler. If done correctly, it is like being attacked by killer bees: everywhere you turn, they're in your face, driving you crazy.

Jalen brought the ball upcourt on the first possession, and the Bearcats immediately pressed him. He lobbed a pass to Howard to try and break it, but Van Exel stole the ball and raced the rest of the way for a layup attempt, which Howard thwarted only by fouling him.

"My bad! My bad!" Juwan yelled, scowling.

Moments later, after Cincinnati missed a shot, Chris grabbed the rebound and turned upcourt, but he, too, stepped into a double-man press and was stripped of the ball. Nelson took it the other way and slammed. Two points.

"All night," Nelson said, passing Chris.

"Keep dreaming," Webber said.

The Bearcats were fast. But they weren't tall. So while their defense played pat-a-cake—and their water-bug guard Van Exel scored seven of the first nine points—they could only watch as Webber tossed in a half-hook over Nelson, then came back with another, as if tossing pebbles over a ship's railing.

Cincinnati was pressing, stealing, forcing turnovers. Michigan was slam-dunking, getting second- and third-shot opportunities. U-M had a lead. Lost it. Cincy had a lead. Lost it.

The halftime score was 41–38, Bearcats.

"Men, that's the best they can play," Fisher told his guys in the locker room. "That's the best, and they're only up three. And you have not played your game yet. We have to get the ball in Jalen's hands more. Let him control it. Eliminate the turnovers and we can win this game."

The Wolverines nodded. But they didn't listen. On their second possession of the new half, Jimmy threw the ball away, and Fisher slammed his foot.

"Talley!" he yelled. In went the junior, out came the freshman. But on the very next play, another freshman, Ray, telegraphed a cross-court pass to Talley that was stolen by Herb Jones, who went all the way for a jam, 44–38.

Fisher shook his head. Dutcher, Smith, and Watson slapped their clipboards and pounded their hands on their thighs. They had talked about this, prepared for this, practiced for this, and now they were making the exact mistakes they were warned about. Michigan went the first four minutes without a basket, and would get only three baskets in the next six minutes. Several Cincinnati players actually began to swagger and talk more junk. Nelson was yakking all night. When Talley fouled Van Exel on a three-point attempt, giving the Bearcats' guard three free throws, Van Exel tapped his forehead.

"That was dumb," he mocked at Talley as he stepped to the foul line. "Dumb. Dumb."

Van Exel made it 50–43, the biggest lead of the game. Some of the Bearcats were actually saying "It's over" when they ran past the Wolverines.

It was hardly over. But it was time for an unlikely hero. Fisher was getting little from Rose. King was on the bench. Jackson was making more turnovers than baskets. With 13:21 left on the clock, Fisher called for the only guy on the team who had delivered an oral presentation in class earlier in the week, entitled "Turbular vs. Laminar Boundary Layers Flowing over a Rotating Football."

James Voskuil.

Junior forward.

Major: aerospace engineering.

And just as Riley had done against Oklahoma State, Voskuil—without a word to anyone—gave the Wolverines a lift, proving that teams cannot live on freshmen alone.

First he got inside on a rebound, went up strong, and drew a foul from Van Exel. He made both free throws, closing the lead to 54–52. Then, on the other end, he blocked a shot by Cincinnati's Erik Martin, which led to a fast break by King, who also got fouled, and made both free throws. Now the game was tied, 56–56.

Voskuil was quickly bringing his floormates to life, lifting their mood, picking up their game. It was hard to say why, maybe just the presence of a new face, maybe the hustle he showed on both ends of the floor, leaping second and third times for rebounds, sticking close to his man on defense.

With under six minutes to go, and the game tied again, 58–58, Voskuil drove past the smaller Van Exel, went up in the air, drew a foul, and hung there for a nervous second, before flipping the ball high up toward the glass. The whole arena seemed to stop breathing as the shot kissed the backboard, ever so gently.

It banked in.

Good! And a foul!

The Michigan bench went crazy, half because the Wolverines now had a lead, and half because they couldn't believe Voskuil made that shot! Chris hugged him. Jalen slapped his back. All season long, he had never been this significant to the freshmen. Now, suddenly, he was saving the day.

Amazing what a guy can do with a little confidence. Next thing you knew, Voskuil was flying in on a missed free throw, grabbing the rebound and drawing a foul. James Voskuil?

Cincinnati made its last surge, closing the gap to 65–63, with under four minutes left. But Voskuil, out at the top of the key, took a pass from Howard and found himself wide open. On another day, he might have held the ball, looked to pass it off. But the good light was on him, he could feel it, so he simply squared, took aim, and as Fisher rose from the bench, his eyes widening, Voskuil launched a three-point shot from 22 feet away.

Swish.

"YESSSSSSS!" screamed Jason Bossard and Chris Seter, two end-of-the-bench Wolverines who both leapt at the same time and turned to each other as if to say, "See? If they only gave us guys a chance!" Michigan now had a five-point lead, and the rest of the game would be Cincinnati fouls and desperation shots. After one such foul, with 33 seconds left, Jalen walked upcourt alongside Martin.

"*Now* it's over," Jalen said.

And it was. Voskuil, the new hero, stayed in until the final

seconds, when he left for a substitution. The Michigan fans rose to
their feet. A standing ovation! James Voskuil! Fourteen minutes, nine
points, four rebounds, no turnovers. For all the trash talk and attitude
that preceded this game, it was the guy who delivered the aerospace
lecture who was most responsible for pushing Michigan into Monday
night in Minneapolis.

"Three . . . two . . . one . . ."

"MICHIGAN'S WON! MICHIGAN'S WON!" screamed
Larry Henry, of Detroit's WJR radio. "THEY'RE GOING TO THE
NATIONAL TITLE GAME!"

The freshmen mobbed Voskuil. Webber hugged him so hard he
almost took his head off. Jalen raised a fist to the crowd. Ray and
Jimmy jumped into a hug, along with Talley and, soon, all the rest.
They were one game away from the pot of gold! One game! Indiana
or Duke! Monday night!

Fisher went to shake hands with Huggins. The Bearcats had
come a long way, and had given Michigan a scare. Now Nelson and
B. J. Ward buried the hatchet with Webber. They wished him luck.
Talk is talk. Part of the game. They all knew it, even if the fans
didn't. They walked through the tunnel together.

Actually, it was Blount who would later sum up Cincinnati's
emotions in the best single sentence:

"Who was Voskuil?"

Meanwhile, a few thousand miles away, in suburban Atlanta, a
few men were watching the game on a health club TV set. One of
them, a tall black man with a gap-toothed smile and a full head of
hair, seemed more interested than the others. When the game was
over, the others asked him about Jalen Rose.

"That really your son?" they said.

Yes, the man said.

"He's got some smooth moves."

He does, the man said.

"He plays a little like you played."

I know, the man said.

Jimmy Walker, who had disappeared from his NBA life nearly
two decades ago, had never met his son Jalen, and—until these televised games—had never even seen his son's face. But he marveled
now at their similarities on the court. That easy gait. The spinning
moves. The confidence when he dribbled. "He's got a lot of me

inside him," Walker thought to himself. And, even if he didn't have a right to do it, he took a certain pride.

When the game was over, and the Fab Five were celebrating, someone in the health club turned off the set. Jimmy Walker got up to go.

"You gonna go see the championship game?" the others asked him.

"No," Walker said. But he thought about meeting his son one day, because it was obvious, quite obvious, the boy was going to be a star. What would they say to each other? he wondered.

9

When you believe in destiny, you don't believe halfway, so there was no doubt in the Michigan players' minds that Duke was going to beat Indiana and advance to the championship. It was meant to be, wasn't it? The only team Michigan hadn't beaten? The one they wanted most to destroy? Jalen had been so sure of this fated rematch that, on his way through the tunnel after the Cincinnati win, he jogged past the Duke players who were waiting to go out for introductions. "See you Monday," he said.

And, of course, that's exactly what happened. Duke ousted the resilient Hoosiers—Mike Krzyzewski, the former student, beating his old mentor Bobby Knight—and the rematch was set. Duke was one win away from repeating as national champions. Michigan was one win away from MTV immortality. The hype machine had 48 hours to crank.

No problem. The press ate it up, and the networks salivated, looking back to the huge ratings the first Michigan-Duke game achieved—and that was before anyone heard of the Fab Five. It was the classic confrontation of youth versus experience, the defending champions against the upstart challenger, Liston against Ali, Connors against Laver. America loves contests like this, and most of the country was on Michigan's side. *Sports Illustrated*, in an article entitled "Boys to Men," predicted a Michigan victory. So did many other experts who liked to go with the underdog.

Well, OK. Not everyone. On one of ESPN's zillion broadcasts,

Dick Vitale and Jim Valvano debated who would win, then pulled out two hats, one Michigan, one Duke.

"Don't pick us, don't pick us, don't pick us," Webber mumbled, watching in his hotel room.

"They won't," Jalen predicted.

Sure enough, Valvano and Vitale both pulled the Duke hats over their heads, and smiled.

"It's the Blue Devils, babeee!" Vitale said.

"Told you," Jalen replied.

"Good," Chris said. "These are the same guys who picked us to lose to Ohio State."

You get a month to prepare for the season, six weeks to prepare for conference play, two months to earn your way into the tournament—and one day to prepare for a championship game. Go figure. Watson and Smith scrambled for information from the past Duke game. Films were already cut. Strategies had been prepared, just in case. But how much could you go over in one day? If you flood the kids' minds, they don't remember anything. Fisher warned them of the obvious. Stop Christian Laettner by double-teaming. Stop Bobby Hurley by taking away his passing lanes. Box out. Get the ball inside.

"We tell 'em the same stuff we've been telling them all year," Smith said, shrugging. "You just pray that it sticks."

Meanwhile, the schedule called for another 90 minutes of press conferences Sunday at the media headquarters. Fisher and the staff gathered the cast together. The NCAA wanted the five starters.

"Steve, Juwan's got a bug," Dave Ralston, the trainer, said.

"A bug?"

"I think he might have a touch of the flu."

"Oh, great."

"Better leave him here."

Juwan stayed at the hotel, in bed, sweating, drinking tea, going to the toilet. The four other starters went to the press conference. On the way over, the coaches were talking about hotels. Jalen leaned forward.

"Hey, Fish, where'd you stay last year at the tournament?" he asked.

There was an awkward pause.

"Oh, that's right," Jalen said, laughing, knowing the answer all along. "You all didn't make the tournament last year."

"Thanks for reminding me," Fisher said, shaking his head. Jalen.

The press conference was typically overstuffed with reporters, TV cameras, rows and rows of newspaper people, not just from America now, but from around the world. The Fab Five—actually Four at the moment—answered the questions sleepily but with enough color to keep the masses happy.

Someone asked why the team was a 6½-point underdog, and Jalen snapped, "Same reasons we're a No. 6 seed."

Someone asked about the last Duke game, and Chris said, "My mother called me after that game and said, 'Don't worry. You're gonna play them again in the tournament.' "

Someone asked what they were all doing last year, as high school students, when the championship game pitted Duke against UNLV. Down the line they went.

Jalen: "I was home in Detroit, rooting for UNLV."

Ray: "I was home in Texas, rooting for UNLV."

Chris: "I was in my living room, rooting for UNLV."

Jimmy: "I was at my friend's house, rooting for UNLV."

The room cracked up.

They were getting awful good at this stuff.

The press conference was also the only chance the players had to see their families, most of whom were staying downtown, 30 miles from the team hotel. Parents pay their own way to these things, and this group was pretty upset that a few stolen moments with the nation's media eavesdropping was all they got with their precious children. Fisher apologized, said, "It's crazy, I know it." Doris and Mayce Webber hung around Chris, as did their other four children, marveling at how many people followed their big brother wherever he went, like mice following the Pied Piper.

Jimmy and Nyoka King stood by the phone bank waiting for Jimmy to get over to them. His girlfriend from home, Tiffany Wilson, was there as well. Ray's parents, of course, were waiting on him, and Jalen's mother, Jeanne, sat in a couch, smoking a cigarette, shaking her head at the mob around her son.

"He really packs a crowd, doesn't he?" she said.

He's just so colorful, someone said.

"I know. He's always been that way. People just like Jay, you know? I think it's because he'll say anything, he doesn't care."

Sleep did not come easy. It also was not necessary. Before the 1989 championship game, Terry Mills and Rumeal Robinson stayed up the entire night. They were too excited to sleep. When you're 19 and 20 years old, you can do that, make up for it with a nap in the afternoon. So Chris and Jalen and Ray and Jimmy and Juwan passed the time talking, watching TV, lying in bed staring at the ceiling. There was no sense of party out in Bloomington, just the sound of dwindling cars swooshing down the interstate.

Down the hall, Steve Fisher kissed his sons good night, tickling them a little, as he always did before they went to sleep. He had been bringing his family with him to postseason games ever since that first magical year in 1989. Mark, the older son, could mark his growth chart by the tournament. Unlike a lot of coaches—who don't want their wives or kids within 50 miles of them when the going gets tough— Fisher found great comfort in establishing a "homelife" in his hotel suite. They ate together whenever possible, room service, hamburgers and fries. Fisher read his kids stories and played board games.

The night before the championship, he wondered what he should say to the freshmen before the game. Should he call attention to the special nature of the night, or was it better to just treat it like another game?

Little did he know that the best words of advice would come from reserve sophomore Jason Bossard the following morning, at the team breakfast. The buffet was the usual fare, pancakes, eggs, bacon, sausage, granola, fruit, cereal, muffins. Most of the players ate the sweetest or fattiest items. Some picked at their food, lost in thought.

At one point, the table conversation got around to nerves.

"Man, I don't want to make a dumb play, you know?" Juwan said, in between bites of toast.

"Yeah, all them people watching," Ray said, "and you be screwing up, and then they replay it."

Bossard listened for a minute, then cocked his head and leaned forward. "Listen," he said, "you guys shouldn't be nervous. You have nothing to be nervous about. You're there. You're out there. You get introduced tonight. You're gonna play a lot of minutes.

w what I would do just to come out in the starting
ɔw what I would give just to step out on the court
...u *miss a shot?*"
He paused. "You guys should be thrilled."
They thought about that, and they nodded to themselves, because it made sense. It really did.

10

*"It's another championship night in the Twin Cities . . . as
51,000 people jam their way into the Metrodome for the brightest
stars in the college basketball universe! After three weeks and 62
games, only two teams survive: the University of Michigan
Wolverines and the Duke University Blue Devils. Tonight, they
play for the NCAA basketball championship. Come on in.
Tonight, let the madness come to an end . . ."*

—Pat O'Brien, CBS, as he opens the championship
broadcast

In a stadium the size of the Minneapolis Metrodome, a basketball
court looks as small as a boxing ring. And on championship night,
it feels like one. It is surrounded by rows of cloth-covered press
tables, like ringside, with cheerleaders on the sidelines, like ring card
girls. Marching bands play all around, tubas, trumpets, trombones,
kettledrums, sometimes two bands at a time, doing battle, leaving
you deaf. The crowd is a sea of faces that starts with the familiar—
family, athletes, movie stars—and thickens, up, up, up into the rafters, blurring into anonymous dots that seem miles away. During
the game, when the crowd reacts—much like at a prizefight—it
makes this weird, faraway noise that crashes above the action and
rains down on the players.
EEEEYYYAAAOOWWWOOHHWAAYYEE.
Is that *for* us or *against* us? Championship noise is nothing like
real college basketball noise, where the throaty screams of the student
sections bounce off the rafters, hot enough to make you sweat. But
then, championship-night basketball is not at all like regular college
basketball; it is surreal, misty, like playing on the moon—hell, you've

played all year in field houses, and now you're in a football stadium! It takes time to adjust.

And as they came out for introductions on Monday night, April 6, 1992, 9:15 P.M., to a worldwide audience estimated at 1 billion people, you could tell the Fab Five of Michigan were still getting used to it.

Because they weren't talking.

"AT FORWARD, 6 FOOT 9, CHRIS WEBBER."

Chris popped off the bench like, well, like a freshman, jogging out with an empty look on his face.

"AT FORWARD, 6 FOOT 6, RAY JACKSON."

A blank expression.

"AT CENTER, 6 FOOT 9, JUWAN HOWARD."

He looked like a choirboy, tapping hands with Duke's Christian Laettner.

"AT GUARD, 6 FOOT 5, JIMMY KING."

He low-fived his teammates.

"AT GUARD, 6 FOOT 8, JALEN ROSE."

Only Jalen even smiled, and it wasn't a wicked smile, just a smile. There was no attitude. No anger. No cockiness. No fire. A whole year of building up this trash-talk, in-your-face reputation, and now, silence. Nobody unloaded on an opposing player, telling him to "send me a tape of yourself playing, and then I'll tell you if you can play with me." Nobody even laughed. Duke's coach, Mike Krzyzewski, had explicitly told his team, "No talking to Michigan. They say something, you ignore it."

He needn't have worried. The Wolverines, for the moment, were acting like they had just entered a library.

They locked arms in their traditional huddle, their hearts racing like rabbits after a loud noise. Up in section 11, where the parents sat, Mayce and Doris Webber clapped like robots. All the years they had driven Chris to his games, waited afterward with sandwiches in the car, and now here was a night that didn't seem anything like the thousand and one nights that had come before it. Was that really their baby out there, with the shaved head? Was he ready for this? The whole world watching?

A few rows over, Nyoka and Jim King were feeling the same thing about their son Jimmy, who just recently celebrated his nineteenth birthday. And Jeanne Rose, who never got nervous about her son's basketball, well, she felt something awfully close to ner-

vousness now. Ray and Gladys Jackson stood on their toes, trying
to read their son's face. He was the youngest player on the floor, 18
years old. Earlier in the day, they had visited a Catholic church and
lit candles for his success. "I'm a Baptist," Ray Sr. said with a shrug,
"but what can you do?"

"Here we go, Blue," the freshmen said in their huddle.

"Let's show 'em."

"No letup."

They broke apart and came nervously toward the Duke players.
Juwan, still suffering from the flu, was breathing through his mouth.
He took his place next to Antonio Lang. Jimmy went thigh-to-thigh
with Grant Hill. Jalen stood flat-footed next to Thomas Hill, ignoring
him, looking straight ahead. Finally, Chris stepped in against Laettner, the guy he hated more than any other star in college basketball,
the guy he wanted to beat so badly he had to keep himself from
lunging. Chris' mouth was dry, his nerves jangling. He leaned in.
Laettner followed.

For an instant, they froze, inches apart, the floor beneath them
painted in the shape of the state of Minnesota, an aerial camera
capturing the image, sending it around the planet, to Brazil, Australia, Israel, Japan, Spain, Taiwan, Turkey, Great Britain. Senior
against freshman, suburban white kid against inner-city black kid.
Reigning champion against raw challenger. Back in the streets of
Detroit and Dallas and Austin and Chicago, long-limbed high school
kids sat with potato chips and bottles of Coke, their Air Jordans
untied, watching the tube, thinking, "Man, that could be me one
day." Why not? Last year, all five of these Michigan starters were
right there, alongside them, saying the same thing.

And up went the ball . . .

Of a hundred possible scenarios, no one would have imagined
what happened next: Christian Laettner, who'd been the subject of
endless glowing profiles in the days leading up to this game, dribbled
the ball off his leg on the first possession. Next time down, he tried
a long jumper from the top of the key—it clanged badly off the
rim. Next possession, he squirted a weak pass across the lane which
Webber easily stole away. Turnover.

"What the hell's wrong with Christian?" Krzyzewski asked
down near the Duke bench. "He's playing like he's asleep!"

Meanwhile, the Wolverines were still finding their feet. Juwan
drew a foul but missed both free throws. Jalen got whistled for going

over the top. Chris made a great move to the hoop, but the ball was slapped away by Grant Hill. The pressure seemed to make both sides jumpy.

After nearly five minutes, the score was 5–5.

Laettner continued his plunge. He tried a step dribble around Juwan, the whistle blew, and all three Michigan coaches jumped up, rolling their hands, like a Temptations routine.

"Traveling!" they screamed.

Three turnovers for Laettner.

Next possession, Ray and Juwan sandwiched him on a double-team, and he threw the ball away again.

Four turnovers for Laettner.

Krzyzewski had seen enough. He sent in his own freshman, Cherokee Parks, and told Mr. Wonderful to have a seat.

The Fab Five took note of this and thought to themselves, "Hmm. They're as nervous as we are." It boosted their confidence. Juwan bullied inside, rolled a soft jumper off the rim, but Chris grabbed the rebound and put it back with a one-handed thunder jam, right in Parks' face. "AAAAH!" Chris yelled, dropping his jaw in fake horror, then smiling at Bobby Hurley as he ran upcourt.

The pace quickened. Hurley hit a three-pointer. Grant Hill hit a three-pointer. Juwan banked in a short jumper and drew a foul, a three-point play. His free throw made it 10–8, Michigan. Laettner came back from his benching, but he was no better, missing a shot badly off the backboard, then throwing another poor pass across the middle, which Jalen stole and took the length of the court for a layup. A few plays later, Laettner again tossed an errant feed which Jalen robbed—*If you're gonna keep giving 'em to me, I'm gonna keep taking 'em*—and took off downcourt with Jimmy on his right. Time for a little fun, Jalen figured. He lobbed over Hurley's head, and Jimmy rose like the old days in his driveway, snared the ball, whomped it through the rim.

"Yeeeeeeaaaaah," King yelled.

Slowly the night was coming to Michigan. The frost had burned off, and the sweat felt good on their bald scalps. The lead went back and forth, but with Laettner such a mess—he was taken out again by Krzyzewski, yelled at, and put back in—it was Michigan, not Duke, that seemed closer to its form. During a TV time-out, Fisher told his guys, "Relax out there. Play the game you know how to play."

And for one memorable stretch, they did. Jalen took another rebound and turned into a football quarterback, chucking a long, lefty pass which flew perfectly over everyone's head and landed in Chris' hands. Chris rose without a dribble and slammed the ball home.

Duke tried a shot, missed, Laettner got the rebound, but Juwan knocked it away. Bang! Jalen was taking it the other direction again. Laettner was so frustrated by this point he didn't even run downcourt, just hung back on his own end and watched as Rose dished back to a trailing Juwan, who banked it home. Michigan led, 22–21. Krzyzewski was livid, not just at the turnover, but at Laettner's nonchalance. Next play, Laettner went for a shot and Juwan slammed him to the floor, staring at him, fire in his eyes.

"Yeah, baby!" Juwan yelled.

"Don't give him nothin'!" Jalen answered. "Nothin'."

The ref called a foul, but Howard didn't care. Michigan was flexing its muscles, feeling all the swell of youth, and if it meant a whistle here or there, the hell with it. Laettner missed the first free throw anyhow, made the second, then his coach yanked him once again and gave him a nice little lecture on the bench.

"You stood there!" Krzyzewski yelled. "You didn't even run!"

Michigan was hitting high gear now. Hurley drove the lane, tried to dish off, but Webber slapped it away, the ball rolled between several players' legs, a scramble, and suddenly here was Chris, up with the prize, and dribbling the other way. He cut, handling the ball like a point guard, and went right around Grant Hill.

"WHOA, DID YOU SEE THAT DRIBBLE!" Billy Packer yelled on TV.

Everyone saw it. And Chris was still motoring down the floor, in full gallop, switching hands with the dribble. He saw Rob Pelinka on the opposite side, out of the corner of his eye, and made a behind-the-back bounce pass—one of the hardest passes in basketball—that went perfectly into Pelinka's hands. It was a pass from the gods, no way you screw it up, and Pelinka spun 180 degrees, raising his arm like the Statue of Liberty—Rob Pelinka was doing this? A 180?—and the ball poked off the glass and fell through the hoop.

"WHOOOOAAAA!!!" screamed Packer.

"WHOOOOAAAA!" screamed the fans.

It was a remarkable move, liquid talent, unteachable, all instinct, and as Webber ran downcourt, Juwan yanked the back of his uniform and made him look him in the face.

"RIGHT NOW!" Juwan yelled. "RIGHT NOW! WE TAKE IT RIGHT NOW, BOY! THAT'S HOW YOU DO IT! RIGHT NOW!"

Chris nodded, and gulped for air, every muscle in his body tingling. Duke walked the ball upcourt, slow enough for the crowd to rise in appreciation of what these unquenchable freshmen were doing. Here, on the biggest stage in the sport, they were defying every notion of history, every theory that says experience beats energy and wisdom beats emotion. Here they were, taking on the defending national champions, and outperforming them, outspeeding them, certainly outjamming them. What if they actually pulled this off? Five freshmen? Winning a championship? Wouldn't the world tilt off its axis?

Their parents were jumping in the stands, the fans in the Metrodome were screaming in amazement, and back in Ann Arbor, the sports bars were packed with fans whooping and hollering at this little miracle on the TV screen.

"I SAID BEFORE THE GAME, WE MIGHT BE SEEING A CHANGING OF THE GUARD TONIGHT . . ." Packer announced to the world.

A changing of the guard? Jimmy hiked his shorts up and dropped into a combat-ready stance. Jalen planted next to Grant Hill.

"We're *on* now, boy," Jalen said. "We're on."

Juwan bumped bodies with Antonio Lang. Chris muscled for position inside. Ray, Eric, James, Mike T, the subs, the scrubs, the coaching staff, Fisher, they were all on their feet, flush with excitement, clapping, stomping, telling them to hang with it, keep it up, this was it, this was the game they'd been waiting for their whole lives, Minneapolis, the national championship, the last team left on the revenge list. Beat them. Go home. Have a parade. Go down in history.

For that one blessed moment, everything in the world, even the unthinkable, seemed possible.

They could win.

They could really win . . .

They didn't win.

Although the Wolverines took a 31–30 lead into halftime, it was one of those leads that should have been more. Way more. And Fisher knew it. Some of the older Wolverines knew it, too. Given Duke's uncharacteristic mistakes—seven turnovers by Laettner alone—Michigan, on a better night, could have been up by 15 points.

No one said this in the locker room, least of all the freshmen. They were all optimistic, yelling, "ONE MORE HALF!" and "TWENTY MORE MINUTES!" After all, Chris and Jalen figured, didn't their high school teams always win the championship? Didn't it always work out? Wasn't this meant to be?

"Stay strong," Fisher pleaded. "You can do this. They'll make a run at us, but we can withstand it."

Duke, meanwhile, was taking a tongue-lashing from Krzyzewski, and deserving every word of it. "You just played the worst half of your life . . . You suck!" the coach told Laettner. He banged a blackboard so hard he knocked it over.

And he walked out.

Message delivered. Duke emerged in the second half as the team the world expected. They clamped down on defense, making the inside game impossible for Webber and Howard. The Wolverines, showing signs of impatience as they neared the finish line, began to opt for outside jumpers, which is not what Fisher wanted. They missed shot after shot.

To make matters worse, Duke was drawing fouls, getting Webber to commit his third with more than 17 minutes to go, and Rose his fourth with 12:45 to go. Cherokee Parks, Duke's only freshman, was the guy who got Rose to bump him ever so slightly on an inside shot.

"Replay that one!" Rose yelled to Packer, while Packer was doing the broadcast. "Replay that one!"

He wanted it shown on the big-screen scoreboard, as if maybe the fans booing would get the call reversed. Packer laughed and shrugged.

Jalen the director.

He went to the bench.

Meanwhile, Laettner had woken up, thanks to some excellent feeds from Bobby Hurley. He hit layups. He hit three-point shots. He committed no more turnovers.

With just under seven minutes left in the game, Duke led by three points, 48–45, but Krzyzewski sensed that the Michigan kids were on the brink. He had talked to his team earlier about a moment when freshmen, if they were losing in a huge game like this, would say to themselves subconsciously, "Hey, we can get it next year. We've done enough just to be in this game."

That, Krzyzewski said, was the time to go for the jugular.

"Do you feel it?" he yelled at Laettner. "DO YOU FEEL IT?"

"Yes," Laettner said.

The play was called for Laettner to throw the ball in, get it back, and fire a three-pointer. But Laettner bobbled the return pass, and, with the open shot gone, he instead drove inside, past Webber and Howard. He lost the ball, fumbled it, got it back, picked it up, and somehow tossed it in backward for two points.

Webber and Howard slumped.

The year was over.

There was no spark. No spring in their shoes. No confidence. No trash talk. Unlike all their other magical nights in this tournament, the freshmen seemed to be without a second wind, just going through the motions. Duke ran a clinic, *scoring on their last 12 possessions*, with Grant Hill getting five baskets, driving the baseline, slamming, hanging on the rim, his team moving, uninterrupted, from a 14-point lead, to a 16-point lead, to an 18-point lead, to a 20-point lead.

The air was gushing out of the Fab Five, and all they could do was take desperate shots and wait for the end. The bench looked like a portrait of plane crash survivors. The freshmen were suddenly the most tired kids in the world, the exhaustion oozing out of their pores. All they had worked for. All they had dreamed about. This whole, crazy, wild ride that had seemed like such a lark, so natural, so fun, and now they were hopelessly behind.

Chris buried his face in a towel. He was sobbing. Fisher tried to tell him, "Be proud. Stay strong. We have nothing to be ashamed of." Juwan stared straight ahead. Jimmy and Ray and Jalen had their heads lowered as Perry Watson rubbed their shoulders. The Duke band was playing "Na Na Na Na, Hey Hey Hey, Goodbye." A Duke fan waved a sign, "HEY MICHIGAN: ONLY THE BEATLES ARE FAB." The horn sounded and the Blue Devils hugged one another on the sidelines as the crowd erupted in wild applause for the history they'd just witnessed.

Duke had just won back-to-back national championships, first team to do so since 1973. Hurley pulled out a shirt from under the bench and yanked it over his torso. It read, "You can talk the game, but can you play the game?" On the back it read, "Duke. We can play the game."

Not that the Wolverines hung around long enough to read it. As they walked through the long tunnel to their locker room, Chris could not control his tears. A TV camera moved right into his face, and all thoughts of manners and public image vanished. He remembered what they had done to some players from Kentucky, after the Wildcats had lost to Duke on a miracle shot. The Kentucky kids were crying, and the cameramen got right down on the floor with them, lenses in their faces. Chris was livid when he saw that. Said TV treated players "like monkeys in a cage."

Now it was his turn.

"Get those cameras outa my face, all right, motherfuckers?" he screamed. "I'm serious, get those cameras out of my face. That's all you want to see is a motherfucker cry? Then you'll see a motherfucker cry on TV. This is a motherfuckin' man here. This is a man!"

He had no idea the footage would be aired on stations back home, and people would criticize him as a poor loser, before his tears had even dried.

Fisher's cheeks were red, as they always get when he is upset. He spoke, hoarsely, about Duke's excellent team. "We're crushed, and we should be," he said, "but it's what Duke did, more than what we didn't do. We needed a spectacular game, and we didn't have it in us."

Michigan fans filed out of the Metrodome, saddened, but not surprised, as if they'd come to see a comet that was *supposed* to be visible, but, hey, you never can tell with comets. The parents of the freshmen wiped away tears and hugged one another and went down toward the tunnel to console their sons.

Not far away, a white-haired man named Arnie Ferrin gathered his belongings. As the former captain of the last team to start four freshmen and win a national championship, he had come to offer congratulations to the Wolverines—if they'd won. Instead, he figured, they didn't want any visitors now. His slice of the record book was still safe. It probably would be for the rest of his life. Arnie Ferrin, now in his 60s, was one of the last surviving members of the Utah Utes of 1944.

He made his way toward the exits, and, like history, left without ever shaking a Fab Five hand.

V

THE SUMMER OF
THEIR DISCONTENT

1

A warm breeze blew through the narrow streets of Venice, Italy, with its green water canals, gondolas, ancient churches, piazzas, cafés, souvenir shops . . .

. . . and Jalen Rose, talking into a video camera.

"This here's Jalen Rose reporting for Stupid News! And here on Stupid News, we show the stupid things people do!"

The camera spotted an old Italian couple, who stared curiously at Jalen's baseball cap and billowing shorts.

"These people," Jalen said, pointing, "are searching for the fountain of youth! Stupid!"

Juwan and Jimmy cracked up.

The old folks smiled, not understanding a word.

"Let's walk."

The camera followed Jalen.

"Now, this is stupid . . ." he said, coming upon a female artist whose leg was in a cast from toe to thigh.

"This is what you call passing time, in Italy, when you can't move."

She looked at him curiously.

"Let's walk."

He bounced through the crowd, sliding in and out. He yelled "FIRE!" just to see if anyone understood him. "Stupid!" he said.

Suddenly a group of Italian schoolchildren, who recognized the Wolverines by their height and T-shirts, came running over for autographs. "Uh-oh!" Jalen yelled into the camera. "Here come more kids who never saw a tall black man before!"

Jimmy and Juwan cracked up again.

Steve Fisher walked ahead, with his wife, Angie, looking in the shop windows, snapping photos of churches, trying to ignore as much as he could. Was this the vacation from hell, or what? They had been like this since they got to Europe, all of the Fab Five, especially Jalen, playing the Ugly American, making fun of everything, moaning about how the food was lousy, the accommodations tiny, the bus rides too long, the stores too expensive. Maybe this wasn't such a swell idea, Fisher thought, taking the team overseas for nine exhibition games, just a month after the NCAA championship defeat. He knew they were tired. He knew the season went longer than anyone expected. But the trip is only available once every four seasons, and he figured this would be a good bonding thing for next season.

Sure. And Mussolini was just misunderstood.

Things were changing. In less than a year, Chris, Jalen, Jimmy, Juwan, and Ray had gone from promising high school stars to worldwide celebrities. People in Italy, Switzerland, Monaco, and France were recognizing them—especially Webber and Rose—yelling, "Fab Feeve! Sign! Sign!" There were articles about them in languages they couldn't understand. There was footage of them in countries they didn't know existed. Although they had lost the championship to Duke, their flamboyance, bald heads, long shorts, and trash talk were remembered more clearly than the Blue Devils' jump shots. They were famous. Rock-group famous. People imitated their style and their moves. Kids were asking for extra-long shorts. Summer was here, and the five of them had a million things they wanted to do with their newfound fame back in America.

And instead they were stuck in—ugh—Europe.

True, the itinerary, for most people, was a fantasy: fly into Venice, sightsee, play a basketball game, go to Yugoslavia, sightsee, play a basketball game, go to Switzerland, France, Monaco, stay at nice hotels, have your meals arranged, spending money provided. The average college student would kill for this trip. But airplanes and hotels were no longer a novelty for the Fab Five; neither was fan attention, or free meals and spending money. And where most of them grew up, strolling the banks of the Seine was about as appealing as Lawrence Welk music.

"This place is terrible, man," Ray said.

"I wanna go home," Juwan moaned.

"I'm what you call a product of my environment," Jalen announced, making a rap hand sign, "and this ain't it."

So they walked around the capitals of Europe with headphones shielding them from conversations, and they arrived in each new city with eyes only for fast food and video arcades. Rob Pelinka and James Voskuil, who both aspired to play in the European pro leagues, took better advantage of the trip, sight-seeing, exploring. The Fab Five laughed at them, then went back to complaining. The arenas they played in were often old and small, some of them no bigger than high school gyms. After the Metrodome? The Final Four? They were supposed to get up for this?

And the teams they were playing? Who were these guys? *Auxilium Palla Canestro? Nice Olympic Select? Billy Desio Basket?*

And the toilets? Well! There were some places where you just had to, you know . . . squat!

"I ain't with that shit," Jalen said.

So to speak.

They moped. They complained. When they finally found a McDonald's, in Paris, they ordered enough food for two weeks. Fisher shook his head at all this—his son Mark was better behaved, and he was 13—and he wondered if this attitude was simply fatigue, Jalen's influence, or a harbinger of things to come. He knew the Fab Five had been to the mountaintop, and after that, most views could only seem lacking. Still, he needed them to grow up a little. They would be the heart of the team next season, now that seniors Freddie Hunter, Chip Armer, and Chris Seter were gone, and Rich McIver had transferred. And Michigan would probably be ranked preseason No. 1, so the media attention would be enormous.

Fisher sighed, and tried to enjoy what was left of the trip. Spoiled? Of course they were spoiled. They had done a great thing in their first season, a remarkable accomplishment. Now came the price: expectations as heavy as a wet blanket, and a what-can-you-show-us-that-we-haven't-already-seen attitude. Next season would be rough.

"IT'S JALEN, BACK WITH MORE STUPID NEWS!" . . .

Assuming they ever got there.

2

Things didn't get much better when Fisher returned to America. Sitting on his desk in Ann Arbor was the news that Donnie Kirksey, the volunteer assistant high school coach who had been instrumental in the recruiting of Juwan Howard, was embroiled in a lawsuit against a Chicago newspaper—and might be dragging the Michigan basketball team in with him.

Kirksey had filed the lawsuit against the *Chicago Sun Times* for an article written a year earlier, by their high school sports expert, Taylor Bell. In that article, Bell claimed the NCAA was investigating Kirksey "and his alleged involvement with the Michigan program."

The article read, in part:

> . . . The NCAA is trying to determine if Kirksey, who is credited with persuading Vocational's 6-10 Juwan Howard to attend Michigan, was instrumental in persuading 6-9 Chris Webber of Birmingham, Mich., to attend Michigan, and whether he attempted to persuade point guard Cory Alexander of Mouth of Wilson, Va., to commit to Michigan.
>
> According to NCAA rules, it is illegal for anyone not directly affiliated with a college basketball program—such as a high school coach, alumnus, fan or relative—to serve as a self-promoted "agent" of the university.
>
> But Kirksey has boasted to friends that he helped persuade Webber . . . to choose Michigan over Michigan State. . . .

Now, the truth was Donnie Kirksey had no affect on Chris Webber's decision to attend Michigan—God knows, Chris had enough people he *really* cared about trying to tell him what to do—but Kirksey did speak to Webber before Webber signed. Phone records showed they had at least one conversation.

As for Cory Alexander—who ultimately chose Virginia—Kirksey did talk to him at the Dapper Dan Classic in Pittsburgh, and *Sun Times* lawyers had in their possession a sworn statement by

Alexander's coach, Steve Smith, that stated in part, "I believe Donnie Kirksey talked to Cory Alexander about the University of Michigan."

This was just what Fisher needed to hear after returning from National Lampoon's European Vacation. Kirksey may well have been acting on his own. But under NCAA rules, he was not allowed to be pushing Michigan to any potential recruit. And if he was, it would ultimately be Fisher's responsibility.

The Michigan lawyers were already on the case. Phone calls went back and forth. The NCAA had indeed conducted an "informal" investigation of Michigan back when the Fab Five signed, but no action had been taken against the basketball program.

Still, a lawsuit is a lawsuit, things get dredged up. Fisher asked his personal attorney to get involved in addition to the university lawyers. For obvious reasons, Fisher wanted this thing to stay as far from him and his players as possible. The *Sun Times* lawyers were digging into everything: Juwan's recruitment, Chris' recruitment, Perry's hiring, and they were calling Fisher's office, seeking to interview him for the case.

Fisher refused.

"I can get a subpoena," one lawyer said.

"Well, that's the only way I'm going to talk to you."

Fisher hung up. If they subpoenaed him, he knew, they would most likely do the same to Chris Webber, Juwan Howard, Brian Dutcher, maybe others. Their depositions would be public record, and who knows what fuss would be made if the press got hold of all this?

Donnie Kirksey! Was Fisher now going to pay the price for indulging this guy? He had, after all, paid him twice to appear at his summer camp. And he had interviewed Kirksey for the assistant coaching job at Michigan—even though Kirksey had no paid coaching experience on his résumé. Fisher had even tried to get Kirksey work with Nike.

In his efforts to court a good relationship with Kirksey—and therefore, a good relationship with Juwan—Fisher had undeniably and perhaps foolishly suggested that Donnie might have a future in college athletics; it was for that future that Kirksey was now suing the paper. He sought damages of $375,000.

In reality, without a star like Juwan under his arm, Donnie Kirksey was of little interest to anyone in sports.

"Listen, Donnie, I really don't want to be subpoenaed," Fisher told him over the phone. "I mean, I would prefer not to have to do that."

"Well, do you think I should drop the suit?" Kirksey said.

"I can't tell you to do that. You do what you have to, I'm just saying I really don't want to have to testify or to have our kids dragged into it."

He hung up.

Donnie Kirksey!

He wondered what was next.

3

"This is the life," Chris Webber figured. American soil. Palm trees. Sunshine. Practice an hour a day. He saw a shirt inside a seaside boutique and went in to ask about the price.

"That's $300," the salesperson said.

"Un-hmm," Chris said.

While Jalen, Ray, Jimmy, and Juwan were back home for the summer, getting reacquainted with their pasts, Chris Webber was getting a glimpse of his future. He was in sun-drenched La Jolla, California—a town so chic it doesn't allow parking meters—part of an elite group chosen to work out the Olympic basketball squad, better known as the Dream Team. Webber and other college stars, including Bobby Hurley and Grant Hill from Duke, Rodney Rogers from Wake Forest, Jamal Mashburn from Kentucky, and Eric Montross from North Carolina, were banging bodies against the greatest collection of basketball talent ever assembled. Nothing like this had ever been tried in Olympic history, and even the practices were media events, covered by hundreds of reporters from as far away as Japan.

The spotlight fell on the NBA stars, but plenty spilled over to the collegians, and the 19-year-old Webber, the youngest player here, was getting plenty of ink—and his first real glance of the good life that awaited in the league. There were shuttle buses to take him anywhere. Good-looking women on every corner. He signed autographs in the open-air lobbies, hung out by the gleaming swimming pools. One day he went golfing with Magic Johnson and Clyde

Drexler. One night he went to dinner with Scottie Pippen. He walked among the palm trees, snapping pictures to show his friends back in Detroit. In a few short months, Webber had gone from dunking on some poor Chicago State history major to defending Michael Jordan.

And he was holding his own! That was the most encouraging part. He had been nervous, until that first night, when Larry Bird, the Boston Celtics' legend, stepped into the elevator with Chris and several college players.

"Hey, fellas," Bird said, pushing his button. "Y'all better get your sleep tonight, 'cause tomorrow we're gonna run your butts off the floor."

Chris blinked.

Trash talk?

"Listen, Larry," he quipped, almost instinctively, "your back's already hurt. Maybe you better relax tomorrow."

Bird laughed.

"Yeah, Larry, you need your rest, man."

"Don't hurt yourself."

"Leave the heavy stuff to us."

So much for intimidation. Webber quickly realized that the rules here were closer to a summer night in St. Cecilia's than a rigid practice in Crisler Arena. This was about getting an edge, playing with an attitude, showing your stuff—and Chris knew all about that. So the next day he dunked on a startled Charles Barkley, he fought for rebounds with Karl Malone, he tried to muscle against Patrick Ewing. They complimented him, taught him tricks, and, as the week went on, told the mob of reporters that this Webber kid was for real.

"Lemme know when he's coming to the NBA," Malone had said, "so I can retire."

By the end of the week, Chris felt larger, older. He was still wide-eyed at his heroes' skill, but he began to relate it to his own. Jordan, the best player in the history of the sport, had only averaged 13.5 points as a freshman at North Carolina. Barkley had averaged 12.7 as a freshman at Auburn. David Robinson had averaged 7.6 points as a freshman at Navy.

Chris, as a freshman, had averaged 15.5 points and 10 rebounds per game.

So he felt good, puffed-up, even bold enough to trash-talk with his biggest idol, Magic Johnson.

"Hey, Magic," he teased one day after practice, "the only reason you got the record for assists is 'cause you were throwing it to Kareem all the time. Even I could do that."

"Yeah?" Magic answered, flashing that world-famous smile. "Well, I got me five rings. Do you have five rings? Do you have *any* rings?"

Magic looked around. "Where's Bobby Hurley at?" Hurley was quickly found. "Hurley, show Chris how many championship rings you got. He needs to see them so maybe he can go out and win one this year."

Webber laughed. But deep down, that stung. He was going to get one of those rings this year, he promised himself. And if he didn't, well, wasn't he good enough to play with these NBA guys already? Coaches were telling the media that had Chris come out in this year's draft, he would have been no lower than the fifth pick. That meant millions of dollars right there.

A safety net was forming beneath Chris' collegiate future. He looked at Magic and remembered that he'd left Michigan State after his sophomore season.

Maybe two years is enough, Chris thought.

4

Meanwhile, in downtown Chicago, a summer league play-off game was set to begin in the packed gymnasium of the Malcolm X Academy. Rob Pelinka and his teammates shot warm-ups on one end. Juwan Howard and his teammates shot on the other. The place was hot, crowded, a typical, boisterous summer gym crowd, anxious to see a game that pitted two homegrown stars against each other. The fans cheered wildly when the players were introduced. Everyone had a good sweat going. It felt like a good, intense summer game coming on.

Only minutes into it, a foul was called, and during the free throw, Rob glanced over his shoulder and saw a group of fans suddenly racing onto the court. "What's this?" he thought. "Are they playing around?"

Then he saw their frightened expressions, and he heard two

quick popping sounds. "GUN!" someone yelled. And everyone ran. Juwan dove toward the bleachers and landed hard on the floor, wood-burning his knee so badly that he still has the scar today. Other players dashed for the exits but changed directions when the mass of people clogged the available doorways. Confusion. More popping sounds. Screaming. Crying. Pelinka was the worst kind of fright-ened, the out-of-his-element kind, and at first he jumped between the bleachers and lay flat, head and belly down, then, when more shots were fired, he raced toward the bathrooms and pushed through the door marked "Ladies" where several other people were also inside, hiding. Rob found lockers in the back and climbed inside one and shut the door. He stayed there, listening to his own breath, for at least 10 minutes. He wondered about his parents, who were in the stands. He wondered about Juwan.

Juwan, at the moment, was hiding in another bathroom, along-side an old woman and two children. The children were crying. He tried to calm them down. He stayed there until the noise died down, then ventured out, found his bag, and looked for his friends. People were still crying and pointing, walking gingerly, as if a footstep might start the whole thing over again. The game was canceled. Everyone was sent home.

"What happened?" they asked, but all anyone knew was that a man had started shooting.

Eventually Rob found his way out to the court, and he saw Juwan. "You OK?" he asked.

"Yeah, you OK?"

"Uh-huh."

"This is for real, Rob."

"Yeah."

"When this shit happens, it's for real."

"I know."

"Man," Juwan said, exhaling. "Man! We coulda died playing basketball. We coulda died playing the game we love. That's fucked-up."

"I gotta find my folks," Rob said.

He went out to the parking lot, where five black men, friends of the program, offered to walk him to his car, just to be safe. He accepted, and, ringing around him like a hula hoop, they moved together, black and white, until he reached his car and found his mother and father there, his mother in tears. She grabbed his wrist so hard her fingers touched one another. And in her grief and relief, she refused to let go.

"Mom, please, that hurts," he said.

Months later, when they looked back on it, Juwan and Rob would shake their heads, maybe even laugh at the way they dove for cover. But it helped bridge a gap between them. It made Rob, who drove back to the suburbs that day, understand a little better what Juwan had grown up with, and made Juwan, who always thought rich white people behaved differently, understand that fear knows no color or economic status.

As summer school went, it was pretty educational.

5

Talent burns like rocket fuel in college basketball. You can be loaded one year and coughing fumes the next. Kids graduate. They leave early. They transfer on you. Suffer an injury. In a sport where one player can make a program, you can never have enough in reserve. And so even Michigan, with the Greatest Class Ever Recruited having finished only its freshman year, needed to replenish.

And it was time for Perry Watson to earn his pay.

Perry may have helped the cause the previous year by keeping Jalen and Chris on the straight road to Michigan, but Fisher was relying on him this summer to dig some new oil wells, particularly with inner-city black players. In addition to Marcus Hughes, a forward from Detroit, and Bobby Crawford, a point guard from Texas, Perry had his eye on two Los Angeles kids, teammates from the same high school.

One was Avondre Jones, a 6-foot-11 center.

The other was 6-foot-6 forward Charles O'Bannon, whose brother, Ed, was already a star at UCLA.

Perry made trips during the summer to watch them play. And he called them during the designated periods. The NCAA had tightened the rules yet again, and phone calls were even more limited than before. This meant that recruiting out of state was an even riskier proposition. Fewer chances for contact. Better odds for the local school. But Watson seemed confident.

"If you ask me," Brian Dutcher, the recruiting guru, said one day, lowering his voice, as if sharing a major tip, "the hardest thing to do is to get 'em to leave home. They say they want to go. They say it right until the time they have to make a decision. Then Mom and Dad or friends or uncles or aunts or whoever says, 'How are we gonna see you play?' and the kid gets scared and he signs with the closer school. I've seen it happen a million times."

Maybe. But Watson was new to this side of college recruiting, and he felt he had a good chance with the L.A. kids, particularly Jones, a shot-blocking center, because (1) Jones had lots of family in Toledo, (2) he seemed enamored with the Fab Five. When he talked to Perry he would say, "How come Chris didn't dunk on that guy the other night?" Or "That was a sweet move Juwan made against Christian Laettner."

Jones was into music, particularly rap, so Perry would encourage him to talk about it. Anything to keep the conversations memorable.

"I'm gonna tell Chris you're a rapper," Perry would say, trying to use Chris' name as much as possible.

"Does Chris rap?" Jones would ask.

"Oh yeah."

"I can rap better than him."

"Well, you'll have to come up here and try it."

"I know I can rap better than him."

"I don't know about that."

"I'll blow him out of the water."

"You'll have to come here to show me that."

"I'll whip him. I got some good raps."

"Yeah? Why don't you do a rap for me now . . ."

Recruiting. Some business, huh?

Of course, it was recruiting that spawned the whole Donnie Kirksey mess. And Kirksey had gotten the message loud and clear from Michigan and its lawyers that they would very much prefer he drop his lawsuit, before players and coaches got dragged into depositions. Kirksey, who has always kept one eye on future connections, later admitted, "I didn't want to get anybody in trouble or mad at me. Those guys had to concentrate on the season. I was just trying to make my point and clear my name."

He dropped the lawsuit.

He got no money. He didn't gain the "future in college coaching" that he felt he'd been deprived of by the *Sun Times* article. The only compensation he received was a letter from the sportswriter, Taylor Bell—which Bell was basically forced to write—loosely apologizing for any misunderstandings and crediting Kirksey for helping Juwan "land in a top-notch program at Michigan."

Kirksey accepted the letter as proof that he'd done nothing wrong. Bell and the *Sun Times* rolled their eyes and shook their heads. The lawyers collected their fees and went on to the next case.

Fisher breathed a sigh of relief.

6

But just when Fisher thought it was safe to go back into summer, a new bomb went off in his beach chair.

Camps.

This would make Donnie Kirksey look tame.

Basketball camps—and personal appearances—have long been a way for players to pick up summer money without doing much work. They go to an event, maybe a clinic, a coach's camp, or a tournament, they speak, teach drills, sign autographs, and go home.

A typical fee is $150–$250 per appearance. It can last five hours, or be over in 30 minutes.

For college kids, it's nice work if you can get it.

And in the summer of '92, Fisher tried to get his players as many camps as he could. With their newfound popularity, it wasn't hard to find takers. One of them was a tire store owner named Rocky Harbison, who invited three Michigan players to his OK Shoot Out, a charity basketball tournament, in Holland, Michigan.

Harbison had arranged everything through the proper channels. He had spoken to Jay Smith, asked for Chris Webber—naturally— and "whoever else you can get," told Smith that the event was nonprofit, to raise money for a 4-year-old boy named Derek Hazelett, who had a hearing disorder and needed an operation.

Harbison and Smith agreed on a fee, $300 per player—a figure Harbison came up with. Smith told Fisher, who thought it sounded good. When Fisher spoke to Harbison, his main concern was safety.

"We don't want our kids slam-dunking or anything and hurting themselves," Fisher said.

"No problem," Harbison said. "We just want them to judge a dunk contest, sign autographs, give out trophies, maybe say a few words."

"OK," Fisher said. "Just no playing basketball."

The event was on a Saturday. Jalen, Chris, and Eric were picked up in a limousine at Battle Creek, a halfway point, and taken the 60 miles to Holland. In the limo with them were two reporters, Jeff Seidel, from the *Grand Rapids Press*, and Gary Brouwer, from the *Holland Sentinel*, who had hoped to get interviews to tie in with the event. Also in the limo were two young boys, one of whom was 11-year-old Nathan Genzink. One week earlier, Nathan had seen his younger brother run over by a car. The organizers thought meeting Webber, Rose, and Riley might cheer Nathan up. He was thrilled. He didn't sleep the night before, and came with pennants, hats, and a magazine for the players to sign. He was a big Michigan fan.

At least he was when he got *in* the car.

Maybe Chris, Jalen, and Eric thought they'd have the limo to themselves. Maybe they'd been out too late the night before. Maybe Jalen was simply in one of his moods. But as soon as they crawled inside, Jalen and Chris took the backseat, stretched out, and went to sleep. The kids sat with their souvenirs on their laps, looking silently at their heroes. Riley tried to make it up to them by talking and flipping to cartoons on the limo TV.

The reporters were shut out completely.

When the car arrived in Holland, Seidel got out, went over to Harbison, who had been waiting, and whispered, "I'm not sure these players want to be here. They act like jerks."

Harbison was worried. It was already hot and humid, and there were maybe 4,000 people on hand, far more than he had expected. The event was staged in the parking lot of an outlet mall called Manufacturer's Marketplace. There were 13 courts, where three-on-three teams competed, bleachers, a refreshment area, and a first-aid station.

As the limo pulled into the center of the crowd, the Michigan fight song blared over loudspeakers. The doors opened. Introductions were made. No accolades were spared.

"LADIES AND GENTLEMEN, THE BEST PLAYER IN

THE COUNTRY, THE ALL-AMERICAN FORWARD, CHRIS WEBBER! . . ."

"LADIES AND GENTLEMEN, THE BEST POINT GUARD IN THE NATION, JALEN ROSE! . . ."

"LADIES AND GENTLEMEN, THE BEST SIXTH MAN IN COLLEGE BASKETBALL, ERIC RILEY! . . ."

Riley nodded. Chris and Jalen yawned and stretched. Already Harbison could smell trouble. For the next 30 minutes, the three players judged a slam-dunk contest. Then, for an hour and a half, they signed autographs and posed for pictures (along with James Voskuil, who lives in the area and came by on his own). The crowd—almost entirely white—was nonstop, going from one line to the next. It was hot and noisy. The seven security guards Harbison had hired could barely contain the fans. When Harbison brought over hot dogs and sodas for the players, someone grabbed the hot dog right out of Webber's hand.

By this point, Jalen was already moaning and making faces. He started talking about leaving early. Chris, as is often his downfall, followed Jalen's lead. They said they wanted a break, and they went to the mall, where they found video games and began to play.

Meanwhile, the people in line for autographs stayed put, sure they would return quickly. When they didn't, the mood began to sour. Where were they? There were so many people waiting!

The announcer came on the loudspeaker.

"PLEASE, FOLKS, LET'S BE PATIENT . . . THESE GUYS ARE SUPERSTARS OF THE FUTURE . . . WE DON'T LEAD THEIR LIFESTYLE . . . WE DON'T KNOW WHAT IT'S LIKE TO BE IN THEIR SHOES . . ."

Jalen, Chris, and Eric were racking up points in the video arcade.

When they returned, there was clearly tension. The players had seen how much the organizers were charging for autographs and pictures, and even though it was all going to charity, they somehow felt abused. Rose insisted they had to go. Harbison said that wasn't the deal. Rose said they had another charity event that night. Harbison said he was told they could stay until 5 P.M. and it was only 2:30. Rose said they needed the limousine. Harbison said he'd have to call the company, because it wasn't due back for several hours.

Things deteriorated. The players reluctantly signed items and handed out trophies while they waited for their lift. Eventually the limo showed up—around 4 P.M.—and they loaded up. Harbison handed each of them a check, $300, as they agreed.

"What are we gonna do with these checks?" Chris said.

"What do you mean?" Harbison said.

"How we gonna cash a check on a Saturday night in Detroit? Can't you pay us cash?"

Harbison reluctantly took the checks back, went to the refreshment stands, got $900 in cash, and handed it to the players.

"We should be getting more," Jalen said.

"What are you talking about?" Harbison said.

"We stayed here longer than we were supposed to. Now we're gonna be late for the next charity thing we gotta do. You should give us more money, so we can give it to the next charity to make it up to them."

Harbison was losing his patience. He asked what charity, and Jalen said it was for another kid. A kid who was worse off than this one. Jalen said Harbison should give them another $400.

Harbison refused.

"If there's really another kid, we'll mail him the $400."

There was no other charity, and he knew it.

When Harbison walked away, the players sat in the limo for a while, refusing to leave. Finally they shut the doors and the car drove off. Harbison was visibly shaken. He saw Seidel and shook his head.

"I thought they were going to punch me," he said.

The whole appearance had been a public relations disaster. Almost everyone involved—Harbison, the children in the limo, the large crowd—had been huge Michigan fans before the players showed up. Now, to say the least, they had mixed feelings. Fans complained. Harbison was embarrassed. Nathan Genzink, the 11-year-old kid whose brother was killed, went home with one basketball signed. He said he didn't ask for anything else "because I didn't want to make them mad at me."

And this, believe it or not, was just the beginning of the problem.

When the local newspaper story ran the next day—which left out many of these ugly details—the mention of a payment sent off sirens in the national media. They were paid? For a charity event? Is that allowed? That much money? Phone calls were placed to the

NCAA. As it turns out, the answer was unclear. One NCAA rule says you can be paid "reasonable" amounts at a charity or educational event. Another says you can lose your eligibility for "awards or benefits over and above normal expenses."

Typical NCAA.

Nobody can understand it.

Fisher, meanwhile, was besieged with phone calls asking what he was going to do about this "controversy." He was stunned. He had no idea anything was wrong. And he resented the fact that the story was already in the papers without someone first checking with him.

Then, to make matters worse, a Port Huron newspaper ran a story that week saying Michigan could be in even bigger trouble, because those same three players, Rose, Webber, and Riley, had been paid to appear together at a camp in Port Huron. This seemed to be in violation of another NCAA rule that says only one player per team can appear at a camp. Believe it or not, the rule was created to keep a team from practicing secretly during the summer.

Right.

Practicing what? Video games?

"Holy cripes, we're getting butchered on this thing!" Fisher said to Bruce Madej, the sports information director. "What the hell is going on?"

"I don't know," Madej said.

"Well, just tell everyone we have no comment until we get more information. I don't want to make this worse."

Fisher spent the last days of warm weather researching NCAA rules, meeting with university officials, and trying to calm down worried parents. He wondered if he'd goofed. He wondered if it was all his fault. Never mind that the charity in Holland had its most successful tally to date—over $12,000 was raised for the boy's operation, thanks at least partially to the players' appearance.

And never mind that nobody seemed to care about the Port Huron thing until the stories about the Holland fiasco came out.

On September 11, as a precautionary measure, Michigan sent a report to the NCAA and notified them of a *potential* violation. "I'm declaring Rose, Webber, and Riley temporarily ineligible, pending the outcome of the investigation," Fisher said.

And although this was a mere formality, and actually a time-saver while the NCAA went through the paperwork, Fisher braced himself. He knew what was coming. Headlines reading, "WEBBER, ROSE, RILEY INELIGIBLE: SEASON IN JEOPARDY."

He was dead right.

Summer really stunk, he thought.

7

Michael Talley shook his head as he drove back to Ann Arbor. This was one ride he never thought he would be making. When he walked off the floor in Minneapolis last April, he figured that was it for his Michigan career. He was gone. Outa here. Transfer. Something.

"I wasn't coming back," he said. "That's why I didn't go to Europe with the team. I didn't want to be part of it. I told James Voskuil and a few other guys that was it for me. I couldn't take it anymore."

But ultimately, what was he to do? He wasn't good enough to go pro. If he transferred, he'd have to sit out a year before he could play again, and then it would only be for one season—and what big school would want him under those conditions? He spoke to his mother and grandmother, both of whom said the important thing was his education, that he had to stay in school to get his degree. They worried that any kind of departure from Michigan would jeopardize that.

Talley and Fisher had talked off and on over the summer. Fisher had told him, "Look. We can bring you back on a scholarship, and you can go to school here, free of charge, without being on the team."

"What's the point of that?" Talley had said. "The whole point is to play basketball!"

"Well, I don't want you on the team if you can't have the proper attitude, Mike."

"What's that supposed to mean?"

Talley knew what it meant. It meant accepting a reduced role behind the Fab Five. It meant playing hard off the bench and being happy with that. Talley still couldn't swallow the fact that he'd been a starter for two years, and now, as a senior, he was reduced to an afterthought. Shit. He had been voted Mr. Basketball in Michigan—

same as Chris Webber—the best in the state. And now he should just go to class and not even play?

He didn't give Fisher a definite answer. He kept saying he'd think about it.

Toward the end of the summer, Greg Stoda, a *Detroit Free Press* sportswriter who covers the Wolverines, called Talley at home, just to see what he was thinking. Talley told him, well, he was going to come back. Stoda tried to reach Fisher for a comment, but Fisher was in Chicago, and didn't get back to Stoda in time. So Stoda printed a small story saying Talley would return to Michigan.

And Fisher went nuts.

It wasn't just because now, with Talley's decision out in print, it all but eliminated any options for Fisher to try and privately convince Talley not to come back. More than that, Fisher felt that he had specific instructions that players were not to be contacted at home by the media. That all requests should come through the basketball office. Never mind that this is a little paranoiac, and without basis, because since when does a school control a player's activities when he's not even in session? Fisher dashed off a letter threatening to close down access to the *Free Press* because of the incident.

It was the first sign that the pressures of managing the Greatest Class Ever Recruited were stressing even Fisher's enormously high tolerance meter. In the one year since Chris, Jalen, Juwan, Jimmy, and Ray had arrived, Fisher had felt the glare of the spotlight intensified like a blowtorch held to his forehead. He'd felt a certain national celebrity, but also the wrath of nationwide criticism. And for the first time in his coaching career, he'd felt the pressure of championship expectations—and hadn't delivered.

On top of that, Jalen was making Fisher's life pure chaos. First there was his embarrassing behavior in Europe.

Then there was his part in this whole summer camp mess.

Then, in early October, just a few weeks before practice officially began, Fisher got a call in his office. It was a police friend in Detroit. A guy named Tom Moss.

"Jalen's been arrested," he said.

"Arrested? For what?"

"He was caught in a drug raid. Now, don't worry, he wasn't doing anything. He was ticketed for loitering, but everything's been taken care of."

"It's been taken care of?"

"Yeah. Don't worry, it happens all the time."

"You sure?"

"Yeah. You just might want to talk to him."

Fisher hung up the phone and never told the press. Never told anyone besides his inner circle. This would come back to haunt him. Many things would come back to haunt him. He was about to enter Year Two of the Fab Five era. And none of them, including Fisher, were quite as young as they used to be.

VI

BLACK SOCKS, BLUE DEVILS, RED FACES

1

Never eat fried chicken from a box. This is a reliable rule, and the man in the Boston Celtics jacket seemed to know it; you could tell from his face as he pulled open the cardboard lid. He sighed, closed the box, and grabbed a container of coleslaw instead. The man in the Sacramento Kings sweater shrugged and did the same. He was followed by a man in a Detroit Pistons pullover, who took two chicken boxes, and another man in an Indiana Pacers jacket, who filled a Styrofoam cup with coffee. They were middle-aged scouts who'd seen far too many basketball games. They eased into their food like factory workers on a break, swigging Diet Pepsi and dabbing their mouths with paper napkins. Now and then, one of them would cough or burp and the others would barely register it, just roll their eyes and say between bites, "Thanks for sharing."

It was just another night on the NBA scouting trail—the adult version of the Great Recruiting Chase—and tonight the majority of the nation's professional scouts had gathered in the basement-level "media lounge" of the Houston Summit, where the No. 1 ranked college basketball team in the country, the Michigan Wolverines, was set to open its season against the unpredictable Rice Owls.

Not that Mr. Celtic, Mr. Pacer, Mr. Piston, or Mr. King gave a hoot about who won or lost. They just wanted to see who could play, who could handle the rock, who could swing his ax with the big boys in the league—and, more specifically, in the case of the Wolverines: who was coming out.

"You think Webber'll go pro this year?" one of them asked a Michigan reporter.

"Dunno."

"I think he will," one scout said.

"Somebody told me he's a lock," answered another.

"They usually come out."

"Guy like him oughta come out."

"What's he got to prove in college after two years?"

They nodded, chewed, took a breath.

"He can play, I'll tell you that."

"Umm-hmm."

"Got that right."

"He can play right now."

"With that body? Shoo."

A reporter asked how high would Webber have gone in last year's draft. As they were all chewing, no one answered, but their eyebrows raised.

"Top five," Mr. Piston finally gushed.

"Easy," added Mr. Pacer.

"I'll tell you this much," said Mr. Celtic, with a gulp. "We had the seventh pick, and I guarantee you he wouldn't have gotten past us."

They nodded, paused for slurps. A worker came by with programs, and they each grabbed one, instinctively flipping to the page with players' vital statistics. Someone cleared his throat.

"What about Rose, you think he's comin' out? . . ."

So the Fab Five had new regulars to add to the cast of M Club boosters, TV crews, reporters, parents, groupies, boyz from the hood, agents, card collectors, rap singers, cheerleaders, talk show producers, high school coaches, old girlfriends, potential recruits, and, of course, the regular-old-ticket-holding basketball maniacs who were following them these days, game to game. Now they had scouts. Last year's Wolverines had no promising senior prospects, and even hard-boiled NBA types don't expect freshmen to jump straight to the league without extenuating circumstances.

But sophomores? That's a different story. Isiah Thomas had gone pro as a sophomore. Magic Johnson had gone pro as a sophomore. So the scouts were hovering now, sniffing out the potential inside those baggy Michigan uniforms.

Exit was possible. The encore could be the finale.

This was only one subtle change in Act II of *The Greatest Class Ever Recruited.*

Here was another:

Black socks.

Black socks?

★ ★ ★

It started that morning, when a friend of Ray's came to visit him at the hotel and brought a gift.

"You should wear these tonight, man," he said. "They're fresh."

Ray pulled on the black socks, then stepped into his basketball shoes. He liked the look. So did Jimmy, who went across the street to the Galleria Mall to buy some for himself.

When Jalen saw them, his eyes lit up. "Where'd you get 'em?"

"Foot Locker."

Jalen went and got three more pairs—just enough for the starting sophomores. Now all that remained was getting them past the coaching staff.

No problem.

"We dress at the hotel," Jalen suggested, "then keep our sweats on until the tap."

"Aw, man, Fish'll be pissed."

"Naw, he ain't gonna say nothin'."

"It's just black footies."

"Yeah. He ain't gonna say nothin'."

They laughed. They plotted. They agreed. And sure enough, early that evening, they got on the bus fully dressed and jogged out for warm-ups with their sweatpants on. Brian Dutcher, who notices such things, made a mental note. *That's strange. They hate wearing their sweats. They usually come out in their shorts.*

He thought no more about it until introductions, when the five sophomores—doesn't that sound strange, five sophomores?—gave the half-empty Summit a lesson in big-time entrances.

"AT FORWARD, 6 FOOT 9, CHRIS WEBBER!"

He trotted out, slapping hands, staring upward with a nasty-faced attitude.

"AT FORWARD, 6 FOOT 6, RAY JACKSON!"

"All right!" Ray hollered, jogging out, hugging Chris as if he'd just come back from the army.

"AT CENTER, 6 FOOT 9, JUWAN HOWARD!"

Another scream, more hugs, arms slapping heads as they embraced.

"AT GUARD, 6 FOOT 8, JALEN ROSE!"

This was classic, a slow strut, bouncing like a marionette, his palms bent back Egyptian style, yelling, "Uh–huh, uh–huh, uh–huh, uh–huh . . ."

The others doubled over in laughter.

"AT GUARD, 6 FOOT 5, JIMMY KING!"

He joined the group and they locked in their private huddle, arms into arms, heads in close. They began to bounce, together, up and down, like a human tire pump, dip and lift, dip and lift, *huuyy-yah, huuyy-yah*, back on the court, back on the court, finally, after all those European countries, all that summer camp nonsense, all those sleepless nights thinking about that one-point halftime lead on Duke and what happened to it, finally, back on the court, *huuyy-yah, huuyy-yah*, enough waiting, enough delay, basketball, just basketball, what they wanted, what they needed, back on the court, back on the court, they couldn't wait, they yanked off their sweats, they jogged to the center—

"Uh–oh," Dutcher whispered. Then louder, "Fish. You looking at this?"

"What?"

He didn't even notice.

"The socks. They have black socks."

"How the hell did they . . ."

"Don't ask me. I didn't even see it until just now."

Fisher sighed. He glanced over at the bench players, hopeful, perhaps, that this was at least a teamwide thing. No such luck. It was strictly Fab Five Fashion. A more hard-boiled coach would have lost his temper, maybe stopped the game right then, pulled them off the floor, told them to get the hell back in the locker room, put on the correct team uniform, and don't try that shit again. In the meantime, he would send in five replacements and take his sweet time putting his big shots back in.

Fisher did nothing of the sort. He watched as the ball was tossed, two bodies went up, and the new season was under way. The crowd yelled, the sneakers squeaked, the sophomores were moving, their black socks moistening with sweat. As he watched the scoreboard register the first Michigan points of the season—Chris catches a lob, one-handed, and rams it through the rim, *whooomph!*—Fisher thought of how unique a situation he was in, really. Having to coach two teams, both wearing the same uniform.

★   ★   ★

On the plane ride home the next morning, the players passed the Houston newspapers back and forth. Most of them just checked for pictures of themselves, read a few paragraphs, and passed them on. They were already tired from a road trip and the season had just started. Juwan, who dressed nicely for travel, wore a black suit, read a few pages from Magic Johnson's book, then dozed off. Chris was already crumpled in a heap, sleeping over two seats, his forehead buried in his sweater. Jalen had on a wrinkled, button-down, white dress shirt, with a red tie, and a blue ski cap on his head. He slept with his mouth open. There is no one quite like Jalen.

It had hardly been a memorable game. The Wolverines seemed far too eager to slam their way to victory, and Rice grew confident watching Michigan make mistake after mistake—bad lobs, silly passes, forced shots—until the Owls actually had a six-point lead in the second half. Michigan finally kicked into gear and ran off 10 unanswered points, Chris slamming in a missed free throw, Jimmy dropping a three-pointer from the corner. The final score was U-M 75, Rice 71, much closer than it should have been, and yet, most of the players expressed little concern over the outcome.

"No way we were gonna lose," Rose had said nonchalantly.

"We're not losing any games this season," Webber had added. He'd scored 20 points and grabbed 19 rebounds—on a mediocre night—and no doubt the scouts from Boston, Detroit, Sacramento, and Indiana were licking their chops. "I'm telling you. We're not losing any games this year. None. Zero. I'm telling you."

Not everyone was so optimistic. Sitting off by himself, looking out the airplane window, Ray Jackson was thinking about Texas. He hated to leave it. But it was hard coming back. The night before, his family and his childhood buddies—"my dogs," as he called them—had all come up to see him play, maybe 30 people, wearing their Michigan hats, making the drive in from Austin, and what happened? Same as last year. He was the last option of the Fab Five. He scored just two baskets. He didn't make any steals, had just two rebounds, no free throws, and five fouls. He fouled out. In front of all his friends? He fouled out? He felt an emptiness in his stomach, as if remembering a lost love. Since when did basketball become so . . . distressing?

"You don't know what it's like," he kept saying to his mother and father, in private, after the game. "It's not what it seems."

"What do you mean, Ray?"

"It's just not what it seems."

"What isn't?"

"You know. Everything. It's not what it seems."

"What are you trying to say, Ray?"

What Ray was trying to say was . . . what was he trying to say? That all the glory and hype of the Fab Five was front-loaded, and the front was Chris and Jalen, and he was in the back? That the attention and the glamour and the network TV cameras were all fine and good, unless your coach didn't trust you to shoot and wanted you to get the ball to the other guys first? Was that what he wanted to say?

Or did he just miss home?

Rob Pelinka sat three rows behind Jackson. He was wide-awake, and reading about Duke in the newspaper. The Blue Devils had also opened their season last night, with a 48-point blowout over Canisius. Duke, like Michigan, had all their best players back except Christian Laettner. The hype for the Wolverines–Blue Devils III was already unbelievable. A record number of media credentials had been issued, over 200, and the game would be televised nationwide.

"I hear they've been camping in tents outside Cameron for a week already," Pelinka said. "Can you believe that? There's still three days to go.

"I would never camp in a tent for 10 days to see anything. Certainly not a sporting event!"

Pelinka was truly a different model than your standard-issue jock. He prided himself on his studies. He worked like a law student—which he was training to be. His notes were meticulous, his schedule was well maintained, he met with professors, lived in libraries, spoke at church groups, and generally cut a figure next in line to Dudley Do-Right.

"You know, when we play the smart schools, I feel lucky when we come out with a win," he said. "I know it sounds funny. But smart players remember plays. It's hard to remember a lot of plays, harder than you think.

"And they know what matters. Usually we unnerve a team with slam dunks and alley-oops, but the smart guys just come right back, like Rice last night. They know each basket is only worth two points, no matter how you got it.

"Believe me, it's tougher to play a smart team, even with limited talent, than your typical state school.

"And that's one reason Duke is so tough every year. They're smart—and they get great players."

He paused, and looked across at Juwan, who had stirred from his sleep and was looking over, glassy-eyed, as Pelinka talked.

"What do you think, Juwan?"

Juwan inhaled deeply, then let it out. "I think," he said slowly, "we should have our own plane."

2

The M Den in Ann Arbor is the Carnegie Hall of Michigan merchandising, decals, banners, posters, T-shirts, coffee mugs, scarves, sweaters, caps, license plates. You walk in, you feel like the world has been recolorized, and everything is either maize or blue.

Dave Hirth, one of the owners, was shaking his head. He thought he'd seen "hot" items before. This was ridiculous. Basketball uniforms? He couldn't keep basketball uniforms in stock? How many people can even *wear* a basketball uniform, for pete's sake?

Apparently that didn't matter. Last April, after Michigan's loss to Duke in the national championship, Hirth had ordered 125 official uniforms from Russell Athletic, yellow fabric, stitched letters, the real thing, same as the players wear. He worried that he might have overordered.

They arrived.

He unpacked them.

He charged $75 for the jersey and $75 for the shorts, $150 for the outfit.

They sold out in a heartbeat.

"It's like feeding shot glasses of water to men in the desert," he groaned, desperately trying to reorder before Christmas. "It's unbelievable."

Unbelievable? The Fab Five had become a merchandiser's fantasy. Almost anything having to do with them flew out the door, especially items that captured their personal flair, such as the shorts. Places like the M Den and Moe's Sport Shops—which never even carried basketball shorts before—suddenly couldn't stock enough of

them. Thousands of pairs were sold in Ann Arbor alone, and everyone who came in inevitably held them up to their waists and said,
"These are the long ones, right?"

The alumni living in Bloomfield Hills and Grosse Pointe may
have clucked their tongues at those embarrassing players—*no respect
for the Wolverine tradition, who do they think they are?*—but boys aged
8 to 18 were plunking down their last quarters to get anything with
"Webber" or "Rose" on it. Webber's No. 4 was far and away the
most marketable number in Michigan history, and stores all over
Ann Arbor sported his jersey on hangers in the front window.

"We're the MTV of college basketball," Brian Dutcher crowed,
not without a certain pride. "Parents might not follow us, but you
can't find a kid who doesn't."

And since Christmas is for kids, as the holiday approached—
and fever for the Duke rematch built—the Fab Five were being
boxed, stuffed, and gift-wrapped. The university's athletic department was looking at a $2.5-million intake from souvenirs for the
year, the lion's share of it thanks to the basketball team.

And not a penny went to the players.

It never does. It never has. College athletes receive no windfall
from any merchandise sold—even if they are the only reason people
buy it—and, to make matters worse, they are not even allowed to
work. Those are NCAA rules. No jobs during the school year. A
scholarship athlete's income is limited to the room-and-board check
($624 per month at Michigan), per diem money on road trips (maybe
$30 for the day), and whatever Mom, Dad, Grandma, or Uncle Joe
can spare.

Needless to say, this hypocrisy is not wasted on the athletes.
Webber and his friend Shonte Peoples, a defensive back from the
football team, were between classes one day, late in the fall semester,
and stopped at a take-out place for lunch. They each ordered a five-
piece chicken meal, two fish sandwiches, and a drink. Then Webber
reached in his pocket.

"Wait a minute," he said to the cashier. He counted his money.
"Uh, just give me the three-piece chicken and one fish sandwich, all
right?"

On the way out, he zipped his coat, looked at Shonte, and shook
his head. "I can't believe this shit, man. I gotta put back food, and
look at that over there."

He pointed to a shop where his jersey hung in the window.

"How is that fair?" he asked. "I mean how is that fair? Will you tell me?"

He opened his paper bag, his breath blowing cold smoke. He tried to calculate how much profit the store made from that one jersey alone. Enough to pay for another fish sandwich, he was sure of that.

3

There were two new faces on the 1992–93 Wolverines' roster. One was Leon Derricks, a skinny, big-eared, 6-foot-9 center from Flint, who signed late, and was mostly brought in for his size and shot-blocking ability. Derricks had an impressive academic record in high school. You would never know it from his behavior. He was mostly silent, and when he did speak, at least to strangers, he was often rude and dismissive. Even people in Michigan's sports information department commented about "what a pain" he was to deal with—and a freshman no less! Fortunately for them, he almost never played, so there wasn't exactly a line at his locker.

The other new face was point guard Dugan Fife, a 6-foot-2 white suburban kid from Clarkston, Michigan, who might have been the only high school star in the country willing to sign early with Michigan the same year it collected the Greatest Class Ever Recruited. Most big-name recruits refuse to go to a school where the starting positions are locked up. Fife didn't even take any other visits. He met with Fisher and Jay Smith, and he said, "I'm coming."

Then again, as Fife admits, "I was born coming to Michigan."

Dan Fife, Dugan's father, was captain of the Wolverines' basketball team in 1970–71. He later served as an assistant coach on the staff. The school spirit was in the genes; when Dugan was young, he wore only blue and yellow clothing, and teased any kid who wore green, because "green is Michigan State's color, and they stink."

Dugan, who had sandy-blond hair and a slightly flipped-up nose—he looked like he stepped off a surfboard in Laguna Beach—became a skilled, fundamentally sound basketball player in high school, not surprising, given his father's teachings. He got his first recruiting letter from Michigan when he was in ninth grade. He cherished it.

He met the Fab Five on his recruiting visit (pretty much a formality) in the fall of 1991; he was paired with Kenyan Murray, a prospect from Birmingham Brother Rice High School. Michigan likes to bring in two recruits at a time. It gives each of them someone to talk to, and at times, as in the case of Juwan Howard and Jimmy King, one actually helps recruit the other.

On Saturday night of that weekend, the Fab Five were heading to a party. So Dugan and Kenyan were brought along.

"It was an all-black party up on North Campus," Dugan recalled, laughing. "We didn't know anybody. I walked in, and some guy put like a stick in my face and said, 'Are you sure you're in the right place?' And I just kind of looked around for the Fab Five and said, 'Well, I'm with them.' And he said, 'Oh, you're all right,' and then he started shaking my hand and patting me on the back. It was weird."

Dugan and Kenyan didn't last very long at the party. The freshmen had dispersed into the crowd, they couldn't find them, and so they just left and hitchhiked back. An Asian driver who spoke little English picked them up.

"You going anywhere near Central Campus?" Dugan said.

"Sorry?"

"Central Campus?"

"Sorry?"

Eventually they got back, and taped a note to Jimmy and Juwan's door, telling them what had happened. Dugan didn't think much about it, but Fisher was angry when he found out. Murray wound up choosing another school—although whether that night had anything to do with it is questionable.

Now Fife was part of the same team as Chris, Jalen, Ray, Jimmy, and Juwan, and life was anything but a night out. In fact, Dugan was getting quite an education. The Fab Five had no problem swinging their weight against the seniors; you can imagine what they did to freshmen.

The very first time he scrimmaged with the team, Dugan took off on a break, with Jalen trailing him, and as Dugan moved into layup form, he heard Jalen yelling from behind him, "BLOCK PARTY COMIN'! LOOK OUT, DUGAN! BLOCK PARTY!"

He flew out of nowhere and slapped Dugan's shot against the backboard.

"Told you," he said as they came back upcourt.

Dugan wasn't used to this kind of stuff—Clarkston is a little more laid-back—but he adjusted. He toughened up.

And when Jalen started teasingly calling him "Dan" after his father, Dugan retaliated by calling Jalen "Jimmy" after his absent father, Jimmy Walker. Jalen hesitated, then laughed.

"Doog's cool," Jalen said.

That was a relief.

Fisher, meanwhile, wished they were all like Dugan. He thought about this as he watched the players practice for the Duke rematch. Wouldn't it be great to have all the kids tell you, "Don't even bother to recruit me, I'm coming to your school. I'll sign right now."

That happened about as often as, well, a national championship. The latest news from the recruiting wars was modest at best. The Wolverines had signed Bobby Crawford, the point guard from Texas. He had come to school with his father, enjoyed the visit, and gave them an early commitment. So between Crawford coming next year and Fife here now, they were covered in the point guard department.

That was the good news. The bad news was that Marcus Hughes, the 6-foot-9 forward from Detroit, had gone to Notre Dame, his first visit, and had signed on the spot. Dutcher and the others had warned him specifically, "Marcus, your first visit is always your best. You see things you never saw before. Just don't get starry-eyed. Come back and take your visit here."

Too late. He was Fightin' Irish now.

Meanwhile Jon Garavaglia, another local star—and big man—committed to Michigan State. That really hurt Fisher. "We should be getting the best local kids," he told his staff. "Garavaglia and Hughes should be coming here."

Perry, meanwhile, continued to work on L.A.'s Avondre Jones and Charles O'Bannon, both of whom came to visit Michigan's campus. Avondre got to hang around with Chris—a big thrill—but Fisher made sure he spent some time with Juwan as well. Juwan is "our best recruiter," Dutcher would say. Juwan loved the school, loved the team, and was easy to get along with. You talked to Juwan, you were sold on the program. Chris might just tell you to be a man, don't listen to anyone, do what's best for you—and that wasn't always Ann Arbor. So he was a little dangerous.

Meanwhile, Fisher was discovering another odd consequence of the Fab Five explosion: high school players wanted Michigan to recruit them, not necessarily because they wanted to attend, but because a visit from "the Fab Five School" meant a certain celebrity, like making a Who's Who list or getting on MTV. Neighbors would come by for Fisher's autograph. Siblings would watch the Michigan highlight film with rapt attention.

But did the kid really want to be a Wolverine?

Fisher tried desperately to separate the serious from the starstruck. It wasn't easy. Jerry Stackhouse, a 6-foot-6 North Carolina prep star and one of the top players in the nation, was considered a lock to stay in the ACC. Everybody knew that, so Michigan had never bothered to pursue him. But over the summer, Stackhouse ran into Juwan Howard at the Nike camp.

"How come you guys aren't recruiting me?" Stackhouse said.

"I dunno," Howard said. "I'll ask Coach."

When Fisher heard this, he scratched his head. Was the kid really serious? Did he really want to attend Michigan—with North Carolina, North Carolina State, Virginia, and Florida State as his other declared front-runners? It didn't make sense. But what should Fisher do? Ignore a top-five player?

He went to see him.

As it turned out, neither that North Carolina visit nor the upcoming one to Duke would prove to be much fun.

4

Michigan-Duke III would be a prime-time event, nine o'clock on Saturday night, with 90 percent of the nation getting it via syndicated TV. Most major newspapers were sending somebody, and 225 media credentials were issued—the largest ever in Duke history. In many ways, this game would "officially" kick off the college basketball season, and the publicity machine was working full blast. Footage from the championship was replayed nightly. Banners hung from dorm windows in Ann Arbor and Durham. "DESTROY DUKE." "MAUL MICHIGAN." The tents outside Cameron-Indoor Stadium went up as early as Thanksgiving weekend, with at least one student required to stay inside at all times in order to hold the place in line for seating.

The Fab Five did their share to stoke the flames. Chris was asked early in the week about Bobby Hurley vs. Jalen Rose. "As far as I'm concerned, Bobby Hurley can't check Jalen Rose. Jalen is the best point guard in the country."

Webber even wrote a prediction for the game: 86–74.

"Which team will have the 86?" he was asked.

"Who do you think?" he laughed.

Jimmy King talked about "waiting a long, long time for this."

Ray Jackson said, "We want some payback."

Juwan Howard said he "pitied" Duke, for what Michigan planned to do to them on Saturday.

This stuff quickly found its way to Tobacco Road, where the two-time defending national champions practiced diligently for the challengers.

"Who knows," Grant Hill, their star sophomore, said, in mock boasting, "maybe *we'll* shock the world."

Ouch. Stealing their material.

5

Hail to the state school champions
Hail to the sophomore losers
Hail, hail, to Michigan
the cesspool of the west

Hail to the slam-dunk players
Hail to the two years players
Hail, hail, to Michigan
We're not finished yet

Hail to the Fab Five criers
Hail to the champions . . .
*   NOT!*
Hail, hail, to Michigan
the bastards of the west

—lyrics to "The Victors" as
rewritten by Duke students

Before the game even started, a flying tennis ball hit Angie Fisher in the head, and someone dumped a soda at her feet. She smiled at this, not because she enjoys torture, but because similar things happened just prior to the 1989 championship game. Maybe it's a sign, she figured.

The Wolverines would take any sign they could get in this haunted building, Cameron-Indoor Stadium, home of the Duke Blue Devils. Cameron is sort of a cross between a gymnasium and a library, with rims, nets, and hardwood, surrounded by oak walls, Gothic windows, and brass hand railings. But during a basketball game, the place is murder, a cramped, hot, hellaciously loud place where the students sit so close to the floor you can smell their breath as you dribble upcourt. So intimidating is the gym that a nonconference opponent had not won there in nearly ten years. Ten years? And on this particular Saturday night, the Duke student fans—nicknamed the Cameron Crazies—who had been sleeping in those tents for the past week, waiting for the best seats (and temperatures fell to the low 30s), were cranky, wet, and intent on keeping that record intact. Known for such antics as throwing Twinkies at fat players, and printing a mock newspaper for archrival North Carolina, with a hole in the middle above the caption "This useless white space is in honor of Eric Montross," the Duke fans have long been the wildest, most creative, and certainly most coordinated fans in college basketball, with chants, cheers, and jeers in a sort of Greek chorus harmony.

For all the wild places the Fab Five had played basketball, they still hadn't experienced anything like this.

The chorus began with a driving drumbeat the moment Michigan came out for warm-ups.

"OVER . . . RATED!"
bum-bum-bumbumbumbum
"OVER . . . RATED!"
bum-bum bumbumbum

that quickly jumped to

"FIVE SOPHOMORES—NO TITLE!
FIVE SOPHOMORES—NO TITLE!"

with half the place holding up five fingers, the other half making a big goose-egg shape.

Even Jalen snickered at that one. What did these kids do, go to basketball cheering class?

In truth, what sat inside the gym was less intimidating than what sat outside, in the lobby: two glass cases housing national championship trophies, the first from 1991, and the new one from 1992, engraved "Duke 71, Michigan 51."

Even though Michigan was now ranked No. 1 in the country, until it eclipsed the edge inside that trophy case, Duke was still the reigning champion. Still the team to beat.

"Let's go! Let's go!" Fisher exhorted, clapping his hands as his players tucked in their jerseys. The five sophomores, wearing their black socks and white shoes again, walked out for the opening tap, looking serious and maybe a little tight, licking their lips for moisture. Cherokee Parks, Duke's floppy-haired center from Huntington Beach, California, stepped up to meet Webber for the jump ball. Parks was the only new starter in either lineup from last April's championship game, replacing Christian Laettner. Earlier in the week, someone had asked Webber if he was glad Laettner wasn't around this time, and he had said, "No, I wish he was back from the Minnesota Timberwolves, so we could beat him, too."

Not smart.

But then, smart had always been on Duke's side of the ledger. So it was no surprise that, when Chris won the opening tap over Parks, Grant Hill, sensing this would happen, snuck in front of a flat-footed Juwan Howard and intercepted the ball as Juwan waited for it. Duke swung into action, Thomas Hill drove, took the first shot, it missed, but once again, Grant Hill raced in front of Howard, who did not box out, too busy waiting for the ball to fall in his hands, and Hill grabbed it, put it back up and in.

Duke had the lead.

And Michigan never would.

Although the Blue Devils could not match Michigan in raw talent, they did a million little things to get a basket here, a free throw there, tossing points on the pile, concerned only, as teams should be, with the final tally. When Jimmy King broke free and drove down the lane, Thomas Hill, helpless to stop him, simply planted himself and drew the offensive foul, negating a layup. When Bobby Hurley lost the ball and Webber led a three-on-one break, Grant Hill again, overmatched, planted himself in front of Webber and drew the offensive foul, Webber's second.

It didn't help that Webber, on that play, was trying to showboat with a wraparound pass. Fisher shook his head and took Chris out of the game.

A three-pointer by Hurley made it 28–25. A Thomas Hill layup made it 34–28. A Grant Hill slam made it 36–28. At one point, the net got tangled, and Jimmy King volunteered to climb a ladder and fix it. When he had momentary trouble untangling it, the Duke crowd launched into

"BASKET WEAVING 101!
BASKET WEAVING 101!"

Jeez. Fix your own net next time.

At halftime, Duke led, 40–33. Michigan had plenty of impressive dunks. But the telling statistic, as in all these Michigan-Duke games, was in two less glamorous departments, turnovers and free throws: the Wolverines had five more of the former, and five less of the latter.

It continued in the second half. Grant Hill banged a 12-footer over Jalen, and on the next play, Jalen, frustrated, was called for pushing Bobby Hurley out of his way.

Wheeeeeett! Hurley and Hill slapped hands at the sound of the whistle and yelled, "All tight! Yeah!" which didn't sit well with Jalen. Twelve seconds later, Jalen knocked Hurley over with an elbow to the sternum.

Wheeeeeet! Another foul.

Rose went to the bench and dropped down angrily. "The only reason they called that is 'cause he's so small and I'm so big," he said.

By their usual standards, the Fab Five wasn't doing much trash talking—it was too loud, and too exhausting a pace—but that didn't stop broadcaster Bill Raftery, who was doing the game on syndicated TV, from criticizing them when they did. After Webber blocked a shot by Antonio Lang, he snapped a few words off. Raftery said, "And now he's gotta tell Lang about it? It's like, just play, Chris. You're supposed to block it!" Later, he criticized Webber for letting Cherokee Parks go past him for a layup.

"Great talent [Chris], but you've got to suppress selfishness . . .

As good as you are, guys are not going to just show up and step back."

So Bill Raftery became the next in line to smack Michigan on the butt in front of a national TV audience.

Not that Duke needed any help.

Thomas Hill snuck inside the Michigan players to rebound a missed Duke free throw—the cardinal sin, coaches always say—and put it back in for two points. Jimmy King dribbled off his leg, and Hurley stole it, threw it downcourt to Grant Hill, who slammed it to an expulsion of noise. That made the score 56–42, a 14-point lead, Duke's biggest of the night, with 13:32 to go.

The Wolverines were sinking, same old story, same old nemesis. They had seemed so sure they would clobber Duke this time, cross them off the revenge list, simply because, well, the Fab Five were sophomores now, and it was time, wasn't it? But they hadn't done the little things necessary, the box-outs, avoiding fouls. They seemed to come in as if entitled to the win. Meanwhile, Duke continued to protect the ball better, slap rebounds out of Michigan's grasp, and go to the foul line at a two-to-one ratio. And when the Blue Devils took free throws, they made them, unlike the Wolverines, who actually missed seven of 11 chances. Between that and their turnovers, they were history.

When the buzzer sounded, Duke had beaten Michigan, 79–68. The Blue Devils remained the Fab Five's downfall, their Achilles' heel. The Cameron Crazies, flush with success, waved goodbye with the now familiar chant:

"FIVE SOPHOMORES—NO TITLE!
FIVE SOPHOMORES—NO TITLE!"

The Blue Devils' mascot ran across the court with a sign: "Duke. We're the Best. Any questions?"

Outside the locker rooms, even the security guards were gloating. One older guard stopped several Michigan reporters from standing outside the door.

"But that's customary at Michigan," the reporters protested.

"Well, that's not how we do it here," he barked, crossing his arms. "I doubt they want to talk to reporters anyway. They did all their talking before the game."

Cripes.

Even the guards had attitude.

In the Duke locker room, the Blue Devils wore those same shirts they wore after the national championship win, which read, "You can talk the game, but can you play the game?" Hurley, the senior guard from Jersey City, was smiling, vindicated. Someone asked him about Webber's comments earlier in the week.

"It doesn't make sense," Hurley said, pulling on a blue sweater. "He's a great player. He has to realize that when he makes those comments, they only help the opposition. Teams put it on the bulletin board, they say, 'Look at what this guy said.'

"That was a mistake. You don't do things to give other players confidence. And besides, Chris talking about Bobby can't check Jalen, that's talking about individual matchups. We don't talk about that, we talk about the team. They need to get away from that stuff."

He pulled a brush through his short wet hair. "You know, they've played together as starters since last year, but they don't always play *together*, you know what I mean?"

Across the hall, Fisher knew this was coming. He knew he was in for several more weeks of discipline-beats-demonstration talk, at least until his team played a real opponent again, maybe North Carolina or Kansas in the Christmas tournament. "Free throws," Fisher moaned, studying the stat sheet, looking at the 17-point advantage Duke had in that department.

The players were angry. Ray Jackson sat by his locker, looking like he was ready to punch it. He had played only 20 minutes, scored seven points, and had four fouls.

"I'm tired of losing to these guys," he said. "They're a good team, but we ought to be able to beat them by now."

Chris said, "They deserve to be celebrating. We deserve to be locked in a closet and not see the sun shine until the next game."

Someone asked Jalen if he thought Duke would be No. 1 now.

"I don't know. I'm not a ranker. That's for, like, columnists, and people like that.

"I know we ain't gonna be No. 1. That's all I know."

On the plane ride home the next morning, they sat in separate rows, trying to sleep, their heads on the seats in front of them or in their laps. Jalen threw a blue blanket over his head, so that all you saw was a white shirt, a tie, and a covered noggin. He stayed that way until they landed.

At baggage claim, in Detroit's Metro Airport, a porter came up to a writer who was traveling with the team.

"That Chris Webber over there?" the porter asked.

"Yeah."

"Tell him next time, put a piece of tape over his mouth, OK?"

6

With the Fab Five now solidly sophomores, there was no questioning their right to start, or, for that matter, to play the entire game. This did not stop the other Wolverines—particularly those at the far end of the bench—from feeling overlooked and unappreciated. There were many ways to measure this. The most interesting was the size of Jason Bossard's muscles.

Bossard, a grinning, square-jawed, rural kid from northern Michigan, was one of those recruits from the hungry year, the year Fisher did *not* get Eric Montross. In fact, Bossard took his recruiting visit the same weekend as Montross, and they roomed together in the hotel.

"You thinking about coming here?" Bossard asked.

"Maybe," Montross said.

"You want to room together if you do?"

"Yeah, maybe."

Montross got the star treatment that weekend. Bossard was pretty much the throw-in. He didn't know what good training that would be.

As a freshman, Bossard played sparingly. But as a sophomore, with Chris, Jalen, Juwan, Jimmy, and Ray in uniform, well, "sparingly" would have felt like heaven.

"This is killing me, man," Bossard told friends during that sophomore year. He was depressed, he didn't want to go to class. He knew he wasn't Chris Webber, but, like everyone in that uniform, he'd been a big deal in high school. Hell, he'd averaged 30 points a game, and once scored 53. So what if it was weaker competition? He had still been a star, and now he was a practice player, who only saw action when the game was a joke, safely in hand or out of hand.

He made four baskets his entire sophomore season. He was angry and tense.

Then he discovered the weight room.

"You oughta lift," his roommates, who played on the football team, had told him. "Get out some of that aggression."

Bossard tried it, and he was hooked. With each frustrating practice, he would run to the bench press, the curls, the leg lifts. "There were times in that weight room," he later recalled, "I tell ya, I got so choked up I had tears in my eyes. I would just stay in there for two and a half hours straight, pushing myself until I was exhausted.

"It's like, you go to practice, you bust your ass, you get good grades, you do everything you're supposed to do, and they're just ignoring you, you don't get to play.

"I needed some release."

Of course, the side effect was that Bossard began to look like a tight end. He came running out for layups lines, you expected him to plow into a tackling dummy. His neck was thick. His arms were solid. The Fab Five teased him about his build, taping pictures of weight lifters above his locker. But he had found an outlet for his frustration. They all had to do something. Mike Talley spent his time sulking, complaining, and making faces. James Voskuil buried himself in his engineering studies. Rob Pelinka vigorously went after law school scholarships. Eric Riley dreamed about the NBA, and how at least he might get paid to sit the bench there.

This was Jason Bossard's way: whenever he thought about his dwindled career, he went down the tunnel and added a new layer of muscle.

Less was more, so to speak.

7

They have to play 40 minutes like the Michigan Wolverines, not the Harlem Globetrotters.

—Charlie Vincent, *Detroit Free Press*, Dec. 8, 1992

A Jaguar that drives like a Yugo.

—George Cantor, *Detroit News*, Dec. 8, 1992

A case of lockjaw for Michigan's players would help friend and foe alike.

—Bucky Waters, Raycom TV network, Dec. 11, 1992

The Wolverines won't make it to the Final Four.

—Al McGuire, NBC, Dec. 10, 1992

In the Fab Five's freshman season, Steve Fisher had been pitied for having to deal with all those young and flamboyant personalities. Now he was condemned for not controlling them. Alumni clucked their tongues. Fans booed when a show-off play didn't work. Most of what Fisher was allowing was the same stuff he'd allowed the year before, but it was viewed differently, like a parent on an airplane with a crying infant, versus a parent who lets his four-year-old run down the aisle with a squirt gun. Fans made no more excuses for the Fabulous Five. They were old enough to know better, they figured.

"Hot dog!" they yelled at Webber.

"Just make the pass!" they screamed at Rose.

The loss to Duke seemed to sharpen critics' tongues—particularly the Ann Arbor critics. They hated the way Duke spanked the Wolverines in front of the whole country. The first time was expected and the championship game was chalked up to youth. But this third time? With all the pregame bragging? This was embarrassing! You got the feeling some Michigan fans wished the Duke players, with their combination of intelligence and athleticism, were the ones wearing the maize and blue, instead of Webber, Rose, King, and company. It was a definite case of Purist Envy.

And it didn't help that U-M's next few games were sloppy, and sometimes sleepy. Oh, the Wolverines won all of them—but who were they playing? They beat Detroit-Mercy in their home opener (Crisler Arena, unlike Cameron-Indoor Stadium, had plenty of empty seats); they got by Bowling Green, although the lowly Falcons actually led Michigan early in the second half; they clobbered Cleveland State—and old friend Mike Boyd—by 32 points, but there was a lot of talking on the court, most of it between Sam Mitchell and his former teammates. Again, the tongue-cluckers had something to complain about.

In the national rankings, the Duke loss had tumbled Michigan

down to No. 6, behind such traditionally disciplined programs as
Indiana and North Carolina. U-M's next game was a Saturday night
affair against Iowa State, and was televised by ESPN, which meant
the return of old pal Dick Vitale, who wasted no time jumping on
the stop-the-swaggering-sophomores bandwagon.

"They're the Muhammad Alis of basketball!" Vitale crowed.
"I've had a lot of people come up to me, Michigan people, who
really feel this is totally unnecessary . . . It's OK to praise your
teammates but you don't need all the histrionics and carrying on.
Absolutely no need for it!"

Dick Vitale, criticizing histrionics.

Go figure.

Fisher did not budge. He would not publicly criticize his players.
He had made his bed. Now he would sleep in it. Fans may have
wanted him to put tape over their mouths, but to do so would be to
reverse what had gotten them all that success last season. And winning was still the thing that mattered most, wasn't it? Fisher had
always felt you don't stifle players' enthusiasm, you use it. The Fab
Five were accustomed to saying what they wanted, doing what they
felt. Most of the time this resulted in victory. Never mind that the
buzz around town was, "Fisher isn't coaching the team, the kids
are."

They were, after all, 4-1.

Still, Fisher began to get testy with the media, and complained
to several reporters about unfair treatment. "I see people calling us a
bunch of egotistical cocky braggarts who don't work hard and try
to intimidate with their mouths," he told one newspaper. "I defy
anyone to prove that."

Problem was, they didn't have to prove it.

That was the image.

And image, as the commercial says, is everything.

The image didn't sit well back in Fisher's hometown of Herrin,
Illinois. Particularly not in his parents' house. Howard Fisher, Steve's
father, who was 81 and in bad health, watched the games via satellite
dish, taped them, then watched them over and over, working the
remote, trying to prove to whoever was with him—usually his other
sons, John and George—that this trash-talk thing was a bum rap.
His contention was not that Michigan didn't talk, but that other

teams did the same thing (interestingly, this would be Steve's defense as well). After countless viewings of the Duke game, Howard concluded that the critics had it all wrong: by his count, Duke had actually out-trash-talked Michigan by 11 incidents.

OK. It may have been a homer tally. But the Fishers were fiercely dedicated to one another. Steve, as a child, had followed obediently when the old man was making him jump rope and run around cones to become a better basketball player. And now the old man awaited Steve's phone call after every game. Sometimes, when he wanted to make a suggestion, he would say, "You know, Steve, John and I were talking, and John thinks you ought to try a different defense . . ." John would be standing right there, never having said anything, his mouth would drop, but his father would wave a hand not to object. Howard wanted to be involved, but he was mindful of interference. So much so that the last time he'd gone to see a game in person was when Steve was still an assistant under Bill Frieder, and Michigan was playing Purdue in West Lafayette, Indiana. The Wolverines lost, and on the ride home, Howard declared the end of all live visits.

"We distracted Steve and Bill from their jobs by asking for tickets," he said. "It was our fault they lost."

He never went to another game.

But he watched them all, even as his health was slowly failing him. He'd had terrible stomach problems—half of his stomach had been removed due to ulcers—and his heart was very weak. He had been in the hospital at the start of the basketball season, but checked himself out, made his sons pick him up and return him to his home routine. They knew he was slipping. They were there the night of December 19, the Iowa State game, in which Ray Jackson, Mr. Fisher's favorite player (remember, Howard had called Steve and suggested he start Jackson against Notre Dame), was doing well, scoring often. Howard watched as long as he could, but started to feel bad. His sons helped him to the bedroom. They came in after the game was over.

"What was the score?" Howard asked, looking up from the pillow.

"We won, 94–72."

"How did Jackson do?"

"He had a career high. Sixteen points."

Howard Fisher smiled. "I knew he could do it."
He rolled onto his shoulder.
And died.

Steve flew home two days later, missing the game against Central Michigan to be at the funeral. He had burst into tears when Angie told him his father was gone. He cried in private; outsiders had no idea how broken up he was. *Play the hand you're dealt.*

Fisher came to Herrin, which was hard in itself, because usually it's like a coronation when he comes home, and he hugged his mother and brothers and he went to the funeral parlor. At the wake, someone actually came up and asked Fisher for an autograph. He signed it, without complaint.

It was four days before Christmas. The team was due to fly to Hawaii on the twenty-fifth. Steve hugged his son Mark, who sat next to him at the funeral, and felt the flush of being suddenly and singularly responsible for what happened in his life, the way people often feel when they lose a parent. Fisher's burden was greater than it had ever been. He had the grief of his father's death, the sadness of his sons losing their grandfather, and a basketball family full of 19-year-olds that, according to his critics, was his responsibility to straighten out.

"We dedicate this win to Coach Fisher's dad," Jimmy King was saying, back in Ann Arbor, where all five starters scored in double figures for the first time in their careers, destroying CMU, 94–69, for their sixth win of the season. "Mr. Fisher was a true Michigan fan."

And, at this point, they would take any they could find.

8

Juwan Howard drove the Toyota through the streets of Chicago's South Side. It was the day before Christmas, and everyone seemed in some kind of a hurry, holding bags or boxes, hunching their shoulders against the blasting winds.

Juwan fiddled with the heat switch. "Man, it's freezing," he said. "Damn!" He was driving through his old neighborhoods with a reporter who was doing a story about his youth. Juwan's friend

Juice Carter was along for the ride as usual, because Juwan rarely went anywhere without him.

He had one day in Chicago before going back to Ann Arbor for the Hawaii trip. He didn't mind. Since his grandmother died, Christmas wasn't really the same. Jannie Mae Howard was born on Christmas Day, so it was a double celebration, birthday, holiday, and they used to gather at her house on 135th Street, with enough food for a week, meat loaf, pork chops, potatoes, greens, pies, cakes. Juwan loved that day, all that family around.

But now, while Chris, Jimmy, Ray, and Jalen went back to the hugs and smothering affection of their parents and siblings, Juwan went back to Chicago and stayed at his old assistant high school coach's house. Donnie Kirksey's house.

"You see that place there?" Juwan said, pointing to a three-story brick building off 89th Street. The place looked vacant, and several of the windows were boarded with wood planks.

"We used to live in that top apartment."

He nodded silently, checking out the wood. "Don't look like nobody's in there now, huh?"

Juwan and Juice decided to drive to their old high school, Chicago Vocational. It is one of the biggest high schools in the country, and one of the oldest. It takes up several blocks in the South Side, a joyless concrete monument to inner-city education.

"Lock your doors," Juwan said, getting out. "This ain't exactly the greatest neighborhood."

They crossed the street, hands in pockets, eyes watering from the bitter cold. The large front door, big enough for a castle, was ajar, and Juwan pulled it open. They headed upstairs to the gym.

"Sometimes when we practiced here," Juice said, on the stairwell, "it was even colder than this. There wasn't no heat or nothing."

"Oh, yeah, baby," Juwan said, laughing. "We practiced no matter what."

Like most high schools, CVS, when empty, seemed eerily quiet, as if everyone had been kidnapped. The gym doors were open and Juwan and Juice stepped inside. It was huge, big enough to land an airplane. The ceiling was an Erector set of iron brackets, holding up assorted backboards. The lights were dim, and several of the upper windows had large cracks patched with tape. On the front wall, someone had spray-painted in red block letters,

PENALTY FOR HANGING ON
THE RIM $10

"Yo!"

The voice echoed. Juwan and Juice glanced over at an older man in the near corner, who was wearing a coat and holding papers. He stood before a dozen or so tall black teenagers, huddled together, shivering, wearing jackets, sweatshirts, and ski hats over their sweatpants and sneakers.

"Nookie?" Richard Cook said.

"Hey, coach!"

"Nookie! Man, what are you doin' here? I thought you was in Florida or something."

"Naw. Hawaii. We're goin' tomorrow."

"Hawaii. Florida. Gotta be warmer than here."

He laughed and hugged his old player. Juwan hugged him back, and waved at the team, said, "Whassup, fellas." The kids knew who Juwan was instantly, and their eyes followed his every move with a mix of awe and attitude.

"Our heat's broken down again," Cook said.

Juwan turned to the reporter. "See? I told you."

"I thought maybe we could go through drills this morning," Cook said, "but it's too cold. I'm fixing to let 'em go home."

A couple of kids nodded at that.

Cook turned to Juwan.

"Yeah. So. Nookie. I saw your game a few weeks ago. Those Duke boys are good."

"Yeah," Juwan mumbled. "We shoulda won, though."

"Why don't Fisher get the ball down to you more?"

"Haha. You should ask him that, coach."

"You gotta get it inside. Get it down low."

"I know it."

"It's the inside-out game, that's what I say."

"You right."

"The inside-out game."

"Yep."

"Tell Fisher I said that."

"I will."

The coach smiled at his old player and put a hand on his shoulder. "This one worked hard," he said. Coaches loved Juwan. He had the

right attitude, he liked to learn, and he liked when someone took
interest in him, as coaches always did. At Michigan, Fisher wouldn't
hesitate to single Juwan out to the other Fab Five, saying, "If you all
practiced like Juwan, we'd be in better shape."

They gave him a hard time about that in private—"Coach's
pet"; "He loves you, Nookie"—but Juwan could take it. He enjoyed
being admired by people he respected. He respected his coaches.

"I gotta get these boys outa here," Cook said. "They're about
to freeze to death."

"Yeah, we gonna go," Juwan said.

"Hawaii, huh?"

"Yeah. It's supposed to be nice."

"It sounds nice. You have a good time."

Juwan and Juice said goodbye, left their old high school, and
went back to the car across the street. The kids on the team, whisper-
ing to one another, grinning secret grins, watched them go. The kids
hadn't said much, but they'd never stopped watching Juwan's moves.
The fact that Juwan Howard, from the Lowden Homes projects in
the South Side, was going to Hawaii tomorrow, to play basketball,
meant that someday they, too, could do the same thing.

In the gymnasiums with the broken windows, this is how
dreams begin.

9

Considering the disaster the last time the Fab Five flew over an
ocean, the coaching staff had reason for concern about the Hawaii trip.
And the early signs were not good. First came word that Juwan had
overslept and missed his plane to Detroit. He would have to fly out of
Chicago and meet the team in Honolulu. So much for togetherness.

Then, after flying to San Francisco and getting on a connecting
flight, the players and staff felt a disturbing pause as the plane was
moving down the runway.

"Uh-oh," Dutcher said.

"Folks, we're gonna turn around," the pilot announced. "We
wanna check a little something here . . ."

Mechanical problems. The flight was delayed. And further delayed. Finally they canceled it altogether. The team was stuck for

seven hours in the San Francisco airport. Seven hours? On Christmas Day? Some of the players took up residence in the video arcade. Others stretched out over seats and went to sleep. What was it with these long trips? Fisher scrimmaged with the airline people long enough to at least get the entire team bumped up to business class, since, after all, they were spending the holiday in the domestic terminal. Still, the flight didn't even depart until after the team was originally supposed to be in Hawaii. Trainer Dave Ralston called ahead to cancel the Christmas dinner he had scheduled. That was replaced by airplane food.

By the time they landed, the Wolverines were dead tired. Twenty hours of travel! A Hawaiian woman in traditional garb met them at the airport and put leis over their necks. They nodded, went straight to the hotel, and crashed.

That the trip didn't turn into another National Lampoon European Vacation was due to two factors:

1. Instead of playing a bunch of never-heard-of-thems, the Wolverines would face three top-ranked teams, No. 17 Nebraska, No. 5 North Carolina, and No. 2 Kansas.
2. Jalen was happy.

True, as a general rule, Jalen didn't like to leave Detroit. But this Hawaii thing seemed cool. Everyone spoke English. The hotel rooms were large. And, most important, the TV worked. Jalen immediately hooked up his video game, opened the windows, and flopped on the bed with his joystick.

"Warm breeze coming in from the ocean while you play your Sega," he cooed, "makes a man feel big-time."

To each his own.

Fisher was relieved. Still aching from the loss of his father, he was in no mood to play baby-sitter. He told his team they'd have fun the first two days, see the sights, and after that, "this is a business trip."

Not that he needed to say it. If there was one thing that held the Fab Five's interest, it was playing against other big-time players. Going head-to-head with Adonis Jordan from Kansas or Eric Montross from North Carolina—then coming home to watch their highlights on ESPN's Sportscenter—was a lot more interesting to them than the tour of Pearl Harbor, although Jalen did actually buy one of those disposable cameras to take pictures.

The beach was right across the street, and James Voskuil, Eric

Riley, Dugan Fife, and Jason Bossard went snorkeling one day during free time.

The Fab Five were not the seafaring type.

"Too much sand and shit," Juwan said.

"I don't want no sharks biting me," Chris said.

"I got everything I need right here," Jalen said, wiggling his joystick.

Still, the warm weather seemed to relax them. And by game day, the world's most celebrated college basketball team was ready for action.

The schedule called for three games in three nights. At no other time of the season are you asked to do this, not during conference play, not during the NCAA tournament. Whoever won this thing would have to play great basketball for 72 hours—and would obviously need a deep roster. Before the opener, against Nebraska, Jalen started getting on Eric Riley, the way he often did when he wanted Riley to have a big game.

"You weak," Jalen said.

"Shut up," Eric said.

"Man, as big as you are, you're terrible. I bet you 10 bucks I get more rebounds than you tonight."

"It's a bet. You ain't outrebounding me."

"Fool. I'll bet you 10 bucks I block more shots than you, too."

"You wanna give me all your money, I'll take it."

"Man, you ain't good enough to play against Nebraska."

"Shut up."

"They gonna dog you all night like you're a punk."

"You're a punk."

"I bet you 10 more bucks I dunk more than you . . ."

This was Jalen's method of motivation. He did it with a lot of the Wolverines, but with Riley, well, he kept going until there was smoke coming from the skinny center's nostrils. But it worked. When Fisher put Riley in the lineup, he sprang to life, scoring 13 points and grabbing 10 rebounds.

The Wolverines easily knocked off Nebraska, 88–73. And Riley outrebounded Jalen, and outscored him. "That was Eric's best game of the season," Fisher said afterward.

"Gimme my money, Jay," Riley said.

Jalen grinned. In his own way, he'd make a good coach—as long as someone bankrolled him.

By the following night, game two, Fisher had gotten in the island mood by wearing short-sleeved Hawaiian shirts on the sidelines, no ties, no open collars, same thing for his staff.

"Coach look like one of them Hawaii Five-O guys," Ray said, laughing.

This casual approach was in stark contrast to Dean Smith, the conservative, legendary skipper of the North Carolina Tar Heels, Michigan's opponent. Smith wore his trademark sky-blue sports coat, white shirt, and tie, and the same tight-lipped expression for which he was famous. North Carolina was another school, like Duke and Indiana, with a tradition of excellence—Michael Jordan, James Worthy, Sam Perkins, to name a few, had all gone there—and it was fueled by the systematic, no-nonsense attitude of the coach. You went to North Carolina, you did things Dean Smith's way.

Not a single member of the Fab Five took a recruiting visit there.

The last time the Tar Heels and Wolverines had met was the 1989 NCAA tournament. It was Fisher's third game as head coach, and U-M upset Dean's Team, and, of course, went on to win the national championship. North Carolina got its revenge the following year, when it signed Montross. In all its previous trips to Hawaii, North Carolina had come home with the crown. The press had jokingly nicknamed it "the Dean Smith Invitational."

"Not after tonight," Jalen predicted.

The Fab Five were hungry to beat a team higher-ranked than they were. Chris couldn't wait to try Montross, whom he had gotten to know at the Dream Team workouts in La Jolla.

"You can't check him," Jalen began.

"Bull," Chris said.

"You can't. He's better than you. You weak . . ."

"Shut up."

"I'll bet you 10 bucks . . ."

The game, from the start, was frantic. There were airballs, steals, bad shots. It was hardly picturesque basketball, and yet was so evenly matched in its mistakes—and dotted with enough brilliant plays by Montross and Webber—that it was extremely competitive. The defense was good on both sides, with rejections more important than scoring. Very physical. Lots of talking. It was a manly game, the kind that needs an action hero.

And coming down the stretch, Jalen pulled on his cape.

First he drove on North Carolina sophomore Donald Williams,

pushed in a bank shot, and got fouled. His free throw tied the game, 62–62. On the next possession, he tossed in a quick lefty three-pointer, 65–62. Next, he broke free on a fast break and dropped a layup, 67–62. Seven straight points for Rose.

But he was just getting warm. North Carolina fought back, grabbed the lead, and with a little over a minute left, Michigan trailed, 76–75. Jalen tried a shot, missed, saw a Tar Heels player catch it out of bounds and try to throw it off of Chris' leg. The attempt was wide, and the ball caromed out toward half-court. Jalen never took his eyes off it. He leapt, caught it, spun around, and from 35 feet away, heaved the ball dead on line with the basket, a high alley-oop, to the one big yellow jersey he'd seen in the middle of all those white ones. It was Chris, who leapt perfectly, caught the ball two-handed, and dropped it in over his head.

"Was that a pass or a shot?" someone asked.

"Who cares?" came the answer. "It was amazing."

North Carolina raced downcourt, needing a basket to win. Derrick Phelps drove the lane and launched a running shot that bounced twice on the rim and fell through. They led, 78–77. All but two Tar Heels players ran back downcourt to defend Michigan's last chance.

Eleven seconds remaining.

No time-outs for the Wolverines.

Chris Webber took the ball.

Ironically, four months later—in another Michigan–North Carolina game, for the national championship—this same situation would have huge significance, the single biggest play in the history of the Fab Five. But here in Hawaii, there seemed only one place that ball was destined to go.

Jimmy King drove the baseline, rose between George Lynch and Eric Montross, and fired a shot—and there was Jalen, watching the whole thing develop, finding a spot in front of the rim where he thought the ball would come off a miss. Perfect guess. He leapt, caught the rebound, and in one motion, with his own man, Juwan Howard, draped over his back, Jalen somehow willed a shot back up off the glass before his feet ever touched the ground. He landed as the ball hit the front rim and dropped through the net. The buzzer sounded.

"YEEEEEEEAAAAAAASSSSSS!" the Michigan bench screamed. The basket counted. They'd won, 79–78. The players ran out onto the floor, and Jalen was mobbed by Chris, Juwan, Jimmy,

Voskuil, Pelinka, all of them, laughing and hugging and shaking fists.

"THE DEAN SMITH WHAT?" Jalen screamed.

"THE NORTH CAROLINA WHAT?" Chris answered.

You could tell this wasn't just some second-round victory in a Hawaii tournament. This was the first really big win they'd had in nine months, since that Cincinnati game in the Final Four.

"I never won a game with a last-second shot like that!" Jalen said afterward. Then, as if to keep his trademark cool, he added, "You know, every game in high school, we blew 'em out . . ."

Honolulu was now his kind of town, and there was no holding him—or the Wolverines—back. They returned the next night, on very little sleep, and simply outplayed the No. 2 ranked team in the country, the Kansas Jayhawks, beginning with Jalen's eye-blinking, 180-degree spin move past the celebrated Adonis Jordan, and ending with Jalen's two-handed, breakaway slam, his twenty-fifth point of the night, just before the final buzzer. Final score, 86–74. Michigan won the game. Won the tournament. Won the trophy. And won back some of the reputation that Duke had chewed away that night in Cameron.

When was the last time any team had beaten three Top 20 opponents in *three consecutive nights*?

And Michigan had done it with two significant injuries. The first was Ray Jackson's separated shoulder, which he suffered early against North Carolina. Ralston had to pop the shoulder back in the socket—one of the most excruciating pains you can imagine—and Ray, with his arm in a sling, was drowsy from painkillers the rest of the trip. He always seemed to have the worst luck against big-time opponents. He would be out now for three weeks. He was miserable.

The second injury almost nobody knew about. It also happened in the North Carolina game. One of the players had banged his wrist hard on a TV monitor. Ralston pulled him aside, worked it over, and saw the player wince. Ralston thought the wrist was fractured. The player said leave me alone, I'll be fine.

And considering how he played, Jalen Rose was right.

The plane left on December 31, which meant they'd be flying on New Year's Eve. A small celebration had been planned, but turbulence was so bad the celebration was canceled. They finally landed in Los Angeles at 2 A.M., on January 1. The players were all starving, and of course, nothing was open. They headed off down the airport corridors in search of vending machines.

All except one. Jalen found a spot in the corner, opened his bag, and removed a soggy carton of Jack-in-the-Box chicken, which he had purchased just before leaving Hawaii. There, by the windows of the world, he treated himself to his first meal of 1993. He smacked his lips and glanced occasionally at the dark western skies, all alone, contemplating the chicken and his own unique place on earth.

10

"You hate to sit there and say a kid should come out of college, but if you think about it, you go to college to earn a living, right? Chris Webber, right now, would be, at the worst, the No. 3 guy in the NBA draft, at the very least, if not No. 2 or No. 1. Now, how can you tell someone to turn down what amounts to $20 to $30 million for six years? . . . If you have to come back to finish your degree, you might as well come back with $20 or $30 million in your pocket, right?"

—Bob Elliott, TV announcer, Prime Network, during
Rainbow Classic telecast

Well. It's hard to argue with that kind of logic. And more and more, Chris Webber was being told don't even try. Wherever he went, people said, "You can jump to the NBA, you should do it now!" And "This is your last season at Michigan, right? You're going pro, right?"

Although he'd been in college less than a year and a half, and had played fewer than 50 games—little more than half a regular NBA season—the consensus was that the kid was ready, and when the time came, he would go. Chris Webber, who was too big for kindergarten, too big for grade school, too big for junior high, and too big for high school, was now, in people's minds, too big for college.

He was 19 years old.

One day he sat in an Ann Arbor pizza parlor and talked about the whole idea.

"Truthfully, the thing with me, more than winning, more than a national championship, more than me being happy in college—and I've never said this before—the thing is, I'm scared of that lifestyle. I'm scared of just being out there on my own. Basketball's more of a business in the NBA. There's no more smiling and having fun and high-fiving. Everybody's bitchin', nobody likes each other—people on teams aren't friends with each other, all of that stuff."

He pawed at his spaghetti and slurped it into his mouth. In his green sweatshirt and baseball cap—and he was sitting down, so you couldn't really tell how tall he was—he looked like every other college kid in the place, even younger than some, because his chin and upper lip had only scraggly whiskers.

"I've talked to a lot of pro players," he said, "like Isiah Thomas. And I found out most people who left early like him left because they needed the money. I'm broke right now, but I'm really not desperate for the money. Derrick [Coleman, his friend from Detroit] waited four years. Steve [Smith, another friend from Detroit] waited four years.

"And then, I know this sounds stupid, but I'm afraid of what I'd miss . . . you know what I mean? Like, say I'm a player in Chicago, and I'm in a hotel next year, and Michigan's about to play Duke—December 11, I already know the date. I would hate that. Know what I mean? It's like I don't wanna leave college. But all these people say I should."

He stopped for a minute for another mouthful of spaghetti. It was suggested that maybe he, like most of us, was in no hurry to grow up.

"Right!" he said, his eyes lighting up. "Exactly! I mean, I *like* acting silly, you know? What's wrong with that?"

VII

CRITICS, CRITICS, EVERYWHERE

1

Whatever tropical magic came with the balmy sunshine of Hawaii, it was gone now in the frigid winds of a Michigan January. Ray and Jimmy, in particular, had no stomach for the cold—"We got to get our ass back to Teh-xas, dawg!" they would yell at each other, hunching their shoulders and shivering as they walked across the parking lot to practice.

January meant the new semester, new classes. And, oh, yes. The Big Ten schedule. Before the season started, the Wolverines had established four major goals:

1. Beat Duke in the rematch.
2. Win the Hawaii tournament.
3. Win the Big Ten.
4. Win the national championship.

World peace, presumably, was No. 5.

So far, they were 1-1 on their hit list, and they felt hopeful, if not confident, about getting Fisher his first conference title. The biggest threats would be Indiana, Purdue, and Iowa, all of which, like Michigan, were Top 10 teams in the country right now, and all of which were on the calendar the next four weeks.

Purdue was first. And even though the Wolverines were without Ray Jackson, who pedaled the stationary bike while his teammates ran through practice, they beat the Boilermakers down at Mackey Arena in the season opener, 80–70. It was the Wolverines tenth straight victory, the longest winning streak of the Fab Five era.

That improved to 11 straight two days later, with a businesslike 98–73 blowout of Wisconsin, also on the road.

And then came Indiana.

And the return of a friendly critic.

★　★　★

"THERE IS NO DOUBT THAT MICHIGAN POSSESSES
THE MOST POWERFUL FORCE IN COLL—"

"Hold it, Dick. We need to take it again. Just relax, Chris, this'll
only take one second, sorry."

Dick Vitale was standing next to Webber inside an otherwise
empty Crisler Arena early Monday evening. He was filming a "tease"
for the opening of Tuesday's Indiana-Michigan broadcast. Vitale had
asked Webber to "help me out, it'll only take a second, thanks, big
fella," and Webber, who was growing more and more distrustful of
the media, was still too polite to say no. So here he stood, posed like
some kind of basketball monster, arms locked behind his back, eyes
locked straight ahead, no smile—just as the producer had requested,
even though Chris felt embarrassed and stupid—as Vitale cranked it
up.

"THERE IS NO DOUBT THAT MICHIGAN POSSESSES
THE MOST POWERFUL FORCE IN COLLEGE BASKET-
BALL . . ."

The cameraman dropped to the floor, shooting Webber up from
his ankles . . .

"CHRIS WEBBER TO ME IS THE PREMIER POWER FOR-
WARD/CENTER IN THE GAME TODAY . . ."

The lens worked up his knees, his waist, his chest.

"HE'S AN AWESOME PRESENCE . . ."

Now his neck, his chin, they were right in his face.

"SCORING, REBOUNDING . . ."

His eyes, that glare, make him look like an ogre.

"AND BLOCKING SHOTS . . ."

Got it.

"Thanks, Chris. We really appreciate it."

"Yeah, Chris, thanks so much."

"You're a GOOD GUY, big fella," Dick said.

Chris nodded and walked slowly back to the locker room, wondering what had just happened, wondering if he should trust the way
it was going to look.

"Why do you agree to do those things?" Webber was asked on
the way home.

"I dunno," he said. "I didn't want to be a jerk."

★　★　★

There are 301 Division I college basketball teams in America. And then there's Bobby Knight and the Indiana Hoosiers.

While most coaches scour the country sniffing for prospects in the Great Recruiting Chase, Knight walks out his back door and hustles up a barracks' worth of in-state soldiers. And while most big schools can't help but let their players become the stars, Knight remains the marquee name on the roster; his players simply cast members lucky enough to work for him. Fab Five? Long shorts? Ha! Hoosiers don't even have names on the back of their uniforms! There is only one star in Bloomington. And he's the guy in the red sweater.

As a result, Knight's teams always feature good role-players, kids who follow orders, and—considering the makeup of topflight programs today—a large number of whites. The 1992–93 squad had seven white players, and six of them were raised in Indiana—including Knight's son, Pat. Most of them looked similar, brush cuts, square jaws, good teeth, like some 1950s navy flight school class. Knight's staff was entirely white as well, no black assistant coaches—Joby Wright left two years earlier for Miami of Ohio—no black trainers or doctors, and only one black student manager, alongside 16 white ones.

"They're like that movie *Hoosiers*, all them white Indiana kids," Juwan said, laughing, "only they're the real thing."

And they win. Which is why Knight's legendary temper, his ranting and raving and even occasional chair throwing, is tolerated in basketball-addicted Indiana. Knight has won three national championships in his 21 years at the school (and that's not counting several near misses in the Final Four), he captures conference titles with regularity (averaging one every other year), and has never, ever, in all his years at Indiana, had a losing season. He wins by getting players who have grown up dreaming about playing for him, who are ready to run through a minefield in their underwear if that's what he wants, and he plugs those players into his personal coaching matrix, where if you trust him, he will make you good. And suddenly the kids are setting picks and box-outs more often than they're shooting.

When Bo Schembechler was considering a replacement for Bill Frieder, it was Knight, not Steve Fisher, who was his first choice. Football types love Bobby Knight's approach.

And not surprisingly, once again, not a single member of the Fab Five was the slightest bit interested in attending Indiana.

Chris Webber was the only one to even set foot on the Indiana campus as a high school player, and that was an unofficial visit, as a junior, when he went to see a friend named Andy Slovis. Slovis was a former high school teammate of Webber's, now a student at IU, and Webber stayed in his dorm room. Early in the morning, 7 A.M., the phone rang.

"Hello . . ." Slovis groaned.

It was one of Knight's assistant coaches. There was a rumor Chris Webber, the high school star, had been visiting. Was it true?

"As a matter of fact," Slovis said, "he's asleep on my floor."

Really? Did he want to come by practice?

Webber eventually did go to practice, and did meet Knight, who said to him jokingly, "Hey, if you want to come here, we can get it done right now. Just go in the office and sign the papers . . ."

Chris laughed. He declined.

Later, Knight called Slovis and asked him to come by the gym.

"What kind of chance do we have of signing Chris Webber?" Knight asked.

"Truthfully?" Slovis said. "No chance."

"See ya later, son," Knight said.

> *Hail to the victors valiant*
> *Hail to the conquering heroes*
> *Hail, hail, to Michigan,*
> *the leader of men . . .*

Knight's Hoosiers were now running layup lines inside booming Crisler Arena, where school spirit was showing itself in color and in volume. Indiana was ranked No. 6 in the country, the Wolverines No. 2, and the U-M fans were unusually raucous, this being the first real opponent they could get excited about in person. They roared during introductions. They roared before the opening tap. And they went crazy when, on the very first possession, Indiana missed a shot, Jalen took off with the rebound, dished to Jimmy, who two-handed slammed for the game's first basket.

"UH-OH, ALREADY, BABEEE, HERE THEY GO, THE

WOLVERINES, WHAT A TRANSITION LAYUP, INCREDI-
BLE SPEED AND QUICKNESS!"

Vitale.

It could be a long night.

As it turned out, Michigan and Indiana battled for 39 minutes
of some of the finest basketball played all season. There were few
turnovers committed and few fouls called by the referees, who
seemed a little in awe of the talent trading blows before them. Webber
had a lob feed knocked away, but scooped the ball off the floor and
monster-jammed it in a single, blinking motion. How did a big man
move that quickly? Calbert Cheaney came off the trademark Indiana
screens and fired soft jumpers from all over the floor, seemingly
firing *down* at the rim. How did he get so high?

The defense, on both sides, was exceptional. It was wonderful
frenzy. Ebb and flow. Give and take. Alan Henderson, the Hoosiers'
best shot-blocker, was hitting his jumpers with tremendous accuracy.
And talking trash. "You guys can't check me," he told Webber. "I'm
on it, you can't stop me." Chris had known Henderson since eighth-
grade summer ball, and he thought about jawing back and decided,
"The hell with Alan. This is too big. I'm staying focused."

That was a switch.

The Hoosiers took a halftime lead of 37–31. Respecting Michigan's talent inside, Knight was having his players sag on defense,
daring the Fab Five to shoot outside.

"Don't take the bait!" Fisher warned them in the locker room.
"Keep pushing it inside. Don't be impatient. And if we do get that
open 14-footer, we've got to make it!"

Fisher wanted his team to work an imaginary "midline," divid-
ing the court. The goal was to force the ball to one side of that line
and keep it there, cut the court in half, limiting the Hoosiers' trademark ball movement. It was smart strategy by Fisher, and he had
the horses to do it. The Wolverines were a smarter team than last
year. More mature. More skilled.

"Twenty minutes! Twenty minutes!" Fisher reminded them.

In the second half Indiana surged to a 10-point lead but it was
quickly erased with a series of exhilarating plays: Jimmy drained a
three-pointer. Jalen hit a jumper. Chris pulled a rebound and took
off like a guard, pounding the ball with that high dribble, faking a
pass, then rising for a delicate finger roll.

"OH! OH!" Vitale yelled, and this was surely the Big Heart Attack, right here. "OH! . . . OH! . . . HE'S AN M&M MAN! HE'S MARVELOUS AND MAGNIFICENT! MR. WEBBER! . . ."

Accolades aside, Michigan was indeed playing a great game, going punch for punch with one of the toughest chins in the college basketball business. The players really wanted a win over Indiana, and the fans really wanted a win over Indiana, not simply because you always want a win in the Big Ten, but because of the type of team the Hoosiers were, which is to say, all the things the Fab Five were not. Controlled. Conservative. Well respected by the national press. Duke was all those things, and most of all, the fans wanted Duke, but if Duke couldn't be around, Indiana was the next best victim. To beat the Hoosiers would be . . . therapeutic.

And, thanks to a screwup by Bobby Knight, Michigan had a chance.

With 14.1 seconds left, and Indiana leading by a point, 76–75, Michigan intentionally fouled Todd Leary. Leary—another crew-cut Indiana white kid, with a face straight out of *Leave It to Beaver*—was a 90 percent free throw shooter, so the Wolverines were already thinking three-pointer once he made the shots. The referee, Phil Bova, handed the ball to Leary, and at that very moment, Knight waved Cheaney off the line, to send him downcourt for defense.

Bova saw this and blew his whistle.

Lane violation.

Knight blew his top.

"ARE YOU KIDDING ME?" Knight screamed. "ARE YOU & %$#! KIDDING ME?"

He wasn't kidding. You can't move your players off the line once the shooter has the ball. Indiana would have to give up possession. And deep down, Knight knew it was his fault. A fundamental thing like that? He had screwed it up? Now Michigan had a chance to win with a basket.

"JESUS CHRIST!" Knight was yelling, pacing the sidelines. "JESUS CHRIST ALMIGHTY!"

Meanwhile, Fisher was calling a play. "Jalen, you drive in, take it to the hole, or look for the options. If you draw the defense, look for the dish!"

Chris pulled Jalen close on the way out to the floor. "You shoot it, no matter what. I'll get the rebound. Don't worry."

Jalen nodded. With the crowd on its feet, he brought the ball upcourt, accelerated to the top of the key, spun out to kill a few seconds, then spun back in again. He drew two defenders but—instead of forcing his way to the hoop, which he had done before, and instead of shooting, as Chris had told him—he dished off to the open man in the corner, James Voskuil. Voskuil squared for the long baseline jumper and released his shot with five seconds left, as Cheaney leapt toward him.

Maybe Cheaney distracted him, maybe not. But the shot had too much arch, not enough distance. It hit the rim, bounced high, Juwan tapped it, Chris caught it, with two seconds to get a shot back up.

I'm going to win the game, Chris actually thought to himself as he lifted off his toes. *I'm going to win the game . . .*

Had he dunked the ball, he would have. But not knowing how much time was left, he hurried to get the ball into the air, and out of the corner of his eye he caught a red blur coming from behind and felt a body and—*whack!*—it was too late. Henderson swatted the ball away just as Chris released it. Chris still had his arms up, toward the hoop, as if following through on an invisible score. *He blocked my shot?* Chris looked at the ref, seeking a whistle, but the ref had his hands by his sides. The crowd groaned. The buzzer sounded.

Game over.

Indiana wins, 76–75.

Henderson went crazy, running past the scorers' table waving his arms at the Michigan crowd. "Whassup now?" he yelled. "Whassup now, baby? How do you like us now?" Fisher would take note of this and bring it up every time someone criticized one of his players for taunting. Never mind that the correct approach would be that *nobody* do it, Wolverines or Hoosiers. If Fisher was looking for a trash talker in a different-colored jersey, there he was, dancing across the Crisler floor. Meanwhile, the Michigan locker room was an angry place. Rose came in cursing and knocked over a gum machine. The glass smashed and the gum spilled all over. Rose was mad about the loss, and he was mad for passing off, especially to Voskuil, even though he didn't say this out loud, and even though, basketball-wise, that was probably the right play. "I shoulda fuckin' shot it," Rose hollered, half to himself but loud enough to be heard. "Damn!"

And Voskuil, who had wanted so much to prove he could do whatever a Fab Five member could do, felt like "coming up the tunnel and just keep going, right out into the night."

★   ★   ★

James Voskuil had been the last non–Fab Five starter in the Michigan lineup. He had also been the last white starter. Voskuil, a good-looking kid with sharp features and straight brown hair, came from a small Christian high school in the Grand Rapids area. He'd been recruited with a lot of promise. Now, like all the veteran players, he struggled with the idea that things would no longer get better as he got older at Michigan; they would get worse, because the superior talent was now younger.

Still, to several of the white players on the team—including Voskuil—that was only part of the problem. On the court, they didn't always feel a part of the action.

"It's funny," he said, "but the basketball court is one of the few places in our society where blacks hold the clear majority. And you definitely feel it as a white player.

"Whether it's true or not, when you're not getting the ball, you start to think, is it because I'm white? Why aren't they passing to me? It's very definite, especially on this team, like they don't trust you to make the big play."

Jalen's reaction after the Indiana game, in Voskuil's mind, had confirmed it. Knocking over the gum machine? Saying things like "I shoulda fucking shot it!" James knew what that meant. He didn't trust Voskuil in the clutch, not anymore—if he ever did—and if Jalen felt that way, he'd influence a lot of people to feel that way.

Including, Voskuil felt, the coaches.

"There's like this double standard," Voskuil said. "If I was closer friends with Jalen, it would be OK. Like, if he had swung it to Jimmy on the other side, and Jimmy had missed, this would have been 'Well, there just wasn't enough time' or whatever.

"They forget, what happened with me, that's exactly what happened against North Carolina in Hawaii. Same play. Jimmy missed the shot, but Jalen got lucky and rebounded it in. But here . . ."

He shook his head. "He made me feel like I was the lowest thing on the planet earth."

What if one of the Fab Five were white?

It was an interesting question. Much of the criticism the sophomores were receiving, for trash talking and showboating, they felt, had to do with race.

"I think our image would definitely be different," Jalen said after practice for the Notre Dame game. "You get a lot of white guys on a team, you get a reputation of playing smart. You get a lot of black guys, you get a reputation of being talented."

Could you be as tight as you are now with a white guy as part of the Fab Five? he was asked.

"Probably not, for the simple fact that he wouldn't have gone through the same things we have."

Chris had a different answer.

"I don't think it would be any different," he said, "because people have already formed their opinion of Michigan.

"But I tell you what would be different. If one of us were playing for one of those other teams. Like, if I were on Indiana? I'd be the greatest person of all time. 'Look at him! He's always smiling! He's got heart! That's what Bobby Knight wants out of his players!' That's what they'd be saying."

Ray gave the question some thought before answering.

"It would depend on the white guy's background. I think there'd be more of an effort to make him feel a part of things, you know?

"You gotta understand, with schools like Indiana and Duke? Those are, like, the white teams. Where I was raised, my friends would be like, 'Boy, don't let no white boys beat you.' Basketball was our thing, you know? More of a black thing. That tends to stay with you through the years."

The Indiana loss took steam out of the Fab Five—and not just on the basketball court. True, their 11-game winning streak was over. Their chance at a Big Ten title had taken a major blow. But on top of that, everyone on campus was talking about it. This meant the sophomores shied away from classes, rather than be bothered with endless questions.

Which was one way basketball affected academics.

The Fab Five had done well academically their freshman year. Although critics liked to imagine them illiterate, sleeping through classes, copying papers, selling tickets to professors, it was not so. Sure, Jalen would brag that "I've never seen the inside of the Michigan library," but that was trash talk, it simply wasn't true.

In fact, of all the Fab Five, Jalen was the most scholastically gifted. We're not talking work habits, now. But production. He got it done when he had to, much the way he played basketball. Jalen missed his share of classes, but he could whip a paper off at the last minute and get by with it. Juwan, on the other hand, was the most conscientious, but probably had to work the hardest. Ray and Jimmy had to fight their occasional tendency to take studying a little too casually. Chris, when he applied himself, was fine.

But the older they got, the less it seemed to matter.

Chris and Jalen had been admitted, as freshmen, to the School of Literature, Science and Art—the major school for undergraduates not declaring a specialty. Ray, Juwan, and Jimmy qualified only for the School of Kinesiology, which, although people at Michigan won't readily admit it, is a sort of safety net for athletes. The standards are a little lower. Ray, Juwan, and Jimmy felt the stigma of that, and they worked hard enough freshman year to make LS&A as sophomores. That was an impressive accomplishment.

But as their fame increased, the Fab Five attitude became more lax. As in other areas, they were sensing things would be taken care of for them eventually, and they often pushed it to the limit. They would register for one class, then switch to another without filling out the "drop/add" paperwork. In their minds, someone else took care of paperwork. Weeks would pass. Then, one day, a report would come in that one of them hadn't shown up for a class in a month, and Fisher's office would go crazy and the phones would explode.

They exploded in Bob Clifford's office.

Clifford is the academic adviser to the athletic department, and he seems built for the job—a big man, with a midsection that comes at you like an offensive line; his hair is often mussed, his shirttails loose, and he has the look of a cerebral adventurer who is flustered by the world of athletics. One coach called him "Raging Bull" mostly because Clifford didn't take any crap from athletes. He was assigned to monitor the basketball and football teams, had been for the last dozen years, and he had seen pretty much every trick in the book.

When the Fab Five started having these "paperwork" problems, he would race up to "the Hill"—the code word for the academic side of the university—only to learn the kid had been going to class the whole time, but not the class he listed. Some other class.

Clifford would find the player and ream him out.

Clifford's screaming matches with the Fab Five became legendary, especially in sophomore year, and especially between Clifford and Jalen, and Clifford and Chris.

That's mostly because Clifford, who controlled their monthly room-and-board checks, would hold them up if there was any kind of academic problem.

"No check until you straighten it out," he would say.

"Aw, come on, man, gimme my money!" Chris or Jalen would say.

"Get it straightened out, and you can have it."

Up the Hill they would trudge, grumbling about "that fat ass-hole." But Clifford was doing his job, and even Fisher, in his private moments, had to admire the way he stood up to them.

Because Fisher never used that approach himself.

"YEOOAAAAAWW!"

Chris grabbed his face. His eyes rolled.

His nose had just been broken.

It was practice at Crisler, two days before the Minnesota game, and Eric Riley had accidentally elbowed Chris in the face. "We know you want more minutes, E, but you didn't have to kill him," Ray would later joke.

Chris was helped off the court, examined, and surgery was scheduled for the next day. Dave Ralston, the world's most prepared trainer, got on the phone and lined up a production of a special mask for Webber to wear during games, a clear plastic thing that made him look like the Phantom of the Opera.

"I'm gonna play against Minnesota," Webber vowed. He hadn't missed a start since arriving at Michigan.

He kept his word. Despite surgery, painkillers, and the discomfort of the new mask, Webber started against Minnesota, got knocked down at one point, right in the face, came back out like a heavyweight fighter, and set his personal best for blocked shots. Seven.

Blocked shots?

With a broken nose?

Michigan won, 80–73.

"Batman!" Jimmy yelled at Chris in the locker room, and they all joined in.

"Batman!"

"Toucan Sam!"

"Jason, *Friday the 13th!*"

Fab Five rehab.

★   ★   ★

Several hours after the Minnesota game, Fisher was still awake in his hotel suite, watching tapes. Angie sat beside him. They both wore sweat suits and had their shoes off. Angie sipped a glass of white wine.

The plane had been canceled, bad weather, so everyone just returned to the Marriott and got the room keys back. Fisher watched the TV and picked from a plate full of chicken fingers and french fries. This was a typical postgame nourishment for Fisher, and you wondered how a guy this thin could have the world's worst eating habits. His favorite pit stop is Dairy Queen, and not necessarily for the desserts; he goes for their chili dogs. Mike Boyd always teases Fisher about the time when they were recruiting a kid, and Fisher just had to stop at Dairy Queen on the way to the home visit, he just had to, and Mike said, "You better be careful eating one of those chili dogs, they're messy," and Steve said he would, but sure enough, the first bite, he oozed a hunk of chili right onto his tie. He tried desperately to clean it with napkins and water. Finally, to Boyd's stifled laughter, he simply kept his hand near his chest during much of the visit. Maybe the recruit thought he was pledging allegiance.

"Look," Fisher said, showing a replay of a behind-the-back pass by Webber. "We get a lot of criticism for that kind of pass, but look . . . see . . . that was the logical pass to make. Most of the time, the passes the kids make are the best way for the ball to get where they want it to go."

More and more, Fisher was taking heat—not for defeats, which were few and far between—but for victories. *The Fab Five let teams hang around too long. They play beneath their talent. They're too cocky. Too many alley-oops and behind-the-back passes.*

Fisher whose team was now 14–2, had heard this so much he either rolled his eyes or took offense and offered comparisons.

"If you look at Kansas, they do as much fancy stuff as us . . ."

"If you look at that Indiana game, you'll see Alan Henderson trash-talking . . ."

It was one of Fisher's least appealing characteristics. Instead of taking a stand and holding his ground—"This is the way I do things, OK? You don't like it, go somewhere else"—he often defended himself with the behavior of others.

Everyone else is doing it. For many critics, this wasn't enough.

The press was coming to view Fisher as almost paranoiac about Fab Five criticism. He would ask beat reporters about quotes in their stories. He would get upset more than he used to. When Fisher was first named the Michigan coach, he was so media-conscious he returned phone calls to out-of-state radio stations while on the way to the White House.

Not anymore. If you asked Fisher a question, he often stared at you for several seconds, formulating an answer, or perhaps trying to figure out your angle. More and more he was saying things like "I think I know where you're heading with this . . ." or "I know what you want me to say . . ."

He—and many of his players—definitely felt the media was out to get them in their sophomore year, and they were not going to just sit there and be accommodating.

2

Rob Pelinka was probably the only member of the Wolverines to keep a diary. He was certainly the only one to get into Harvard Law School. An Academic All-American with a 3.9 grade point average—he blamed his only B on the flu during exam week—Pelinka left many of his teammates scratching their heads. How did he do it? The Fab Five used to see him rushing home to study, or working on the road on 20-page papers, or reading books on the airplane just for the fun of it, and he became, for them, symbolic of a category, almost alienlike. They would say, "Well, you know, if you're a Rob Pelinka type . . ."

But Rob Pelinka, whose face is a cross between Rob Lowe's and Robert Downey, Jr.'s, was a basketball player, too, and like all of them, he'd been a big deal in his high school. He'd come to college expecting the big deal to continue. Granted, he didn't have the monster size of a Chris Webber or a Juwan Howard—he was 6 foot 6, average frame, average speed, average jumping ability—but he worked like a demon, and he followed directions well.

And he could shoot.

He came early to shoot. He stayed late to shoot. He attended every shoot-out on the road, even the optional ones. He could bomb from three-point range with terrific accuracy, and he more than held his own when the players would get an informal contest going in practice.

With Ray Jackson still hurt, Fisher decided to start Pelinka against Ohio State. It was a big deal for Pelinka, who, now a senior, had never started a Big Ten game before. And since the game was at Crisler, it was even bigger, because it meant his father would be there.

"My dad might not even mind the drive this time," Pelinka said.

It was some drive. Bob Pelinka was a schoolteacher in Lake Bluff, Illinois, a good five hours by car from Ann Arbor. But every afternoon of every evening home game, he left school early and made the trip down I-94, Chicago to Ann Arbor. He was there when Rob came out for warm-ups, and he gave him a little wave. Sometimes Rob only played a few minutes. Sometimes he barely touched the ball. But the father thought it was important for the son, and so he came, and he left at the buzzer, in order to get back before sunrise. "It's funny," Rob said. "We never even get to talk. I wish he had a car phone, so I could at least thank him for coming."

On Tuesday, January 26, Pelinka ran out during introductions and heard the crowd applaud his name. It felt good to slap hands with guys like Chris, Juwan, Jalen, and Jimmy, and stand there with them for once, part of the starting unit. He gave a glance to his father, who was grinning.

Pelinka's first shot was a three-pointer. He made it. His second shot was a three-pointer and he made it again. His third shot, a two-pointer, swished. He was perfect going into halftime, and Michigan had a 16-point lead.

And then, when the Wolverines suffered what was becoming a disturbing pattern—opponents that should be dead coming back to life against them—Pelinka was there again. He sank six free throws in the final two minutes to ice the game, 72–62. He finished with 16 points, his career high. He also grabbed three rebounds. The coaches patted him on the back.

"It was the greatest decision in the history of Michigan basketball," Fisher said jokingly, of the move to start Pelinka. "Other than that, it was no big deal."

Pelinka was surrounded by reporters, so he stayed longer than usual. He was one of the last players to the parking lot. As he approached his car, he blinked; parked next to his Jeep was his father's Jeep, with his father sitting inside, just waiting for him.

"I didn't know you were here," Rob said. "I would have come—"

"I wanted to give you a hug," Bob Pelinka said, getting out and doing exactly that. "I was just so proud of you tonight."

"Thanks, Dad."

They talked for a few minutes. Then they looked at their watches, and the father climbed back inside his vehicle. He drove off into the dark, five hours of late-night highway ahead of him. Rob watched him go, wiping his eyes.

Sometimes the best moments in college basketball are the ones nobody sees.

After an upset loss to No. 11-ranked Iowa, Michigan was 16-3. Breslin Center—home of the Michigan State Spartans—was hardly the place they wanted to go next. The Spartans were not having a good season so far, and in the frozen depression of a winter night in February, the chance to spank those hotshots from Ann Arbor was reason enough to pump the Spartans' fans.

In the opening minutes of that game, Chris took a nice inside feed and slammed home a patented monster dunk.

"ASS-HOLE! ASS-HOLE!" the crowd chanted in unison. It sounded as if every person in the place were joining in.

"ASS-HOLE! ASS-HOLE!"

The chant was repeated whenever Juwan or Jalen tried a show-boating move. "ASS-HOLE! ASS-HOLE!" Juwan, especially, was the target of curses, and one fan yelled, "Go back to the ghetto, nigger!" loud enough for reporters to hear it on press row.

Midway through the game, a group of MSU male students, dressed as floozy women in flimsy dresses, went racing through the stands waving bright orange construction signs that read:

CHRIS, YOU SAID YOU LOVED ME
KING IS A QUEEN
JUWAN, I'M PREGNANT

It wasn't that the players were bothered by the signs—or even saw them. But the taunters stopped right in front of the Michigan family section, in plain view of Jeanne Rose and Angie Fisher.

Earlier in the week, Angie had said, "I know we're winning, but this really hasn't been a very fun season, you know what I mean?"

Sitting there in the shadow of these hairy-armed cross-dressers, you got a pretty good idea.

Despite the rain of hatred—or, who knows, maybe because of it—the Wolverines won the game, 73–69, holding form down the stretch of a rather sloppy evening that featured *23 missed free throws.* Had they simply walked off, the Spartans' fans would have had little to gripe about besides their own team.

Ah, but what fun would that be? A group of the Wolverines— including Jalen and Juwan—defiantly wandered out to half-court and a few sat on the green and white "S" in the middle of the floor. Didn't just sit, but rolled around, and . . .

Well, a letter from a Michigan State anthropology professor sent a week later to Steve Fisher—and several area newspapers—said it all:

Dear Coach Fisher:

I am a longtime—21 years—faculty member at Michigan State University and I am also a sports fan. . . . I have been unable to forget something which occurred following the MSU/U of M basketball game in East Lansing last week: it was, I believe, the most egregious example of poor sportsmanship I have ever witnessed. . . .

. . . four University of Michigan players ran to the middle of the floor and fell down and began rolling around, laughing . . . they were, in fact, rolling over and rubbing their genitals on the "S." As a further indignity, one player . . . squatted and simulated defecating on the "S." It was disgusting to watch. . . .

If the players on the University of Michigan basketball team wish to divest themselves of their "playground" image, this is surely a poor way to do so. . . .

Loudell F. Snow, Ph.D.
Professor of Anthropology
Michigan State University

On the other hand, who said they wanted to "divest themselves" of anything?

3

Controversy didn't hurt sales. In fact, the more controversial the Wolverines became, the quicker their merchandise flew out the doors. The long yellow shorts were everywhere: you saw students in the intramural leagues wearing them, you saw them hanging in bookstore windows. Chris' No. 4 was the biggest-selling jersey by far; women, men, everyone seemed to want one.

And the fever wasn't limited to clothing. The Michigan athletic department introduced Wolverines basketball trading cards, $5.95 per pack, and they were gobbled up almost as fast as they were printed, nearly 30,000 packs in the state alone. Some people opened them and sold the cards separately—with Webber's card fetching as much as the whole pack at some card shows—while others bought the pack and never even broke the seal, holding out for the day it became a collector's item.

"How much you think they're making off these?" Chris asked Ray one day, fingering through the cards in the locker room.

"I dunno, dawg," Ray said, studying his card, "but I haven't got any checks, know what I'm saying?"

"The worst part is when people come in and get 'em signed after a game," Jimmy said. "Then they go out and sell 'em for even more. So we're losing money twice."

They shook their heads. And they didn't know the half of it. Had unbridled merchandising been allowed—the NCAA is strict on the type of item, number of items, and legality of items—there could have been Fab Five dolls, Fab Five comics, Fab Five cereal, Fab Five candy bars. They were that popular. And this was *before* the NCAA tournament and *despite* the fact that they trailed Indiana by two games in the Big Ten. It didn't seem to matter. The Fab Five weren't just about winning, they were about attitude and style. High schools and junior high schools across America were reordering their own uniforms to look more like Michigan's baggy, loose, long shorts. "We want the Fab Five look," they told their sales reps.

With their bald heads, black socks, long shorts, and highlight film style, Chris, Jalen, Juwan, Ray, and Jimmy had tapped into a vein of American celebrity, the one that runs straight to the hip pocket, the one that makes kids buy Air Jordans and wear their baseball caps backward and hang posters on the wall and stand in front of them in mock poses. They were cool. And cool meant money.

Just not to them.

"Hey, C Webb," Ray said, smiling, "when you go to the league next year, you gonna hook me up right, you gonna buy me a house, right?"

Chris laughed. "I'm not buying you anything."

"Come on, dawg!" Ray held out a handful of cards. "I'll let you have some Ray Jacksons, free of charge . . ."

4

Sunday, February 14, was Valentine's Day, and several of the Fab Five's girlfriends didn't hesitate to remind them. Flowers would be nice. A phone call? A visit?

"Sorry," the players said, "got a game."

Not just a game. *The* game. Maybe the last game that mattered in the regular season. The rematch with Indiana. Sunday afternoon, on CBS-TV, down in the madhouse known as Assembly Hall, where Bobby Knight's red-clad image seems to loom like Godzilla, making opposing players clank their shots and referees swallow their whistles. Lately, Knight had been more iconoclastic than usual. On his weekly TV show, he announced that Indiana had received a commitment from 6-foot-8 Ivan Renko, who used to play for the Yugoslavian National team. Hoosiers fans got very excited. A new recruit is cause for a parade in Indiana.

One problem.

Ivan Renko didn't exist.

Knight made the whole thing up.

He never explained it, either. He seemed to revel in the fact that not only could he fool people with such nonsense but he was so big he didn't even have to answer for it. Knight was a man who needed a long visit to the real world.

But his team, once again, was top-shelf. Ranked No. 1 in the country. Undefeated in the Big Ten. Michigan's only hope was to win in Bloomington, then hope another team could knock the Hoo-

siers down as well. Sunday was huge. The newspapers began writing
about it four days in advance. It was yet another Fab Five showdown
with a "disciplined" team, and the sophomores were so sick of hearing the comparisons they could spit.

Jay Smith, the tall, bespectacled assistant coach, who used to be
a decent college player himself—and still held the Michigan high
school state record for career points—tried to figure out a way to get
the sophomores properly psyched. Showing them Alan Henderson
after the last Hoosiers win ought to do it. He made sure he had that
part of the Indiana tape cued up.

Smith was a stickler for details. He was also the most health-
conscious of the coaching staff, running every morning or afternoon,
eating smart, staying slim. Then again, he would joke that he couldn't
afford to eat well. Under new NCAA rules, the third assistant coach
on a staff can only earn $12,000 a year, and can only receive a maxi-
mum of $4,000 a year more for working at his boss's summer camps.

This meant that Smith, who spent just as much time as Dutcher
or Watson scouting teams, running practices, and studying film,
made less than a third of what they made in salary.

"It's ridiculous," he said. "I'm lucky my wife works, or I
wouldn't even be able to afford groceries."

Smith stayed with it because he loved it, the way Doogie Knoll,
the student manager, kept knocking on doors and setting up video
games for the players. Because he loved it. All they asked in return
was that the team win.

And Smith was trying to goose them to it now.

"Here's a picture to take to bed with you tonight," he said,
running in slow motion the tape of Henderson screaming to the U-
M crowd.

"That bitch," Chris whispered. "Look at that bitch. Look at
him, you see that, J?"

Jalen nodded. "And *we* get in trouble for talking."

Smith tried to build on the anger. "You gonna let him dance on
your house like that?"

"Naw, man!"

"You gonna let him show you up like that?"

"We gotta get this bitch tomorrow!"

"Yeah! Come on, Blue!"

Fisher listened, not saying much. He needed emotion. They

played well on emotion. Of course, if they didn't listen to what he'd told them about defensive switching, and fighting through the screens, and boxing out, boxing out, boxing out, well, they could forget it. Indiana was too good.

"Yo, coach," Chris said, heading toward his room. "If we win tomorrow, you gotta do the moonwalk, OK?"

"You do?"

"No, you."

"I do?"

The players all laughed, walking down the hall, throwing their arms around each other. "Fish, man . . . the moonwalk . . . that'd be funny . . ."

Fisher just grinned, and wondered, for a moment, how the hell you do the moonwalk anyhow.

5

The latest word on Avondre Jones was good. Perry said the kid was telling him, "I'm coming. You're my school. I'm coming." Fisher hoped he was right. A 6-foot-11 center would look pretty good right now, especially since everyone kept talking about Chris leaving after this year.

Meanwhile there was this little matter of revenge and a Big Ten title to take care of . . .

"Take the action to them, put yourself in an attack mode on both ends of the floor," Fisher told his troops minutes before the Indiana game. "Poise under pressure! But most importantly, remember you are a special group that has the rare ability to play its best in important games."

He put his hands together. "Let's do it."

"ONE-TWO-THREE, NUT UP!" they yelled.

Fisher watched them walk out, slapping each other's heads, bouncing, chanting slogans. He was not a fire-and-brimstone speechmaker, he never had been. He felt that if he got them to believe they were special, they would be. Some coaches insult you and dare you to prove them wrong. Fisher complimented you and challenged you to live up to it. That was his style.

The Fab Five, of course, had their own.

Chris: "Let's do this, boy!"
Jalen: "Let's go holler at these bitches!"
Ray: "Don't nobody leave it in here!"
Juwan: "LET'S GO BREAK THEIR HEART, BABY!"

Hearts would be broken, but the wrong ones, as far as Michigan was concerned. Oh, the Wolverines came out in the first half like a team possessed, playing perhaps their finest basketball since the Fab Five arrived. Under the baleful glare of Knight, who truly can't stand losing in his own building, Michigan was hitting outside shots when the Hoosiers sagged off, and inside shots when there were one-on-one matchups. When Juwan came down on a fast break and hung in the air, adjusting his hands for perfect form, then dropped a soft four-footer, the Michigan lead was 26–14.

In Bloomington?

"Great job! Great job!" Fisher said during the time-outs. "Keep going to the boards. Keep helping out defensively."

The only thing bothering the coaching staff was the officiating. As per usual in this building, the fouls were piling up at a two-to-one disadvantage ratio. It went that way right to halftime.

When they took the floor for the second half—their lead having been whittled to 46–44—there was a new Hoosier in the lineup. A freshman named Brian Evans, who had the perfect Indiana look: crew cut, poky-eared, toothy grin, he looked like a kid out of *This Boy's Life*. His shoulders almost drooped and his midsection seemed decidedly nonathletic. Yet there he was, in the lineup, one of Knight's coaching-by-instinct moves. And it turned out to be deadly.

Michigan kept the lead well into the second half, and had a 70–61 edge with under 11 minutes left. But then the whistle started blowing. Foul on Pelinka. Foul on Jackson. Foul on Riley. Foul on Pelinka. Those four fouls took 89 seconds to be called, and suddenly Indiana was in the bonus free throw situation with more than nine minutes to go, and the crowd was shaking red and white pom-poms and screaming as if welcoming Michigan to hell.

And hell it was. For six of the last seven minutes of the game, the Wolverines would not score a point. Not a basket. Not a free throw. Nothing. Their side of the scoreboard sat at 78 while Indiana's went from 76 to 79 to 81 to 84 to 85 to 87 to 89. Michigan was standing around, watching shots hit the rim, and the Indiana players would sneak inside and steal the rebounds away.

"BOX OUT!" Fisher pleaded. God! They had worked on this all week! "BOX OUT!"

Meanwhile, Evans, the freshman, was going nuts. He dropped a three-pointer from the right corner, then stole the ball from Jimmy King, then stole a pass from Jalen, then sank another three-pointer from that same right corner.

Brian Evans?

"We're sending you guys home," Cheaney said to Webber. "You all can't come in here and beat us."

"You all can't come in here and beat us," Webber mimicked, then rolled his eyes at Rose. Cheaney couldn't trash-talk as far as they were concerned. He sounded, Chris would say, "like a nerd."

But his team was obviously going to win.

And it did, by one point, 93–92.

The Indiana players hugged one another and waved to the thundering crowd. They had survived Michigan's challenge, remained undefeated in conference play, and were almost sure to win the conference crown. The Fab Five would get no rings. Not from the Big Ten anyhow.

"How disappointed are you?" someone asked Jalen in the subdued Wolverines' locker room.

"Well," he said, pulling out his headphones, ready to disappear into a world of rap music, "I look at it this way. There's still the NCAA tournament and the national championship. That's our big dream. Indiana just won the silver medal. We're going for the gold."

6

Bob Clifford rubbed his forehead and waited one more ring, then hung up the receiver and sighed. They were disappearing on him now, the Fab Five. He noticed it right after the Indiana loss. They were missing classes. They were not answering the phone. When he left messages on their answering machines, they didn't always get back to him.

"After Indiana, they really lost interest in a lot of things, not just schoolwork. That loss really knocked the life out of them."

The problem was, there was still a month to go before the

tournament. And in the minds of the Fab Five, at least, nothing else counted. Sure, Fisher got all over them about "staying focused" and "finishing strong" and "earning a No. 1 seed." That was their big goal now. A No. 1 seed in March Madness.

But how excited can you get over a seed? Michigan defeated Penn State, Minnesota, Ohio State, and Iowa, and as far as the average fan was concerned, who cared? Indiana was going to win the conference.

With no place else to go, the spotlight seemed to fall on the peripheral issues of the team. Chris' NBA plans—will he stay or will he go? Jalen Rose—is he really a point guard? Steve Fisher, his coaching ability—is he a genius or a baby-sitter?

Bobby Knight, of all people, had an interesting theory on that. He told his friend Bob Hammel, of the *Bloomington Herald-Times*, "Steve has done a really good job with that team. You don't know what it is to have to coach a group of kids with all the baloney that is written about them . . .

"I've never had to contend with all that, all the hype on a group of kids. I think Steve's done a marvelous job."

Fisher appreciated that. Of course, he would have appreciated beating Indiana more.

In the rematch game with Michigan State, at Crisler, in early March, Michigan won in overtime by six.

Which the critics admired.

Then Chris and Ray jumped on the scorers' table and did a victory dance in front of the cheering throng.

Which the critics hated.

"Why do they have to rub it in?" people asked on the radio talk shows. "Why do they have to be such hot dogs? Who do they think they are?"

The next day, the players shrugged off the criticism. They were tired of it. They had heard it all before. The Fab Five were not even finished with their second year in college, and already they were cynical about the media, the public, and the whole idea of public image.

"You know, if I go out, and I try to be real quiet and polite," Chris said, "you know what happens? I hear back that someone said I was stuck-up. But if I talk too much, I'm some kind of show-off. I can't win.

"After last season, I just said forget it. We're young, we're having fun out here, we love to play basketball, and we like to let it show. If people have a problem with that, so be it. At least we're entertaining."

They were an enigma, loved and hated, criticized yet followed with a passion. They were 24-4 on the season, ranked No. 4 in the country, attracted huge TV audiences, and sold more merchandise than any college team in the country.

And all you ever heard was how one day they're gonna fall hard, and a lot of people are going to be smiling.

7

The 'hood, no matter,
for better or worse,
comes first.

—Naughty by
Nature, one of
Jalen's favorite
rap groups

Mick McCabe, a bearded, easygoing, high school sportswriter for the *Detroit Free Press*, had heard enough in his 23-year career not to be surprised anymore. But he was surprised at this. A woman he knew was on the phone, saying, "A cop just told me Jalen Rose was picked up in a crackhouse."

"A crackhouse?"

"Yeah. He couldn't believe it."

McCabe made a few calls. One was to someone he knew in the police department.

"This is probably crazy," McCabe said, "but do you know anything about Jalen Rose and—"

"It's true," the officer said. "That's all I can tell you."

McCabe went to Jim Schaefer, who covered the police beat for the *Free Press*, and the two of them began a search that would take them in 50 different directions, with a surprise waiting at almost every turn. First they learned that Rose had indeed been ticketed for something during a drug raid, but not necessarily at a crackhouse, and not recently; it happened back in October (and this was late February). Then they found that while the log of his ticket could be traced, the ticket itself had vanished.

Or someone had made it vanish.

Nobody wanted to talk. The police tips all came off the record. At one point, McCabe and Schaefer were pretty much out of information, other than the name Garland Royall, one of the other men ticketed in the same raid. They went to the apartment building where Royall supposedly lived, with his mother, on the West Side of Detroit.

"Check the names on the directory," Schaefer said as they entered.

McCabe frowned.

"There are no names," he said.

They were actually considering going door-to-door, which was as ridiculous as it sounds, when they saw a middle-aged woman out near the curb, wearing a jogging suit, gold chains, and eyeglasses. She was the only person around. She seemed to be waiting for a ride.

"Should we ask her?" Schaefer said.

"Why not?" McCabe said, chuckling. "Maybe that's his mother."

They approached her. Introduced themselves.

"You wouldn't happen to be Mrs. Royall, would you?"

"I sure am," she said, smiling.

So it began.

Several days and two dozen interviews later, here was the story they pieced together: Back on October 4, 1992, the police had raided a suspected drug house at 8044 Cloverlawn in Detroit. The house belonged to a high school friend of Jalen's named Frederick Hogan, a heavyset youth whose only available photograph, when the media was searching for one, was a pose of him holding a machine gun, grimacing, and grabbing his crotch. Police were granted authority to raid the house—which Hogan inherited when his mother died—because the day before, an undercover cop tried to make a cocaine purchase there, and was told to come back at night, and he would be "served."

When the police came through the door, yelling, "Police! Search warrant!" (they did not kick down the door, by the way; it was unlocked and open), they found five young men, including Lamont

Wheeler, who had four packs of crack cocaine in his pockets, Hogan, Royall, Daman Holmes, a freshman at Ferris State University, and a tall, skinny kid named Jalen Anthony Rose. The cops knew who Jalen was immediately. One of them later said, "It killed me. This kid is my son's favorite basketball player, and here I am, popping him in a drug raid."

Jalen was only doing in that house what he does almost always when he's not playing basketball—playing video games, "John Madden Football" to be exact—but there were packs of marijuana on the dining room table and a briefcase with marijuana next to it, and there was a large marijuana plant in the corner, and so the tickets were written up and the young men were charged. "Loitering where drugs are kept or stored" was the ticket issued to Jalen, Daman Holmes, and Garland Royall. It is a misdemeanor charge that carries a maximum $500 fine and 90 days in prison. At some point, Jalen held that ticket in his hand, even as he watched Hogan and Wheeler arrested and taken away for more serious felonies.

The next day, Steve Fisher got the call from Thomas Moss, a civilian deputy police chief. Moss has long been a friend to University of Michigan sports. His office walls are adorned with pictures of him shaking hands with Fisher and Gary Moeller, the football coach. He helps get summer jobs for college athletes working with the cadets programs.

One of the athletes he employed the previous summer was Jalen Rose.

"Steve, there's been a problem, but everything's OK now," Moss had said.

Fisher listened. Moss told him "it has been taken care of," dismissed. He said the police had done this "at least 500 times."

Maybe a more streetwise coach would have asked what Moss meant by "taken care of." Maybe he would have asked if Jalen was being given preferential treatment over the other guys ticketed for the same charge—who had to go to court. Maybe he would have asked if this was something that could come back to haunt them later. John Thompson, the coach at Georgetown, had an incident once where a suspected drug dealer was hanging around with one of his players. Thompson didn't just talk to his player; he dragged the suspected dealer into his office and told him, "You stay the hell away from my kids, you got that?"

Fisher is cut from a different cloth. He heard the words "Don't worry" and figured Moss, who is, after all, in the police force, must know what he was talking about.

He accepted it.

And he never said anything to the press.

And for nearly five months—while Michigan played Duke, while Michigan went to Hawaii, while Michigan embarked on the Big Ten campaign—neither did anyone else.

When a reporter from the *Free Press* first confronted Jalen with the story, in late February, and asked if he was in that house on that day, you would have thought he'd accused him of being from another planet.

"Never in 10,000 years," Jalen said.

Jalen wasn't the only one lying. Moss also said he knew nothing of the incident.

But, a few weeks later, the evidence—which included a Xerox of the original police log, with Jalen's name on it—was too substantial to deny. The funny thing is, the story, the real story, was not that Jalen did anything wrong, but that someone in the police department buried his ticket. Thought they were doing him a favor. Had Jalen taken that ticket, gone to court, and had it dismissed—as it almost certainly would have been—he might have avoided the insanity that came next.

The story ran in the *Free Press* the morning of Tuesday, March 9. It was followed up by the *Detroit News* the same afternoon. It went out over the national and international wire services, and pretty soon, every media outlet in the country was screaming, "Jalen Rose arrested in a crackhouse!"

Fisher was livid. He felt the media blindsided both him and Jalen, confronting them only hours before the story was going to be published. Of course, Fisher had been happy when nobody knew anything for five months.

A press conference, out of sheer necessity, was called that afternoon, inside Schembechler Hall, and at least 30 reporters arrived, along with half a dozen TV cameras. Again, they knew Jalen's actual "crime" was minimal, and no one was suggesting otherwise, but the room already had that buzz of "there's more here than meets the eye." Theories were traded. Rumors flew. A suspected cover-up, no matter how small, is news, and a suspected cover-up involving a member of the Fab Five was more than news, it was your lead story.

Jalen and Chris—Chris came for moral support—pulled up to the building in Jalen's car. They parked in the No Parking zone. They were laughing when they came inside, and they were still laughing, albeit nervously, when the cameramen stormed like paparazzi.

"Scarface is here," Jalen said, looking at Chris.

"Public enemy No. 1," Chris said.

Jalen delivered a statement. He admitted he had been in the house (so much for his "Never in 10,000 years") and apologized to "my family, my teammates, and my friends . . .

"I would like to say I did nothing wrong, I'm not in trouble with the law . . . hopefully this can end today, and we can go on with the rest of the season, get a No. 1 seed, win the championship, and I can get me a championship ring. That's what I'm here to do . . .

"I'd like to end by saying I did nothing wrong."

He walked out, without taking questions, and in the hot light of the TV cameras, Chris threw an arm around him and said, "You did all right, man."

And Jalen said, "Scarrrrface!"

Chris had been in that house before. He had played video games on the same TV set. Had the police come on another day, it might have been Chris' reputation that was dropped in the mud. And the night the story broke, his father, Mayce, called at 4 A.M. and pleaded, "Please, don't go near any of those guys. If Jalen's hanging around bad people, you gotta stay away. You got too much to lose."

Chris told his father not to worry, he was smart. Neither he nor Jalen would indulge in drugs just because there were people around who did. But exposed to them? Hell, they had known drug users almost half their lives. Jalen even knew about pickup basketball games in which teams were selected by competing drug dealers, large wagers were placed, and the dealer that won "paid" his players for bringing home the loot.

"I'm from Detroit," he says, by way of explanation.

And Jalen Rose would rather be thrown off a bridge than give up his friends in Detroit. All attempts to convince him otherwise meet with a smirk and a quick dismissal. After the ticket incident, his older brother Bill told him, "You got to lose those guys. And stop dressing like some kind of rap gangster. What's with that shit?"

His mother told him, "Those boys are not your friends, they will only drag you down."

Jalen shrugged and said he knew what he was doing. And with the emotional loyalty of a 20-year-old, he refused to turn his back on his roots. "Those are my boys," he said. "They're my true friends, they always will be."

So for the first two years Jalen was a Michigan student, he never developed any real friendships in Ann Arbor, not outside of the basketball team. He defiantly wore big hooded sweatshirts and ski caps and oversized pants and medallions on chains, straight off an album cover by Geto Boys or EPMD. His demeanor said, "I'm from the city. You people don't get me. Don't even try."

This was his identity. You could not question it.

The Illinois fans were about to learn that.

"Crackhouse!" someone in the crowd yelled.

Jalen ignored it.

"Crackhouse!" someone else yelled. Then a small group. Then a whole section. "CRACKHOUSE! CRACKHOUSE!"

He launched the first free throw. Swish.

"JUST SAY NO!" came the new chant, spreading around the building. "JUST SAY NO! JUST SAY NO!"

He launched the second free throw.

Swish!

There were nine minutes and 13 seconds left in the game when the Assembly Hall fans decided to get stupid, decided to see how far they could push this bald-headed kid from Detroit. Everyone was talking about the incident. Jalen had been shielded from the press. The Michigan staff had tried to make it easier for him. But now, on his way downcourt, Jalen raised a hand to his ear, and looked at the enemy fans as if to say, "I can't hear you . . ."

And from that point, until the final seconds of overtime, he was a beast. He drove and scored, drove and scored, he drew a foul and thrust a fist in the air. He yanked rebounds over people's heads. He slapped the ball out of would-be scorers' hands. He tied the game in regulation with a leaning baseline jumper. He forced overtime by stripping the ball from Illinois' Andy Kaufmann. He rebounded his own missed shot late in overtime, made the basket, got fouled, and tied the game at 91–91.

He scored the final winning points at the free throw line. Six seconds left. When he sank the last one, he jogged downcourt, looked at the crowd, and put a finger up to his lips as he smiled.

"Shhhhhhhhhh."

He had shut them up. Typical Jalen.

"He's a man-child," Perry Watson marveled after U-M's 98–97 victory.

"He's a keeper," Fisher added.

Jalen had played all 45 minutes. Led all scorers with 23 points. Had more rebounds (eight) than anyone on the Illinois team. On a night when distractions swirled like bugs around a summer light, he was the most focused of them all.

"I was just trying to let the crowd know they weren't gonna bother me," Jalen said. "When someone doubts me, I'm gonna prove them wrong."

He sat by his locker as if this were just another night.

Fisher, meanwhile, had barely slept before the game. He looked like hell. He didn't know what to expect anymore, press conferences about drug raids, ugly headlines wherever they went, crowds that hated them, boosters that resented them, a tournament that began in eight days, and a team that was 25-4, and would probably earn a No. 1 seed and who still nobody could figure out, except to say that they always played their best when someone poked them in the chest.

"I'd just as soon we didn't need this kind of pressure to win," Fisher sighed, heading for the bus. Who was he kidding? If he'd learned anything in this whole crazy Fab Five experience, it was that pressure was as reliable as a TV commercial: you know it's coming, just give it a minute.

VIII

THE PROMISED LAND,
ONE MORE TIME

1

Muhammad Ali did not come to Tucson. But then, the Fab Five no longer needed celebrities in hotel lobbies for inspiration. One year after their first tournament appearance, Chris, Jalen, Jimmy, Juwan, and Ray had themselves *become* the celebrities in the hotel lobbies. People mobbed them, and they often sneaked in through back entrances.

Tucson, where the Wolverines would play their first two rounds of March Madness this year, was actually a pleasant change; outside of dude ranch workers, retirees, and the student body of the University of Arizona, who would bother them? They had been awarded the No. 1 seed in the West bracket, sharing top honors with North Carolina (No. 1 in the East), Indiana (No. 1 in the Midwest), and Kentucky (No. 1 in the Southeast). The Wolverines went to the airport Wednesday afternoon, said a few words to the TV cameras, and got on the plane. From the players to the coaches to the student managers, they were simply relieved to finally get this tournament started.

And, of course, they liked the idea of going someplace warm.

"I'm a *big* fan of the selection committee now," Jimmy said, pulling on a pair of shorts and a T-shirt when he got to the hotel.

Never mind that the critics were predicting a letdown before they ever reached New Orleans. Never mind that Bill Walton had called them "one of the most underachieving teams of all time." Here in Tucson, they stayed at the Viscount Suites, with a huge atrium lobby, so they could hang over the railings and see everything and everybody, but with a bodyguard on their floor, nobody could hassle them. This was good.

Michigan would play its first game Friday night, against the Coastal Carolina Chanticleers, a team that few ever heard of. A loss to them would be devastating to Michigan. On Thursday, several backup players were hanging around the pool. Jason Bossard had his shirt off, getting a tan. Dugan Fife was working with a Spanish tutor. Rob Pelinka leafed through a hardback copy of John Grisham's *The Client*.

"It's my future," he said. "The story of a yuppie lawyer."

"YO, ROB! GET OUTA THE SUN!"

Pelinka squinted. It was Jalen yelling down from his balcony. Pelinka forced a laugh, but Jalen said it again.

"GET OUTA THE SUN! SUN TAKES AWAY YOUR ENERGY!"

Pelinka ignored him, and eventually Jalen went back inside. Five minutes later, however, Pelinka got up and went in, too. *You know, if Jalen is taking things this seriously . . .*

Coastal Carolina, from tiny Conway, South Carolina, was tough to take seriously. Under tournament play, the No. 1 seed draws the No. 16 seed, No. 2 draws No. 15, No. 3 draws No. 14, etc.—so Michigan was, theoretically, facing one of the four weakest teams in the field. The Chanticleers' regular season schedule included Radford, Towson State, and Liberty. And they lost to all of them. The Chanticleers had a 6-foot-7 starting center who averaged one basket per game. Their mascot was a large chicken.

Still, none of that compared to their star player, a four-time Big South Conference Player of the Year named Tony "Slam" Dunkin.

"They gotta be shitting us," Jalen whispered in the first film session. "Slam Dunkin?"

"Slam Dunkin," Chris repeated.

"Someone gave me that nickname," Juwan said, "I'd give it back."

Still, Dunkin was the enemy, this was the tournament, so when Michigan arrived Friday afternoon at the McKale Center arena on the Arizona campus, Jalen wasted no time in checking him out. Dunkin was a 6-foot-7 small forward with low eyebrows that made him look constantly worried, and a protruding lower lip that seemed to be sewn on his chin, like a large piece of macaroni.

Jalen found him, nodded "Whassup" and began to talk.

"You're kinda thin," Jalen said. "You need a little time in the weight room."

Dunkin laughed. "I heard about you guys."

"I'm serious, you need to lift some weights. Maybe go sleep on that weight bench a little."

"Haha."

Chris was standing near them now, dribbling, listening.

"Tell you what," Jalen said, "I'm gonna let you choose which way you wanna die."

Dunkin looked at him curiously. Jalen held out his left arm.

"This is the hand with the jump shot," he said.

"And this"—holding out the right—"is the hand I'm gonna freak you with the layup."

He locked them both behind his back.

"Go 'head, pick one."

Chris was laughing so hard he had to walk away. He shook his head and went "Hooooooo." A lot of people criticize Jalen's behavior, but they never knew how therapeutic he was for Webber. Chris was the type to worry about everything, to think of the worst-case scenarios, all the things that could go wrong. He couldn't help it, his brain worked that way.

Jalen, on the other hand, was always sure he was going to win, so talking had no effect on his performance. In fact, it helped his confidence. And by the time Chris was done laughing at Jalen, some of that same confidence had rubbed off and soothed his otherwise worried soul.

Dunkin never did pick a hand, but it didn't matter. The Fab Five had introduced themselves. With the arena only two-thirds full, and the noise level low, the Michigan sophomores walked out for the start of the most important three weeks of their careers, and Chris kept looking over at CBS' broadcaster Greg Gumbel, "just to make sure it was really the tournament."

Webber dropped into a crouch, the ball went up . . .

And the Wolverines gave the Chanticleers the assortment pack—one of everything. The first basket was a sweet, pull-up jumper by Ray Jackson, then Juwan banked one home, then Chris slammed and Jimmy hit a three-pointer, and very quickly it wasn't a game, it was a mercy killing. Coastal was not ready for prime time, clanking jumpers and missing dunks. The Chanticleers shot 25.8 percent for the first half, and didn't improve much in the second. With Ray guarding him much of the time, Slam Dunkin was embarrassed, missing 16 of his 20 shots.

"Weight room," Jalen said as he ran past him.

The final score was 84–53, their biggest blowout of the season. The Coastal coach, Russ Bergman, later said, "We knew we'd have to give up something at the start."

Yeah. Hope.

The nicest moment of the game actually came long after the outcome had been decided. Fisher cleared his bench, giving Dugan Fife, Jason Bossard, Leon Derricks, and Sean Dobbins some tournament playing time. Dobbins was a senior who had walked on the team during the 1989–90 season, almost never took off his warm-ups, and had never scored a basket in game competition. His entire career? Never scored a basket? And he was about to graduate? The sophomores were yelling, "GET DOBBS THE BALL!" Finally a foul was called with four seconds left, and Chris and Jalen had an idea.

"Let's get Dobbs down here and hide him."

"Yeah, let him cherry-pick for a layup."

"Hurry up, hurry up!"

They were like summer campers on a panty raid. They caught Dobbins' eye at the other end, where the free throws were being shot, and motioned for him to come down. Dobbins, a neatly groomed kid with this perpetual smile on his face, jogged over as if coming out of the game.

The Fab Five players stood out on the court, pretending to be watching the action, all the while hiding Dobbins behind them. When the free throw was made, they hopped back, revealing Sean Dobbins, all alone.

"THROW IT!" Chris yelled.

Pelinka heaved a pass, Dobbins caught it, and, nerves rattling, he dribbled to the hoop and laid it in. The buzzer sounded.

"YEAAAAHH!"

"DOBBS! WHOOOO! DOBBS!"

You would have thought they'd won the title. They mobbed him. Rubbed his head with their fists. "BIG TIME!" they yelled. "BIG TIME!" Even Fisher had to bite his lip to keep from smiling. Here, they had just passed their first step toward a national championship, something the whole world was daring them to do, and all the Fab Five wanted was to lift up this reserve player, this kid who wouldn't last five minutes in a real game—"You shoulda dunked!" Jalen yelled—and Dobbins was sheepishly turning red and laughing harder than anyone had ever seen him laugh.

The crowd was halfway gone. The CBS announcers were talking about upcoming games. The shame of this team was that it always seemed to be at its best when no one was watching.

Back in the hotel, when they watched the highlights together, the players would tease one another about how they looked on TV.

"There goes E.T.!" Jimmy or Chris would say when Jalen's face appeared on the screen.

Jalen would laugh. "Look at how I'm milking that camera time. I'm all that, baby!"

This was part of the tournament as well. Every member of the Fab Five—and most big time college players, to be honest—were quite aware of the TV camera. And they knew when it was on them. After layups. During time-outs.

"Free throws," Juwan said. "You know that camera gonna be on you for as long as you're getting ready to shoot a free throw. Sometimes you just take a few extra dribbles, you know what I mean?"

He laughed. Juwan would occasionally wink at the camera. Chris would occasionally stare into it after a jam. Jalen played it cooler than that, but he knew it was on him after he made a basket, and he would run back upcourt with his wrists hanging in a loose, defiant way.

"TV time," they would whisper to each other during the big

broadcasts, reminding each other that March was, after all, the time for living large.

Of course, March Madness also means the TV never turns off, not on weekends, not in hotel lobbies, not in sports bars, not in players' rooms. There are always games, updates, more games, more updates, and the Wolverines spent much of Friday and Saturday watching the action, checking out their friends on other teams, saying, "Told you" and "I knew they'd win." Already, there had been several surprising exits, and most of them, to Michigan's delight, were in their West bracket. The highly ranked Arizona Wildcats once again did a postseason belly flop, losing to No. 15 seed Santa Clara, so U-M would not have to face Arizona. Meanwhile, lightly regarded George Washington surprised New Mexico, and Southern upset Georgia Tech, a Final Four team a few years back. That meant either the GW Colonials or the Southern Jaguars (who?) would be Michigan's third-round opponent, if U-M won its second-round game against UCLA.

"We can't look past anybody!" Fisher warned in Saturday's practice. "One loss and it's all over. You see it happening all around you. Pay attention."

At the press conference in the afternoon, the players were asked, of course, about Walton's "underachiever" label ("He's entitled to his opinions," Jimmy said) and they were asked about whom they'd like to play further on in the tournament. Naturally, the politically correct answer was "Whoever, it doesn't matter." But deep down, the Fab Five wanted one more crack at Duke, the only major team they'd played and hadn't beaten at least once.

So you can understand why, Saturday night, at a Tucson restaurant, when word came to the players' table that Duke was in danger of losing a second-round game to California—"*It's on TV, in the bar, hurry up*"—well, everyone left their plates.

"Whatsa score, whatsa score?" they whispered. Juwan, Jalen, Chris, Rob, James, Ray, Jimmy, and Dugan all slid into the cramped bar area, finding stools, trying to get a closer view of the small set, which hung on the wall. Juwan looked around and realized how much taller they were than the other customers.

"Can you see, ma'am?" he said to a woman at a table.

"Yes, yes, I'm fine," she smiled.

Juwan. Always the gentleman.

They watched as the game ticked away, and Jason Kidd, the phenomenal Cal freshman, made a huge play, scooping up a loose ball and laying it in and drawing a foul that gave Cal a two-point lead. They watched Bobby Hurley try to win it with his trademark jumper—as he had done against them several times—but now he missed, and missed again. And suddenly the announcer yelled, "IT'S OVER, THE DEFENDING CHAMPIONS HAVE BEEN DE-FEATED."

Duke had lost. The cameras caught Hurley walking sadly off the court, his college career over. The Fab Five sat motionless in their chairs; Jalen, who had so many encounters with Hurley, and Jimmy, who had refused to give Hurley credit before their rematch this year, and Chris, who had endured Hurley's ribbing in La Jolla when Magic said, "Show him your rings, Bobby." They watched now, some-where between emptiness and glee. This is the game, they told them-selves. Sometimes you own it, and sometimes it owns you. When the broadcast went to commercial, they exhaled and got up.

They would just have to beat someone else for the champion-ship, that's all.

"The King is dead," Perry Watson said as they walked back to their food.

"Long live the King," Fisher added.

The King—Jimmy Sr.—had a hard time sleeping. He'd been in Tucson for several days, but nerves always got him the night before one of his son's big games. He woke up at 4 A.M the day of the UCLA game and took a walk around the hotel. "I don't know why. I got a funny feeling. First I tried ESPN, but they had a fishing show on. I can watch most anything, but I can't watch fishing."

The Kings, like most of the Fab Five parents, had their lives interrupted by the tournament. They took off work. They answered a million phone calls. They flew to the games—paying their own way, thanks to NCAA rules—and they flew back and, if they were lucky, made arrangements for the next round.

Back home, like the Jacksons and the Webbers, the Kings had become famous in their own right. When Jimmy Sr. arrived to fix someone's phone line in Plano, wearing his Michigan cap, they would get to talking, and soon it would come out that he was indeed

Jimmy King, father of the other Jimmy King and, next thing you know, they're giving him a sweatshirt for Jimmy to sign and mail back.

"I'm worried about the team," Jimmy Sr. was saying now. "I don't like the way they're playing. They let too many teams they should beat back into it."

What does his son say? he was asked.

He sighed. "He says, 'Dad, don't worry, we're gonna win.' "

Steve Fisher liked to break down March Madness into three separate weekends, treating each like its own mini-tournament. The reason: it's easier to achieve a two-game goal than a six-game goal. Last year, he refused to use the name "Final Four" in front of his players. He called it "the Minneapolis Invitational."

This was one way Fisher was a deceptively good coach—and one way his coaching style reflected his personality. *The less fuss you make, the more likely it will work out.* Of course, setting up a game is one thing, and enduring one is another.

The Wolverines' second opponent was UCLA.

Which stood for Utterly Catastrophic Loss, Almost.

"Men, we're in the finals of this little tournament," Fisher said before the tip-off, using his methodology as he addressed the team. "And I want you to remember something out there tonight. The mark of a great team is what they do when things aren't going their way. When you're turning the ball over and starting to lose your concentration—those are the tough times. You have to fight through them.

"We've all had 'em. And you may have some today . . ."

He was right about that.

UCLA was once synonymous with college basketball championships. In the John Wooden era of the 1960s and '70s, the Bruins actually won seven national titles in a row, which, in Wall Street terms, is like picking 1,000 winning stocks without a single loser. It's that incredible.

Back then, the Bruins were the team to beat. But they had fallen on leaner times. Wooden was long gone. The Bruins had several disappointing postseasons. Michigan was the team to beat now. And UCLA—which brought an entire band and complete set of cheerleaders to the Tucson game—licked its chops at the upset role, the chance to be "the school that shuts up Michigan." Certainly Bill Walton, one of UCLA's most famous alumni, projected that hope.

"NUT CHECK!" the Wolverines had yelled in the final huddle before the game. And a nut check was soon needed. The Bruins began by stealing a Ray Jackson pass and going all the way for a layup. Then, like some wild animal drawing first blood, they ripped into Michigan with a sharp-toothed frenzy.

Forward Ed O'Bannon—older brother of Charles O'Bannon, one of Michigan's most-hoped-for recruits—nailed a three-pointer, threw in another, drilled another. He shot with such unwasted motion it seemed the ball was sucked in by a vacuum. O'Bannon alone had 10 points in the first four minutes. And while Michigan was matching UCLA's pace with slams and drives, the look on the Fab Five's faces said, "They can't keep this up, right?"

Wrong. O'Bannon hit again. And again. It didn't matter who was defending him. He made six straight baskets and was perfect on his three-pointers. Bruins fans were going berserk, shaking pompoms, singing with their band. Their team had never played this well—the Chicago Bulls don't play this well—and despite Michigan's excellence, UCLA began to pull away.

During a TV time-out, with Michigan trailing, 31–26, the U-M coaching staff noticed O'Bannon was sitting down for a breather.

"Thank God," they thought. "Nobody can be that hot."

Except the rest of the Bruins. Freshman Kevin Dempsey, a boyish-looking Northern California blond, dropped a bomb from three-point land. That gave UCLA an eight-point lead. He then stole a pass and fed guard Shon Tarver for a slam. Ten-point lead. Dempsey got the ball again in the corner, said "Why not?" and fired. Three-pointer! Thirteen-point lead. Jalen took a weak three-point attempt and missed. Michael Talley—just in the game and too anxious to make his presence felt—clanged a shot off the rim, and here came Tarver, racing downcourt, hanging in the air for an awkward jumper. Good! Fifteen-point lead. It was like watching the Harlem Globetrotters against the cast of *The Wonder Years*. O'Bannon, with 17 points, sat on the bench clapping. They didn't even need him! Talley made a dumb pass across the middle, which Tarver stole and took to the promised land.

Slam!

Seventeen-point lead.

It had taken the Bruins less than three minutes to score 12 unanswered points. Fisher dug his hands in his pockets and called time out, the thundering roar of upset-loving fans in his ears. McKale Center didn't begin as a partisan place for the Bruins, but it was certainly turning into one.

"Let's go, Bruins!"
Bum, bum, bum, bum, bum.
"LET'S GO, BRUINS!"

"Maintain your poise," Fisher told his players. "Let's do what we do best. Let's get the ball inside."

At times like this, Fisher's persona was a blessing. A more volatile coach might not have controlled himself. Down 17 points? In danger of being laughed at all summer? And if the coach loses it, the players usually follow. Which is why Fisher, to the outside eye, looked completely serene.

This, even when UCLA moved to 19 points ahead, 52–33, with just 1:52 left in the half. It was the worst Michigan had been behind any team since last year's championship blowout by Duke. The TV announcers were already tying this into all the other upsets of the tournament. Could it be that the Blue Devils and the Wolverines, last year's finalists, would both be knocked out by California schools, within one day of each other?

"Shit," Ray Jackson said to himself, scowling, as he took his place on the free throw line. "We gotta do something."

And he did. Eric Riley missed the front of a one-and-one—UCLA should have had the ball with a chance to go up by more than 20 before halftime—but Ray leapt over two Bruins, grabbed the rebound, spun, and tossed the ball high and in for two points.

He then made a couple free throws. And UCLA got called for traveling. Eric Riley tipped in a James Voskuil drive at the buzzer, and the 19-point lead—which should have been more—was whittled down to 13. It was the kind of unnoticed thing that turns games around.

Fisher felt as if he'd just won the lottery.

"I need everybody's eyes and ears, right now!" he yelled in the locker room. "Right now! Listen! They have waylaid as hard as they can waylay anyone, and we've been part of the fuckin' problem."

Fisher didn't like to curse, but when he did, it was usually for effectiveness.

"They were seven for eight from three-point range—seven for

eight. But you know what? They're all good shots 'cause we're not getting out and closing . . .

"Fight through the screens. Hell, these guys can't screen you. But you've gotta defend. You gotta defend! You make it too easy for 'em. Seven uncontested three-point shots and 10 layups? Shit, a junior high team can do that."

He watched their eyes. He knew what he was doing. Make the other team's success seem like luck.

Then tell your guys how they can win.

"OK, perimeter people, too much standing around . . . Juwan, you gotta work to get yourself open . . . Chris, I want you doing better in position, too . . .

"But, men, more than anything else, you gotta say 20 minutes is an eternity. I don't want you out running all over the floor going crazy. One possession at a time. Twenty minutes is an eternity!"

Hell, he thought, the first 20 felt like one.

"And fellas," Fisher added, "if ever I want to hear what NUT CHECK means, it's right now."

Chris looked at Jalen and allowed a tiny grin.

Maybe Fish *was* listening.

Here, apparently, is what nut check meant: Chris grabbing an offensive rebound and slamming it down. Lead cut to 11. Juwan tossing a short alley-oop to Chris which he one-handed through the rim. Lead down to nine. Juwan spinning for his own short jumper. Lead down to seven. Chris scoring a free throw and another monster dunk. Four. Jalen steals the ball, leads a fast break. Two.

And finally, with just under eight minutes left, Jalen stands at the top of the key, as if thinking up an idea—"Hey, I bet I can shoot from here"—and he heaves a three-pointer that slurps the net.

Michigan had the lead, 67–66.

Had it ended right there, this would have been a wonderful game, with extraordinary surges by both teams—UCLA shooting 70 percent in the first half, Michigan shooting 73 percent in the second. But as it turned out, all that jousting was just to get to Act II.

Which came in the final seven seconds.

Tyus Edney, the Bruins' small, lightning-bug guard, drew a tripping foul on Ray, made both free throws, and tied the game, 77–77. Michigan had no time-outs left.

Juwan ran under the basket to bring the ball in, Jalen broke to get open, with Shon Tarver all over him, and Juwan led Jalen with a pass, but Jalen's legs got caught up with Tarver's—"He tripped me," Rose would later claim—and they both went crashing to the floor. Edney picked up the loose ball and raced back toward his hoop—six seconds, five seconds. Jalen was on the ground watching, helpless. All Edney had to do was go for the layup past Juwan and win the game—four seconds—but Edney, a point guard used to dishing off at the sight of big men, ducked under Juwan and made a bounce pass to a streaking Ed O'Bannon—three seconds—except that Jimmy King—*Jimmy King? Where did he come from?*—dashed in front and intercepted the pass, squeezed it to his chest, like an infant he'd just pulled out of a river—two seconds, one second—

"Nuh-uh, nuh-uh, nuh-uh," Jimmy gasped, shaking his head, as the buzzer sounded, overtime, and at least the dream was not dead—maybe shocked, but not dead. Edney slapped his hands and grimaced, he should have shot. O'Bannon shook his head and walked to the UCLA bench. Jimmy held the ball for another few seconds, as if making sure there were no defenders hiding behind the basket support. Finally he let it go.

"Oh, my heart!" Jimmy King, Sr., panted up in the stands when his breath came back. "I'm gonna need a new valve, I know it."

"Jimmy saved that play," Mrs. King squealed. "He saved it. Jimmy saved it!"

He said not to worry.

And then came Act III.

The overtime went back and forth, that intense, lead-changing basketball that leaves your armpits wet even when you're watching at home. Ray lays one in. Edney hits a jumper. Webber lays one in. O'Bannon hits two free throws. The TV announcers were hoarse, telling people, "What a game! What a game!"

Finally Michigan called time out with 9.4 seconds left and the score tied again, 84–84.

"Chris, you get it on the inbounds, get it to Jalen, and pick for him," Fisher said. "Jalen, you drive, and if you can't get a shot, get fouled."

Once again, in the critical situations, Fisher was going with the kid he least understood, but whose basketball instincts he trusted the most.

The play worked, right up to the shot part. Jalen drove, stopped, lifted, and fired a leaning banker with 4.5 seconds left. It hit the backboard, then the front rim, came off, and in an almost exact reverse of what happened in Hawaii against North Carolina, Jimmy rose to rebound Jalen's miss, caught it in midflight, and kissed it off the glass for a basket with 1.5 seconds on the clock.

The place came unglued.

"YEEEAAAAH!" Ray yelled, grabbing his Texas buddy and jumping into his arms.

"THAT'S IT!" yelled Juwan, doing jumping jacks.

Jimmy's parents hugged in the stands. The Michigan cheerleaders were crying.

"IT'S OVER! IT'S OVER!" Chris hollered.

But it wasn't over. The referees were huddling at the scorers' table, and they were waving and gesturing madly, and the scorekeepers and timekeepers looked like everything had just switched to Russian. Now what? Jim Harrick, the UCLA coach, was screaming that Jalen's shot didn't beat the 45-second clock, and that the follow-up basket therefore couldn't count, because the ball should turn over to UCLA after the buzzer.

"NO WAY!" screamed Fisher.

The referees pushed him back.

"NO WAY!"

Again they signaled.

"NO WAY!"

No way?

Harrick, meanwhile, was screaming on the other side. "HE DIDN'T HIT THE RIM! IT DIDN'T HIT THE RIM."

The refs pushed him back. It was mass confusion. The crowd was half booing, half cheering. Someone told Fisher they just saw the replay and it was clearly a good shot by King.

"Watch on TV! Watch on TV!" Fisher screamed at the ref. "They got it on tape! They got it on tape!"

The referee said he couldn't look at tape. Harrick, on the other end, was urging the same thing.

"Rose got it off before the buzzer," the ref told him.

"That doesn't make a difference!" Harrick screamed. "It has to hit the rim!"

"Go back to your huddle," the ref said.

"WHAT IF YOU'RE WRONG? YOU GOTTA LIVE WITH IT FOREVER!"

They weren't wrong. Not about Jalen's shot. He clearly beat the buzzer on his release, and as long as the shot eventually hit the rim—which it did—there is no violation. Jimmy's put-back was therefore legal. Basket counted. But the refs did give UCLA the 1.5 seconds, because several players had signaled for a time-out following the score.

So after trailing by 19 points, coming back to take a lead, blowing the lead, surviving what should have been a layup that eliminated them from this tournament, and finally having gotten a miracle put-back from their own personal Emperor of the Air that they all thought won the game—now the Wolverines had to play 1.5 more seconds and pray that nothing else went wrong.

And praying is exactly what Chris Webber did. As he watched David Boyle heave a long pass to O'Bannon, and as he defended O'Bannon while he rose outside the three-point line, and as he jumped with O'Bannon while he released a desperation shot, all that time, as is his custom, Chris was praying.

"No, God, please God, make him miss, God, don't let him make it, God, please God, I'll be good, God . . ."

It hit the glass.

No good.

Michigan wins.

Michigan wins? The greatest comeback of the Fab Five era? The greatest comeback in Michigan tournament history? How many points had they been down? Nineteen? They won?

Chris hugged Ray. Jimmy hugged Jalen. They marched off together, waving at the crowd, having advanced to yet another one of Fisher's mini-tournaments, the Sweet Sixteen, in Seattle. Two wins away now from their destiny in New Orleans.

"I know you doubted us," Jalen cooed into the CBS cameras, "but we're bringing it home, baby."

"We're bringing it home, baby," Jimmy repeated.

And lest you think Jimmy's cockiness was simply something he picked up from his close proximity to the Master Blaster, know this: just after King hit that historic bank shot, and the crowd went bonkers and Fisher felt his heart lift and Ray came running over almost in tears, he was so happy—while all that was happening, Jimmy King raced over to the scorers' table and found student manager Gabe Brown, who keeps the stats.

"That's a rebound, too," King said, pointing. "Don't forget."

2

A two-hour plane trip from Ann Arbor and a twenty-minute rent-a-car drive down I-284 brings you to the Sugar Creek Golf and Tennis Center in suburban Atlanta. You can leave after breakfast and be there before lunch. The weather on this particular day was stunning, warm with spring, a light breeze bringing the smell of pine needles. When the breeze died, you could hear the *thwock* of tennis balls from the courts on the hill.

Shortly after two in the afternoon, a beige Mitsubishi Diamante rolled down the long entrance road. It pulled carefully into a parking spot, and the driver's door opened. A tall mustached man in a white tennis outfit stepped out and came around the front of the vehicle, past the license plate that had, as its first two letters, "JW."

Jimmy Walker.

Jalen's father.

He walked with the same pigeon-toed gait as his son and had the same lifted tilt of his head. He carried tennis rackets over one shoulder and a large gym bag over the other, a high-collared white T-shirt peering out from his designer sweat suit, which was zipped to just below the sternum, the collar folded down neatly. He looked younger than his 45 years, with few lines on his face, and a full head of hair, cropped short, the hairline low on his forehead, same as Jalen. He had Jalen's mouth and Jalen's slow, deliberate way of looking at you. Sunglasses rested on the bridge of his nose. He carried a cellular phone.

He seemed cautious, and suggested a picnic table up near the clubhouse as a place to sit. "I play here regularly," he mentioned. When informed that finding him was extremely difficult, that most people who used to know him or played in the NBA with him had, over the years, lost complete track of him, so much so that they now called him "a mystery," he grinned and said, "I'm no mystery."

Jimmy Walker, once the No. 1 pick in the NBA draft, had indeed disappeared from the stage after his pro career ended, rather ingloriously, when he was released by the Kansas City Kings in the late '70s. He floated around. He opened a nightclub called JW's in Kansas City, with former teammate Sam Lacey. It failed and quickly closed. There were reports of him in Virginia and even back in Boston. The IRS had repossessed his auto for back taxes.

And then nothing. He seemed to drop out. Phones were disconnected. Addresses were no longer valid. Friends like Dave Bing, who used to room with him on the road with the Pistons, tried to get in touch with him, but had no idea where he was. Bing did get a Christmas card every year that was signed "Jimmy Walker," but it never had a return address. That, he believed, was intentional.

"I've done this and that," Walker said now, when asked about the last dozen years. "I've got some investments in real estate, like the house I'm living in. I spend time with my mother, she's in a nursing home now."

But what happened since 1978?

"Nothing happened. I'm doing fine now, so it had to turn out all right, right?"

Did you work?

"Well . . ." He grinned. "How do you determine what work is?"

He definitely shared Jalen's gene pool.

Of course, as far as Jalen was concerned, Jimmy Walker never disappeared, because he was never in the picture. They had never met. Never spoken. Walker bolted when Jeanne Rose got pregnant, same as he bolted on a number of other women in his life when the children came: no personal involvement, no financial involvement. Only 15 years later did he hear, through the grapevine, that the son he'd left behind in Detroit was turning into a pretty good basketball player. Soon he started seeing Jalen Rose on television, with the Michigan Wolverines. Walker watched with interest. He followed the games, he studied the boy's moves and saw many of his own instincts. People who knew Walker in Atlanta remarked, "If he's your son, he's got it all backwards. The father is supposed to be the one who's bald. The son is supposed to have the hair."

One time, Walker said, he thought he passed Jalen in an airport. There was a group of tall young men, carrying bags, moving through the terminal the way sports teams do, and Walker saw a face, the eyes, the expression, that he was almost sure was his child.

He said nothing.

What would he say anyhow?

"I'm sure Jalen is apprehensive about meeting me," Walker said. "And I understand that. I consider myself to be a pretty well-balanced person, but during the time that Jalen was born, I really do think that 'acting silly' was putting it mildly.

"I didn't handle the situation well. I think, when Jeanne told me she was pregnant, being the immature person I was, I said, 'Stop kidding.' Or 'No, you're not.' You know, I was married at the time I met Jeanne, and my former wife is putting me under all this pressure . . .

"I remember Jeanne being angry . . . We didn't communicate right, and now Jalen has gone 20 years without meeting his father . . .

"For all Jalen knows, I could be an asshole."

That, it was safe to say, had been assumed more than once.

But as Walker removed his sunglasses, leaned forward, and talked about his own life, it was obvious that, for better or worse, father and son shared more than genetics. Walker was also raised without a father, in the decaying Roxbury section of Boston. His mother worked five days a week in a laundry. Had he not met Sam Jones of the Boston Celtics—the way Jalen met Sam Washington of St. Cecilia's—he might never have escaped the city. Jones took a liking to the then-teenage Walker and helped get him enrolled in an academy in North Carolina, where high school would be safer and more controlled. Walker wasn't sure he wanted to go. Then one night, while walking with his best friend, Bill Wooten, making plans to get Chinese food, they bumped into two men coming out of a liquor store. The men were half-drunk and yelled at the kids to get out of their way. They moved on. Jimmy and Billy thought no more about it. They flipped a coin to see who would go get the Chinese food and who got to go home and change clothes.

Billy lost.

As Jimmy walked up Maywood Street back to his apartment, he heard a gunshot. He ran back down and found Billy lying in the street with a hole in his chest.

"I'm cold, man, I'm cold," Billy kept saying.

He died in Walker's arms.

Three weeks later, Jimmy went to North Carolina.

By the time he reached college, at Providence, he was as talented and as cocky as, well, as another freshman would be 20 years later. Freshmen weren't allowed to play with the varsity back then, so Walker led the Providence freshmen to an undefeated season. When the team was 16-0, Walker and the others presented their coach, Dave

Gavitt, with an inscribed watch. It said, *"From your undefeated 21-0 freshmen."*

They hadn't even played the last five games.

"Don't worry," Walker had said. "We'll win 'em."

So the confidence—and even the trash talking—that Jalen practiced today was prefaced by his biological father. "Next time!" Walker used to yell when someone tried to block his shot, and "That's two right there!" when it swished. Walker made the NBA All-Star team three times and was once paired with Jerry West in the backcourt when West won the MVP award. Jimmy finished second in the voting. "Jerry," Walker said as they came off, "don't you think I should have shot more?"

He drummed his fingers now on the picnic table. A breeze blew. Jimmy had made a lot of money and had broken a lot of hearts, and he claimed he was doing fine, but several times during the conversation, he suggested that maybe he should be getting paid for talking.

"You know . . . maybe some form of . . . compensation? You know what I'm saying? Like, how much is this conversation worth to you?"

Then he shifted subjects, talked about philosophy, laughed, talked about "being real," laughed some more.

He talked about meeting his son, maybe even making a trip to see him during the tournament.

"I don't want to create the impression that I'm getting ready to contact him now because he's following in my shoes, you know, he's getting ready to be a millionaire, and now I wanna be seen with him. It's not like that. But it's time, probably, for us to talk . . .

"If I had it to do over again, I would have stayed in touch. I would have found out what I could do as a person, you know, like, if you need me, I'm here, I'm a telephone call away."

He fingered the portable cellular phone, which had stayed in its case the entire conversation. The sounds of tennis balls were diminishing as the afternoon lost its heat.

"You know what's gonna happen when Jalen and I first see each other?" Jimmy Walker said. "I'm gonna tell you. I already pictured it in my mind. He's gonna be walking toward me, I'm gonna be walking toward him. We're not gonna really know whether to say hello, shake hands—and we're gonna end up hugging. I guarantee it."

He said he had a match to play, that he played a lot of tennis now, he was quite good, a top-level amateur in his age group, and that a psychiatrist once told him he hit tennis balls to release his aggression. For whatever reason, it seemed to work. As he got up to go, he was asked about his own father, whatever happened to him.

"I think," he said, "he got burned in a fire."

Where?

"I don't know. Somewhere in Virginia."

How old were you?

"A sophomore in college."

Same as Jalen?

"Yeah."

Do you remember feeling anything when you heard the news?

"I felt that a person just died, that's all. Just a person."

He walked toward the courts, then stopped, took a pen, and wrote something on a piece of paper.

"You know," he said, "I don't have any regrets or apologies about Jalen. That's just the way things happen sometimes."

He handed over the paper.

"You can give him my number. Tell him to call me, if he wants."

3

REPORTER: *Are you the first team to wear long shorts?*
JALEN: *No, we're the first team to get criticized for it.*

In a perfect world, this is how sports journalism would work: The editor would assign a story about a team. The reporter would have at least two weeks. He or she would spend an hour with all the principal characters. And watch at least three different games. And explore the perception of the team. And be prepared to refute it— even if it meant the story was less interesting.

Yeah.

And if elephants had wings . . .

Very few, if any, newspapers—or television stations or radio stations, for that matter—have the time, budget, or desire to do things this way. Editors often assign pieces with a preconceived notion. "Get us a story on the way they trash-talk . . ." "Get us a story on their arrogance . . ." Reporters, with limited time and budgets, often settle for telling an already told tale in their own words. They use previous articles as research. They ask questions that have been asked a million times before. Not surprisingly, in the brief five minutes they get with an athlete, they hear the same tired answers.

Before you know it, a "national image" is spread, based on the weight of all these slapdash reports that seem to conclude the same thing.

What was that old Elvis Presley album—*50,000,000 Elvis Fans Can't Be Wrong*?

How about 20,000,000 Fab Five critics?

This is what it felt like by the second week of the 1993 tournament. The stories about the Super Sophomores were now in cookie-cutter production. *"They're brash! They're bored! They're boorish!"* Bill Walton's remark—"They're one of the most overrated and underachieving teams of all time"—got more attention than any sports quote since Reggie Jackson's "I'm the straw that stirs the drink." The funny thing was, who was Walton to make that criticism? Nobody had paid much attention to anything he'd said before. He had only recently begun a career in sports broadcasting—after being a notoriously difficult interview himself in the NBA.

Besides, Walton, when he played for UCLA, was not even allowed to play varsity when he was a freshman. So how would he know how difficult that was?

But his words struck some kind of chord, maybe because a lot of people who saw Michigan's big shorts, bald heads, alley-oops, and on-court celebrations—and this includes white fans who saw five black ghetto kids doing their street thing—wanted to believe what Walton suggested. Yeah. They underachieve. Yeah. They're overrated. Never mind the Rainbow Classic, or their 28-4 record.

Last year at this time, the Fab Five were the most cherished story in the tournament. *"Who Are These Crazy Kids?"*

This year, it was *"Who Are These Bored Big Shots—And Will They Ever Achieve Their Potential?"*

As Rodney Dangerfield would say, tough crowd, boy, tough crowd.

And yet, they continued to do things to inspire this criticism. They didn't stop showboating. They didn't stop taunting. They didn't stop coming out for introductions as if coming out for a concert.

"You know, when I first started being interviewed a lot, I thought it was cool," Jimmy King said the day before the team departed for Seattle. "They would open the locker room doors, and all those guys would come running in, like in the movies, when a murder happens.

"But now, well, you know, I'm just as happy if no one shows up. I almost don't want to say anything, 'cause I know I'm gonna be disappointed when the story comes out. It's like they know what they want to say before they even ask you."

This pigeonholing, by the way, was happening all over March Madness. Most of the Sweet Sixteen teams were labeled something (although usually something more complimentary than "under-achievers"). Kentucky, for example—which was blowing out everyone it played—was Rick Pitino and the "Bluegrass Resurgence," a once-crippled program now back to glory. California-Berkeley was "the New Bohemians" with a 29-year-old coach, Todd Bozeman, and a freshman point guard, named Jason Kidd. Indiana was the continuing saga of Bobby Knight, who seemed to be getting weirder with age. North Carolina was Dean Smith's quest for his first ring since the Michael Jordan jump shot.

And George Washington? The team that Michigan would play on Friday night?

They were the last miracle story, the lowest surviving seed, the team nobody expected. They were Cinderella.

Which made the Wolverines the Wicked Witch.

"Hey, Vonnie," Perry Watson had said to Avondre Jones when he called him in L.A. after the UCLA game. "Did you see that win?"

"Yeah. That was good," Jones said.

Coaches never missed a chance to call a recruit after a big victory—especially if they had just beaten a school that was familiar to the kid, or may even have been recruiting him. Avondre Jones, Perry kept saying, was on the verge of picking Michigan. Avondre kept telling Watson, "You're my school."

But USC was in the picture—just as UCLA was leaning hard on Charles O'Bannon, Ed's brother—and faraway coaches always worried about local schools, because the kids can come visit anytime, and there's so much area influence to suggest the kid commit. It had worked for Michigan with Webber and Rose.

"Vonnie, if you come to Michigan, you'll get a chance to play in the Final Four, just like we're gonna do this year," Perry said.

"Yeah. I want you guys to win."

"We're gonna do it."

"I'm rooting for you."

"We really want you to come to Michigan."

"I'm thinking about it."

"Good," Perry said. "So how's your rapping?"

Even in the middle of the tournament, you can't stop worrying about next year.

Steve Fisher stepped off the bus into the cool Northwest air. The last time he was in Seattle, he was cutting down the nets. Rumeal Robinson had hit the free throws, Seton Hall had missed the last shot, and Fisher, the undefeated coach of the new national champions, was telling Brent Musburger, "I'm the happiest man alive."

He was still trying to get back to that nirvana. Maybe this year, he thought. Some things about Fisher had barely changed since that 1989 title: his deliberate way of talking, his slow rise to anger, his blank expressions when his players acted up.

But other things had changed dramatically. Instead of being an overlooked genius of basketball talent, Fisher was now seen as an ineffectual guardian of impolite youth. *Who's coaching those smart-ass players? Why doesn't he do something with all that talent?*

Compared to Tucson, everything was stepped-up in Seattle. The press conferences were much larger. Practices at the cavernous Kingdome, with its massive Teflon roof and football-sized rafters, were spacy, oversized affairs. Nearly 10,000 fans showed up for the dunkathon Thursday afternoon. Michigan put on a show, but less enthusiastically than it had done last year in Lexington. The routine was old now.

Meanwhile, their hotel lobby was crawling with people, and not just fans. You could see vans parked around the corner, where opportunistic collectors unloaded dozens of basketballs, posters, and trading cards to innocent-looking children, paying them $5 to get Webber or Rose or Howard to sign as many as they could. The distributors would then re-collect the merchandise and sell it at assorted card shows.

"Can you believe that shit?" Webber said. "I mean, I know what's going on. How come a kid needs 14 cards? There's only one of him."

As this type of thing increased, the team drew inward and tended to relax only around each other. They felt most of the outside world was against them, anyhow, and they prepared for criticism every time they picked up a newspaper or saw a reporter coming. The youthful joy they had taken into last year's tournament was replaced by a burden of expectations. And rip-off artists in the lobby.

In the interest of team spirit, Fisher scheduled a team meal the night before the George Washington game. The Metropolitan Grill is one of Seattle's finer restaurants, and most of the players even donned dress shirts with a white Michigan sweater over top.

"God," Jason Bossard marveled, "I feel like I'm on Indiana or something."

The restaurant arranged a TV set near their table. Naturally, it was tuned to the games. Jalen pulled a chair up close.

Ray looked for a minute, then leaned back in and shook his head. "I hate watching basketball," he said.

"I get nervous when the games are tight. It makes me too anxious to play myself."

Juwan nodded. "I hear ya. I just wanna get out there."

"You get nervous, too?" Ray said.

"Hell, yeah."

"On the court, too?"

"Naw, once I'm on the court I'm cool."

"Yeah."

"Except the other night, against UCLA, I was nervous as a mother!"

"Aw, man! My heart was in my foot!"

"Yo, I was the one who had to make that inbounds pass. That would have been on my conscience forever, man."

They looked at their teammates, some of whom were nodding along.

"Chris, you get nervous, man?"

"Hell, yeah."

"Jimmy?"

"Sometimes."

"Man," Ray said again, slapping the table, "I'm nervous all the time. I'm nervous right now."

★ ★ ★

On paper, it was George Washington who should have been nervous. The Colonials were in uncharted waters—never in school history had the basketball team gone this far—and many of the players were still learning about American basketball pressure. GW's roster sounded like a United Nations roll call—Omo Moses, Sonni Holland, Adamah Kah, Kwame Evans—and it featured several overseas players, most notably starting center Yinka Dare, a giant freshman from Nigeria who once threw up six consecutive air balls on free throws. When you're 7 foot 1, 265 pounds, they keep giving you chances.

Michigan was favored by 13.

When they got to the Kingdome, the players dressed routinely, the Fab Five pulling on their black socks and black shoes, Chris and Jalen rubbing their shaved heads. They tried to get psyched for something that didn't feel as big as game three of the tournament should feel.

"I wouldn't say this if I didn't mean it," Fisher told his team in the locker room, "but as I watched those guys out there, I said to Perry, they're scared. George Washington is *scared* right now. They've never been here before. Get into 'em with your defense early—effort! Defensive effort! That's what I want, right from the start."

The start was not the problem. Michigan ran off 15 points before George Washington even realized the game had begun. The Colonials did look scared—Fisher was right—and they missed their first 10 shots. Billy Packer and Jim Nantz, the CBS broadcasters—who, you remember, were there for the Fab Five's first Michigan-Duke game, and last year's championship—told a nationwide audience that a blowout was likely, with the score 15–2.

"I think it's over already," Packer said.

Dare, the Nigerian newcomer, was wasted. Webber overwhelmed him, stole the ball, bumped him around. Dare took a seat on the GW bench with the sweaty, dazed look of a prizefighter who just took a blow to the head. Michigan was breezing to the quarter finals of March Madness.

And then something happened. It began, curiously enough, with a Wolverines basket seven minutes into the game, when Jimmy King caught a beautiful alley-oop from Jalen and slammed it with authority. He then slid into the face of GW's Sonni Holland with a primal scream that provided Holland a long view of any dental work Jimmy might have had done recently.

"YAAAAAAAAHHHHHHHHHH!"

Jimmy laughed, flashed a huge gap-toothed sneer, and turned upcourt. Had the game been broadcast only on radio, the announcer might have said, "King slams . . . tells Holland about it . . . ball upcourt now . . ."

Instead, TV cameras captured the whole thing, and when it was replayed, in slow motion, to a national TV audience, Nantz lowered his voice to a schoolteacher-lecture volume and said:

"This is the problem a lot of people have with the Wolverines."

The picture, 100 percent pure trash talk, spoke for itself.

"This is the problem a lot of people have with the Wolverines."

This is the problem a lot of people have with the Wolverines.

More than anything from the broadcast, more than any basket or rebound or jump shot, that sentence, in Nantz' deep, mature, I-hate-to-have-to-say-it-but-we-all-know-it's-true voice, stayed with the viewers, which meant the nation.

And from that point on, Michigan could only sink.

GW cut the lead, then cut it some more. Michigan was playing the way it had against teams early in the season, letting GW back in it, making mistakes, turnovers, lazy passes. Suddenly the GW players were running to the tunnel at halftime smiling and slapping hands. They trailed by only two points, 35–33.

And everyone in the place was rooting for them.

"They've got 35 shots, we've got 21!" Fisher yelled in the locker room. "They got 14 more frigging shots than we do because they've gotten 12 offensive rebounds to our three! They've got 12 offensive rebounds to our three! You guys gotta go to work!"

Fisher peppered his normal calm with angry jabs. But his words did not help. The Wolverines were in a funk, they couldn't shake it. The Colonials were playing a quick-tempo, pressing game, without Yinka Dare in there, and they were crashing the boards and getting second shots. Michigan, meanwhile, was turning the ball over on inbounds passes!

Finally, when Sonni Holland—the guy Jimmy embarrassed—spun between Chris, Ray, and Michael Talley for an awkward layup, the George Washington Colonials, who had taken an ad out in the

Seattle newspapers asking for area alumni to come and show support, were now leading the most famous college basketball team on the planet, with just over 10 minutes left in the game.

"What the fuck is going on? . . . Come on . . . let's do this!" Chris exhorted during huddles at the free throw line. At one point he banged his fists on Jimmy's and Jalen's shoulders and buried his head in Jalen's pectorals. But the Wolverines suffered right to the end—as if being punished for their arrogance. They led by just two points with 90 seconds remaining when they found the only way that fate was going to let them have this game.

At the free throw line.

Rebounding misses.

Chris banged the second of two free throws off the back rim, but Ray eyeballed it the whole way, and chased it down for possession and a fresh shot clock. He was quickly fouled and went to the line, where he, too, clanked the second shot off the rim. But his roommate, Jimmy King, came from the far side of the lane, snuck past three Colonials on the baseline, and grabbed the ball as it came down. Another new shot clock. The Colonials fouled again, Ray made both shots, and the air finally went out of GW's upset dream.

When the buzzer sounded—final score Michigan 72, GW 64— Jimmy and Ray hugged and the bench cheered but it was an empty celebration. Chris walked over to the Colonials, shook their hands, and walked off with little emotion. He put the best spin on the evening as he passed the press table, rolled his eyes, and shrugged.

"At least no one can say we've peaked."

Last season, the press conference between games of the regional finals was where Michigan wooed the nation's media, their coming-out party, where they went down the line when asked if they expected to win four national championships in their time at Michigan and said, "Yes . . . yes . . . yes . . . yes . . . of course."

Well. H. L. Mencken—a journalist, of all people—said the only thing you need to go from being applauded to being hissed is to live long enough.

Freshman to sophomore years, in some cases.

"How do you guys explain your poor performance last night?" came the first question in this year's version of the Big Press Conference.

Chris, who barely slept after the win, he was so upset, let his frustration out. "You guys act like you have all the answers. You act like we *tried* not to play like Michigan. Arizona played bad and didn't advance. Seton Hall played bad and didn't advance. We played bad and we advanced.

"I know we looked like a bunch of junior high kids last night. But it's no big panic. I can guarantee we won't play that badly again. I just wish everyone didn't assume like we're trying to look bad out there, like we don't care or something. People who say that don't know what they're talking about."

So much for the sweetheart relationship with the media. Michigan's opponent in the regional final would be Temple. And John Chaney, the Temple coach, was filling reporters' notebooks with his homespun philosophy. The fickle press was now enchanted with the Temple Owls, not the Michigan Wolverines. About the only moment comparable to last year was when a TV reporter asked the Fab Five to go down the line and answer the following: Would they be back at Michigan next year?

Chris: "I'm not even thinking about that now."

Jalen: "I'll be back."

Juwan: "Me, too."

Jimmy: "Yup."

Ray: "Me? . . . You *know* I'm stuck here."

With the team meal having proven no inspiration, Fisher let the team out on its own Saturday night. Someone arranged for tickets to the Seattle Supersonics–Indiana Pacers game, and most of the players decided to go.

"It'll do them good to get away from the college hoopla for a few hours," Dave Ralston, the trainer, said. Ralston was the designated adult chaperone. Fisher went to a prearranged dinner. His assistants worked on film of the Owls. The players seemed to enjoy the freedom, and the enthusiasm slowly returned to their bodies and their smiles. When they got to the Seattle Center Coliseum, a staff member took them up to a private auxiliary press box, way, way up in the rafters, so that the players looked like toy army men, and the crowd noise was all beneath them, muffled and distant.

Jalen, James, Rob, Dugan, Leon, and Juwan traded comments about the players and chowed on pizza and Cokes as they imagined themselves one day out on that floor. Chris watched the action most intently. He saw Shawn Kemp, Seattle's dominant power forward, slide inside the man-to-man coverage for several monster dunks. He saw Indiana's Detlef Schrempf do the same.

"Man, you know what I could be doing out there with those defenses?" Chris said. "The NBA is a players' game. That's what I like. College is a coaches' game.

"All these zone coverages and double-teams in college? I wouldn't have to put up with that in the NBA. Just my talent against someone else's."

It sounded, someone observed, like he was making a decision to go pro.

"Nah," he sighed, and leaned over the railing. "It just gets frustrating sometimes, you know? All this crap we have to deal with."

He saw Kemp slam just before a time-out, then heard the funk music over the loudspeakers and watched an ad for a soft drink flash across the scoreboard.

"If it feels like a job, you oughta get paid for it, right?" he said.

4

For Juwan Howard, it was a guy named Vic. He used to dread seeing him pounding the basketball on the asphalt of their Chicago playground. The projects where Juwan lived were divided in sections, first, second, and third—having something to do, Juwan thought, with income—and the third was the poorest, with the toughest kids. Vic was from the third.

He clobbered Juwan when they played. Knocked him down, cursed at him, talked junk. Through his punishment, day after day, Juwan learned how to play tough.

Chris got a similar education from Luwan Bell. The coach they both worked with as kids told Luwan to take it to Chris, toughen him up. "He's too soft," the coach whispered. So Luwan had permission to go wild, and he did. Chris would hit the deck, get up, hit the deck again. "You weak," Luwan would taunt. "Shut up," Chris would answer.

Pow!

Down he went.

Jalen, of course, played so much basketball he'd seen it all, felt it all, come home with the scratches and the bloody T-shirts and even landed in the hospital one time in high school when Southwestern played archrival Cooley, and he got clotheslined and came down on his head and was unconscious and the doctors ran a brain scan.

So physical play was nothing new, not to the Fab Five. Which was fortunate on Sunday afternoon when they played Temple in the Seattle Kingdome, the last game of the tournament regionals. North Carolina, Kansas, and Kentucky had all already earned a spot in the Final Four, playing excellent basketball. Now all eyes were on the West. It was like a prizefight. One survives. One dies.

Michigan-Temple would be about muscle.

Fisher had suspected the Owls might get physical. And 10 minutes into the first half, Chris drove the lane, switched to his left hand, laid the ball up, and was smacked across the face by Temple's huge freshman center, William Cunningham. Bam! Chris fell to the floor. And no foul was called! Three referees, no whistle. It was as blatant an infraction as you would ever see.

"HOW CAN YOU NOT CALL THAT?" Fisher yelled. "COME ON! HE CLOBBERED HIM!"

Chris got up, shook it off. A few minutes later, he head-faked and went up again, only to encounter both of Cunningham's arms now, across his head and neck, yanking him to the floor as if pulling him off a ladder. This time the refs called a foul—not on Cunningham, but on Temple guard Vic Carstarphen—and Fisher was livid.

"THAT WAS INTENTIONAL! C'MON! INTENTIONAL FOUL! THAT SHOULD BE TWO SHOTS!"

Chaney, the droopy-faced, saggy-jowled Temple coach, who was encouraging exactly this type of aggression from his players, jumped up and screamed at Fisher.

"SIT YOUR ASS DOWN!" Chaney screamed.

"INTENTIONAL FOUL!" Fisher yelled.

"SIT DOWN AND SHUT UP, YOU PUSSY!"

"INTENTIONAL! THEY'RE HITTING THEM ON PURPOSE!"

The coaches were doing more trash talking than the players.

This was the way it went all afternoon. Temple was playing the thug—particularly the young center, Cunningham, a 6-foot-11 brick wall with sleepy eyes and no points in the tournament. He was out there to foul, a designated goon, but he was only following orders. The day before, in a press conference, Chaney had challenged Cunningham in front of the national media.

"William, are you going to attack Chris Webber?" Chaney asked.

Cunningham laughed, embarrassed.

"Answer," Chaney instructed.

"Yes," Cunningham said sheepishly.

Chaney raised his hands and smiled. "We win."

This, from a man who spouts more philosophy about fair play and character than the next 20 coaches in line. It's funny. You get 'em within a win of the Final Four and suddenly they all follow the same playbook: whatever it takes.

And Chaney, with less talent than Michigan, figured it would take physical domination.

"GET HIM!!" he yelled whenever Webber or Howard came driving the lane. "PUT HIM ON HIS ASS!"

And his players—who already followed Chaney through a disciplined regimen that included 6 A.M. practices—listened to what he said.

With 3:15 left in the half, Jalen drove the lane and Cunningham again put a thick arm across his neck. Down went Jalen. Perry Watson leapt to his feet, having gone through this with Jalen in high school. Fisher was screaming. The TV announcers—the same crew who admonished Jimmy King for yelling in a player's face on Friday night—marveled at the brutality.

"Boy, Cunningham lets you know that's his territory when you go through there," said Billy Packer.

"No such thing as a ticky-tack foul with Cunningham, is there?" said Jim Nantz.

Had they chosen to criticize Temple for deliberate thuggery, the audience would have followed their suggestion, and perhaps even felt a tug of sympathy for the usually unsympathetic Fab Five. But, power of the media being what it is, the physical play was portrayed as necessary, and Michigan went into halftime with no sympathy and an eight-point deficit, 35–27.

Fisher was incensed. His face was red. His shirt was sweaty. He felt cheated, as if Temple were being allowed to get away with murder. But he had also coached long enough to know self-pity gets

you nowhere. If this was Chaney's approach, and the refs were going
to allow it, his players would have to get tougher, or say good night.

So Fisher did something he'd rarely done since the Fab Five had
arrived.

He yelled at Chris Webber.

"What's the matter with you?" he screamed. "You're playing
like you're in *high school*! You men have to go to war and, Chris, it
starts with you! Look at the fucking baskets they've scored, Chris!
Derrick Battie has got four baskets and every fuckin' one of 'em is
because you're standing around. You gotta get down and get your
ass out there and play. You gotta play passionately and uninhibited.
You let me do the complaining and crying. You guys get in there
and hold your ground and get the ball! Play with some heart! The
ball goes up—go get it! . . .

"Men, they outfought you for 20 minutes, and it's disgraceful
for us to let that happen. You go back out there, and you go to war
with this team!"

It was an unusual speech for Fisher—and you wonder why he
didn't give it more often, like when his kids acted like spoiled brats.
But basketball was always where Fisher first put his energy, and
everyone in the room felt the same about the next 20 minutes. They
had come all this way since last year's Duke finale, all the spotlight,
the pressure, the tough losses to Indiana, the off-the-court controver-
sies, the Bill Waltons, the "villains of the tournament" tag, and now
here they were, one 20-minute half away from the Final Four. And
someone was trying to beat them up and take it away?

"You hear the way Chaney dogged Fish, man?" Juwan whispered to his teammates as they headed down the tunnel.

"Yeah," Chris said. "We can't let 'em dis Fish like that."

"Their coach is crying," Jimmy said. "He's weak."

"I can't believe it. I used to respect that guy," Juwan said.

"We're gonna take this thing," Ray said.

"One, two, three . . . NUT CHECK!"

And when the second half began, it was Vic and Luwan and
Cooley High all over again for the starting sophomores. They got
physical. They joined the war. They pounded inside, on rebounds
and on defense. Chris went up with Cunningham for a rebound and
wrestled it away. Juwan pushed between three Temple defenders for

a short, hard bank shot. Ray made a scoop layup with a Temple defender all over him and drew the foul, then punched the air and hollered, "Whassup! Whassup!" The eight-point deficit was cut to six, to four, to two, and finally, Chris stole a rebound right out of Cunningham's hands and, while the big kid was looking around for the missing basketball, Chris jumped and laid it off the glass.

The game was tied, 41–41.

"THAT'S WHAT I WANT!" Fisher yelled. "KEEP IT UP!"

Cunningham, like many of the Temple players, seemed to gradually lose his spirit. The refs whistled him for two fouls on Chris in 12 seconds. A few minutes later, with more than nine minutes to go, he fouled Ray, and the scorekeeper yelled, "THAT'S HIS FIFTH." Cunningham lumbered to the Temple bench, having scored no points, taken no shots, and committed five fouls—more if you count the ones that didn't get called. The Michigan student section did its traditional "aaaaaaaaaaAAAAAAAAAAHHHHHHHHH"—until he sat down, then screamed, "SEE YA!"

And from that point, the Fab Five seemed lighter, back to form. The rainbow was in sight, and they picked up their energy to reach it. Jalen stripped the ball from Eddie Jones, raced downcourt, with Jimmy on his right, and pushed it into the air with two hands as if tossing a volleyball over a net. Jimmy caught it midflight and slammed it down.

"OH, THEY LOOK LIKE THEY'RE HAVING FUN NOW!" Packer told the nation.

"THAT'S THE MICHIGAN OF LAST YEAR!" Nantz added.

With less than three minutes to go, it was 66–58, and Temple was history. All that remained was for Chaney to blow his stack, which he did, drawing a technical foul—for profanity—and then verifying it with a few "bullshit," "fuckin' shit," and "son of a bitch" remarks while shielded by his assistant coaches. Chaney would later refuse to shake Steve Fisher's hand and would blast Michigan in the postgame press conference for, of all things, taunting—which is astounding from a coach who yelled "GET HIM" much of the afternoon.

No matter. One year before, the Fab Five had beaten Temple to gain their first-ever tournament win. And now they were beating Temple for their second straight Final Four entry. It had been a dramatic, remarkable, at times poorly and at times brilliantly played series of games. And the sophomores had been responsible for almost all of it.

In their three tough tournament matchups—UCLA, George Washington, and Temple—the Fab Five played all but 76 of the 625 available minutes, and scored all but 18 of the 235 points.

Yet when the buzzer sounded in the Kingdome, and the Michigan band launched into the millionth rendition of "The Victors," the whole team leapt into this huge heap of bodies—Webber, Rose, King, Jackson, Howard, Voskuil, Pelinka, Talley, Fife, Riley, Bossard, Derricks, Dobbins—and they sang "HEYYYYY . . . HOOOOOOO . . . HEYYYY" as they swayed with their arms together. The ladders were brought out, and they climbed to the rims and cut down the nets. Fisher found Angie and his kids and hugged them, as he had done on this floor four years ago. Jalen found his mother in the stands and draped his piece of net cord over her neck. Chris put his cord under his cap, which read, "Michigan— Final Four 1993," and did a dance like you would do in front of your mirror when no one is looking.

"I said yesterday I felt like a 20-year veteran," he said, "but now I feel like I'm 20 again! It's like, I'm 20! I'm 20! I'm 20!"

They were going to New Orleans.

For the end of their story.

IX

SHOWDOWN ON THE BAYOU

1

Jalen took the news that his father was alive and offering his phone number with typical suspicion.

"Where'd you see him?" he wanted to know.

"What city does he live in?"

"Is he coming to the tournament?"

If there was excitement, he hid it; if there was fear, he hid that, too. Jalen had the unblinking poker face of a million pickup games, where you first measure your opponent with your eyes. His father, all these years, was just an image on a wall in a Detroit gym, dribbling to the sound of a silent movie projector.

Now he wants to get in touch?

"I can't get him no tickets," Jalen warned.

When told he didn't want any, Jalen said, "Oh."

So, did he want to talk to him?

"If he comes around, I'll see him."

What would he say?

"I dunno."

Would he want to hit him?

"Nah. I might ask him where he's been all these years."

But he wouldn't be angry?

"I dunno. He's still my father, right?"

How about the telephone?

"Lemme think about it."

He walked away, and joined the rest of the team as it headed for the airport.

He didn't take the number.

2

New Orleans, some say, is the perfect city for national sports championships. Football types strongly suggest the Super Bowl be held there every year. And if the Final Four must be played in a stadium, the Superdome is a popular choice. Not only is it centrally located, but the city around it is perpetually ready for a party, warm enough, musical enough, and big enough to absorb not only players, celebrities, media, and fans but all the flotsam and jetsam that follows huge sporting events in this country. The party simply flows into the steady stream of human traffic on Bourbon Street and is swallowed by the night.

The Michigan players, who felt they missed a lot of last season's Final Four being stuck out in Bloomington, found accommodations more pleasing in New Orleans. They stayed at the copious Hilton Riverside, on the banks of the Mississippi, where lighted boats could be seen floating by at night. Even better, the hotel was attached to River Walk, an elongated plaza of shops and restaurants and docks— "Aw right! A mall!" the players yelled—and upon arriving, Wednesday night, they wasted no time checking out the scene. Fisher let them eat on their own, and they scouted the endless arcade offerings of Cajun food, pralines, beignets. They passed all of that, however, and kept going until they reached the food court, the fast-food places you find at any American shopping mall. Here they sat and ate pizza and hamburgers. In New Orleans. And they were happy.

Chris, as usual, was the star among stars. Mobs followed him. People called his name from across the street. New Orleans was, this weekend, college hoop heaven, and Webber was likely the most famous face in the city (next to Dick Vitale, of course, whose duties here included hosting the broadcast of an ESPN slam-dunk contest and judging the annual "Dick Vitale Sound Alike Competition" at a local sports bar).

Meanwhile, for the first time since the Duke championship last year, Michigan was a decided underdog, between five and seven points depending on where you looked. The Kentucky Wildcats were eating up the college basketball world: nobody challenged them, nobody even stayed with them. They had beaten their four tournament opponents by an average margin of 31 points, while Michigan was struggling to get past UCLA, George Washington, and Temple, none of which was higher than a No. 7 seed. Critics looking for ways the Fab Five could lose didn't have to rely on them blowing the game anymore; they now had an opponent who, some were saying, could blast Michigan out of the water.

So the Wolverines were back to being the hunter, and they relished the role. It felt like last year. On the River Walk arcade, Ray Jackson, wearing a Nike T-shirt, was stopped by a group of tourists.

"What team do you play for?" they asked.

"Kentucky," he said, straight-faced.

"Really? Oh, you guys are gonna kill Michigan."

"I dunno. Them Wolverine boys are good."

"You guys are better."

"Yeah. You're right."

The crowd walked away and Ray broke up laughing.

It was starting to be fun again. Here they were, at another one of Fisher's two-game tournaments—the New Orleans Invitational—and the competition was first-rate, just like Hawaii, the way they liked it. Kentucky was the No. 1 seed from the Southeast. North Carolina was No. 1 from the East. And Kansas, the No. 2 seed from the Midwest, had reached New Orleans by beating Indiana and Bobby Knight, so nobody doubted its credentials. It was a summit meeting for college basketball, best against the best, and the Fab Five, to a man, could not wait.

"Did you read the paper?" Bruce Madej, the sports information director, asked Fisher Thursday morning, when the coach came down for breakfast.

"Which paper?

"*USA Today.*"

"No." Fisher had his arm around his son Mark, and he eyed Madej suspiciously. "Why?"

"They killed us," Madej said, taking these little steps as he talked, one to the right, then one to the left, which he did when he was agitated. "They just *pasted* us. They said we were the Fab Frauds, and the Gab Five, that we whine, that we're smug, that Kentucky is gonna kill us."

Fisher looked at him blankly, with his trademark hesitation.

"You know what?" Fisher finally said. "I'm hungry."

And he took his son for breakfast.

USA Today, in a feature article by Curry Kirkpatrick, the long-time *Sports Illustrated* writer who'd recently left the magazine, had indeed spewed his venom at the Wolverines:

> Last year as freshmen, Michigan was a team of boundless joy and effervescence. Now the Woe-Is-Us Wolves are smug, haughty, paranoid, too good to block out or cut and screen or focus or respect anybody or play hard for 40 minutes. . . .
>
> Fortunately—for the Fabs' own good as well as the tournament—Kentucky's terrorizing press, sturdy discipline, work ethic and sheer numbers, plus all those threes, should blow Michigan back to reality.

The funny thing was, Kirkpatrick was the guy, the year before, who had joyfully predicted in *Sports Illustrated* that Michigan would beat Duke. "Youth Will Be Served" was the headline.

What did Mencken say? From applause to hiss, in two semesters?

And yet, despite the critics, Michigan was still the people's choice, at least if souvenir sales were any indication. You could go to almost any sports store, hotel lobby, or Athlete's Foot in New Orleans, and find plenty of Kansas T-shirts and sweats, all sizes available. Same for North Carolina and, to a lesser extent, Kentucky.

Michigan?

"All we have left is small and extra small" was the common refrain.

It was true, what Brian Dutcher once said: they were the MTV of college basketball. Parents couldn't stomach them. Kids couldn't do without them. When the Wolverines' bus arrived at a practice or pulled up in front of the hotel lobby, you could feel a vibration, the ripples went out, sucked people in like tide.

Of course, nearly all of the attention was on the sophomores. People barely recognized Rob Pelinka, James Voskuil, or Eric Riley, and Michael Talley, at only 6 foot 1, could have walked past most of the fans unnoticed. They were all seniors, these four, and this would be their last weekend in a Michigan uniform. Yet—except for Pelinka—they were all averaging less statistically than they had two years earlier.

"Well, this will be our last hotel room," Voskuil said to Riley Friday afternoon.

"Yeah," Riley said, "and our last plane trip."

"And our last team meals."

"And our last team curfews."

"And our last team meetings!"

"I'm hip to that."

They high-fived, but Talley ignored them. He had been getting less and less time in the tournament and hadn't played at all in the Temple game. That night, whether out of frustration or coincidence, he got into it with Chris Webber. The Wolverines had a team meal at Ralph and Kacoo's Restaurant, in the French Quarter, a private room upstairs where excited waiters, in between asking for autographs, brought mountains of crawfish, fried catfish, frog legs, blackened mahi mahi, and trout. Fisher was not present, having a banquet obligation. And there was always a little more jawing when Fisher wasn't around.

"C Webb, where did you live again?" Mike T said.

"You know where I lived," Webber laughed.

"Well, you keep saying you're from the city."

"I lived right near you."

"Oh. I thought you lived at Country Day."

The others laughed. Chris hated that Country Day stuff.

"I get it. You hard core, right, Mike T?"

Talley shrugged. "I'm just saying I didn't see you 'round the neighborhood, know what I'm saying?"

"You hard core. You in a gang, right?"

"I just lived in the city, you know? In the *ghet*-to?"

"Yeah, you live next to an ammunition store."

"Well, here's what I'm saying, C Webb: I never saw your house, you know what I mean?" He threw his hands up and closed his eyes, like a woman gossiping in a beauty salon. "I mean, you say it's there, but I never saw it, OK?"

The others cracked up.

Chris was half-amused and half-upset. "I lived right near you! I lived like two miles from you and you know it!"

"You sure about that, chief? 'Cause I never saw your house. Maybe you lived at Country Day."

"Aw! Aw! I ain't even talking to you now!"

"Maybe you lived in the city during the summer?"

"OK, hard core."

"Like in between semesters or something?"

The others were laughing hard. "He got you, C Webb!" they yelled. Talley was grinning. And his little triumph might have continued had Chris not been interrupted by several waiters who slid pieces of paper in front of him for his autograph.

"You gonna go pro?" one of them asked.

"I dunno," Chris said, looking down as he signed.

"You ought to, man, you'd be the No. 1 pick."

"Yeah, you're better than Jamal Mashburn."

"Thanks a lot," Chris said, handing them back their paper.

Talley grabbed a crab leg and bit into it with a smirk.

Back at the hotel, Rob Pelinka, another senior, found Chris and did something a little nicer than Talley. He gave Webber his championship ring from 1989.

"Wear this for a day," Pelinka said. "See how it feels. Look at it. Think about getting one of your own this weekend. You're the guy who can make it happen for us. I know you can do it."

Webber smiled and took the ring. He slipped it onto his pinky finger—the only digit on his huge hands that it would fit—and he looked at it from all sides. That night he slept with it under his pillow. He dreamed of victory.

3

Earlier in the week, at a practice back at Crisler, Steve Fisher had screeched the whistle, pulled his team off the floor, and angrily told them if they kept practicing this way they would lose to Kentucky. They would lose, OK? Kentucky was that good. They were practicing that badly.

"You either listen to what I'm saying, believe in what we're tellin' you here, or you're gonna play these guys and lose," he said.

The players blinked. Lose? They had rarely heard the word, not in two years, not by this coaching staff, which always stressed the positive. *Lose? Coach said, "Lose"?* The phrase itself seemed to stun them, and they leaned over, pulled on their shorts, and looked at each other.

"Now," Fisher continued, "if you're ready to listen, we're gonna concentrate on breaking this full court press that they use, and we're gonna do it right . . ."

Lose? Coach said, "Lose"?

From that point on, the team's focus narrowed like a laser. The Wolverines, after a year's worth of being favorites, were finally back to being the underdog, expected to lose, and they used this to inspire themselves. They actually enjoyed it. Fisher prepared more thoroughly for the Wildcats than he had for any team all season. With six days, he and his staff had the time. They studied every ounce of Kentucky's success, and the morsels of their failure. Fisher noted that in some of their defeats, they had still played well, which gave him hope; it meant they could lose on a good night.

Fisher still had nightmares of the last run-and-gun team he'd faced in the NCAA tournament, Loyola-Marymount, three years ago. His players convinced him they could match the Cowboys shot for shot. He let them try. They lost, 149–115.

That was Fisher's first postseason defeat. It cut him. He bled all summer. He would not go down that way again.

"They'll throw 10 or 11 guys at you, so forget about trying to outdo your man," Fisher lectured his players, at practices and at film sessions. "You're not playing men with Kentucky. You're playing the system. Got it? The system! The system!"

And that system, at the moment, was a raging wildfire. Kentucky was the sudden darling of college basketball nuts everywhere. The Wildcats were fast and fun. Rick Pitino, the charismatic coach who had taken Providence to the Final Four and the New York Knicks to the NBA play-offs—before jumping to Kentucky to resurrect the most fanatical program in America—liked his basketball furious. His teams pressed on defense for 94 feet. They bombed away from three-point land. They moved personnel in and out like a subway turnstile. Watching Kentucky was like watching a hurricane.

In their four tournament games, they had jumped out and stayed out. Nobody touched them. They led Rider, 29-9, they led Utah, 27-8, they led Wake Forest, 34-8, they led Florida State, 27-17. Thirty-one points? That was their average margin of victory? Thirty-one points?

Fans fought for them in their Final Four pools. Las Vegas made them five-point favorites over Michigan, then six, then seven as the week went on. Why not? Wasn't Kentucky a basketball avalanche? Couldn't every Wildcat shoot? And didn't they have junior Jamal Mashburn, who had already announced he was turning pro after this season, one of the best players in the country—who, at 6 foot 8, with greasy moves, was also one of the hardest to defend?

"Should we put Ray on him?" Fisher asked at a staff meeting. Dutcher and Watson nodded. Ray was the defensive stopper.

Jay Smith wanted Juwan.

"Ray's quicker, but he's shorter and Mashburn will automatically try and go inside," Smith said. "Juwan's bigger. He can keep him on the perimeter. I know Mashburn's a good outside shooter, but I'd rather have him doing his stuff from 25 feet than from six feet."

Fisher thought about it. This was asking a lot of Juwan, who was also going to handle the ball more than usual, because Jalen would be swarmed by the press. But Fisher loved Juwan Howard, he had from the moment Juwan said, "I'm coming to Michigan."

And more than any of the Fab Five, Fisher trusted Juwan to listen to his coaching.

"Jay's right," Fisher said. "Juwan on Mashburn."

And let us pray.

Saturday morning, Fisher did pray, he went to church, as he usually does during the tournament. And Saturday afternoon, a few hours before the game, he found a pay phone in a deserted hotel corridor, and called Bo Schembechler in Ann Arbor. He did this now and then, almost like a good luck charm. Schembechler, now retired from college sports, was still the guy who gave him the job, still the guy who believed in Fisher in 1989. All the other coaches here—Pitino, Dean Smith, Roy Williams, none of whom had any more success than Fisher in the postseason—had the press celebrating them, and fans mobbing them for autographs, believing in their legend. Now and then, Fisher liked to hear someone believe in him, too. Schembechler did.

"Steve, I know you guys can do it," the old coach said over the telephone. "If you can get your kids to respect the ball, cut down on the turnovers, you can beat Kentucky."

"I think so, too." Fisher said.

"You have the talent."

"I hear ya."

"And you're doing a good job with 'em. I know it's not easy."

"Thanks, coach."

"And Steve?"

"Yeah?"

"Don't worry about the media crap."

Fisher hung up and walked slowly back to his room. The players were just getting up from their naps. The bus would leave in an hour or so. Everything was either ready or it wasn't. Two wins from a championship.

When Fisher got back to his room, Angie and the boys were waiting, dressed in their Michigan colors. Jonathan, the youngest, handed Fisher a doll he had gotten on the River Walk, one of those plastic trolls with the orange hair and the devilish expression.

"Take it, Daddy," Jonathan said. "And you'll have good luck."

Fisher smiled, and stuffed it in his pocket.

"THEY DON'T BELIEVE US! THEY DON'T BELIEVE US! SEVEN-POINT UNDERDOGS!"

Chris Webber was yelling in a deep, booming voice as the Wolverines, with their arms on each other like a human train, chugged past reporters. It was a long way to the court in these football stadiums. You exited the locker room, went down a corridor, through this open space where reporters worked, and finally out to what seemed like an empty indoor parking lot, which you hiked across to the court. It was at least a four-minute walk.

"LOOK AT THESE GUYS!" Webber hollered, pointing to the media but talking to his teammates. "SEVEN-POINT UNDER-DOGS! THEY DON'T THINK WE CAN DO IT!" He got in Jimmy's face. "THEY DON'T THINK WE CAN DO IT!" He got in Ray's face. "THEY DON'T BELIEVE IN US!" Ray yelled, "IT'S GOIN' DOWN!" Jalen grinned and yelled, "WE'RE COMIN' HOME WITH IT!" Eric Riley began to bounce, and even Rob Pelinka and James Voskuil got a skip in their step, as they crossed the end zone area and approached the rear of the court. They looked up and saw the bodies all around the upper deck levels, rings of people, 64,000 hysterical faces, growing more real as they approached.

And then the swirl of noise began, rock-and-roll concert noise, echoing in the rafters. Ray did an exaggerated march like a windup soldier and Juwan raised two fists. Chris dropped his head like a prizefighter and jogged into the deafening roar.

The band exploded at the sight of them.

"HAIL TO THE VICTORS VALIANT.
HAIL TO THE CONQUERING HEROES . . ."

Someone tossed them basketballs, and they slid into layup drills as the hysteria rang in their ears. Drums pounded. Trumpets blared. Across the floor, the Wildcats were warming up in their blue and white sweats, and several of them looked over at the bald heads and black shoes they would be facing. For all Kentucky had going for it, its players had never played the Big Room at the Final Four.

Somehow, watching the Fab Five glide so smoothly onto the stage, you knew that would matter.

Ray made the first basket for Michigan, Juwan made the second, Jalen made the third and fourth, Juwan made the fifth, Chris the sixth. They did not miss a shot for the first five and a half minutes, and on nearly every play—just as the coaches designed—the big men, Howard and Webber, touched the ball at least once. They were patient. Slowing it down. Working for the best shot instead of matching macho with Kentucky's speed. On defense, the Wolverines slid and helped, slid and helped, and Jimmy King was so glued to little Travis Ford, Kentucky's purest three-point shooter, that Ford didn't even get a good look at the basket, much less make one.

Jamal Mashburn fouled Chris, and as he stood at the line Chris spoke to himself, out loud. "Relax. You can make these. You can make these." He'd been shooting 57 percent on his free throws in the tournament, and Fisher had told him that was inexcusable. He exhaled. Aimed. Fired.

Swish.

Swish.

"Hallelujah," Jay Smith mumbled on the Michigan bench.

The Wolverines led 14–7. So the first chink had been made in Kentucky's armor. The game was seven minutes old, and the Wildcats weren't leading by 20 points. They were behind.

Fisher gave Juwan a quick breather—he was playing Mashburn tightly *and* taking the ball whenever Jalen got double-teamed *and* making good passes on offense *and* scoring points—but as soon as

Howard sat down, Mashburn went wild, scoring and drawing fouls on Eric Riley. Fisher quickly sent Howard back in. Kentucky scored nine straight to take a lead, but Juwan shut them up with a flipping hook shot.

The teams stayed close for the next few minutes, and even the TV analysts remarked how differently the game was going from what was predicted.

"Michigan is having its way inside," Nantz said.

"They're playing with more intensity and concentration than I've seen in them all year!" Packer marveled.

And they were keeping Kentucky earthbound. The Wildcats were not racing up and down the floor, bombing away, as *USA Today* and so many others had foreseen. They were, instead, being swarmed by the taller Wolverines, and defended out near the three-point line. Fisher was playing it smart. When Chris scored on three consecutive plays, Fisher yelled, "SLOW IT UP!" because he saw his star breathing hard. And a tired star commits fouls and makes mistakes.

Fisher treated every possession as critical. Kentucky was staying close thanks to Mashburn's excellence (he had 17 points in the first 18 minutes). But the Wildcats were getting outrebounded. And Ford was a blank, 0-for-2, thanks to Jimmy's defense.

Kentucky set up the final play of the half, working the ball to Dale Brown, the only guy to hit a three-point basket so far. He squared, fired, and missed badly off the rim, symbolic of the Wildcats' sudden chill.

Michigan led, 40–35, as the horn sounded. It was the first time all tournament that Kentucky had to leave the court trailing.

"Twenty minutes!" Riley yelled in the Michigan locker room.

"We can do this, fellas!" Juwan added.

Fisher was all business. "Men, you must stay strong mentally. If you're tired, let us know, we'll take you out for 30 seconds . . .

"Jimmy—Jimmy and Rob—you guys have done a great job on Travis Ford. He doesn't have a field goal. You gotta have that same type of defense for 20 more minutes . . .

"Juwan, Eric, you have to attack inside. Juwan, on Mashburn, try and get one more step on him, like this, make him step one more back.

"Jalen, Ray, throw it in hard, no soft lob passes or they'll steal it . . ."

The players listened intently, sweat still dripping down their foreheads. Watching Fisher instruct them during that halftime, moving his body, simulating the action, showing guys twice his size how to hold their legs and arms, his eyes intense, as if holding a live grenade, you could see his passion, the hours he spent watching film and not understanding why everyone in the country didn't find this equally fascinating. For better or for worse, Fisher was addicted to the sport. And if all he had to worry about were these halftime sessions, well, this might be the greatest job on earth.

"I believe in you," he told them.

"NUT CHECK!" they yelled.

The second half tilted quickly toward Michigan. Jalen, who'd taken only four shots so far—something seriously wrong there—figured it was time to get the numbers up, and he hit a jumper in the lane and a jumper from the baseline, then made a driving flip shot. "You didn't forget me, didja?" he teased Dale Brown.

The Fab Five were rolling. Jimmy came soaring through the air, scooped underneath Kentucky's Andre Riddick, and banked the ball high off the glass. It dropped through—pure highlight film—and the Michigan faithful went wild! The Wolverines had an 11-point lead, 52–41, and if they held it for 13 more minutes, they would play for the championship Monday night. The North Carolina Tar Heels, who had beaten Kansas in the first game, were dressed now and in the crowd, watching their would-be opponents along with all the other ticket-buying customers.

Kentucky bounced back, and briefly rediscovered the reason it was here—the three-point basket—with Mashburn hitting one, Ford hitting his first, Brown hitting another. Quickly, the score was even.

"FIGHT THROUGH THE SCREENS!" Fisher yelled during the time-outs. "DON'T LET THEM HAVE THOSE SHOTS!"

Back and forth now, Michigan up a point, Kentucky up a point. As the game moved into the stretch, it was obvious this would be a battle of wills—and possessions. Mashburn committed a reach-in foul on Webber, who took a deep breath, and once again made both free throws. He was six-for-six from the line.

"THIS IS A FUCKING 64 PERCENT FREE THROW TEAM AND THEY'RE MAKING EVERY GOD DAMN SHOT!" Pitino yelled at his staff. They shrugged. It wasn't *their* fault. Michigan was doing a lot of things it hadn't done well before. Working the shot clock. Using Juwan as a ball handler. Even boxing out. It was their finest game in months.

Webber upstaged Mashburn again by blocking his drive, and Mashburn, frustrated, poked at Jalen on the way back upcourt. The whistle blew. Another foul on Mashburn. Jalen and Chris could see the Kentucky star beginning to fade, and they gave him a little lip at the free throw line.

"Jamal Mashburn averages 21 points for Kentucky," Chris said, looking straight at Jalen.

"Yeah," Jalen said, looking back, "and 8.5 rebounds."

"And he's shooting 49 percent from the field."

"That's right."

Reciting a player's stats, without looking at him, was one of the Fab Five's pet tricks. Make the guy feel self-conscious. Mashburn, who'd heard pretty much everything—he did grow up in the Bronx—tried to ignore them. Rose made the free throws; Michigan led, 60–57.

The final five minutes were chaotic. The Wolverines did an excellent job on defense, helping out, denying the easy shots, but they had committed too many fouls, Kentucky was in the double bonus, and each Michigan infraction, no matter how slight, now brought two shots. Kentucky made the free throws to match Michigan's rebounds and tip-ins. And with 21 seconds left, Michigan led by just a basket, 71–69.

And Kentucky had the ball.

"No three-point shots!" Fisher yelled. If they have to make something, he figured, let it be a two-, and we'll go to overtime . . .

Kentucky worked the ball around, the clock down to 16 seconds, 15, 14, Travis Ford came off a screen, got the ball for a three, head faked, spun away awkwardly, without dribbling—

"OH, HE WALKED!" Packer screamed into the microphone. "TRAVIS FORD WALKED AND GOT AWAY WITH IT!" He did walk. But it was King who paid the price. He was whistled for a reach-in foul, his fifth. He was out of the game. Michigan would have to win without the clutch performer who had saved them against UCLA.

Jimmy yelled "NO! NO!" at the refs, then walked off, biting his lip.

Fisher patted him on the back.

Ford hit both free throws.

Jalen tried a last-second shot, drawing contact from Rodney Dent.

"FOUL! WHERE'S THE DAMN FOUL!" Fisher yelled.

No foul.

The scoreboard read 71–71.

They were in overtime.

Again.

If Fisher had thought about it, he might not have minded so much. This was U-M's fourth overtime in their last eight games, and they'd won them all. Kentucky, meanwhile, hadn't had to sweat much recently beyond the opening tap.

Mashburn gave KU a quick lead in the overtime, sinking a layup and then drawing a foul. He had 25 points and was the go-to guy now for Kentucky. Pitino was basically clearing everyone out to let him do his stuff (a common strategy in the NBA, where Pitino had come from and where Mashburn was going, right after this season). Still, Jalen and Chris were not impressed. They remembered playing against Jamal back in eighth grade, in the summer AAU Tournament, when he was on the New York City Gauchos, and Chris and Jalen played on Super Friends from Detroit.

As Mashburn lined up his free throw, Jalen sneered, "This ain't the Gauchos, Jamal."

He missed the shot.

And 25 seconds later, he fouled out.

When the whistle blew, Juwan shook a fist, while Pitino, down-court, kicked the floor in anger. Kentucky had just lost its star, and the Michigan defense was so suffocating that no other Wildcat had the confidence to lead. Slowly the Wolverines came from three down, to one down, to a tie game, to one ahead, and finally, on two free throws by Jalen—"Make these and we're playing North Carolina," Juwan had whispered to him at the line—Michigan had a three-point lead, 81–78.

They were 21 seconds away from Monday night.

Kentucky ran a weave, praying for someone to find an open shot. As the clock ran down, Gimel Martinez, a 6-foot-8 backup center, tried an awkward three-pointer, it missed, went out of bounds off Michigan, and now there were four seconds left.

Four seconds to the national championship game.

Four seconds to their destiny.

Time to do something fabulous.

Rodney Dent tried to inbounds the ball, Chris knocked it back at him, laughed, shrugged, put his hands up again, leapt at the release, and knocked it again, this time up in the air. *He blocked the inbounds pass? Twice?* Yep. And then he caught the ball and tossed it up high, so the clock kept ticking. In a game that was supposed to showcase a "system," natural ability provided the finishing touch. Fisher clenched his fists, Jimmy King punched the air, and two heartbeats later, it was over. The hottest team in the nation had just met the angriest, and the angry one was now leaping and jumping and saying, "WE DID IT! WE DID IT!"

Chris was mobbed by the bench players. Jimmy, who had watched the overtime near tears after fouling out, found his roommate, Ray, mugged him, and Ray yelled, "WE DIDN'T FORGET YOU! WE DIDN'T FORGET YOU!"

It was as close to a perfect game as the Fab Five had played in the tournament—or played, period, for that matter. Juwan carried the burden of his assignments and still scored 17 points. Chris had 27 points and 13 rebounds, nearly twice the boards of any Wildcat. Ray—who had a huge rebound, a critical layup, and a set of free throws in the overtime—was becoming the biggest clutch player on the roster. Michigan held "unstoppable" Kentucky to just 35 percent shooting in the second half—"Nobody has done that against us," Pitino moaned—and both the system, and the star, Mashburn, had been neutralized.

"Jamal is a great player, and I wish him well in the NBA," Chris said, laughing and waving at friends. "Oh. And I hope he gets me some tickets."

Fisher was beaming. They had followed his plan, they had stayed focused. They were the team he had dreamed about when he recruited them. In the locker room he applauded them, said, "You were fantastic! You were fantastic!" Even James Duderstadt, the tall, bespectacled president of the university, came in and said a few words.

"That was one of the greatest victories in Michigan history. You had to overcome the officials, the press, you won it for yourselves, and you won it for Michigan, and we're really proud.

"A year ago you said you'd be back. You're now back. And two days from tonight you're gonna win it all."

"YEAH, BABY!" Juwan said.

"HELL, YEAH," Jalen said.

Duderstadt grinned and left. The players looked at one another. Maybe all it took to make your school proud of you was getting back to a championship game.

Outside in the press area, journalists were typing their accounts of the evening. A number would say "Fisher outcoached Pitino."

That may have been true. Or, it may have been karma. After all, on this same day, four years earlier, in another overtime game, in another domed stadium, Fisher had run onto the court in celebration with his Michigan players.

April 3rd, 1989.

This was the anniversary of his championship.

So it might have been that, Fisher admitted. That, or the troll in his pocket.

4

So now there was one team, North Carolina, and one game, the championship. That was all that remained in the longest season of the Fab Five's lives. The press was already hyping Monday night as a rematch of Hawaii, where Jalen made his last-second shot to end "the Dean Smith Invitational." And TV stations were running side-by-side highlight footage of Eric Montross and Chris Webber, the two Monsters of the Middle, the recruit Fisher got and "the recruit Fisher let slip away."

Some things never stop haunting you, Fisher figured.

No matter. They were here. They were back to Monday night, and just equaling last year's distance was phenomenal, considering the pressure and distractions. Michigan had actually gained a little media respect by beating Kentucky. It was a huge win, and even cynics could not deny it was done with intelligence and patience— not just streetball.

The Fab Five also scored media points during the grueling two-hour press conference Sunday afternoon, taking questions from hundreds of reporters with patience and good humor.

Reporter: "Chris, will your father shave his head if you win tomorrow night?"

Chris: "Maybe. I think Coach Fisher might go bald, too, if we win."

Fisher: "Well, I'll think about it."

Juwan: "He's already bald! HAW!"

Reporters were even more pleased when each player was sent to his own meeting room for individual sessions. Chris held a packed crowd spellbound with stories about his childhood, and his friendships with Jalen, Montross, and everyone else who ever played basketball. He spoke about the lure of the NBA. He spoke about fame and racism. He was always good talking to large groups. It was kind of like performing.

Someone asked if the season would be a failure if Michigan didn't beat North Carolina.

"Yes," Chris said without hesitation. "The only goal I had all year was not to have the feeling I had last season after Duke. That feeling has stayed with me for 364 days. It was the worst experience of my life."

Someone asked what he'd say if Bill Walton showed up right now.

"I'd, uh, ask him for his autograph."

Everybody laughed.

"He's delightful," whispered Ron Rapoport, the columnist for the *L.A. Daily News*. "Why does he get such a bad rap?"

Down the hall, Jalen was also entertaining the troops, albeit with fewer words. Someone asked what would happen if the Fab Five played the 1989 Michigan championship team 10 times: how many would the Fab Five win?

"Ten," he said without blinking.

"How is Coach Fisher different off the court than on it?"

"He curses more on it."

"What do you fear most in life?"

"Death."

"Why?"

"Because I can't imagine the world without me in it."

The room cracked up.

Jalen looked at them like, "What? What'd I say?"

Sunday night, 24 hours from destiny, began the longest part of championship weekend. Practices were over. Press briefings were over. Now all that remained was the waiting. Fisher, Dutcher, Watson, and Smith viewed tape constantly, looking for little tendencies that might help beat the Tar Heels. Fisher left the players on their own for dinner. "I'll see you at the 10 o'clock meeting tonight," he said.

The Texas kids went off with their parents, Jimmy visiting his now bald-headed father, who had shaved his head in honor of the Fab Five look—"I still can't believe you let him do that, Mom," Jimmy said—and Ray, as usual, hanging with his mom and pop. Ray had almost missed curfew the night before by going to his parents' room, and lying on the bed, in front of the TV, just like at home.

"Ray, don't fall asleep, Coach Fisher will be mad," his mother warned.

"I won't," Ray said, his eyes half-closed.

His father looked at him lovingly and laughed. "He's just a big baby. He's the same big baby he always was."

Most of the other players took refuge in the River Walk arcade, blending into the foot traffic, shopping, people-watching, eating fast food. All except Chris, who couldn't blend anywhere anymore. He wanted to buy a birthday present for his youngest brother David, but the two of them, and their friends, were followed and surrounded from the moment Chris appeared. He walked to a watch store, a mob walked behind him. He entered a clothing store, a mob entered with him. He signed autographs as he moved, trying to keep up conversation with David and his friends, but he kept losing them in the crowd. Finally they found a table in the food court area and had some Mexican food. Chris teased David about being old enough now to talk to girls.

"I can talk to girls," David said defiantly.

"Oh yeah?" Chris said, grinning. "Go talk to that girl over there."

He pointed to a woman working one of the food stores.

"Aw, man," David said, "she's 80 years old."

Chris laughed. He loved being the oldest brother. It suited him. He was the only oldest child on the Fab Five—the rest were all babies of the families—and the difference in responsibility showed. When David made a joke about not having a sweat suit like a friend of his, Chris reached in his pocket, took out all the money he had, removed a $5 bill for himself, and gave the rest to David without a word.

"Thanks!" David crowed.

The people kept coming at Chris, even as he ate. *"Who's gonna win? What will you do to Montross? When are you going pro?"* One cute girl slipped Chris her phone number on a personal check. But just in case, she wrote "VOID" through the dollar amount.

"What does she think I'm gonna do, try and cash it?" Chris asked.

He threw the check in a trash can.

At one point, Chris walked into a video arcade and was so mobbed when he tried to play a game—*"What's he playing? How's he doing? Who's he playing against?"*—that the manager offered him refuge in a giant, modulelike ride called the Simulator.

"No one will bother you in there," the guy said. He opened the chain and let Chris, David, and several friends inside. The module was dark, like a submarine, with half a dozen seats and a screen in front. "I'll run it for you, you'll like it," the guy said, shutting the door.

Suddenly the screen lit with the speeding images of a roller-coaster ride, and the seats swung back and forth, rumbling with the pictures. Then the screen turned to a downhill ski slope, the seats jerking forward, then a speedboat, the seats bouncing with imaginary waves.

Chris was yelling "WHOOOA!" and so were the others, squealing and occasionally screaming, "I'm gonna be sick!"

When the ride finally stopped, everyone sat for a few seconds, breathing hard, collecting their stomachs. "That was unbelievable," someone said. "I was so dizzy."

"Kind of like my life," Chris said softly.

An hour before the last official team meeting, Jason Bossard and Michael Talley had been looking for the hotel's health club. Jason wanted to work out. Mike didn't have anything else to do. They found the facility, on the upper level, and accidentally opened a door to reveal a small, rooftop basketball half-court, lit by floodlights. The far side was a high fence that kept the ball—and the players—from going over the ledge.

Bossard looked at Talley and said, "Let's do it, man!" Next thing you knew, they had their shirts off and were shooting with the hotel's rubber basketballs.

"Whoa, outdoor ball, chief!" Talley said, firing a jumper in the night breeze.

"This is the most shots I get all year," Bossard said.

"Now I'll show you my magic, chief."

"You can't shoot like me."

They banged shot after shot, playing with the loose invention of every kid who has ever been on a playground. They laughed and fed each other for shots.

"What time is it?" Bossard kept asking. "I don't want to be late for the meeting."

"We won't be late for the meeting," Talley clucked, annoyed. This was the last night of curfew in his life, the last night he took orders from Steve Fisher or anyone else at Michigan. He was having fun, just shooting hoops for once. He and Bossard made an odd pair, Bossard, from the rural small towns of northern Michigan, and Talley, from the heart of urban Detroit, but they had one thing in common: they sat the bench. Talley had not played since the UCLA game, when he made several mistakes and the team fell behind by 17 points. Bossard had not played since Coastal Carolina, and that was just garbage time.

So here, on the roof, they played H-O-R-S-E and when Talley missed a few, Bossard said, "What's the matter with your shot?"

"Nothing wrong with my shot, it's the school I go to."

Bossard laughed.

"YOU GOT H, chief!"

"You got O!"

"You got HO, you Ho!"

They broke a good sweat. And for a moment, they seemed to remember what it was they loved about the sport. Even in a city gone mad for basketball, it was an unlikely scene: a hotel rooftop on a spring night on the bayou, a couple of lost shooters trying to find their light.

Jalen asked for his father's phone number.

A sudden request, on the day of the game.

When asked why, he said, "I changed my mind."

When asked about talking on the telephone, instead of in person, Jalen said, "You gotta start somewhere."

He took the number and said, "That's in Atlanta, right? He's in Atlanta?" Then he took the number back to his room. It was written in pen, on a ripped piece of paper, and he felt a little like the kid he once was, with the baseball card he used to carry around. A paper father. Always a paper father.

Walker was home in Atlanta, this was the time of day to get him, and had Jalen gone through with the call, he would have heard his father on the other end. He would have at least heard his father say "Hello? Who is this?"

Several times, Jalen picked up the phone, then put it down.

What if he tells me something that gets me geeked for tonight? he thought. He liked the idea. He envisioned scoring 30 points.

Then he thought again.

What if he says something that gets me upset? Puts me off my game? What if he's . . . an asshole?

He put the phone down, picked it up, put it down. He looked at the paper, sighed, and finally stuffed it in his pocket and left the room.

5

The buses pulled into the service entrance of the Louisiana Superdome. It was less than two hours to tip-off. The Michigan players unloaded, wearing maize and blue sweat suits, their ears covered with Walkman headphones, a few of them bopping and singing out loud. Across the dock, the North Carolina players got off their bus, wearing suit coats and ties, as if heading for a sales convention. They were big, four 7-footers on the roster, and Montross cut the most imposing figure, freakishly tall, with pinkish-white skin, protruding cheekbones, and a tight crew cut/fade that suggested the fictional Russian boxer Ivan Drago, whom Sylvester Stallone fought in *Rocky IV*. Montross smiled at a worker, and even smiling, he looked ominous.

Of all the teams Michigan had faced, the Tar Heels were probably closest in personnel. They were studs. Prior to Fisher's collecting the Fab Five, many thought Dean Smith's 1990 recruiting class of Montross, Derrick Phelps, Cliff Rozier, Brian Reese, and Pat Sullivan was the best crop of college recruits in years. They were featured on the cover of *Sports Illustrated*. Smith, like Fisher (and unlike Bobby Knight), used the nation as his recruiting backyard, getting Montross from Indiana, Phelps and Reese from New York, Sullivan from New

Jersey. He had a player from Germany, a player from Holland, one from Texas, one from South Carolina. George Lynch, the Tar Heels' muscular, large-jawed senior forward, was from Virginia. The night before the championship, Fisher had run into Mike Krzyzewski from Duke—his rival in last year's title match—and Krzyzewski, who plays North Carolina twice a year in the ACC, said, "Steve, believe me, the guy you gotta watch for is Lynch. He's the killer. He's a warrior. He's the one."

And he was a senior. Dean Smith liked his seniors. The winningest coach in college basketball, with well over 700 wins, Smith is a hybrid—a "system" guy who believes in collecting the best talent available, but making it wait its turn. Smith's alumni include Michael Jordan, James Worthy, Sam Perkins, and J. R. Reid. They were all stars. And they were all subject to the rules: Freshmen carry bags. Freshmen don't speak to the media until after their first game. Freshmen very rarely play, that's why God invented seniors. Jordan had only averaged 13.5 points as a Tar Heels freshman. Montross, for all his ability, averaged only 5.8 his first year.

Needless to say, none of the Fab Five were seriously interested in attending North Carolina.

And needless to say, Smith outshone Fisher in the media spotlight.

Which was OK with Fisher. He looked up to Smith. Thought he was a gentleman, worthy of his legend. Besides, for all the hype, Fisher was undefeated against the guy, having beaten the Tar Heels in 1989, en route to the championship. And of course, Michigan had tripped North Carolina in Hawaii. The Honolulu broadcasters mentioned Fisher's 2-0 mark against Smith when Fisher was interviewed there, and Fisher had laughed.

"That's it. I quit. I'm never playing him again!"

Now Fisher, in a dark blue suit, followed his players quietly to their locker room, and Smith went the other way with his. The maintenance workers looked after the two teams, marveling at the bodies, then went back to work.

"TEST ONE-TWO, ONE-TWO . . ." a voice boomed over the loudspeakers from the main floor. "TEST ONE-TWO, ONE-TWO . . ."

By 8 P.M., New Orleans time, a football-sized crowd had filled the stadium, and the noise was so deafening, people could be yelling at you from two rows away and you couldn't hear a word. CBS was broadcasting to 20 million viewers around the world, and they opened with a dramatic, MTV jump-cut introduction set to Ike and Tina Turner's "Proud Mary (Rolling on the River)," with enough two-second clips of Webber, Rose, Montross, and Lynch to turn them into movie stars.

Pat O'Brien welcomed the audience to New Orleans, "for a Cajun special!" The cameras zoomed in on Michigan cheerleaders with "M" decals on their young cheeks, and North Carolina students, their bodies painted blue, with small rubber basketballs stuck on their noses. The bands blasted fight songs. The crowd was already screaming. Back in Ann Arbor, Crisler Arena was stuffed with students and fans watching on the giant screen. Every sports bar in North Carolina was tuned in and juiced up. It was typical championship night insanity, and the buzz was primarily the Fab Five, the Fab Five. Their fans were sure tonight was the night they kissed their destiny.

Chris and Jalen had promised, after last year's tighten-up against Duke, that if they ever got back to the national championship, they'd have fun, laugh, talk junk. But again, here, they were unusually quiet. They marched through the open press area they had turned into a verbal rifle range before the Kentucky game on Saturday—but there was no yelling now, no swagger.

"Quite a difference," one reporter whispered.

"That's 'cause we picked 'em to win," said another.

Nerves? Focus? Fatigue? The Fab Five said nothing during their introductions. Jimmy and Juwan even bit their lips. In black socks, black shoes, bald heads, and determined expressions, they huddled up one more time.

"LET YOUR NUTS HANG!"

And when the game began, the loosest team you ever saw was tight as a marine.

Chris missed the first shot, a flat three-point try. Jalen tried a drive but got nothing. Lynch, meanwhile, grabbed two quick rebounds, blocked one of Juwan's shots, and drew a charging foul on Ray.

"Come onnnn," Fisher moaned. Lynch hadn't even scored yet, and in two minutes, he was everything Krzyzewski had predicted.

Montross was winning the early battle inside, dropping a layup and three free throws. Michigan seemed fatigued, out of sync. Finally

Webber slipped inside Montross for a powerful dunk, and it appeared to juice him up. He snarled on the way downcourt, "Get used to that. I'm here all night."

But the only thing that was there all night was choking defense and scoring surges. North Carolina jumped to a 9–4 lead. Michigan scored the next 11. North Carolina closed it to 18–13, Michigan scored five straight to make it 23–13. Lynch was playing well, his thick torso seemingly glued to the ball, rebounding, shot blocking, laying it up. "This guy's a bitch," Jay Smith whispered. Behind Lynch's efforts, the Tar Heels tied the game, then pulled ahead, 31–28. Michigan used jumpers by Jimmy and Jalen to reclaim the edge, 32–31.

Still, the scoreboard seemed of less interest to the coaches than the personnel and the foul situation. Fisher took Webber out during U-M's best run of the half, because Montross went out, and Fisher was playing a chess game with Smith's players, much as Smith was doing with his.

"Both coaches are playing this first half to get it over with," Packer observed. "You can tell by the substitution pattern."

It was grueling, possession-by-possession basketball. At one point, the pattern actually had Pelinka, Eric Riley, and Michael Talley, three seniors, on the floor at the same time. It had been a long time since the Wolverines saw that in a first half.

Still, the evening felt funny, as if Michigan were wearing someone else's clothes, or, heaven forbid, short shorts. The Fab Five had almost no fast breaks, and very little joy in their game. It was almost as if the weight of expectations were strapped on their shoulders, so that even the simple things required double effort.

To make matters worse, Jalen was getting burned by little Donald Williams, the sophomore shooting guard. Sometimes, on defense, Jalen had a tendency to turn his head, and you simply couldn't do that with Williams. He was such a pure shooter, and so damn quick, hell, you couldn't swallow without giving him an advantage. Fisher had told Jalen before the game, "Make him go to his left, his left, his left!" Williams canned two baskets in five minutes—from his right. Interestingly, Williams was the only player Dean Smith recruited the year Fisher got the Fab Five. In the national high school rankings, he had been listed behind Chris, Jalen, Juwan, and Jimmy.

You'd never know it by the way he shot.

With under two minutes left in the half, Michigan trailed, 37–36.

Montross came charging downcourt and banged into Riley, knocking the thinner player to the floor. No whistle. "HEY! FOUL!
COME ON! FOUL!" Fisher pleaded. Montross, meanwhile, was
wide open as the ball came in, and Ray Jackson raced over to help.

Now the whistle blew.

"FOUL, 21, YELLOW!" the ref bellowed.

"NAW! NAW!" Ray screamed. That was his third personal,
and his face contorted almost to tears. This was exactly what he
didn't want to happen tonight. Stinking fouls. They had ruined him
last year. They had ruined so many games for him. Foul! It wasn't
his fault! They should have called it on Montross!

Fisher took him out and put an arm around him.

"DAMN!" Ray hollered, then buried his face in a towel.

Montross made his free throws. And with 49 seconds left, Donald Williams fired another three-pointer over Jalen—from the right
side.

Good!

The Tar Heels went to halftime with a six-point lead, 42–36.

"Eyes and ears on me," Fisher said in the locker room. He saw
the frustration in their faces. What was it with these championship
nights that sucked the life out of you?

"Look, I never once got a comfortable feeling in that half, but
I look at the scoreboard and we're still right there. We're right there.
And I don't think they can play any better . . .

"You need to box out more. You need to fight on the offensive
glass. Jalen, we gotta be more careful on Williams, gotta make sure
we're out on him . . .

"And all of you need to relax a little." He took a breath himself.
"You know, sometimes, in life, you try too hard to grab something,
and it squeezes out of your fingers. But if you just reach up for it
like a feather"—he held his arm up high as if pulling something from
the air—"like this, like a feather, you get what you want."

He could have been talking about himself. He could have been
talking about the way he recruited these kids, or the way he handled
them. Or simply the way he went through life. Steve Fisher, without
even realizing it, was sharing with them, at their most needful moment, a philosophy of his life: when in doubt, go back to acting
natural.

"Chris, you got that?"

Chris looked up at his coach and nodded.

"OK. The fight is good! The fight is good! Now you gotta put the head with the body. You got yourself in the mood to play a perfect half, now go out and play one!"

Juwan clapped his hands. "Twenty minutes to the championship!" he yelled.

"Let's bring it home!

"One, two, three . . ."

If you ask the members of the Fab Five today to describe the second half of Monday night, April 5, 1993, you will inevitably get a shrug, a sigh, and a sad-eyed look about the ending. Beyond that, the details fade. Few of the players have watched the tape. All they are sure of, they'll tell you, is that it was grueling, suffocating, physical play, and that God must have had something in mind for Chris Webber, or there's no justice in the world at all.

Webber kept them living in the second half. Without him, Michigan would have been wheeled out. The Tar Heels came out fresh, as if they'd showered and shaved. Montross flipped in two early hook shots for an eight-point Carolina lead. But Webber fought back, the sweat dripping down his bald scalp. He muscled in a layup, set a thick screen for Jimmy to hit a jumper, grabbed long-armed rebounds of shots that never should have come back to Michigan, and took an alley-oop from Juwan to slam life into their offense.

North Carolina continued to forge ahead—thanks largely to Donald Williams' eating up Jalen and Jimmy with more right-side baskets—until Webber, of all people, arrived to take Williams down a peg. Encountering him on a switch at the top of the key, a chance meeting between tree and twig, Webber reached over Williams' unsuspecting head, poked away the ball, then beat him to it and chugged downcourt, blowing air like a locomotive—*"Look at Chris run!"*— and he finished with a walloping slam. The Wolverines were within a point, 53–52.

"LET'S GO!" Webber exhorted, waving his fist. "NOW! LET'S GO! LET'S DO THIS!"

His enthusiasm was contagious, and Michigan fought North Carolina blow for blow, a bloody draw. For the next three minutes, no Tar Heel scored a basket, no Wolverine scored a basket. To the thumping cries of "DEEE-FENNSE!" (*bum-bum*), "DEEE-FENNSE!" (*bum-bum*), shots were stuffed, bodies collided, rebounds were fought for like a piece of meat between dogs. Montross slapped away a Juwan jump shot, Ray and Chris clobbered Montross underneath. Jimmy had a baseline drive rejected, Juwan leapt for a rebound and whacked Lynch in the stomach.

Once again, it was Chris who dragged them back onto the scoreboard. He hit a power layup. Then spun around for a one-handed reverse. He took a lob from Howard and rammed it home. He had 21 points. No outside shooting now. This was pure brute basketball. Webber's eyes were fire. He was carrying his team toward the national championship, sucking air, too tired to even talk. There were less than five minutes left, Michigan had the lead, and the announcers quickly pointed out that "these Wolverines have never lost when leading at the five-minute mark."

The Tar Heels, meanwhile, were juggling personnel so fast their bench looked like fourth down on a college football sideline. Situation substitutions. Rest everyone, even for a few seconds. This was how you coached these championship nights, the games that won't let you pull the rip cord until inches from the ground. No detail too small. No move too insignificant. Dean Smith knew this.

Steve Fisher knew it, too.

But in the heat of the moment, people forget things . . .

"Ray, get James!" Fisher yelled.

Ray Jackson ran out, tucking his shirt into his long shorts. With four minutes and 31 seconds left, he joined Chris, Jalen, Juwan, and Jimmy on the floor. The Fab Five were together again.

For the last time in their lives.

Ray passed to Jimmy, his roommate, who passed to Jalen, his close friend, who dished to Juwan, the kid who started the Greatest Class Ever Recruited, who found Jimmy again for a 17-foot jumper from the left side.

Swish.

"YES!" Fisher yelled, clapping his hands. The Wolverines now led by four, 67–63. The pressure should have been on North Carolina. Instead, the Tar Heels inexplicably began to roll. First, Jimmy made a mistake—he let Williams escape his defense. The sophomore guard drained a three-pointer as if shooting in his driveway.

"JE-SUS!" Fisher yelled.

It was 67–66.

Now Jimmy seemed intent on making up for his error. He fired a three-point attempt from the corner, it clanked the rim, Michigan got the rebound, the ball worked again to Jimmy, he tried another baseline drive and missed everything. Two shots, two misses. North Carolina took off the other way. Derrick Phelps drove on Jalen, the ball hung on the rim like a coin standing on its edge, trying to make up its mind . . .

It fell through.

The Tar Heels were winning, 68–67.

Three minutes left. Jimmy again tried to fix things. His three-point shot from the top of the key went up, came down, and hit nothing.

"AIR BALL! AIR BALL!"

North Carolina grabbed it, worked it downcourt to Lynch, who hit a fadeaway jumper, four feet, over Juwan, good.

A killer. Just as Krzyzewski predicted.

Tar Heels 70, Wolverines 67.

Things were disintegrating. The ceiling was caving in. Jalen tried to drive to the middle and simply lost the ball! Nobody even touched him! North Carolina grabbed possession, and, moments later, Montross slipped away from the Michigan defense and made an easy dunk for a five-point lead, 72–67. The Carolina players were leaping into each other's arms, pounding fists.

There were 63 seconds left, and they smelled a title.

They were early. Ray got the ball, and he knew what he was going to do. Fuck it. He'd watched his team sink last year from the bench and he wasn't gonna watch it now. He squared. He fired. Bang! An 18-footer, just inside the three-point line. Fisher, Rose, and Jackson immediately signaled time out.

It was their last.

"OK, NO TIME-OUTS LEFT," Fisher said, screaming to be heard over the bands and the crowd. "WE WANT TO PRESS THEM, LOOK FOR A TURNOVER. IF WE DON'T GET IT QUICKLY, WE'LL HAVE TO FOUL."

In the days and weeks that followed, fans would debate whether Fisher had ever mentioned the time-out situation during that break. He had. Clearly. He mentioned it at the start, and he mentioned it at the end. Chris Webber sat just a few feet away, he listened, he heard. But Chris' mind always raced at times like these. Here he was, 46 seconds from the end of the rainbow, and the colors of his life were swirling. Never mind the three-point deficit; Chris was sure they would win, he had this feeling, he just knew it would happen. He had felt this same way back in Hawaii, and he felt it in overtime against Michigan State, and when they were down 19 points to UCLA and when everyone said they couldn't beat Kentucky. They would find a way to win. It was meant to be. Not long before they'd left for the arena, Rob Pelinka had stopped by Chris' room and said, "It's weird, but for the first time, I am absolutely convinced we're gonna win. I'm not even nervous." And Chris had smiled and said, "I was just thinking the same thing."

Now Fisher was putting Pelinka in the lineup, for three-point accuracy. Rob looked at Chris, a private glance, and they almost smiled again.

They just knew it.

And so they turned up the defensive pressure, and sure enough, North Carolina committed an unthinkable turnover—Brian Reese stepped on the out-of-bounds line. Michigan ball! Dean Smith almost tore his eyebrows out, as Chris and Ray clapped as if applauding an opera performance. *"Very good! Very nice!"*

And then Chris sucked in a rebound off a Jalen three-point try, one of those reach-back-and-grabs that no one but Chris could pull off, and he laid the ball in, and it was 72–71, the crowd was going crazy, the noise beyond thunderous, and the Wolverines felt it now. They felt it so much, it was so contagious, this maize and blue fever oozing all over the arena, that after Pelinka intentionally fouled Pat Sullivan with 20 seconds left, hoping he'd miss the one-and-one free throws, and they all took their places on the line, the Tar Heels' reserves holding hands on the bench, heads down, praying, this is what Pelinka did:

He talked junk.

"This is for the national championship, baby," he sneered at Sullivan, imitating the swagger he'd heard from his famous team-mates. "Don't nut up."

Don't nut up?

It would be the last line of trash talk in the Fab Five era. Rob Pelinka, from Lake Bluff, Illinois, had said it.

Sullivan launched the first shot. Swish. A two-point lead. But the second—*don't nut up!*—was too hard. It hit off the back rim, ricocheted upward, and the whole scene was a tapestry before them:

two-point deficit, 20 seconds left, Michigan was still alive, still alive, the angels calling, now, *now*, the ball bounced high into the air, up for grabs, free to the highest bidder . . .

6

Twenty . . .

The clock matched Chris' age when he pulled down the rebound. But as the seconds ticked away, he seemed to grow younger with them.

Nineteen . . .

His first thoughts were of victory, how his whole life had been geared to this moment. "We will win," he told himself, cradling the ball against his chest. "We will make a basket and we will win!"

Eighteen . . .

He spun, and seemed to grow confused. He made a hand signal to the referee, then saw Jalen clapping. Jalen, Chris thought, relieved. Jalen. He went to pass, but saw a defender, and he pulled the ball back while dragging his foot, as awkward as

Seventeen . . .

"WALK!" Dean Smith screamed, leaping in the air.

"WALKING! THAT'S WALKING!" Tar Heels players sprang from the bench in unison, as if 100,000 volts had just shot through their sneakers. "WALKING! WALKING!"

Sixteen . . .

Now we're definitely gonna win, Jalen thought, watching all this happen. The ref let us have that traveling call, we must be supposed to win. Jalen wanted the ball, but Chris charged past him in a hurry, pounding that conga-drum dribble. Jalen took off after him, backcourt mates, like the old days, when they were

Fifteen . . .

"Over here, Chris!" Pelinka was thinking. He had floated to the left, he was open, he was ready. It was spooky. Someone had told him earlier he would win the game with a three-point shot. Rob was tingling. "Over here, Chris!"

Fourteen . . .

What's Chris doing? Juwan thought, waving his arms, as Chris dribbled past him on the right, headed toward the corner.

Thirteen . . .

What's Chris doing? Jimmy thought, muscling under the basket, as Chris picked up his dribble in a sandwich of defenders.

Twelve . . .

What's Chris doing?

Eleven . . .

What's Chris doing?

Chris heard no questions, just this funny sound, like thunder, and these half-words from the bench area: "Ttteeahhhouut . . . tiiah-hhhnooo . . . tyyynoooeeehhh." He had brought the ball this far, protected it from harm, now he felt the stalking of the two Carolina defenders, Lynch and Phelps, and for a second, the noise, the sweat, his heartbeat, he lost track of it all, the clock was taking his basketball life in reverse, from 20 to 11, the year it all began, the year he met Jalen, the year he learned the game, and in learning the game they teach you this: when you need help, you call for help, when you need help, you call for help, you call for help, call for help . . .

Eleven . . .

"Time out!" he signaled, poking his hands together in a "T" as he spun to the baseline. "Time out! Time out!" The referee blew the whistle and made a "T" sign right back at him. The Carolina defenders looked at Chris like a car thief being offered the keys.

Then they jumped.

Michigan had no time-outs.

Chris had just turned it over.

A technical foul? Two shots, plus possession? Time out? He called time out? When he had no time-outs?

It was the national championship, wrapped in a bow.

"OH! OH! A HUGE MENTAL MISTAKE," Packer told the world.

Eleven . . .

And over.

"GOD DAMN IT! WHY'D YOU MAKE ME CALL TIME OUT!" Chris had yelled at the bench when the fog cleared and he'd realized what he'd done. His eyebrows had furrowed, his head had begun to throb. He looked decades older, a bald angry man. He turned back again. "WHY'D YOU MAKE ME DO IT?"

He yelled this in the direction of Michael Talley, who held up his palms and said, "Don't worry. Don't worry." Talley, perhaps as confused as Webber, had signaled for a time-out when Chris came upcourt—he even clapped when Chris made the call—until Brian Dutcher, standing next to him, threw his head back in disbelief. Had Talley yelled "Time out"? Had Webber heard him? He said he heard somebody. He said he was confused.

"Why'd they make me do it?" Chris repeated to himself. He wanted to run away, jump into a black hole, pull that moment back before it ever reached heaven and was officially recorded.

Heaven.

Chris thought of God.

"Why did you do this to me?" he asked. "Why me? Why?" He saw the Carolina players hugging each other in exaggerated happiness, like a family winning a game show. Did people always look so stupid when they were happy? He wiped his eyes. He felt the whole world watching. He heard the Carolina fans singing "WEB-BER! WEB-BER!" as they tapped their foreheads, mocking his intelligence. He saw the referees huddling. He put his hands on his hips, and there was Jalen, from somewhere far away, yelling at him, "Come . . . on . . . boy! . . . This . . . ain't . . . over . . . yet . . ."

But it was over, he'd played enough basketball to know that, for Christ's sake. The Fab Five would get nothing. The Fab Five would have another terrible summer. He had handed away their destiny. He went through the motions of the final seconds, the jolt of the buzzer, the pats of his teammates, their mumbled "Don't worry about it" and Fisher's heartfelt "I'm proud of you, you did nothing wrong." But all that was just data now, like the final score, 77–71, North Carolina, just data collecting on some shelf inside his brain. His soul had left his body, left the court, left the building, flying around somewhere high above New Orleans, and it stayed up there for the next hour, through the short, mumbled press conference, through his hiding in the locker room, through the clothes that someone slipped him so he wouldn't have to come out. Finally the security people led his empty husk down the corridor, with one guard behind it, one in front of it, and five newspaper and TV people around it, saying nothing, too sympathetic to ask a question. It was almost to the door, almost to the bus, when, from behind a railing, Chris' father, Mayce, and his younger brother David, slid under the rope and stepped in front, and opening their arms, they touched him, and his soul came rushing back, like the end of a falling dream, hurtling from space and landing with such a jolt that he froze, stiffened, then slumped into their shoulders.

He wept like a baby.

7

The French toast sat untouched inside a silver tray, a mountain of it, alongside equally full trays of eggs, bacon, sausage, hash browns, muffins, fruit, cereal, toast. Pitchers of orange, cranberry, and apple juice were filled to the brim, still waiting to be poured. Place settings sat neatly arranged at every table.

There was no one in the room. The bus was scheduled to leave in five minutes, back to the airport, and the last official Final Four function of the Fab Five—"team breakfast, hotel, third floor," it read on the schedule—was in danger of being a no-show.

Finally Juwan Howard wandered in, wearing socks and sandals, along with Jason Bossard and, moments later, James Voskuil. It was early Tuesday morning. They didn't speak. Just helped themselves to a piece of something small, and ate it while blankly looking at the table in front of them. The clinking of their silverware seemed unusually loud.

"Well," James finally said, "I guess as of this moment, I'm no longer a college basketball player."

Bossard nodded as he chewed, saying nothing. Juwan didn't even look up. Voskuil was asked how he felt.

"Very average," he said.

Suddenly Juwan banged his right fist on the table so hard the coffeepot moved.

"DAMN!" he yelled.

He froze for a moment, then went back to his clinking silverware.

Down by the bus, Ray and Jimmy said so long to their parents and got on board. They pulled on Walkman earphones and disappeared from the world. Eric was already in his seat, as were Rob and Dugan and Leon and the others. When Juwan, James, and Jason got there, only Jalen, Chris, and Fisher were missing. The engine was running. A crowd of people gathered near the curb, waiting for a peek at something, a last look at this uncrowned team . . .

Fisher had gone back to his hotel room after the loss Monday night. He gathered there with Angie and his brothers and several close friends and they sat around the table like a funeral. They tried to talk about other things. Summer plans. The latest news on members of the family. There was soft, polite laughter, never too loud. Fisher's face was red and haggard, and he stared off into space. Now and then, he'd say, "Man, oh, man . . ." and his voice would die. The TV was not on. There was no music. It was a wake.

The next morning, Fisher went to church, same as he'd been doing since he got to New Orleans. Angie did not go. She felt nothing thankful in her heart, and while she knew it would pass, she couldn't bring herself to go and pretend. Nothing benevolent would have caused what happened to Chris and to her husband. That's how she felt. She marveled at Steve, who had every right to be angry, and, maybe even for several hours, agnostic. But Fisher was calm. This was the hand he'd been dealt. He went to church and never said a word about playing it.

X

"T" IS FOR THE END

1

Jack Dempsey, the legendary prizefighter, was never as popular in victory as he was in defeat. The infamous "long count" loss to Gene Tunney changed his image forever. By failing to go to his corner after knocking Tunney down—a simple mistake—Dempsey gave his opponent enough time to recover from the blow and get up to defeat him. He had been perceived beforehand as a brute. But as he cried in the rain of Chicago's Soldier Field, Jack Dempsey became human, and was embraced by his country.

Chris Webber was college basketball's answer to Dempsey. The outpouring of sympathy after the time-out call was voluminous: The President wrote him a letter. The First Lady mentioned him in a commencement address. *Sports Illustrated*, which had never done a full feature on Webber before, wrote a three-page story about how well he was coping with his heartbreak. Mail flooded the basketball office. Requests came for him to speak to churches, youth groups.

Wherever he went, people hugged him, or wanted to. They told him what a great athlete—even better, what a great person—he was and always had been.

"It's strange," he would observe a week after returning home, "all these people seem to like me more because I screwed up."

It grew, day by day. Through a single, youthful mistake, Chris Webber was transformed from one of the nation's more resented college athletes to its most beloved.

And, to a degree, he pulled the Fab Five into that good light with him. Short of a championship, that may have been the nicest thing he could have done for them.

Steve Fisher sat next to Webber now, on a plane, heading for L.A. It was several days after the championship game. Chris was sleeping, his head buried in the seat, his mouth open. Fisher wondered when he should bring the "other" subject up. He knew once they got to L.A., for the John Wooden Awards banquet, it would be the usual madhouse: interviews, shaking hands, they'd be separated for sure. And after that, who knows? Would Fisher even get a chance to talk to his star player again? Would Chris just call him one day and say, "Thanks for a good two years, but I'm outa here"?

The question of whether Chris Webber would stay in college had been like the question "What should we do the day *after* the prom?" There was always such concentration on getting to the Final Four that it was easier to table the issue, forget about it. Hey, maybe they win it all and everything looks different.

Now the flight attendant made an announcement, and Chris stirred, yawned, and stretched his long arms, his wingspan seemingly extending from window to window. Fisher smiled, made some small talk. Finally he asked.

"What are you thinking about the NBA?"

Chris sighed. "I don't know. I haven't decided. I know I'd like to come back and finally win one of these championships."

Fisher nodded.

"But, you know, if we play well all next year, and lose in the Final Four, I'm gonna feel like a failure."

Fisher stared.

"If I did go," Chris said, "it would open things up more for the other guys. They'd get a chance to show how they can play, you know?"

Fisher said nothing. All those years of trying to sweet-talk recruits, you get pretty good at reading kids. Fisher was reading one now. He was reading bad news. He thought about the team returning next year without the four seniors—Riley, Voskuil, Pelinka, Talley—and, unless they got Avondre Jones, not much of a recruiting class. He tried to imagine that team without Chris Webber in the middle. It was an empty picture, and it made Fisher sad.

"Take your time before you make a decision," the coach said, and as the plane landed, Chris said he would.

Actually, Chris did more than take his time: he thought about it every waking moment. He thought about it driving, he thought about it during final exams, he thought about it while playing video games.

When he wasn't thinking about it, he was talking about it.

He talked with everyone who would listen. Jalen, Juwan, Jimmy, Ray. He talked with Jamal Mashburn, the Kentucky junior who was coming out, and Anfernee Hardaway, the Memphis State junior who was coming out as well.

"Why are you doing it?" Chris asked Hardaway.

"Because all that stuff about staying and enjoying another year of college, that's all bullshit, man," Hardaway said. "That's just people messing with your mind. Yeah, you give up a year of enjoying college, but $4 million should ease the pain, you know? If we weren't basketball players, if we were doctors or something, they wouldn't even ask, they'd just say go."

Chris visited Oakland, hung out with Cal guard Jason Kidd, went to a recording studio, talked to rappers. Everyone there told him he should go pro. When he got home, he called Shaquille O'Neal, who had left LSU after his junior year and had received the biggest rookie contract in the history of the NBA, six years, $40 million.

"How is it in the league?" Chris asked.

"It's great," Shaq said. "You should come out."

The opinion was overwhelming. In fact, every NBA player and professional athlete Webber asked—and that included Magic Johnson, Isiah Thomas, Joe Dumars, Terry Mills, Andre Rison— advised him to come out. Not one said he would regret the years he didn't have in college.

And still he kept searching. Another week. Another week. He knew, in his heart, that he wanted to be in the league, to live the life, to buy his father the car, get his mother the house, take his brothers and sister to the mall, go into the store and say, "Listen, here's my credit card, whatever they want, let 'em have it," and then just walk out, casual, like a gunslinger in the Old West. Could he really go back to college? After all that had happened? Could he delay his dream one more year?

Or did he have to do it now?

He waited for a sign, a burning bush, a thunderclap.

He got it, not surprisingly, from the work of his father's hands: a Cadillac.

Chris, who, despite all the advice, had been leaning toward coming back, was on the street on a Monday afternoon when a shiny

Caddy drove by. He admired it. It stopped. A middle-aged woman, who had recognized him, got out and ran over, asking for an autograph. He obliged, she squealed, thanked him, and drove off.

"Now, that's messed up," he told himself. "I'm wishing I could get a car like that for my father, and she jumps out and asks *me* for my autograph."

Something snapped. He went home, looked his mother in the eye, and said, "It may not be your first choice, but I've made up my mind."

He told his teammates next. He saw Juwan in the apartment building parking lot, and said, "I'm outa here," and Juwan grabbed him and hugged him, the way you do with a member of your family. Jimmy and Ray, already back in Texas, called with their congratulations and their wish list for gifts. "Don't forget I want a house, I want a swimming pool . . ."

Jalen answered the phone when Chris called.

"I'm gone," Chris said.

"I'll be right over."

They talked for hours. They shook their heads. "Man," Jalen said, "I can't believe it. It's like now you're older than me."

There was one more person to tell.

On Tuesday, May 11, Steve Fisher drove to the Webbers' house.

It had not been a great month for Fisher. The word had come from California that Avondre Jones, after telling Michigan for nearly a year "I'm coming, I'm coming . . . You're my school," chose another school instead. Southern Cal. Right in his backyard. Same for Charles O'Bannon, who chose UCLA. Like Dutcher always said, location, location. Skeptics said Webber's hesitation about returning may have scared off Jones, who, like all of them, wanted to play right away. Fisher figured that probably had something to do with it. But what was he supposed to do, tell Chris to hurry up?

Now, as he pulled up to the Webbers' house, he could only hope a flood of sentiment had washed over his star player, and he would return for one more year. The minute Fisher walked in the door, he knew he was wrong. Doris and Mayce shrugged. Chris shrugged. Fisher stared blankly when Chris finally said the words "I'm gonna leave," then the coach told the biggest recruit he'd ever landed, "Chris, we were lucky to have you as long as we did." And, as is his custom, he got red in the cheeks, and said little else.

A press conference was called for the next day, and once again, reporters stuffed a room for Chris Webber. Cameramen, columnists, radio hosts—many of the same people who came to the 1940 Chop House two years earlier to hear Chris' college decision. He was like this lightning rod, every couple of years, another big press conference, everyone shows up.

For his part, Chris spent the final minutes of his amateur life shooting hoops with a couple of friends on the Crisler floor. He shot from the outside, no dunking necessary, and he swished a few and he had a few laughs. Then he sauntered into the press room, basketball sweat dripping through his long-sleeved silk shirt.

"I've decided to go to the NBA . . ." he began.

The Fab Five was no more.

From that point on, Chris' life was a blur. He visited several NBA teams, and they picked him up in limos, paid for fancy meals, nobody asked about rules or violations. A trading card company cut a quick deal with Chris—who hadn't even picked an agent yet—and suddenly he had a contract worth close to a million dollars for, essentially, the use of his picture. It was more money than his parents had earned in the last 15 years. His aunt cut him his first check, which he proceeded to spend, quickly, on a down payment for his father's car, a shopping spree for his father in a clothes store, and a bracelet for his mother. When his aunt told him, "Chris, don't spend it all, you have to pay taxes on it," Chris squinted and said, "Nuh-uh. Nuh-uh. You only have to pay taxes on your salary and stuff."

This was his first real job.

He didn't know any better.

It was Lesson No. 1 in the real world. There would be plenty more. On a trip to Nike headquarters in Portland—ostensibly to talk about a shoe contract and possible agent representation—the executives wined and dined Chris and Mayce, then before leaving, took them into the huge employees' store, where all Nike merchandise from shoes to carry-on bags was on display.

"Pick out anything you want," the executive told them.

Chris and Mayce looked at each other, grinned sheepishly, and each selected a pair of shoes.

"No, no," the executive laughed. "Anything you want. Everything you want."

Everything?

Mayce picked up a bag. He looked for approval. Go ahead, the executive said. A couple shirts. A jacket. Help yourself, he said.

Next thing you knew, they were loading up with as many shoes, shorts, and sweat suits as they could carry, filling carts, the stuff bulging under their arms. A month earlier—when Chris was still a college student—even accepting dinner would have been improper. Now, in a half-hour shopping spree, they were taking home merchandise that, on the open market, was worth a semester's tuition at Michigan.

No strings attached.

Living large was just beginning.

2

And so, we're back to where we started, draft night at the Palace of Auburn Hills, with Chris in his camel-colored suit and Jalen, in turquoise, right beside him. It was just as they had planned as kids. Only one was going, and one was staying.

"Next year, this is you, right?" people kept asking Jalen as he stood and watched Chris pose for pictures.

"Naw," Jalen sneered, "I'm staying in college five years."

Juwan and Jimmy—who flew in from Texas—would show up later, and so would Fisher and Perry and Donnie Kirksey and Ed Martin and almost all the cast of Webber's life. But, for the moment, Chris and Jalen, childhood buddies, sat together in the VIP area, with a buffet spread and all the drinks they wanted. Chris had his own table for family and friends. So did each of the top projected draft picks. The Webber table was next to the Jamal Mashburn table and the Anfernee Hardaway table and not far from the Bobby Hurley table and the Shawn Bradley table and the Calbert Cheaney table. A league photographer gathered all these players together, in their silk suits and gold tie clips and expensive leather shoes, and posed them for a group shot.

How strange. Chris had seemed mortal enemy to so many of these guys during the season. Cheaney from Indiana? Hurley from Duke? Mashburn from Kentucky? How terribly had he wanted to beat them and their teams?

And yet now they chatted and laughed as if they'd all been part of this big stage production and they were only reading their lines. Mashburn, Bradley, and Webber teased about the first time they all met each other, in that AAU tournament back in eighth grade. Tonight the eighth graders got the keys to the kingdom.

"We think Chris is gonna be No. 1," Mayce, his father, said, pacing nervously, getting the latest data. "We think Orlando is gonna take him."

"Does it matter?"

"Not really. He'll play anywhere. He just really wants to be No. 1."

They sat at their table. People came by, agents, well-wishers, business types dropping off business cards. Everyone slapped Chris' back, everyone wanted to make some contact. Finally, to the sound of applause from the sold-out crowd, the announcement came that the draft had begun. It was televised live across the country, and highlight footage of Webber and the others dominated the opening moments.

On the other side of the VIP area, representatives from all 28 NBA teams sat on a four-leveled, newly constructed platform, behind team insignias, like panelists in a game show. They grabbed telephones, hung up telephones, redialed telephones, sometimes talking on two phones at a time. David Stern, the NBA commissioner, came out to read the first selection card, and a buzz went through the 19,000 spectators in the Palace, and TV cameramen swarmed around the Webber table and the Bradley table and the Mashburn table and the Hardaway table, covering all bases.

"Here you go," Jalen whispered, as if they were starting another game. Chris pursed his lips and looked down at the table, locking his gaze. Suddenly this really mattered, being No. 1, proving to himself he had not made a mistake, proving it was the right decision.

"WITH THE NO. 1 PICK IN THE NBA DRAFT . . ." Stern announced.

"We know who it's going to be," Jalen quipped.

"THE ORLANDO MAGIC SELECT . . ."

"We know who it's gonna be."

"CHRIS WEBBER, OF MICHIGAN!"

"Told you."

The Palace exploded. Chris leapt to his feet and so did most everyone at his table, his father bursting into tears, burying his head in Chris' shoulder, grabbing his neck, his arm, his hands, as if seeing him for the first time in a decade. Doris kissed him on the cheek and looked stunned. His brothers slapped hands. His sister waited for a hug. The music from *Chariots of Fire* burst over the loudspeakers, stirring, majestic music. Someone signaled for him to hurry, go to the stage, the world was waiting, and slowly he disengaged from his loved ones and began a solo walk down a makeshift corridor, a red carpet, toward the stage of his future.

"My dawg did it!" Ray said, watching TV back in Austin.

"Our boy did it," Jimmy and Juwan said, high-fiving in the stands.

"Told you," Jalen said, sitting at the table.

The No. 1 pick in the nation. At age 20. The last Michigan person to do that was a kid named Earvin Johnson.

"GO GET PAID, CHRIS!" fans yelled as he walked to the stage.

"GET THE MONEY, CHRIS!"

He looked up into the noise and smiled.

In the next half hour, things would get crazy. Orlando would trade Chris to Golden State for Anfernee Hardaway and three No. 1 draft picks, and Chris would take off the Orlando hat and pull on the Golden State hat, he would tell his father and his friends that this was exactly what he wanted, and the party down at the State Theatre would kick into gear, Jalen, Juwan, Jimmy, and the whole world, it seemed, coming to shake his massive hand.

But for those few seconds, it was just Chris in that corridor, walking toward the vision he—and almost everyone he played with—had been nurturing from the day they took their first dribbles. He was all of the Fab Five at that moment, reacting the way they each would react. In the din of the crowd, at the base of his rainbow, it all came back to him, the midnight sessions of orange juice and sandwiches with Curtis Hervey in that empty gym, Luwan Bell smacking him to the ground to toughen him up, the AAU leagues every summer, the reporters coming around in eighth grade, the high school selection, the high school state championships, the boxes of recruiting letters, the press conferences about his college decision, the first pickup game against Michigan's upperclassmen, the road trips in college, the jeering mobs, the tournament, the second tournament, the TV cameras, the reporters, the preseason polls, the hot nights against Duke, Indiana, Michigan State, North Carolina, the pressure, the exhaustion, the laughter in the locker room, every element of this tapestry he had woven was unraveling for him as he walked down that corridor, the No. 1 pick in the nation, the best of the best, and here is what he was thinking in the middle of all that, the heart of the athlete, the soul of a competitor, there was really only one thing to be thinking:

I won.

EPILOGUE

Late summer, 1993. Jalen sat in his mother's small house on Appo-line, eating french fries and bacon from a local breakfast joint. The grease leaked through the Styrofoam container, and Jalen licked his fingers as he talked.

"I never told you about the first time we met?" he said.

No, he was told. He nodded, smacked his lips, and tried to remember the date. The sound of a thumping basketball came through the open window, two kids playing in the street on a makeshift hoop made of lumber, cinder blocks, and a bent rim. Jalen, who learned the game on a hoop much like that one, now wore a large gold "5" around his neck, and a diamond stud earring—"from a friend"—in his left ear. Behind him stood a giant blowup photo of him during a Michigan game. There were magazines with his picture on the cover strewn around the room. Several of his trophies were alongside the old couch. The TV was playing silently, a music video program.

"Oh yeah, I remember," Jalen finally said. "It was just before school started freshman year. I had never met Ray, and he came up, and the other guys called and said, 'Come on, Ray's here, we gotta all get together.' So I jumped in my car and drove out to Ann Arbor. I had never been to the dorm before. I figured I'd just ask somebody where it was.

"I got all messed up. Lost. So I called Jay Smith from a pay phone. He said, 'Where are you?' I said, 'I'm here in Ann Arbor, but I can't find this dorm I'm supposed to live in.' So he came out and met me, and I followed his car in my car.

"Finally I parked in this No Parking space, and as I'm walking to the building, I hear Chris and them yelling, 'They gonna tow you! They gonna tow your car!' And I look up and I see all of them hanging out the window, Chris, Jimmy, Juwan, and Ray—and I never seen Ray before—but it was like we all knew each other already. Like we already knew we was special.

"And when I got in the room, they said, 'J, this here's Ray,' and I said, 'I know.'

"And then we just talked for, like, an hour, just sitting on the floor of that room. We were laughing like we'd all been together forever. And I was feeling like 'Man, we're live! It's all happening now. It's coming together . . .'

"And I knew I made the right choice."

He nodded, smacked his lips, and had another french fry. His hair had grown in, and he looked older now. In a few weeks, he would pack up and move back to Ann Arbor, start the pickup games, see what the team looked like. The 1993 Wolverines—after losing all those seniors, and Chris—would only have nine scholarship players, and one of those was a smiling small forward named Olivier Saint-Jean, from France, who only committed over the summer after his father, who lived in New York, called the basketball office and asked if Michigan would be interested. As Fisher's staff had lost out on Avondre Jones, and Jon Garavaglia and Charles O'Bannon and pretty much all the big-name recruits, they were ready to consider Saint-Jean.

He visited.

They signed him.

Two years earlier, it was the Greatest Class Ever Recruited. Now it was a kid from France, on a phone call from his dad.

Fortunes change. So do coaching staffs. Perry Watson was gone from Ann Arbor. He quit to take over the head coaching job at the University of Detroit. Although he hadn't exactly reeled in any new big-name recruits for Michigan in his two years there, he did parlay the job into a better one. Part of Perry's magic. Now he would compete for some of the same high school talent as Michigan. Brian Dutcher was already watching out for him.

Dutcher spent the summer, as usual, watching high school studs play all over the country. Jay Smith worked basketball camps to supplement his limited income. Doogie lived in the film room, cutting tape until way after dark, listening to Tigers games, eating sandwiches.

As for the players? Riley got drafted, in the second round, by the Houston Rockets, who eventually signed him to a three-year contract worth a reported $1 million, including $600,000 guaranteed. So his son wouldn't have to worry about baby-sitters for a while.

Voskuil and Pelinka were not drafted. Both tried NBA rookie

camps, and both were cut. The European market was jammed, and at last word they were each going into their fields of study.

No one heard from Michael Talley. He spent draft night at his house, with his Detroit friends, watching himself go unmentioned to nobody's surprise but his own. He had skipped the Wolverines' end-of-season basketball banquet—the only player to do so—by telling Fisher's office he was in Arkansas with his sick grandmother. Fisher told that story to the banquet crowd. So he was quite embarrassed when, later that evening, a reporter called Talley's house and got him on the phone—and wrote about it.

Even gone, Talley was still dogging Fisher.

Jimmy and Ray both spent the summer in Texas. Neither worked. They were "concentrating on our games." Tiffany said Jimmy had taken a new turn toward the romantic; he actually took her to San Antonio, and they just walked around the river, holding hands.

Juwan Howard took summer classes, in Ann Arbor, and stayed on line to graduate, as he had promised his grandmother. He spent much of the summer with Donnie Kirksey, who at last word was trying to get work with a major shoe company.

Chris, of course, was negotiating his contract with the Warriors, seeking somewhere around $45 million for eight years.

Steve Fisher did his normal recruiting, basketball camps, and personal appearances. He took several vacations with his family. His son Mark attended Michael Jordan's basketball camp in Illinois, and Jordan, a North Carolina graduate, teased Mark whenever he saw him, by making the "time out" signal.

Fisher didn't watch the tape of that championship loss until one night in his office as the summer was about to end. "I don't know if I want to see this," he said, but he pushed the play button and stood back.

The TV replayed those final 20 seconds, starting with the free throws, Chris muscling for position on the line. When the camera cut to Fisher, standing there, hands in his pockets, for the first time he admitted, "Maybe we should have been reminding them about the time-outs right there. Yelling it. Making sure they heard us."

He sighed.

"Hindsight. Hindsight."

There's a story about that game that most people don't know. When the final buzzer sounded, and Fisher had to swallow his emotions yet again and make that short walk to congratulate Dean Smith, one Michigan player waited for him to finish. Jalen Rose. He stood on the far end of the court, watching, even though his teammates had already gone down the tunnel, and even though the North Carolina fans mocked him by pointing and singing their fight song. Jalen waited until Fisher came back, and he put his bony arm around Fisher's shoulder.

"Don't worry, coach," Jalen said. "We'll be back here next year."

Fisher looked at him—Jalen, of all people!—and, choking up, he said, "We damn sure better be."

Now, back on Appoline, his breakfast finished, Jalen closed the Styrofoam carton and leaned back in the couch.

He never did call his father. He mentioned it to his mother, and she took offense. "We've been looking for him for 20 years. He wants to see you, let him come up here."

Jalen figured nothing was worth upsetting his mother. After all, she'd done the work on him, not Jimmy Walker. "I'll meet him eventually," he said. "I lived this long without a father.

"Anyhow, he knows how to find me."

He got up and stretched. Chris was flying back to town from California this weekend, and the two of them had plans to get together, have some fun, shoot some hoops. Then it was back to school for one, and off to the NBA for the other. When asked about the Fab Five, Jalen said it wouldn't be the same now, what with Chris and Perry gone. But that was OK.

"Even though we never won a championship, they'll be talking about us for 20 years."

Why? he was asked.

"Because," he said, surprised, as if explaining the obvious, "we were *original*."

They were original.

There will never be another group like the Fab Five. But then, nothing ever truly repeats itself in sports. Things just seem to happen. Right now, as the summer heat fades to autumn, there's a thumping outside the window on Appoline, and down on Biltmore, where the Webbers live, Chris' younger brother Jason, who is 16, got his first recruiting letter the other day. He took it upstairs, closed the door, and read it over and over.

ACKNOWLEDGMENTS

The author wishes to thank the following people who were invaluable in putting this book together:

Kerri Langen, Adam Schefter, Sharon Marion, and Bill Wickett, whose enormous efforts were above and beyond the call of both friendship and professionalism.

Ali Nesser, for his tireless work with the photos.

David Black, Lev Fruchter, and Susan Raihofer, who are no doubt tired of my calling.

Larry Kirshbaum, Harvey-Jane Kowal, and all the other very patient people at Warner Books.

Mike Littwin and Tony Kornheiser, for their editorial assistance.

Also, Jay Smith, Brian Dutcher, "Doogie" Knoll, Karen Beeman, Bruce Madej.

Angie Fisher, the Webber family, Jeanne Rose, Bill Rose, Nyoka and Jimmy King, Ray and Gladys Jackson, Thelma Howard.

Dave Robinson, Gene Myers, Neal Shine, and Heath Meriwether, for letting me go, Chris Kucharski, as usual, Buzz Van Houten, Mick McCabe, Greg Stoda, Laurie Delves, Bo Schembechler, Kurt Keener, Taylor Bell, Freddie Hunter, Bob Wojnowski, Chip Armer, Loy Vaught, Sean Rivers, Kevin Robinson, Rocky Harbison, Dave Hirth, Jeff Seidel.

Leslie, for the fruit salad.

The Maize "N" Blue Deli, CMB Property Management—everyone should write a book in one of their apartments—Denny Iott.

Mike Stone, Ken Droz, Elvis.

Janine.